IAN BRADY

The untold story of the Moors Murders

DR ALAN KEIGHTLEY

ROBSON BOOKS

First published in the United Kingdom in 2017 by
Robson Books

ISBN 978-1-86105-754-9

A CIP catalogue record for this book is available from the British
Library.

10 9 8 7 6 5 4 3 2 1

Printed and bound by CPI Group (UK) Ltd, Croydon, CR0 4YYY

CONTENTS

PREFACE

The BBC Television news was on when I returned home from work one day early in May 1966. The main story was about a man and woman from Manchester sentenced to life for killing children. I knew that the case was thought to be too horrifying for detailed daily television reports about the trial, but I couldn't help wondering just how awful it was. The black-and-white photographs of Ian Brady and Myra Hindley were shown on screen for a few seconds.

I sat down for tea and thought little more about them when the newsreader moved on to another item. Few viewers that night would have thought that the story of the Moors Murders, as they came to be called, would still be helping to sell newspapers – week in, week out – more than forty years later. And I had no notion that 25 years after Brady and Hindley were jailed, I would have a minor walk-on part in the Moors Murders drama, as many thousands of others were to have.

As unlikely as it may appear to those detectives, psychiatrists, authors, criminologists, journalists and the victims' families, who have long sought in their own ways for decades to discover it, the chapters that follow reveal what they wanted to know. I am not saying that, therefore what follows is the absolute truth; my only purpose is simply to reveal what was presented to me to be the truth.

This is the first account of the Moors story told in detail by Ian Brady. It has never been revealed or published before. In these few opening paragraphs I have to say how this became possible, so that readers are able to understand the circumstances in which Brady's disclosures were made. Some – perhaps many – may say I shouldn't have bothered to be in the position where I could receive them. They could well be right.

One of the prevailing, unchanging patterns of Ian Brady's life, from the very beginning, was the compulsion to live his life in compartments. His acquaintances and friends in one compartment wouldn't be aware of his behaviour towards – or even the existence of – individuals in another. As the story unfolds, I will try to describe the walls he erected in his life: his life with his foster family; life with his natural mother; his criminal life with others in theft; life with Myra Hindley, to mention just a few.

After Brady's capture, there were the compartments occupied by a whole range of people, including detectives, warders, journalists and fellow prisoners. If you were such a person, you were simply not in the compartment of his life where he would disclose to you, for example, details of precisely how the victims died. It was as simple – or as complicated – as that.

I approached Ian Brady only after some prompting by the parents of a victim of the Moors Murders. I went to their home and they came into my classes in the college where I taught. If there is one single theme that can be distilled from the chapters that follow, it is that the campaign waged by the relatives of the victims, over decades, has been completely vindicated. *They were right all along*. This was particularly so in their claims about the role of Myra Hindley in the whole ghastly nightmare.

Brady's story seeped slowly into my mind over several years – usually in very small drops. These came in many letters, telephone conversations and face to face during my visits. Brady had an extraordinary memory. Sometimes, he would recite spontaneously long passages from Shakespeare. He could recall dialogue, word for word, from the distant past. Where dialogue and detailed quotations appear in the chapters which follow, they have been constructed from what Ian Brady said or wrote in letters to me, or from notes he sent or handed to me.

Over the years Brady returned again and again to the people, themes and events described in this book. This was inevitable over such a long period. Usually, however, his comments added something new to the topics he had spoken about several times before. A great deal of ground can be covered during five-hour monthly visits, fortnightly letters and daily telephone conversations spread over many years.

I drew up lists of hundreds of items – themes, individuals, incidents, etc. – and added material under each heading as I learned something new. Naturally, the information entered under topics such as the planning for a murder, and the murder itself, eventually became quite detailed. The topic would have sparse material under its heading at the outset but be quite full more than ten years later. I always had many questions in my mind to ask Ian Brady during a visit. This accounts for the biographical detail in the chapters which follow.

Brady always wrote a letter to me the same evening of my earlier visit that day; to thank me for coming and for the cigarettes and other small items that I brought him. Immediately after a visit in July 1994 he wrote: 'You ask a lot of questions re the past. I don't really mind, except that when I slip into the past, I become it. A stream of consciousness leads to a process of abreaction, or osmosis, which in turn generates a resentful invective which reflects my consciousness of the dichotomy taking place – half of me in the past, the other half in the present. Also certain inertia, rooted in the impossibility of destroying the myth, the ever-increasing mountain of invention heaped upon me by the media over three decades, creates an obtrusive style of delivery.

'I just mention this to illustrate that I am conscious of the process and its causes, and how it manifests itself – a strident Jekyll and Hyde at first glance, unless you know what currents are running beneath the surface. Do you understand this? I'm also aware of repetition at times, which I deliberately use as reminders of what I'm getting at, a telegraphic style to punch points home, or to delineate the line of logical extension. In short, I'm not running wild though it might appear so from the audience viewpoint at the time.'

Several of the passages in Brady's letters and notes to me may have been sections or summaries from the draft of his autobiography. I do not know if this was the case and I never raised the subject. His autobiography may be published at a future date but nothing I have written in the chapters that follow consciously quotes from the autobiography, by default or otherwise. Although a version of Brady's manuscript – on typing paper I gave him – lay in the vault of my local bank for some years, I didn't see the text. Brady said to me more than once that he often felt like destroying everything he had written of the autobiography, as he had done already with the manuscript of a novel he had written in Wormwood Scrubs prison.

In the first year or so of my contact with Ian Brady I had no notion that I would be writing a book on the Moors Murders. Consequently, I destroyed material Brady had handed or sent to me. I still have some of these notes and, of course, I extracted the significant details from the notes I discarded before I destroyed them.

I do know that Brady lifted passages from his word processor to send to more than one person and relieve him from the chore of having to write everything from scratch for his different correspondents. In the Introduction I will mention the courses I taught, some of which examined the formative experiences and influences that led an individual to take other human lives. Brady was happy to supply biographical material for these courses.

I once quoted to Ian Brady Nietzsche's remark in *Thus Spake Zarathustra*: 'Whoever fights monsters should see to it that in the process he does not become a monster. And when you look into an abyss, the abyss also looks into you.' Brady said that he was, of course, familiar with the quotation and added: 'It must occasionally pass through your mind that, by introducing [the students] to the works of Nietzsche, you are risking their looking into the abyss. Did that possibility engender the question you put to me about the effects of Nietzsche?' I had, in fact, raised the question with Brady because the Nietzsche quote had been typed on a postcard and sent to me anonymously at the college where I taught.

Ian Brady often mentioned letters he had received from teenagers doing projects at school. I am sure that these were at a more harmless level than my own dealings with him. He often said that the biographical first half of his autobiography was much less appealing to an American publisher, compared with the second part with its account of the murders.

So he regarded the material about his life before he met Myra Hindley as less exclusive than the second part of his book. Besides, in his final few years he had lost interest in virtually everything and simply didn't care any more. Even before this mood set in, I found that he enjoyed talking about his early years in detail. It was a happy time for him and an innocent one – if it is possible to use that word in the same sentence as the name 'Ian Brady'.

I had only an hour or so after work each day to sift through the material. It has taken years to put the fragments and listed details into the form of a coherent, plausible picture within the given framework of events that are now part of the public record. I had access to all of Brady's property during the writing of this book and I shall have the same access to whatever remains after his death. These items, particularly his book collection, were invaluable – despite their lurid associations – in adding detail to the story you are about to read.

Brady had no knowledge of my writing a book about him. I realise that not everyone will want to know about his and Myra Hindley's diabolical crimes. But, alas, they have left a permanent stain on the pages of British criminal history.

The Moors Murders have been analysed, publicised and condemned to a degree that is unprecedented in British criminal history, with the possible exception of the murders of Jack the Ripper that retain their fascination largely because the case is unsolved.

The consensus – among authors, criminal psychologists, television crime profilers and journalists – is that the Moors Murders were the work of a psychopath; a sadistic sexual predator, with the rare distinction of having a compliant girlfriend who would have been a loving mother to her children, had she never met him. Their crimes, it is said, were fuelled by the pornography of the Marquis de Sade and Nazi ideology.

The emotional reaction of the man and woman in the street has been that of unrelenting revulsion, even though Myra Hindley had many supportive friends. I cannot think of a single individual who was sympathetic to Ian Brady, with the possible exception of Lord Longford. Most people who know anything about the Moors Murders would have said that Brady and Hindley should have been hanged. Nevertheless, as journalist Duncan Staff, writing in the *Guardian* on 29 February 2000, observed: 'Our strong emotional response has never been matched by a proper understanding of the case.'

If a child were told, in simple terms, the story of the Moors Murders, they would know what most adults know. It is one thing to cause another person to suffer in the course of trying to achieve some other goal, as in violent robbery. It is another matter to cause a person pain for no other reason than to make them suffer. It is pure malevolence. This is the gut level feeling of revulsion people have felt towards Ian Brady and Myra Hindley.

Revulsion is a natural reaction, but the relatives and friends of the victims may still wish to know what happened to their loved one in the moments before they died.

People of a reflective mind, and not directly involved in the pain of the lost ones, might wonder what kind of universe it is that gives birth to Buddha, Socrates and Jesus of Nazareth, but also to Ian Brady and Myra Hindley. Still others may wonder what goes on in the mind of a notorious serial killer.

Almost from the outset of my contact with Brady, I realised that there was a philosophical dimension, however perverted, running through the Moors saga, and in a way that is virtually absent from most cases of cold-blooded murder. His murderous crimes aside, Brady cannot be put into the same intellectual category as the likes of many British serial killers of recent times – the Yorkshire Ripper, the Black Panther, the Cromwell

Street killer couple, to mention only three cases. Brady would lose Peter
Sutcliffe and Donald Neilson after a few sentences, and the Wests after his
opening remark.

Whether we agree with him or not, Brady was saying that he was a
new kind of killer, the kind of which we would see more and more. These
killers would be products of the secular atmosphere that pervades many
dimensions of life in the West and which appears to welcome the decline
of religion and, perhaps unconsciously, the disappearance of the
absolutes that held sway just a generation ago. To regard Ian Brady as an
evil, sadistic psychopath may well be a true judgement. But to leave
the matter there is simply a failure to respond to the complexity of the
Moors Murders.

Brady and Hindley were both at ease in using the word 'spiritual' when
talking about their lives and crimes. For this reason, I have included a
chapter – 'To Deny Our Nothingness' – that would appear to be out of
place in a book on true crime. Some readers may wish to skip over the
chapter. Nevertheless, I believe that the philosophical and spiritual
dimensions of the case beg for something to be said about them, however
briefly. The chapter represents my case for saying that Ian Brady, in his
intellectual convictions, was catastrophically mistaken.

By implication, it also rejects the widespread pessimistic assumptions
about life's purpose and meaning that are now casually accepted over
coffee by academics without batting an eyelid. This is precisely why –
rightly or wrongly – Brady thought of himself as someone who was a
product of our times, in a way he could not have been of any other.

Right up to the day she died, Myra Hindley evoked more mass hatred
than Ian Brady. Brady resigned himself to permanent imprisonment with
no hope of release even before the Moors trial judge announced the guilty
verdict. Brady often said to me that he didn't deserve any sympathy and
had no wish for it. He believed that nothing he could say or do would make
any difference.

In contrast, Myra Hindley was never resigned to her fate of dying in
prison. This is possibly one of the reasons for the unrelenting hatred
she had to face. Another reason is that she did not admit to any involvement in the murders until twenty years after her sentence, leaving two
families to suffer the long, agonising uncertainty about what happened to
their children.

The public hatred of Myra Hindley was also fuelled by the fact that she
was never damaged by her imprisonment in the way that Ian Brady clearly

was. If anything, Hindley was one of the success stories of the prison system. She also had a long series of passionate lesbian affairs that relieved the boredom, and a network of friends outside who were there for her. To my knowledge Ian Brady had no kind of sexual life in prison and very few friends, if any.

My own association with Ian Brady is described in the body of the book, but a few words here may anticipate a question some readers might wish to raise already. Many writers on the Moors Murders have assumed that Brady is an atheist or an agnostic and basically anti-religious. My own assumptions about human existence are fundamentally religious – not in any 'born-again' sense, but in the timeless tradition of the perennial philosophy, the awakening or transformation of consciousness to be found in the deeper levels of the world's religions and individual teachers.

This was never a problem in my relationships with Ian Brady. It's significant that the only person Brady allowed to visit him for a number of years was Lord Longford, a devout Catholic. Nevertheless, Brady often said to me that nobody has the answer. When he did so, I couldn't help thinking of Gertrude Stein's comment on the same theme: 'There ain't no answer. There ain't going to be any answer. There never has been an answer. That's the answer.'

Religion, like everything else in this universe, has its good and bad dimensions. It has produced saints and perpetrated cruel murder. Yet, even one of Ian Brady's existentialist anti-heroes, André Malraux, said that the 21st century would be religious, or there wouldn't be one.

As strange as it must seem, one of the things that became clear to me, through my years of contact with Brady, was that he was temperamentally 'religious' in the way his philosophical hero Friedrich Nietzsche is often said to have been. Nietzsche announced the 'death of God' but was fascinated by the post-mortem signals emitted from the deity's grave. No one believes in God like an atheist. Brady said to me once that he had known several major criminals who had an 'innate Christianity' – and, of course, a bad conscience because of it.

Brady reflected, when talking about the kind of religious education he received as a child and young teenager, that, 'I was offered "God" in a very tedious and trivial package which was empty when you opened it. To be compelled to believe in a deity made no sense to me.'

Another question the reader may have in mind at this stage relates to how far Ian Brady's physical presence in a one-to-one encounter is indicative of his fundamental state of mind. He has been described in a number of ways: an incurable, heartless 'psychopath'; 'the Daddy of the Devils'; 'the most evil man alive'. I shall take up the question of 'evil', as it is used of Brady and Hindley, at appropriate stages as the story unfolds. The term 'psychopath' is now used so widely and loosely in popular parlance that it can mean almost anything.

From Brady's point of view, a 'psychopath' is someone who is primarily concerned with ambition and is driven by a ruthless, often humourless, quest for power at the expense – if necessary – of anyone who happens to be in the way. Brady would claim that it is not only serial killers who are motivated in this way. According to him, we rub shoulders with socially acceptable, clinical psychopaths every day without realising it. Very few of them actually commit murder.

Professor Malcolm MacCulloch, Ian Brady's psychiatrist for some years, remarked to journalist Duncan Staff (*Guardian*, 29 February 2000): 'There are lots of people with very tough personality types who do great and brave things or who are extremely brave. Under other circumstances they might be labelled as abhorrent psychopaths and do dreadful things. It's really a question of whom you meet and what happens in the circumstances.' Brady observed that they are often 'successful' people who have become so because of their total absorption in their own ego-besotted selves. They regard this as 'normal' behaviour and are blind – through habit – to their own fundamentally psychopathic nature.

I was talking with Ian Brady once about the psychology of Carl Jung. Brady commented: 'He's the only theoretician I find relevant.' In his book *The Psychology of Nazism*, Jung appears to agree with Brady's understanding of 'psychopath':

> I am aware that the word 'psychopathic' strikes harshly on the layman's ear, and that it conjures up all manner of horrors, such as lunatic asylums and the like. By way of explanation I should like to state that only a very small fraction of so-called psychopaths land in the asylum. The overwhelming majority of them constitute that part of the population which is alleged to be 'normal' . . .
>
> . . . So anyone whose ears are offended by the word 'psychopath' is at liberty to suggest a soft, soothing, comforting substitute which correctly reflects the state of mind that gave birth to National Socialism.

The author Colin Wilson once exchanged letters with Ian Brady for a long period and, in his foreword to *The Gates of Janus*, comments that Brady could be an explosive and difficult correspondent. I never experienced this in my relations with Ian Brady. He may have thought that Colin Wilson's high profile made him fair game.

Brady is the most complicated man I have ever met. He was fond of saying that 'nothing is ever what it seems at first. We have to remove the patina of self-deception.' Brady was clearly intellectually gifted and could often surprise or startle you with a genuinely original slant on an issue; he is probably one of the most articulate killers in the long, infamous line of British murderers. This counts for nothing, of course, in the light of the cruel killing of a child. Ian Brady's actions have completely eclipsed what virtues he may have possessed.

Ian Brady craved for only two things in the years I knew him – anonymity in life and oblivion in death: 'It's oblivion for me. Only bores go to heaven.' His craving for anonymity could never be satisfied. The final crime of a serial killer is their fame. Yet to forget his victims is for them to die a second time.

INTRODUCTION

A MAN OF SECRETS

I glanced at the clock on the wall: 1.55 p.m. It was a bright Sunday afternoon early in March 1994. I was in a small interview room on Newman Ward in the grounds of Ashworth Hospital for the Criminally Insane in Maghull, a dormitory town for Liverpool and Merseyside. I was waiting to meet Ian Brady for the first time and reflecting on what had brought me there. I had seen the various prison security photographs of him over the years. In some pictures he was bloated; in others he was skeletal. I had been writing to him for just two years but had no idea what he looked like now.

I was a little nervous, standing in what was said by some to be the most dangerous few square yards in the United Kingdom. Ashworth Hospital had been in the news several times over recent years with reports of 'no-go' areas where staff were afraid to venture.

A man with dreadlocks blocked my path on the way to the interview room and asked me what I was doing there. This was no-man's-land for a stranger. Several men were walking around freely. I learned later that almost all of them had committed murder. As a visitor penetrating this wilderness, I was an object of curiosity.

I was looking at the clock again when Ian Brady walked into the room on the stroke of 2 o'clock. He looked much younger than I had expected and had a full head of hair. He was at least six foot – another surprise. We shook hands and sat down. He was wearing a black polo neck sweater, blue jeans, a blue coat and shiny black shoes. Before he spoke, I saw my own reflection in his dark glasses. Shades of Alfred Hitchcock. In the years that followed, Brady broke his glasses several times and sent them to me for repairs.

1

Visiting time was from 2 to 4 p.m., but I was still there at 6.30 p.m. There were no other visitors to the ward. I handed Ian Brady chocolates and several blue packets of Gauloises, his favourite untipped, strong French cigarettes. He gave me a book, *New Pathways in Psychology*, by Colin Wilson. Wilson had sent the book to Brady with a written dedication. Brady had made his own notes in the margins.

I had read all the available books and many of the articles on the Moors Murders. My mind was flooded with questions, not least the simple one that has lingered in the minds of many thousands of people for decades: what actually happened? I was sitting no more than a yard away from one of the two people on earth who could tell me.

Brady introduced the very first topic: 'How many instruments of murder do you think are in this room?' I was taken aback by the starkness of the question and struggled for a reply. After he had enlightened me, I asked my first question: 'Why children?' He answered immediately: 'Existential exercises.'

It would be some time before I learned the full meaning of his words. After explaining himself briefly, he went on to tell me in great detail how he had planned to kill Myra Hindley's former fiancé, Ronnie Sinclair, and David Smith, the man who finally reported Brady to the police. I was surprised at the amount of intricate, precise detail Brady covered in telling me about those two men who were, apparently, lucky to be still breathing as we spoke. As with many other themes, during our communication over the years Brady added to the detail of this first account of the plan to kill Ronnie Sinclair, referring to conversations he had with Myra concerning it, and so on.

Ian Brady had strained his back in the kitchens just before I arrived and he stood up from time to time in order to stretch. He towered over me as I looked up – a view shared by his victims in their dying moments. Brady demonstrated how easy it was to strangle someone. He claimed he could do this with one hand. He quoted Robert Walker's lines in Alfred Hitchcock's *Strangers on a Train* explaining the virtues of strangulation: 'Simple, silent and quick.' Brady recalled seeing the film at the Claremont cinema in Manchester.

Brady's parting words to me at the close of this first meeting were, 'I haven't become stooped and white haired, so I must be mad . . . Until whenever.'

As I reflected on the encounter while driving south for home, one of the things that had most surprised me was the sheer detail in his descriptions, particularly those concerning Ronnie Sinclair and David Smith. This was to become a familiar experience for me. I imagined that since these conversations were not taped, he was free to vent whatever he wished. When his descriptions and stories were repeated in more detail over the years I began to feel I knew them better than him. Sometimes he would ask me what he had said about such and such.

Later the same day, I wrote down everything I could remember of what Brady had said. I did so after every visit. I had a good memory for remembered dialogue, as did Brady. I couldn't have known that years later I would have the dubious privilege of inheriting Ian Brady's property. When I eventually sifted through it I found an illustrated leaflet entitled, 'Where To Strike'. It reminded me of the very first question Brady put to me. In the course of time, he claimed to have used a variety of means to kill people – knives, a hatchet, his bare hands and guns. I learned from Brady that the best way to defend yourself, if suddenly attacked, is to kick your assailant's kneecaps.

As I have already mentioned, Ian Brady always wrote to me the same evening, after my visit, to thank me for travelling to see him and for the cigarettes and sweets I gave him. This was to be a regular pattern for several years. On the evening of my first visit he wrote; 'I think the visit went well. Occasionally I had to use mental blocks, when you asked a question about my case, especially a leading question.'

After spending four or five hours in dialogue with Ian Brady, you certainly felt it. I will expand on this much later in the book.

My first meeting with him had its origin in courses I taught in a sixth-form college in the West Midlands. The government had clarified the law on the study of religion in state schools. Sixth-form colleges should now offer courses in religion, in addition to the usual range of examination subjects at Advanced level. I was Head of Religious Studies at the college and taught courses in religion that led to an Advanced level certificate, as did all courses in the various academic fields.

The new ruling meant that non-examination courses had to be offered to all students in the college. The students were perfectly free to opt out if they wished. Many colleges in the country ignored the government ruling, assuming that the majority of students would opt out. Colleges would almost certainly have to find money for additional staff to teach the courses in religion.

My own college had its origins in the sixteenth century and was very aware of its traditional values. It responded positively to the government's new ruling and we discovered that hardly any student wished to opt out of the non-examination courses in religion. As a result, a new member of staff was appointed and he joined me in offering a very wide range of courses from Zen Buddhism to the religious symbolism in Bob Dylan's songs.

One of the most popular courses was a study of evil from religious, philosophical and psychological perspectives, using material from murder cases that cast light – or darkness – on the human condition. John Hick, the professor who supervised my doctoral studies at Birmingham University in the early 1970s, was one of the world's leading philosophers on evil and religion and had written the standard work on the subject. The book – *Evil and the God of Love* – is still a highly acclaimed bestseller and known by thousands of students as 'Egol'. I was, therefore, quite familiar with the material to be explored by students at my own college.

No written work was required on any of these courses. Since there were no examinations to prepare for, the sessions were periods in which students could relax and be free for a time from the academic grind. These courses were not meant 'to lead to something'. Consequently, we could invite guests to talk to the students informally on the chosen topic for the sheer hell of it, and we made full use of this freedom. If there was an underlying purpose for the courses, it was to give the students a range of vertical glimpses into the great minds, the great traditions and the great lives, in the context of the horizontal experience of belonging to this moment, in this century, in this place.

In addition to sessions on evil, I taught a course on miscarriages of justice. The college was just a couple of miles from Yew Tree Farm, near Stourbridge, where Carl Bridgewater was murdered as he was delivering a newspaper. The Bridgewater Four were jailed for life for the crime. Ann Whelan, the mother of one of the Four – Michael Hickey – had campaigned tirelessly for years to free her son, who was still in prison when she visited the college. She came with Teresa Robinson, the wife of Jimmy Robinson, another one of the Bridgewater Four. Some time before, a former governor of Gartree prison, John Berry, talked with the students, and had been at Gartree when Michael Hickey made his 89-day roof protest at Gartree through the winter of 1983–4.

Dick McIlkenny, one of the Birmingham Six, came and spoke very movingly about his own case, about the brutality, forgiveness and the joy of freedom after more than sixteen years' imprisonment for something he didn't do. Unprompted, Dick McIlkenny told me that he made late night drinks for Ian Brady in prison. Years later, I mentioned this conversation to Brady, but he had no recollection of McIlkenny providing such a service. Michael Hickey was eventually transferred to Ashworth. Ian Brady told me that Hickey had given him the papers on the case and that the Bridgewater Four were obviously innocent.

We had a number of fascinating visitors on the 'Evil' courses. The options were offered to students under titles that changed from year to year to capture the passing mood. Britain's last surviving hangman, Syd Dernley, came every year to talk about capital punishment and his part in executing – among others – Timothy Evans, sentenced to death in 1950 for his role in the murders of his wife Beryl and their baby daughter Geraldine. Evans was pardoned some years after John Christie was executed for the murder of a number of women whose bodies were found at number 10 Rillington Place in London. Christie confessed to the murder of Beryl Evans before he was hanged.

I used to get out of bed very early and drive north to Syd's home in Mansfield, Nottinghamshire and have breakfast with Syd and his wife Joyce, before driving Syd back south to the West Midlands for a day of sessions at the college. Syd showed students wooden models of the execution procedure. All the way down the motorway and all the way back, he told me fascinating, unrepeatable stories of the executions he had been involved in. Staff and students alike knew him affectionately as 'Whispering Syd', a real character who would put his feet up on a chair in the staff room and smoke his pipe heedless of the 'No Smoking' signs. I had tea at Syd's bungalow before driving back south and he usually gave me bottles of his home-made wine, which would fetch paint off the walls.

One morning I answered my classroom phone in the middle of a lesson. It was Joyce Dernley. She said, 'Syd's just dropped dead.' All of Britain's hangmen were now deceased. Students didn't believe me when I told them that about a dozen people were hanged in England every year when I was a child. Syd never missed an opportunity to say that he would come out of retirement to hang Ian Brady and Myra Hindley.

Brian Masters, the author of the acclaimed book on Dennis Nilsen, *Killing For Company*, spoke with the students when he was fresh from attending the trial of Rosemary West and shortly after the publication his book on the case, *She Must Have Known*. Among other books on the dark side of human nature, and acute contributions to several television documentaries, he had written on the case of Jeffrey Dahmer, who was killed by a fellow prisoner. I mentioned the Moors case to Brian Masters. He said, 'Brady's mad.' Nothing more.

Geoffrey Wansell had also attended Rosemary West's trial and written his own book on the case, *An Evil Love*. He had listened to recordings of Fred West – Rose's husband – talking for many hours about his crimes. Wansell told the students that he had been driven to question radically his own assumptions about life after his involvement in what came to be called the Cromwell Street Murders. It was clear from the students' reactions later that Brian Masters and Geoffrey Wansell had made an impact.

Jonathan Goodman, the author of many books on past crimes, agreed to visit the college. I was still teaching when he arrived and I found him looking at a poster outside in the corridor, announcing that the football legend, Stanley Matthews, had visited the week before. A hard act to follow. Jon gave a fascinating talk on murder and answered questions on the cases he had written about. He was brilliant and had an enviable natural charm. He had edited the official transcript of the Brady and Hindley trial and introduced it with his summary of the case. It was published as *The Moors Murders*. A student asked him about his feelings on the case. Jon replied that in the course of writing it he had been offered the opportunity of meeting Myra Hindley. He turned the offer down. 'Evil is contagious,' said Jon. The Lesley Ann Downey tape had extinguished any sympathy he may have had for her.

Peter Timms, former governor of Maidstone prison and the man to whom Myra Hindley first confessed, visited the college every year. Ann West – the mother of Lesley Ann Downey – came to the college with her husband, Alan, to give a view of Myra Hindley bitterly opposed to that of Peter Timms. It was on the occasion of the Wests' visit that they prompted me to approach Ian Brady after their correspondence with him had ended. Without their suggestion I would never have contacted Brady. The roles of Peter Timms and Ann West in the lives of Ian Brady and Myra Hindley are described as this story unfolds.

Before my own involvement with Ian Brady, as I have already observed, I had read the various books devoted exclusively to the case, in addition to magazine articles and chapters in books of collected cases. The Moors Murders were guaranteed a chapter in books with such titles as *Killer Couples*, *Child Killers*, *Women Who Kill*, *Sex Killers*, and so on. And there is certainly a steady market for this area: Emlyn Williams' book, *Beyond Belief*, sold more than 250,000 copies.

It was only after I made contact with Ian Brady that I learned just how inaccurate some of the material on the Moors case was. The bare facts of the Moors Murders are awful enough without their flights of fancy. When an author states what seems to be a fact about Ian Brady, for example, it invariably means nothing more than that they have read it somewhere else. The inaccuracies are compounded when the material is reproduced from publication to publication.

As far as Brady's childhood is concerned, there is an assumed body of 'facts' without which no book or article is complete: he was a 'loner'; he had been brought up in an unloving, dysfunctional family; he was sexually abused; he escaped the emotional vacuum of his childhood in the fantasy of films of violence and torture; he imprisoned cats, crucified frogs, sliced up caterpillars with razor blades, beheaded rabbits; tied up friends and set fire to them; killed and buried a child on a bombsite and collected Nazi memorabilia from when he was about eight years old.

It sounds like heresy to say so, but it is quite likely that none of these things are true. To say so is not to whitewash Ian Brady, but to point out that almost anything can be written about the Moors Murders and be believed. It has to be stated emphatically in the opening pages of this book that the family Brady grew up with – the Sloans – were particularly loving and caring. Whatever else happened in the life of Ian Brady, he never forgot what the family had meant to him. He never forgave himself for how badly he had repaid them.

In an article for the *Sunday Times*, two days after Myra Hindley's death, in November 2002, Jean Ritchie claimed that Ian Brady had experienced a strange and damaging childhood. As an illegitimate child, she explains that he was 'farmed out' to a kind family. In spite of this, she adds, Brady felt like a 'cuckoo in the nest'.

The *real* reasons underlying the Moors Murders have been obscured by the almost irresistible temptation to gild the lily with malevolence and impute horror at virtually every point, from the early childhoods of Hindley and Brady onwards. Locating the roots of the Moors Murders in the childhoods of Brady and Hindley passes over the fundamental reasons for these murders. The truth is, in a sense, far worse.

The sustained media coverage, over decades, of Ian Brady, Myra Hindley and all aspects of the Moors case, is unprecedented in British criminal history. The case is also one of the longest-running stories in the history of British journalism. Murder has always sold newspapers, the murders carried out by Brady and Hindley more than any other: 'If it bleeds, it leads.'

Brady himself makes the point in his book *The Gates of Janus*: 'Murder . . . the most popular primal form of public entertainment there is or ever shall be.' He added that demand was outstripping supply. Writing in March 2000, the *Guardian*'s columnist, the late Hugo Young, wrote: 'The Moors Murders have no parallel in the culture, no equal in the almanac of foul remembered crimes. A vast publication industry has been built on their continued existence unhanged, after butchery which 10 years earlier would have sent them to the gallows.'

In a letter to me Brady mentioned the *Guardian*'s survey of the news coverage of murder cases: 'The Moors Murders have received an average of 151 reports a year in the British press – three reports a week for 30 years. Why? Rampant greed. It sells newspapers. The Yorkshire Ripper, arrested 15 years after me, is second in the league table of newspaper money spinners, with a mere 34 reports a year.'

In another letter, Brady referred to the media's current obsession with serial killers and spoke of 'the "designer" irrationality of the mystique'. In response, I asked him to explain the massive press interest in the Moors Murders. Why Brady and Hindley? Why not others? Brady replied: 'Why Jack the Ripper – a mere five murders over a hundred years ago? I suppose there is a parallel mystique, even a romantic gestalt; the foggy, gas-lit cobbled alleys, and the menacing, misty desolation of the moors, present an amorphous dimension of "evil", reflecting the shrouded dark thoughts in every individual.'

Life sentence murderers are usually left to serve their time in obscurity, with very occasional media interest in a high-profile case. The eventual release of killers from prison is reported only rarely. The Moors Murders have never been far from the public's interest. Some reactions took the form of wild comparisons.

At the time of the Moors trial, one politician said that the Nuremberg war trials faded into insignificance by comparison. Another said the same of the Japanese torture of their prisoners of war. John Stalker, the former Deputy Chief Constable of Greater Manchester, and later a media pundit on crime, captured the more reasoned mood of many when he said: 'Nothing in criminal behaviour, before or since, has penetrated my heart with quite the same intensity.'

Peter Topping, the detective who reopened the Moors Murders investigation in 1986, was walking on very thin glass in his dealings with Ian Brady. He added that finding a way into his mind was, 'like getting a crowbar into a crack.' Topping added that Brady was always thinking three moves ahead. I mentioned Topping's comment to Ian Brady. He replied, 'Topping wasn't even on the playing field, let alone three moves behind.'

From my very first meeting with Brady, I knew he was a man of secrets. His very life force appeared to depend upon knowing terrible secrets known to no one but himself. My contact with him had begun, after the prompting of Ann and Alan West, out of a desire to know why he and Myra Hindley committed the murders and to hear his version of what had actually happened on Saddleworth Moor and in number 16 Wardle Brook Avenue. I'm sure that many people wrote to him with the same motive.

It had been obvious for years, to people who had more than fleeting contact with him, that the prospects of Ian Brady confessing to a 'screw', a detective, a journalist, a criminologist, a fellow patient, or a doctor at Ashworth Hospital were zero. The cleaner stood more chance. Peter Topping reflected on his interviews with him and concluded that he would never talk about the murders.

Topping was mistaken. After a few years, Ian Brady slowly began to reveal more and more to me in visits and in letters, particularly in the period before his outgoing mail was opened and read. On many of the letters he wrote 'DESTROY' in red block capitals. For a long period, in circumstances I will describe later, he phoned me every day and at weekends more than once. I also phoned him in Ashworth.

I had a few things in common with Brady. Like him, I had come from a working-class background and had become a 'lunchtime student' after starting work. We were both half-self-mis-educated. We began clerical work at the same time: he in Manchester, I in a railway office in the Black Country of the West Midlands. I left school at fifteen with no qualifications, as did Brady. I have already commented upon Ian Brady's intellectual gifts. Whatever else we may wish to say about him, this dimension of his character has to be accepted if we are to understand the factors which underly the phenomenon we know as the Moors Murders.

Brady had no regrets about not attending a university. He couldn't see any point in absorbing information in a formal setting and reproducing it on demand for the sake of gaining a certificate. He had read widely before he went to prison, making use of any odd moment. In the prison years Brady was able to read most of the classics of world literature, philosophy and religion: 'I have read quite a bit of theology and philosophy and can even appreciate the attraction of Christianity without religion described in the writings of Dietrich Bonhoeffer and Leo Tolstoy.'

The story told in the chapters that follow may be as near as we shall ever get to knowing how the Moors victims died and what happened in the relationship between Ian Brady and Myra Hindley. In my own relationship with Brady I found that he had extraordinary powers of recall; he once commented, 'I've almost a photographic memory for people, places and dialogue, needing only the smallest accurate detail to trigger recollection.'

Music triggered memories for the Moors Murderers. I discovered that one of the unspoken features of the Moors saga was its link in the minds of both of them with the passing contemporary pop scene. I have referred to several editions of *British Hit Singles*, and listened to many hours of music taped by Brady to date stages in his relationship with Myra.

If Brady's autobiography is ever published, I believe it will confirm much of the substance – if not the detail – of the story you are about to read. Brady longed for oblivion and nothing could make matters worse for him. As he often said to me: 'The world and times I knew has gone. No longer being in the game myself, I can observe the passing comedy with the detachment of a ghost and the equanimity of the hopeless. I am finished. I have no reason to lie. Myra's letters to me still exist and will confirm my version of the events.' In his book *The Gates of Janus*, which I will return to later in this story, Brady wrote: 'I am not under the least obligation to please by deceit any individual whomsoever. To all practical intents and purposes, I am no longer of your world – if, as you might suggest, I ever was. I am now simply a curious observer, resistant to "thirty years of blur and blot".' In a letter to Home Secretary Jack Straw in 1997, at the time of Myra Hindley's High Court appeal against a ruling that she should never be released, Ian Brady commented, 'I myself have never applied for parole and never shall, which is why I can afford the luxury of veracity and free expression.'

Brady told me that he wanted his autobiography to be published under the title *Black Light*. The significance of this should become clear as the cloak-and-dagger story develops. Once, when we were talking about the autobiography, Brady said that it was a product of his editing from a copious manuscript penned during his decades in prison: 'I've tried to relive the past by means of a stream of consciousness. I have worked on myself to remove mental blocks which I consciously built over time for my self-protection. This is the only way I could present an authentic account. Regular, daily medication has enabled me to raise the barriers which would have remained firmly in place and the story untold. It has been a real task to recreate the ways I thought, talked and acted so far in the past. In those dim and distant days I reached the point where my mind knew no limits. It was a state of total mental fragmentation.'

I asked him if his autobiography covered events up to the present time: 'No. There's nothing about the prison years, during which I have been nothing more than a ghost. The book is in two parts. The first covers events from birth up to my meeting with Myra Hindley. The second half describes my relationship with her and the murders.

'When I tested the waters with some American publishers I was told that people would be interested in the murders rather than my early life. I laid down a condition from the beginning. It is to be published *in full* or not at all. There is a legally binding contract to ensure this is done.

'It is to be published precisely in my own words. Unlike Topping I do not require a ghost-writer or a newspaper hack to write for me.'

I have some tattered, faded, A4 yellow notebook covers that Ian Brady obviously kept through the prison years and in which he recorded short passages from the books he had read. One of his hand-written quotations is from Charles Dickens' *Sketches by Boz*. Brady told me that the passage, particularly the italicised words, was a perfect encapsulation of how he looked back on his life when he picked up his pen to write his autobiography: 'There are strange chords in the human heart, which will lie dormant through years of *depravity and wickedness*, but which will vibrate at last to some slight circumstance apparently trivial in itself, but connected by some undefined and indistinct association, with past days that can never be recalled, and with bitter recollections from which *the most degraded creature in existence cannot escape*.'

In my conversations with him Brady said he wanted this passage as a frontispiece for his autobiography. He did tell me once that – Moors Murders apart – he hoped that his writings would convey to future generations some flavour of life in Glasgow in the mid-twentieth century and particularly that of the Gorbals, which had meant so much to him. It was clear to me from the very first visit that Brady enjoyed talking in intimate detail about his life in the Glasgow days. It was the happiest time of his life. Brady said, 'Although the Gorbals was a sprawling grimy cathedral of ramshackle tenements, it was a shrine of innocence for me.'

Brady told me that writing his autobiography had been cathartic for him: 'It helped me to pull a lot of threads together for me and my squandered life. As Emerson wrote: "The years teach much that the days never know." '

The life of Myra Hindley is infinitely more transparent and accessible than that of the secretive Ian Brady. Before she met him, her life was unremarkable and followed the predictable pattern lived out by countless of her working-class contemporaries. In contrast, it is futile to look for a similar pattern in Brady's life. It was kaleidoscopic – an image he often used. With each tick of the clock the pieces of experience come down in new array. In another metaphor, he spoke of the growth of a vine of scarlet and black in his life. But it wasn't always black.

What little has so far been known about Brady's life and thought has had to bear the weight of interpretations that it cannot support. Umpteen writers have ascribed the Moors Murders to Ian Brady's obsession with Nazism and the writings of the Marquis de Sade. Several times, in conversation with me, he has scoffed at this interpretation.

The fundamental cause and reason for the events known as the Moors Murders lies in Ian Brady's lifelong conviction that life is meaningless and the universe is without purpose. Therefore, nothing matters. Brady didn't need to read the books of the Marquis de Sade to convince him that life was purposeless. He had come to that conclusion long before he read de Sade.

Knowing Brady's passion for the books of Dostoevsky, I once reminded him that Alyosha, the central character in *The Brothers Karamazov* – Brady's favourite novel – had feared the consequences of complete relativism: 'Without God everything is permitted.' In a letter of October 1992 Brady wrote: 'Yes, Alyosha has reason to be worried by the notion that "everything is permitted". People fear the Unconditional, the realm of total possibility; they crave for any illusions, religious or otherwise, that will stave off reality, give meaning to their existence. Subconsciously they fear they will implode if the inner emptiness is not filled by the artificial substance of illusion. We accepted gladly the indifference of the universe; it provided a power source, explosive and implosive.

'You may argue that such is only another form of illusion, a negative one. But I say it is facing up to reality, squaring up to the void, and turning it into a source of active energy to ascend above the pie-in-the-sky believers. When I enter the stream of consciousness to accurately capture the gestalt, the ethos of times past, I feel the invulnerability of the contempt and indifference.'

I shall discuss the specific question of meaninglessness in the Moors case in a later chapter. But this question hangs like a shadow over the life of Ian Brady from his earliest days and over Myra Hindley's life as a young adult. It's necessary to devote a few paragraphs to the issue here so that its importance can be recognised by the reader from the beginning of the story they are about to hear.

A day was set aside every year at my college for the students to listen to visitors from universities and colleges who were specialists in their own field. The visiting lecturers would talk about the attractions and rewards of studying their subject at degree level. I had the job of looking after the visiting philosopher for the day. I knew that I would never meet them again and so was bold enough to ask, over coffee, if their students ever stayed behind after lectures to ask them if philosophy had given them any clues or convictions about the purpose of existence. Every year, to a man – they were all men – the reply was that life has no meaning other than what you give it in your allotted span on this earth. They were in the tradition of the English philosopher A J Ayer and thousands of others like him. For most of his life Ian Brady has said exactly the same.

In conversations, Brady often returned to the point that we are no more than insignificant ants in a purposeless universe. Again, the conclusions of many scientists seem to confirm Brady's view, even though they put it less graphically. In *The Gates of Janus*, Brady comments:

> The serial killer, essentially conceiving life as meaningless and death as nothingness, is consequently not afraid to die or kill in a final vainglorious attempt to introduce some degree of design . . .

> [Serial killers] create their own spiritual or aesthetic microcosm. Metaphorically gods in their own kingdom, whimsically sampling everything that was once forbidden, eventually taking the lives of those who have entered their private domain, witnessed their darkest desires and, therefore must never be allowed to leave or testify.

Many scientists rule out even this desperate gesture. William Provine said: 'Our modern understanding of evolution implies that ultimate meaning in life is nonexistent.' Steven Weinberg agreed: 'The more the universe seems comprehensible, the more it seems pointless.' The Nobel Prize winner Jacques Monod said that the systematic denial of purpose is the cornerstone of science. Pooh bear's boast – 'I can trace my ancestry to a protoplasmal globule' – is turned on its head. Science has made all truth provisional – or so it seems to many academics.

The American behaviourist B F Skinner argued some years ago that, 'man always behaves as his self-interest requires.' Men are trousered apes. Skinner added: 'The goal of science is the destruction of mystery.' In my view, this has to be one of the most fatuous, idiotic statements of all time. Since this was written, the Nobel Prize winner Francis Crick, in his book *The Astonishing Hypothesis*, concluded that human feelings are no more than the behaviour of nerve cells. The thought behind the old put-down, that violinists are only scraping catgut with horsehair, could now be applied to the cosmos itself.

Shakespeare's line in *Macbeth*, on the tragedy of the human condition, could well be a perfect distillation of the conclusions of many contemporary scientists and philosophers: 'Tomorrow, and tomorrow, and tomorrow . . . a tale / Told by an idiot full of sound and fury, / Signifying nothing.' Ian Brady couldn't agree more: 'People with wealth and fame commit suicide, tramps breathe on in misery. In the end, nothing really matters and is all illusion or delusion. We each do what we believe is best, that's all.' In June 2001, having been force-fed for twenty months by that time, Brady paused in the middle of a letter he was writing to me to ask himself: 'Why bother to write anything at all in view of the perception of meaningless reality? Answer, something to pass the time away that's all, as I sit here at the end of a force-feed tube, exemplifying the accuracy of my observations and the essential absurdity of all life. I wonder if anyone will ever write or think something that hasn't already been done? Even if someone stumbled on the meaning of life, who would know or wish to believe them anyway? Much better for most to dream of afterlifes and other religious concepts of comforts and rationalisations obfuscating oblivion. The most one can say about life is that it's an interesting experience, and the only one. Death is the meaning of life, the race against oblivion; man being the only animal who is conscious that he will one day die; there lies the seed of self-destruction, greed for more, even if only to be remembered a short time longer than others, as if it mattered to the other walking dead. As I sit here writing, peripheral vision catches shapes moving around like aimless somnambulists, ears snatch conversation drivel, all about as significant as dust on the carpet, the microbes in the air.'

In recent times, a strident note can be heard in the pronouncements and prose of some academics. This is particularly so in the writings of scientists such as Richard Dawkins and Peter Atkins of Oxford University. Dawkins was once asked about the purpose of life and he replied: 'Well, there is no purpose and to ask what it is, is a silly question. It has the same status as "What is the colour of jealousy?" ' Dawkins wants to rid the world of the 'childlike inability to distinguish what is true from what we would like to be true'. In his book, *A Devil's Chaplain*, Dawkins gives a detailed account of religion itself as a 'virus of the mind'.

Atkins would go as far as putting fellow lecturers at Oxford University on the dole. With all the gravity of a papal pronouncement, he said: 'It is deplorable that in modern-day Oxford the study of theology is taken so seriously that there is a professorship. It is a chair in the study of fantasy.' There was a time when only popes were allowed to pronounce on their own infallibility. Even the Catholic Church granted a sort of pardon for those who could not help being 'invincibly ignorant'. There used to be no salvation outside the Catholic Church. Now, it seems, there is no salvation outside science.

In my own long experience of studying and writing about religion, I have not encountered an uninformed dismissal of religion and life's purpose that has been expressed so abrasively and savagely as it is in the writings and pronouncements of Dawkins, Atkins and lesser-known believers of this modern-day religion of scientism. Dawkins and Atkins and many others who believe in this pseudo-religion are as depressingly predictable as Mr Gradgrind in *Hard Times*: 'In this life we want nothing but Facts, sir, nothing but Facts.' In Dawkins' religion theologians are banished to the hell of worthlessness, where there is much weeping and wailing and gnashing of selfish genes.

I shall have a little more to say about the aggressive reductionism of Dawkins, Atkins and others later in the book as I consider what would be the alternative to Ian Brady's views. As we shall see, Brady could find no meaning in life, but he never thought it was 'silly' to search for it. As far as Christianity was concerned, Brady read the Bible and some theology, as he claimed in a comment I have already mentioned.

On one occasion Brady put his own view very concisely. Religion was, to him, 'the self-flattering delusion of mankind that some supernatural force is in the least interested in the life of ants on a speck of dust in the universe.' Many philosophers would agree with him.

In a purposeless universe, many academics want to deny other people their brand of meaninglessness while retaining their own. Dawkins accepts the ruthless indifference of the process of evolution. It is neither kind nor cruel, but indifferent. Yet he claims he is not inconsistent with his own acceptance of the brutal facts by showing revulsion against its implications.

Dawkins says there is no inconsistency in 'explaining cancer as an academic doctor while fighting it as a practising one.' The ruthless career of evolution has blundered unwittingly on its own negation. We have a brain endowed with the gift of understanding its own origins. Therefore, we can plan the very opposite of natural selection's massive wastage and its blindness to suffering.

Dawkins is, after all, making an assumption, a value statement about the intrinsic worth of the human state and he is not averse to using religious concepts to do so. Commenting on the British government's proposals to encourage the creation of faith schools, Dawkins called them 'evil'.

But there is nothing 'evil' in a purposeless universe, unless the word is used merely to mean disapproval of some sort. By his own lights, 'evil' is just a colourful word used by an organism reacting to a feature of its territory that it wants to eliminate. Dawkins accepts only one kind of truth – scientific truth. Ludwig Wittgenstein toiled in vain.

It is, of course, no argument against their reasoned claims to the truth to say that they are false because the implications are bleak. Brady believed the truth to be as bleak as it could be. Nietzsche, whom he admired, wrote: 'The best is not to be born; the next best is to die soon.' Another of Brady's philosophical mentors, Schopenhauer, concluded that 'Life is something that should not have been.' But we are stuck with it. Brady often commented, as I have already noted, that crime in general, and murder in particular, paradoxically entertains millions of individuals, making life bearable on the way to their own oblivion.

As I implied earlier, Ian Brady sometimes spoke to me about the new kind of serial killer that will become more and more a feature of modern life: 'An existential killer is emerging. Perhaps "the medium is the message". Serial killers are becoming increasingly part of show business, and this is creating a self-conscious artistry; the difference between a brutal daub and a finished canvas. He has design and purpose. He takes a page from de Quincey's essay, as it were. They are in great demand by the public, their very victims, each of whom believes it will only happen to some other person, not them. So, paradoxically, they are getting what they deserve, being treated as empty canvases, or the very source of the colours the existential killer may choose to use.'

Some would claim that, until now, there has never been such a consensus, among the most 'intelligent' of the human species, that there is no final, eternal context in which kind, humane actions are good and selfish or murderous acts evil. After all, behaviourists would claim that killers are doing what they have been programmed by nature to do: to behave as their self-interest requires.

Denials of the bleak implications of the academic bad news are sometimes based on the plain evidence of the senses. In Woody Allen's film *Annie Hall* there is a scene in which a young boy tells a psychiatrist that there is no point in doing his homework because the universe is expanding and will eventually break apart. His mother screams, 'What has the universe got to do with it? You're in Brooklyn and Brooklyn is not expanding!'

*   *   *   *   *

In my conversations with Ian Brady, he returned again and again to the subject of professional philosophers who, 'always stop halfway. If they didn't, they'd abandon attempts to discover a universal philosophy. Once you believe in chaos and absurdity, all but individual philosophy becomes meaningless, absurd and chaotic.'

This is why Brady called himself an 'existentialist': 'The majority of people are afraid to face stark eternity. They create veils of meaningfulness to hide it from themselves. No matter how vast a philosophy is fabricated, the ego always pops up to laugh at the absurdity of it all.' Brady asked, 'Why does my action strike them as hideous?' He was quoting from Dostoevsky's *Crime and Punishment*, a book that casts a long shadow over the Moors Murders.

Ian Brady uses Dostoevsky's words to describe the targets of his vitriol: 'tuppenny ha'penny philosophers'. In another translation they are called '5 copek philosophers'. The philosophers spell out the same grim facts as the scientists, in Ian Brady's eyes, and both groups, according to him, seem blind to the implications.

Yet, often, individuals without philosophical pretensions see the implications only too clearly. Some years ago I was teaching a small group of sixth-formers studying the philosophy of religion. One of the girls in the group was absent from the class one day. She was attending the funeral of a close friend. The following day she told me that she had read a quotation from Bertrand Russell's *Mysticism and Logic and Other Essays* in her textbook an hour or so before the funeral. The passage filled her with despair. This is what she read:

> That Man is the product of causes which had no prevision of the end
> they were achieving; that his origin, his growth, his hopes and fears,

his loves and his beliefs, are but the outcome of accidental collocations of atoms; that no fire, no heroism, no intensity of thought and feeling, can preserve an individual life beyond the grave; that all the labours of the ages, all the devotion, all the inspiration, all the noonday brightness of human genius, are destined to extinction in the vast death of the solar system, and that the whole temple of Man's achievement must inevitably be buried beneath the debris of a universe in ruins – all these things, if not quite beyond dispute, are yet so nearly certain, that no philosophy that rejects them can hope to stand. Only within the scaffolding of these truths, only on the firm foundation of unyielding despair, can the soul's habitation henceforth be safely built.

Ian Brady's own brand of unyielding despair would be at odds with that of Bertrand Russell, but he would agree with everything in the passage. Brady used fewer words: 'Why do we yearn for something that will outlive us, when we know that, eventually, all living things will disappear and leave nothing behind to show that there was once something there? Our deluded yearnings for immortality are comical and preposterous. Life, like death, doesn't give a damn about us.'

Shakespeare's *Hamlet* put Brady's view more succinctly:

> Imperious Caesar, dead and turned to clay,
> Might stop a hole to keep the wind away.

After a three-part television series on the Gloucester murders committed by Fred and Rosemary West, a journalist writing in the *Daily Mirror* wondered why West was referred to as 'Fred' throughout. He asked, 'Can you conceive that anyone could call Brady, "Ian"?' Myra Hindley had her own problems in using other people's Christian names. When Lesley Ann White interviewed her for the *Sunday Times* in December 1994, Hindley admitted that it was difficult for her to address the journalist by her Christian names. She was also ill at ease when she had to address any man as 'Ian':

At the Moors trial in 1966, Ian Brady challenged one part of a statement to the police attributed to him on the grounds that he couldn't have referred to the last victim – Edward Evans – as 'Eddie'. Brady said, 'I never used anyone's Christian name until I knew them very well.' In the chapters that follow, I usually refer to Ian Brady as 'Ian' for the years before his life of serious crime began and sometimes also in his later years with Myra Hindley.

In a television documentary on the search for Keith Bennett's body, his brother, Alan, who visited Myra Hindley in prison, commented that it would have been pointless to be face to face with her and call her a 'murdering bitch'. He would have learned nothing. No relationship would have been established with the person who may have held the key. Similarly, anything I learned from Ian Brady was only possible on the basis of a certain kind of relationship in a compartment of his life where such things could be discussed. Brady himself had a long correspondence with the brother of Keith Bennett, the third victim of Moors Murderers.

Many people may well say that Brady and Hindley should have been left to rot in their little rooms. It's a point of view that is often passionately put. But, again, we would have learned nothing from them about the facts of the Moors Murders or the nature of the minds that conceived and committed the murders. Thomas Hardy once wrote, 'if a way to the better there be, it exacts a full look at the worst.' Brady himself sometimes quoted Tennyson:

This truth within thy mind rehearse,
That in a boundless universe,
Is boundless better, boundless worse.

In books of this kind, the author is tempted by the page to add personal moral judgements on actions or events they have described. Without overt disapproval, the reader might think the author unsympathetic to the victims. In the literature on the Moors Murders, self-serving indignation is never far away. It's as though a biographer related the tale and couldn't resist the temptation to add comments in brackets: 'That wasn't very nice, was it?'

With the exception of the final pages and the occasional paragraph where I couldn't resist the temptation, I hope I have allowed the actions of Brady and Hindley to speak for themselves. Beyond that, I have tried to lay bare their thoughts and words. These too speak for themselves. It would be patronising for me to point out what is blindingly obvious to everyone I know – that, as even Brady's own supreme mentor, Dostoevsky wrote, crimes against children are the worst kind it is possible to commit on this planet. However, the reader would find it tiresome for me to say so on every page.

On the questions of life's purpose, or lack of it, Ian Brady's views were completely at odds with mine. He believed that the philosophical and religious news was unbelievably bad while I believed it was unbelievably good. We agreed on a truce: we wouldn't try to convert each other.

It has to be said, nevertheless, that Brady felt philosophers and scientists would eventually come to a consensus, sooner rather than later, about the utter purposelessness of human life. This is not to imply, of course, that those academics would sympathise with the views of Ian Brady. But it would be naïve not to consider the moral climate of a world inhabited by humans who tacitly assumed that there was no point to it all. The collective, subconscious awareness of the possible horrors of such a world has cast a shadow that the story of the Moors Murders has served only to darken even further. To be unaware of this is to be blind to the central core of the story I am about to tell.

The key to unlocking the mysteries of the Moors Murders lay with Brady. Myra Hindley, who was clinging on to the faint hope of freedom one day, had too much at stake to reveal the truth. This book is largely taken up with Brady's biography, his actions and his state of mind. It is a story that has so far remained unsaid. The story which develops in this book is based on my direct contact with him over a number of years; through visits, telephone conversations, letters and material found in his property. It has to be said, however, that he was a man of secrets to the end. There are things about Brady and Myra Hindley we shall never know.

Looking back over my correspondence and conversations with Brady, two of his sayings stay in my mind. When I left him after a visit or when he signed off at the end of a letter, he would invariably say or write, 'Until whenever'. When he regained his composure after a rage, he often said, 'Richard's himself again.' This seemed to be a quotation from Shakespeare's *Richard III*. Yet the quote is strangely absent from the accessible texts of the play. When I was sorting through Brady's property, I found a video of Laurence Olivier's performance in the film *Richard III* that contains the elusive sentence. He had watched the film as a boy:

> Conscience is but a word that cowards use,
> Devised at first to keep the strong in awe:
> Conscience avant.

Richard's himself again.
March on, join bravely, let us to it pell-mell;
If not to heaven, then hand in hand to hell.

Brady's parting words to me at the close of a visit during April 1994 were (expletives deleted): 'I would be like Jesus Christ if I could work miracles. As it is, I'm Richard III.'

CHAPTER ONE

BLACK SABBATH IN THE GORBALS

It was a warm Friday afternoon on 31 May 1996 in Ashworth Hospital. Ian Brady and I had been talking for an hour. There was a lull in the conversation. Then Brady said, 'You know, there's one thing I just can't stand.' I asked, 'What's that?' 'It's the way my mother's so deferential to the staff here when she comes. That's the worst thing,' he replied. It was fresh on his mind. 'She came yesterday. She's frail now after a fall. She's eighty five.'

A year or so before, Ian had told me about his early recollections of his mother. He called her 'Peggy'. She had prematurely grey hair with an ash-blonde effect. People remarked about her close resemblance to Rita Hayworth, the Hollywood film idol of the post-war years. As he grew up, Ian noticed the resemblance himself. I had seen a photograph of Ian's white-haired mother taken for an article in the *News of the World* of October 1994 in which it was alleged that she was breaking a thirty-year silence about her son.

The face that peered out to the Sunday morning readers was lined with care, but the features Ian Brady had inherited were plain to see. Her son had inherited the lips, puckered and pained in Mrs Brady's case, although down-turned and cruel in his infamous first police security photograph of October 1965. In the late 1980s Peter Topping, Manchester's head of CID, said that meeting Ian Brady's mother was almost as distressing and moving as meeting the parents of her son's victims. Fifty years before all of this, and where our story begins, Peggy naturally had no foreboding of the misery the years were to unfold. Never mind the future; she had a present to face.

It was Christmas 1937 in Glasgow – under the dark, threatening clouds of war in Europe. Peggy, full name Margaret Stewart, was 28 and heavily pregnant. The baby was expected in Hogmanay, but there would be no wise men or journalists to witness this birth. It was a time when it was shameful to be illegitimate, and even more shameful to be a single mother. There was no father on the birth certificate and Peggy's first name was given as 'Maggie'.

Peggy gave birth on Sunday, the second day of January 1938. In later years Ian Brady grew to loathe the first day of the week of all days in the Scottish calendar. Shops stood religiously closed and barred on Sundays according to the law, except for newsagents peddling puerile Sunday papers to the undiscriminating masses. 'Pubs,' said Brady, 'were closed to prevent any prospect of merriment on the Sabbath, made miserable by Scottish law. The pubs were grim and faded in the daylight. Cinema entrances – every departure from which, Monday to Saturday, brought a small sense of dying – were barred and shuttered – beggared of mystery or magic, offering no flickering entrancement, no vicarious adventures, to ease the boredom and drown out the trite, meaningless funereal noises reverberating from depressing, dilapidated churches. Sunday was a day not to be out in or born in. Especially not this Sunday, on which day I found myself "illegitimate" before taking my first breath. In my case, of course, most people would prefer the term "bastard".'

Decades into the future, Ian told me of the steps he had taken to plot the murder of the leading member of the Lord's Day Observance Society in revenge for the miserable Sundays he had been forced to endure as a child.

Maggie Stewart's baby was born at 12.40 p.m. in the Rottenrow Maternity Hospital, Glasgow. The birth itself was without complications and the boy weighed eight pounds. He was christened Ian Stewart a week later. In *Beyond Belief*, published thirty years after Ian Brady's birth, Emlyn Williams wrote: 'From the day of his birth, the spell had been woven. And nothing could have changed him. Nothing.' As an adult and in captivity, Brady laughed at Williams' fatuous Calvinistic view of predestination.

More than once, Brady talked about the trauma experienced by any mother who tried to bring up a child without a father in the 1940s: 'The social consequences of the stigma were bitter and unforgiving, whoever you were.' Brady often alluded to Dickens when he spoke about his first few weeks of life: 'After all, what were orphanages for if not for the likes of me?' Some writers have falsely and curiously reported that Ian Brady was raised in an orphanage, fostered, and then returned there. Not true. Peggy Stewart decided to keep her child. She scraped together a paltry living as a tearoom waitress in a large fashionable hotel in Glasgow but didn't know whether she would still have a job there after giving birth. Social Security support as we know it now was decades into the future. It was Hobson's choice for Peggy. She had to have a job, whatever it was.

Ian Brady was untroubled by the identity of his father. The one certain fact was that his father was a journalist, a piece of irony that will escape no one who has even the slightest knowledge of the drama of the later chapters of this book. All of the books, magazine articles and newspaper reports on the Moors Murders are confident that Brady never saw his father. This may not be true. A few comments are necessary here, even though they anticipate the story a little.

Ian was about six when Peggy introduced him to a man she called 'Peter'. He was tall and fair-haired and, with hindsight, Ian thought that this man was probably his father. This feeling was reinforced a short time later when Peggy and Peter asked Ian if he would like to go to Australia with them. At the time, it was possible for British citizens to emigrate to Australia for a nominal sum of £10 under a government-aided scheme. It was a one-way ticket. This meant nothing to the young Ian. He had grown to love and feel safe with the people he later discovered were his foster family, the Sloans. The subject of Australia was never raised again. Peter, whoever he was, disappeared from Ian's life. He was never mentioned or thought of again.

Peggy held on to her job but had to move from her home at number 8 Huntingdon Place. She found a single room in a brownstone tenement in the Gorbals, the notorious slum area in Glasgow. It was a first-storey room on the corner of the junction of Crown Street and the Caledonia Road, a main tramcar route into the heart of the city.

For the first few weeks after the birth Peggy could only work part-time. The drop in income meant that she could not afford the bare necessities of motherhood – food and clothing – quite apart from the regular bills for rent and fuel. The only solution was to work full-time and pay for someone to look after Ian. She put a note in a newsagent's window offering to give £1 per week to anyone willing and suitable. Peggy's wage was less than £3 per week and so £1 was hardly the pittance it seems today.

Peggy never told Ian how many people answered the advert, only that she chose with care. As it turned out, she chose more wisely than she could have known. Ian was destined to spend the next sixteen years with his new family – the happiest time of his life.

The woman chosen was Mrs Mary Sloan, a small housewife in her late thirties, a person who had, as Ian was to tell me many years later, 'an unaffected dignity about her, and unconsciously exuded this quality whatever fate dealt for her.' Her husband, John Sloan, was of average height with a sinewy physique that made him well suited to his job as a grain-mill worker at a firm, just a few minutes' walk from home, number 56 Camden Street in the Gorbals.

Although John Sloan was mild and unpretentious, he could be firm when the occasion demanded. One of his favourite sayings was that everyone 'should have a trade at their fingertips.' No doubt he said this because he had never been taught a skilled trade himself. Meagre though it was, what knowledge he had was gained by his own efforts. The books he possessed – albeit few in number – were kept in a small locked glass-fronted cabinet in the living room. The largest book in his collection was an illustrated medical encyclopaedia, useful in the years before the National Health Service. Ian's school prizes eventually found their way into the cabinet. When I inherited Ian Brady's possessions over fifty years later, they included some children's classics such as *Kidnapped*, *Treasure Island*, *What Katy Did Next* and *The Little Prince*.

The Sloans had three children, a son and two daughters. All the books and sources on the Moors case state that there were four children in the Sloan family when Ian was taken in. This is not true. A fourth child, John, was born four years after Ian's arrival.

The eldest child was Robert Sloan, who was twenty years old. He was tall and, as Ian recalled, had Gregory Peck good looks. He served in the Royal Navy on HMS *Swiftsure*, a destroyer. His natural intelligence eventually gained him an executive post in a substantial company.

Next in line was his sister Jean. She worked in a large tobacco factory on the north side of the River Clyde. Ian remembers her as happy, outgoing and a girl who would weep easily over a slight. As he grew up, Ian sensed a melancholy and sadness in Jean that her ready laughter couldn't hide.

Jean's younger sister, May Sloan, had not yet left school and, because of her age, seemed to attract more attention in the family. Jean probably resented this a little. May could argue when she felt her elders and betters were unjustifiably putting her in her place yet she was the calming influence in a crisis.

The brownstone tenements in Camden Street were three storeys high. Each level had three apartments and a shared toilet. Apartments facing each other on the landing had two rooms, one back and front. The central apartment had one front room – 'single-end' as they were called in the Gorbals.

The Sloans had a two-room apartment on the first storey of number 56, a brownstone tenement rented out, as all tenements were, by a Factor – an agent of the landlord. Families had to bribe the Factors with 'key money' to obtain rented rooms. Ian explained that this was usually the considerable sum of £25. The police were familiar with this corrupt arrangement but no action was taken. It was simply the way of life in the Gorbals of those years.

A year had gone by since Ian's arrival at number 56 when Britain declared war on Hitler's Germany on 3 September 1939. At the same time, Ian was fighting his own little war with a bad case of measles – it may well have been the German variety. In those days the disease could affect the sufferer's eyesight, unless certain precautions were taken. Mrs Sloan fixed a sheet of brown paper across the cot, above Ian's head, to protect his eyes from any glaring light. Despite her best efforts, Ian's eyes from then on were extremely sensitive to bright light.

As an adult, Ian took to wearing prescribed tinted lenses that were often mistaken for sunglasses. He wore them on every occasion I met him in his years of captivity. Ian hated to have the harsh strip lighting switched on and, during the autumn and winter months, my sessions with him were often in darkness after two or three hours. He commented once: 'My curtains are permanently closed against daylight. I am a night person,' and concluded a letter; 'Well, it's now 3.30 a.m. and dawn will soon be up, so I must retire – sounds like Dracula, or Hitler in the Bunker!'

Ian's first words were 'Da' and 'Ma' – Mr and Mrs Sloan, and he would address them in this way for the remainder of his life. The rest of the family were sisters and brothers. He knew nothing else. (Emlyn Williams incongruously records Ian's first word as 'Auntie' for Mrs Mary Sloan.)

Maggie Stewart came to see her son whenever she could. All the Sloans called her 'Peggy' – and so did Ian. She preferred this to 'Maggie'. Ian Brady realised many years later that this way of addressing his real mother created a psychological barrier that was only finally overcome when she stayed loyal to him after the Moors trial.

Ian was gradually introduced into the world beyond Camden Street, even though it was only a short open pram ride to the fascinating thoroughfare of Cumberland Street with all its teeming variety of shops and pubs. All human life was there – enough, at least, to fascinate a toddler.

Years before having contact with Ian Brady, I had read the novel *No Mean City* by A. McArthur and H. Kingsley Long, a fictionalised – some would say romanticised – account of the lawless culture of the Gorbals. This gave us some point of contact. A copy of *No Mean City* was found in Brady's house after his arrest. The book was first published in 1935. Its anti-hero is Johnnie Stark, the 'Razor King' of the pre-war slum underworld of the Gorbals, into which Ian Brady was born.

Time and time again Brady extolled the immediacy that these Glasgow slums gave him, while he was there and when he visited them regularly after settling in Manchester. Sixty years after being trundled down Cumberland Street, Brady asked in *The Gates of Janus*:

> Did you ever share the same innocent obsession that I have? Forever being drawn back compulsively to places of childhood. Localities of spiritual renewal. Touchstones to recharge the flagging batteries. Places where the feet itched to make contact with the soil of your roots, hands ached to caress the texture of old buildings and trees you once knew well but had almost forgotten? They look much older and smaller than you remembered them, of course, more vulnerable, in need of tactile comfort. It is mutual. A touch of sympathetic energy spans the lapsed years. For that moment you forget your quarrels with the world. You are innocent again.

Brady goes on to recall:

> . . . those occasions when I returned to childhood haunts as an adult, I couldn't get enough of people, roaming the old bars and cafes, soaking up the atmosphere and delighting in overheard conversations. I felt truly alive, all criminal inclinations and ambitions forgotten, erased by temporarily regaining the vitality of seeing the world through the eyes of a child. That microscopic form of vision where nothing is unimportant and almost everything is fascinating.

A few years before this was written, Brady wrote to me about his dual-consciousness in relation to the Gorbals: '. . . on one hand as a child, and on the other as a cynic who was bored with life and desired the brief respites of illumination and illusion. Whatever the clinical diagnosis may have been, those excursions home to the Gorbals contrived to cast a wholesome influence over me when nothing else could. Myra often told me that I was a changed man whenever I returned to Glasgow; energetic, relaxed and happier, feeling an inner warmth in the presence of strangers.'

In young Ian's day the Gorbals was usually referred to as the South Side, sounding like 'Soo Side' in the Glaswegian of the time. Ian Brady laughed when he pointed out to me that this sounded like 'suicide'. One obvious boundary of the Gorbals was the River Clyde to the north. The west and east sides merged less perceptibly into endless tenements of other districts of Glasgow. The high redbrick wall of the Govan Iron Works, locally known as Dixon Blazes, marked the southern boundary.

The Sloans, like all families in Britain, were having to cope with the blackout and rationing. May Sloan was fourteen by now and had left school to work in a major printing and bookbinding firm in the centre of Glasgow. She was marking time until she was old enough to begin her true ambition: training as a nurse. Jean Sloan continued to work at the tobacco factory and enjoyed one of the perks of the job – particularly in the years of the German blockade on shipping – packets of cigarettes with her wages on Friday.

Ian Brady recalled this many years later when an anti-smoking campaign published the tar content of cigarettes in order of strength. The strongest was Prize Crop, the very same brand that Jean brought home to number 56 Camden Street.

In the Glasgow parlance, the colloquial 'mam' or 'mum' was 'ma' and 'dad' was 'da'. Da Sloan was too old for the call-up and worked at the grain mill throughout the war. The mill was known as Motherwells. Ian told me that he used to go to meet Da coming back from work. Inhalation of the fine grain dust would eventually bring his life to a premature end. Ma Sloan kept house as usual and enjoyed a free Prize Crop cigarette in the calm that descended after everyone had left for work. Then it was 'the messages', as shopping was known in the Gorbals, and young Ian's initiation into the mysteries and smells of fresh food, fish and meat in the open displays of those times. The Brady of later years particularly remembered the tangy smell of fresh sawdust on the shop floors.

What then of these first two or three tender years in the life of Ian Brady? As I had come to expect, his own recollections of these very early years bore no relation to the accounts of numerous authors and journalists

written in the decades following the Moors Murders trial in 1966, one of
these being the distinguished actor, Emlyn Williams. *Beyond Belief*
released a hare in 1967 and the hounds have dutifully chased it. Emlyn
Williams can be forgiven for his inaccurate head count of the Sloan family.
But he parrots a slur on the caring, working-class Sloan family, who
always treated Ian Brady as an equal member, which would be libellous in
a different setting:

> Two daughters only even, or two sons, might have joined to
> champion the wee thing; they might have taken him by each hand
> and swung him down the stone stairs and into the adventure of the
> street, a secure child breathless with delight and trailing bare toes in
> the Gorbals grime. But there were two sons and two daughters, all
> older, and that is too complete an entity to reach outside itself,
> especially in a society where the fight for existence is unremitting.
> They were kind, as a family is to a pet.

If Emlyn Williams can be so spectacularly wrong about this, we are bound
to wonder how reliable he is in the hundreds of pages that follow in the
remainder of his book. Without giving any evidence for saying so, he adds
to his criticism of the Sloan family:

> There was never even the roughness which an overworked mother
> has to fall back on sometimes, the brisk smack-bottom and the lusty
> yell. Kindness all the time, even though it was, in the last analysis,
> the kindness of indifference . . . Where there should have been love
> there was only solicitude; they were sorry for him. The glass wall
> between him and the world was nebulously forming.

Williams casts one eye on the future horror of the Moors Murders and
concludes that 'the theme of the unwanted child is to trace itself
indelibly.' Williams could not have been more mistaken.

CHAPTER TWO

DEATH OF A CLYDESDALE

Hitler was bombing Glasgow and the young Ian came to expect – even look forward to – hearing the sirens and being part of the scramble downstairs to the relative safety of the close outside. The Gorbals, as we have seen, was sandwiched between the Govan Iron Works and the docks on the Clyde – both prime targets. Stray bombs were a fact of life in the Gorbals. In his fifties, Ian Brady recalled one memorable night in particular. The sirens sounded and the families on the ground floor – the Camerons and the Flannigans – were first into the street, followed by the elderly Mrs Brannigan.

The plump, white-haired Mrs Rae, who lived on the same floor as the Sloans, peeped through the asbestos curtain of the shelter and saw a large angel-like shape in the sky. Then there was the sound of a huge explosion. It was a parachute mine that had destroyed the redbrick church at the end of Camden Street and had left untouched the buildings either side of it – a factory and a large prehistoric launderette, a communal washhouse called the Steamie. By the time the all-clear sirens had sounded there was broken glass underfoot in the close and soot had blown down the chimney in the Sloans' apartments.

Ian was now allowed to play in the yards behind the tenements. Ma Sloan could keep an eye on him as she worked at the sink in the back room. Wartime meant that there were no fences that isolated a backyard for the use of any particular tenement. There was one long, non-territorial playground known as 'the Backs', where children made mud-pies and shouted to their mothers to send 'doon a piece' – slices of bread and butter or jam, or butter sprinkled with sugar.

30

Ian was four years old on 2 January 1942. Ma Sloan went into hospital in the summer of that year and gave birth to her fourth child, John. At about the same time, Hettie Hindley of Gorton in Manchester was in labour with her first child. Myra Hindley, like John Sloan, was a war baby. She was born Wednesday, 23 July 1942. In the final minutes before she died, sixty years later, Myra would call for her mother.

Ian vacated his cot for the baby John and slept in the front room with May and Jean. In the Sloans' front room there was something of a rarity for the Gorbals and for those days – an upright piano. May Sloan had taken lessons and was able to teach Ian the scales. He was soon playing by ear and his earliest repertoire included 'Old Man River' and 'I Don't Want To Set The World On Fire'.

He celebrated his fifth birthday and started school at Camden Street Infants School, less than a minute's walk from home. As might be expected, some of the children in the class were crying on the first day, but right from the start Ian enjoyed his introduction to the mysteries of learning: 'As young as I was, on that first day, I sensed that knowledge was power. I felt it.'

He could read before he attended school. His reward for fetching a packet of ten Woodbines cigarettes for Ma Sloan from Pettigrew's newsagents, a few yards from number 56, was two pence for a children's comic. Ian's familiarity with the *Hotspur*, *Rover*, *Adventure*, *Beano* and *Dandy* eased his path into learning.

Ian's natural mother, Peggy, visited him regularly. By this time she had moved from her tearoom job to become a capstan operator at Albion Motors, fully geared for the demands of the war.

One of the first things I discovered about Ian Brady was that he had an encyclopaedic knowledge of films. In the days before the television era cinemas were almost as numerous as pubs. The Gorbals had many of them and they were within walking distance of Camden Street – the Bees, the Crownie and the Paragon being the most popular. There was actually a cinema close by – the Palace – which still had curtained-off private boxes from its days as a theatre.

There were many other cinemas just a little farther afield – the Cinerama, the Calder, the Maryhill and the Majestic. May and Jean Sloan used to escort the wide-eyed Ian to these theatres of dreams. In our earliest conversation, Brady told me that the first film he ever saw was *The Road to Morocco* starring Bob Hope and Bing Crosby – like Webster's dictionary they were Morocco bound.

Ian still recalled the Paragon cinema, where he saw the Hope and Crosby film, a converted church that had pews for seats. He remembered also seeing *The Wicked Lady* and *Odd Man Out* there. In captivity he enjoyed watching re-runs of the classics of those days: *Citizen Kane*, *Casablanca*, *The Maltese Falcon*. Years later, I gave Brady a large picture poster of the final scene of *Casablanca* with Humphrey Bogart on the airport runway – 'the start of a beautiful friendship'. In the prison years he laughed again at the vintage Marx Brothers films. *A Night At The Opera* was the second film he saw with Jean and May.

Part of the enchantment of a cinema visit was walking there and back in the blackout of the war years, along streets that had no name, although the grimy Errol Street was unmistakable at any time of day with its rats the size of cats. Peggy took Ian to the cinema regularly, as did May and Jean. He particularly remembered seeing Claude Rains in *Phantom Of The Opera* with her, and Merle Oberon with Laurence Olivier in *Wuthering Heights*.

The Sloans' youngest child, John, had become the focus of the family's affection and attention, a position that Ian had enjoyed until then. Ian said that he never resented this: 'I was popular at school and so I was hardly likely to have feelings of inferiority. But, of course, I still wanted to be accepted and loved by those I loved.'

After a few months in Camden Street Infants Ian moved into its Primary section – a graduation, which meant that pens and books replaced chalk and slates. He discovered that he could hold a small group of attentive listeners in the playground with his narration of the previous night's film. Ian had no difficulty in attracting followers in what he called the 'pagan territory' of the school playground: 'I was never a loner, even in my youngest days. Whatever it takes to be a loner, I can't see what's wrong with being that way. Loners probably experience life at a more profound level than the self-consciously gregarious who know nothing of individuality, or who lack the courage to go their own way. But for journalists it's a demeaning, almost pathological term, lulling both the writer and reader into a smug, consoling sense of effortless superiority.'

One of the stories of Brady's childhood that is often repeated is the response he made to a teacher's question in the Religious Instruction lesson. She asked whether there was anyone in the class who didn't believe in God. Only Ian's arm was raised. When I raised the subject, Brady commented that this was one of the few stories about his childhood that was true. The film *Moby Dick* had been shown on television the day before I visited and Brady quoted Captain Ahab's words: 'Is it I, God or who that lifts this arm? If the great sun cannot move except by God's invisible power, how can my small heart beat, my brain think such thoughts? Unless God does that thinking, and not I?'

I heard Brady quote these words on more than one occasion. It was his way of saying that his raised arm to the teacher's question was instinctive rather than down to any metaphysical precocity. In fact, the Ian of those tender years prayed regularly and would do so until he was eleven years old. He revelled in Christmas, the carols and everything that went with it, and he was particularly proud when he was able to bring coloured paper to school for the decorations – paper supplied by May Sloan's printing firm.

Brady had vivid memories of prize-giving days at Camden Street Primary. The ceremony took place in a church hall near the school. He enjoyed the tension of waiting for his name to be called. He remembered the books he received as prizes, particularly *Black Beauty*, duly displayed in Da Sloan's locked cabinet.

Another memory of this period is that of a small café just around the corner from school in Caledonia Road. Its attraction was a small box-shaped novelty machine fixed to one wall. It had two brass handles that gave the customer a mild electric shock for a penny. When pennies were scarce, Ian's friends were only too willing to link hands and complete the circuit so that everyone enjoyed the forbidden fruit – a tingle in the arms. I remember using the same kind of contraption in an arcade on Blackpool's Golden Mile. Its manufacturers would be jailed today.

One of the most frequently plagiarised stories of Ian Brady's childhood is his alleged attempt to set fire to one of his pals. I asked him about this and he remembered the incident. He claimed it was harmless role-play with his friend John Cameron, who lived on the ground floor of the Sloan tenement. The victim was loosely tied and released himself when a few pieces of paper had been lit.

Ian had been at school a year when Ma Sloan decided that it was safe for her foster child to eat sandwiches at school rather than go home to dinner at number 56. This was his first taste of freedom, an elixir that would disappear from his life forever just over twenty years later. The time was an hour in the middle of the day. The place was the sprawling cemetery known locally as the 'Southern Necropolis' that had literally edged up to its limits at the walls of the Govan Iron Works, the southern boundary of the Gorbals. It was an exuberantly overgrown paradise for children.

Ian was beginning to be drawn into street games taught him by his elders. He described these to me – 'White Horse', 'Tick-Tack', 'Jumping the Dykes' and a few others. There was one game, however, which provided his first encounter with death. This was called 'catching a hudgie' and involved jumping on the rear of a van or lorry and holding on to the spare tyre or whatever there was to grip. Ian and his pals waited on street corners for vehicles to slow down. One boy in the group jumped but couldn't hold on. He rolled under a following lorry loaded with crates of empty bottles. A crowd gathered. Ian looked through the forest of adult legs and saw nothing but a brown child's shoe filled to the brim with crimson blood. Decades later he would think of this sight when crimson blood gushed from the throat of a girl he had just murdered on the high barrenness of Saddleworth Moor.

Billy Wallace, who lived a few tenements away from the Sloans, met with a similar fate. Ian was allowed to look in the open white coffin – a practice I knew from my own experience that was common at that time. Brady commented that these, and other fatalities, did nothing to discourage him and others from 'catching a hudgie'. There but for fortune . . .

In his sixth year Ian took housekeeping money from Ma Sloan's purse and was ashamed of it ever after. He wrapped silver coins in a ten-shilling note and hid it in a mouse hole on the landing. Twenty years later he took Myra Hindley to see what was left of the ruins of Camden Street and the small hole was still there. Ian managed to live down the theft.

John Sloan had learned to walk at the same time that Ian was forced to hobble on one leg after an accident in the school holidays. He was playing with a balloon in the kitchen, where Ma Sloan had spilt water while peeling potatoes. Ian missed his footing and broke his leg. He had to go to Glasgow Infirmary for treatment. It would be the only occasion he would enter a hospital, outside prison, in his whole life.

Because he was instinctively protecting his leg, Ian lost interest in playing street football and had no interest in it as a spectator in later years – as I discovered from his expletives while I was with him when everyone else on the ward was watching a World Cup final on television. Brady told me that his leg injury had no lasting effects, but as I watched him walk down the long corridor that led to his room, at the end of a visit, one leg was always slightly splayed as he walked.

One of Ian Brady's memories of this stage in his childhood stayed with me for years after he told me about it. I used it many times as a way of introducing teenagers to the subject of death. One afternoon, Ian was walking in the ruins of the church demolished by the parachute-mine and saw a bird on the ground in front of him. It was moving slightly but showed no fear of the young human stranger. The bird seemed to be breathing contentedly and Ian touched it gently with his foot. He smelt the odour of death as it fell on to its side. It was a seething mass of maggots. He built a brick tomb around the bird.

Some time later, Ian was introduced to something that had the same fascination for him as the cinema. John Fraser, a school friend, offered him the chance of going to a music hall show at the Metropole theatre in the centre of Glasgow. They had seats in 'the gods' and saw the old-time musical performer G H Elliot, billed as 'The Chocolate Coloured Coon' – a title unthinkable today. Brady remembered two of his songs: 'Hello Susie Green' and 'My Lily of Laguna'. John Fraser's father paid for the treat.

Less exotic than the theatre was the nightly entertainment provided by the wireless, encased in a large wooden frame and sitting in the corner of the back room in number 56. The diet of programmes is now part of broadcasting history. Every night there was the serial *Dick Barton Special Agent* and a range of comedy shows throughout the week – *Much-Binding-in-the-Marsh*, *Take it from Here* and *ITMA* ('It's That Man Again'). Valentine Dyall, 'your storyteller, the Man in Black', brought the Sloans 'an appointment with fear'. When Da Sloan was in a generous mood, the family were allowed to listen to the German propaganda broadcasts of Lord Haw-Haw, William Joyce, executed by the British after the war.

There was a children's play area in Hutchestown Square en route to Camden Street School. Ian was playing on a swing one day when the back of the wooden seat hit a small child walking by. Brady told me that he saw the child was bleeding profusely but ran from the playground in panic. He assumed that he had killed him.

Brady repeated the story to Peter Topping, Detective Chief Superintendent, head of CID in the Manchester police force, who thought that the fatal outcome was unlikely. However, Brady told me of another incident which happened at about the same time and which proved to be very significant. The memory of it will enter our story at a much later stage. He briefly referred to this event with Topping, who was inclined to give this occasion more credence. Many years later this incident had lethal consequences. This is part of Brady's written account of it in a letter to me: 'Ma sent me every morning for hot rolls and milk from a dairy in Florence Street. One morning – very frosty in the Gorbals under the leaden hue of the Glasgow sky – I was holding the hot rolls to my chest on my way back and saw a crowd of people huddled in a circle on the corner of Cumberland Street and Crown Street. I was inquisitive and pushed through the mass of gawking heads to discover the cause of the commotion. I was within touching distance of a huge Clydesdale horse lying flat on its side in the road. It was still tethered to the cart.

'It had slipped on the icy road and was badly injured. It lay there with its massive sides heaving and its breath steaming in the frosty air. I was near enough to touch the large head. I can still see the great liquid eyes rolling in terror, looking up to the grey Glasgow morning sky. Its great fetlocks raked the air, bedraggled and wet. A man appeared from nowhere to erect a canvas screen around the Clydesdale.

'They were going to kill the horse. Even I knew it. My chest was bursting and I began to cry. I fought my way through the mass of bodies and ran to Camden Street, trying to hold on to the bag of hot rolls with my hands clapped over my ears. I sat on the tenement stairs until the tears dried up before taking the rolls into Ma. I was afraid to wander near the spot where the horse had died. I couldn't bear to see the remains of bloodstains and hairs. I couldn't rid the event and scene from my mind.

'Many years later I saw something in a dark railway arch that triggered the image of the wet, straggling fetlocks of the Clydesdale, suddenly changing my relaxed mood to one of ice-cold fury and leading to a frenzied knife attack on a man in the street. I didn't hang around to check whether it was fatal. It was enough for me to feel that the Clydesdale had been avenged.'

Before I knew Ian Brady I was aware that the German philosopher Friedrich Nietzsche and the Russian novelist Dostoevsky played an important part in his adult years. Strangely, Dostoevsky influenced Nietzsche himself in a similar way. In one of his letters, Nietzsche writes that by chance he found a book by Dostoevsky. He wrote: 'A few weeks ago I did not even know the name Dostoevsky. The instinct of kinship spoke immediately, my joy was extraordinary.' In *The Twilight of the Idols*, Nietzsche comments: 'Dostoevsky was the only psychologist from whom I had anything to learn: he belongs to the happiest windfalls of my life.'

Dostoevsky was, in a catastrophic sense, a windfall in the life of Ian Brady too.

Brady gave me a copy of Carl Pletsch's *Young Nietzsche* and I remarked on the strange coincidence of events involving carthorses in Nietzsche's life and Dostoevsky's writings, on the one hand, and their place in the young Ian Brady's life on the other. This conversation prompted him to give his account in the passage quoted above.

Nietzsche's final collapse into madness is closely linked to an incident early in January 1889. As he left his house he saw on the Piazza Carlo Alberto, where horse-drawn cabs were waiting for customers, an exhausted old horse being brutally beaten by a cabman. Nietzsche rushed over and flung his arms around the horse, burst into tears and collapsed. He was carried back to his room but never recovered. The Dostoevsky incident is in *Crime and Punishment*, a seminal book for Brady. The central character in the book is Raskolnikov, who has what is described as a terrible dream:

> It was a dream about his childhood, back in the little town where they had lived. He was about seven years old and he was taking a walk with his father. The road passed close to the drinking house. And by the entrance stood a cart – but it was a strange sort of cart. It was one of those big ones that are usually drawn by great carthorses. He had always liked watching those enormous cart-horses with their long manes and brawny legs, moving at a tranquil, measured pace. It was a strange thing, however, that in the present instance one of these massive carts had been harnessed up to a small, thin, greyish peasant jade. "Come off it, Mikolka, have you lost your brains, or what? Harnessing that little filly to that great cart!" "Get in, I'm going to take you all!" Mikolka said, leaping into the cart first. "Flog her to death!" . . . "It's come to that. I'll do it myself!" . . . "Whip her on the muzzle, on the eyes, on the eyes!" Mikolka shouted. "That's the end of her!" people shouted in the crowd. "Papa! The poor little horse. Why did they kill it?" He sobbed, but his breathing was choked. His chest felt so tight, so tight. He felt he wanted to draw breath, to scream, and woke up.

When Ian Brady first read this passage in *Crime and Punishment*, he thought of the frosty morning in the Gorbals when he had witnessed a Clydesdale horse dying. In his own copy of the book, when he was in captivity, Brady wrote in the margin of the dream description: 'Crystallized immorality of violence; almost too painful to read.'

On Saturdays Da Sloan would sometimes take Ian to the stables of the grain mill to sit on a Clydesdale. If we are to believe Ian Brady, this and several other incidents show him to have tender feelings towards animals that belie stories of his cruelty, stories faithfully repeated in many of the books and newspaper articles on the Moors Murders. For example, immediately after the trial in May 1966, the *Daily Telegraph* reported the comments of a man who claimed to have lived immediately below the Sloans' apartment in Camden Street in the Hutchesontown area of the Gorbals: 'Once Ian threw a cat out of the top-floor window, and on another occasion boasted he had buried a cat under a gravestone because he wanted to see how long it would live. We released the animal.' Ian Brady told me that these and other such stories are simply part of the collection of myths that have become attached to the Moors case over the years. 'In fact,' he said, 'Myra and I used to scan the papers and make a note of people convicted of cruelty to animals. Why? For future reference . . . '

The date 8 May 1945 was Victory in Europe day. The war was over. Ian was seven years old and the celebration and the images of anarchy in the Gorbals were etched in his mind. The flames from the street bonfires of VE night competed with the newly ignited furnaces of the Govan Iron Works. Anything flammable and to hand was used. Ian saw a fat lady terrified when some youths tore down the door of the outside toilet she was using.

His main concern was to be part of the chaos as far into the night as possible by avoiding the eyes of any member of the Sloan family – Ma and Da at the front window of number 56. It was May who eventually dragged the exhausted seven-year-old to bed in the small hours.

The next morning Ian and his friends sifted through the debris in the streets looking for 'luckies', Gorbals slang for anything that could be converted into cash. Empty bottles for return could bring in one or two pence. A soda water siphon was a gift from the gods. More ingeniously, the gang put a piece of soap on to the end of a broom handle and retrieved coins that had dropped through grills in the pavement. Even sewer grills – 'stanks' – were not overlooked. Well-tried 'luckies' were copper coins covered in silver paper that were occasionally passable as shillings.

A few days after VE night Ian was alone when he found a rifle, complete with a khaki lanyard, which had been discarded behind waste bins in a midden. It was a .303 Lee Enfield. Such finds were not unknown in the immediate post-war years, as I know from my own experience. Ian played with the rifle for a few hours before selling it on to an older boy for a shilling, a sum spent within minutes.

The final act of Ian and his gang in the immediate post-VE celebrations was the perilous journey across the Albert Bridge into the forbidden heart of the city to see the neon adverts – 'the lights' – in Argyle Street. This was a new experience for the boys, who had known nothing but the blackout. They returned to the cobbled streets of the Gorbals and gaslight.

The blackout – the perfect cover for many of the gang's adventures – had gone, but the dense fogs remained. Almost sixty years later, writing to me in captivity, Ian Brady said: 'We relished the pea soup fogs in the Gorbals. We would step out of the cinematic fantasy warmth into the cold streets and the night of solid murk and real adventure. We had the perfect excuse to stay out late since no trams were running. We ran a hilarious and mysterious obstacle course of follow the leader and dodging adults coughing and spluttering. For some reason we invariably came to some old night watchman sitting in his guard box in front of a glowing brazier of charcoal, before which fellow explorers would be gathered around, toasting their hands and radiated like shadow-eyed goblins.'

The Sloan sisters were now buying records to play on an ancient wind-up gramophone. Jean was a fan of Steve Conway and May worshipped the new crooner on the scene, Frank Sinatra. Whenever the machine was free, Robert played Gigli and Bing Crosby records. Ma and Da Sloan's idea of entertainment was watching Nelson Eddy and Jeanette MacDonald musicals. They also sat through *The Jolson Story* several times during its long run at the Bedford cinema.

When Ian wasn't out with the gang or at the cinema, he played the piano in his own untutored way. At this stage his *pièce de résistance* was 'My Blue Heaven'. After the Moors trial, a London musical about the case featured a scene in which the Ian Brady and Myra Hindley characters danced to this tune.

Perhaps the most memorable event for Ian during this year of his childhood was seeing *King Kong*, a film first released in 1933 and now a classic. Ian was mesmerised throughout and was devastated as the inevitable outcome dawned on him. He cried as Kong took care to make sure that the heroine, played by Fay Wray, was safe before he fell to his doom. I heard Brady quote the closing words of the film several times: 'It wasn't the airplanes. It was beauty killed the beast.' I found two videos of the film among his possessions many years later. The young Ian was slowly realising that, perhaps, there were more snakes than ladders. In the next few months he directed his sympathies on to another creature in the unequal struggle between man and beast.

During the gang's foray into the city to see 'the lights', Ian saw what, to modern sensibilities, was an incongruous sight. In the busy thoroughfare of Argyle Street, opposite Central Station, was a flight of stone steps leading up to Wilson's Zoo. Two weeks later, Ian and his friends walked into the city centre – 'doon toon' – to pay their threepence entrance money and walk round the Zoo. It turned out to be one benighted, squalid room with cages occupied by monkeys, tropical birds and a solitary tiger.

Brady told me that he was overwhelmed with anger and pity, most of all at the plight of the tiger. But all the animals in that room seemed completely resigned to their fate – motionless, withdrawn and defeated. During his prison years Brady would witness men in the same state. On this first viewing, however, Ian said that he felt ashamed at the sight of flecks of sawdust on the tiger's coat that seemed to demean it more than the captivity itself. A young customer standing nearby tried to evoke some reaction from the tiger by flicking a used matchstick through the bars. Ian kicked the youth and punched him in the face. Some adults rushed to intervene and the gang left in a hurry.

During his own captivity, years later, Brady used a Braille machine to translate the works of William Blake for a blind woman. He thought of Wilson's Zoo when he came to what had become his favourite poem, *The Tiger*:

> Tiger, tiger, burning bright
> In the forests of the night
> What immortal hand or eye
> Could frame thy fearful symmetry?
>
> In what distant deeps or skies
> Burnt the fire of thine eyes?
> On what wings dare he aspire?
> What the hand dare seize the fire?
>
> And what shoulder and what art
> Could twist the sinews of thy heart?
> And, when thy heart began to beat,
> What dread hand and what dread feet?
>
> What the hammer? What the chain?
> In what furnace was thy brain?
> What the anvil? What dread grasp
> Dare its deadly terrors clasp?

When the stars threw down their spears,
And water'd heaven with their tears,
Did He smile His work to see?
Did He who made the lamb make thee?

Ian visited the zoo for another month or so. He found the tiger's squalid captivity unbearable. In the prison years, he had a small, framed picture of a tiger's head on his cell wall. Later, I found the picture among his property.

The war had been over for some months when Ma Sloan complained that she could not hear very well. The doctor said that it was caused by her intake of nicotine. Ma saved her cigarette ends and used a small rolling machine. She was given a harness for back pains but made no burden of keeping house for everybody.

Peggy still visited Ian regularly for treats. He recalled two of these in particular. The first was to see a circus at Kelvin Hall in the city. This merely revived his anger at Wilson's Zoo, particularly when there was only sawdust and dung in the ring at the close of the performance.

The second treat was a visit to the Museum and Art Gallery in the city. Ian was fascinated by a model of the steamship *Queen Mary* and the suits of armour, but was totally intrigued by a tableau called, 'Who killed Cock Robin?', with the bird in question pierced by an arrow. Some years later Brady enthused over this to Myra Hindley and they made a special effort to see it. The tableau had long since disappeared, but the huge whalebones that formed an arch over the main staircase were still there. As he stroked them, Brady, now with more appreciative eyes, drew Myra's attention to the curves of Rodin's *The Kiss*. They looked at Salvador Dali's *The Crucifixion* and watercolours by Lautrec, almost two decades after Peggy first showed her son that such wonders existed.

Life slowly returned to normal in the months after the war. Peggy took Ian to see a captured German submarine. They joined the queue of fascinated Glaswegians and descended into the U-boat's claustrophobic and intricate interior. American submarines and ships were moored in the Firth of Clyde and American servicemen were a common sight on the streets of Glasgow's city centre. Local girls went to the Locarno dance club to mix with them and hope it was their night of nights for a pair of priceless nylon stockings.

The likes of Ian's gang were more realistic in their pursuit of the tall American soldiers – 'Any gum, chum?' Ordinary Glaswegians were content if they were able to get their hands on that other great wartime scarcity – bananas.

After a few months Robert Sloan returned on leave from the Navy with a white kitbag stuffed with gifts for the family. Da Sloan was given a bottle of rum. Robert knew that his father preferred this to whisky and liked to pretend that he was drunk from time to time. Ma was handed a black silk Japanese kimono with a red dragon motif. May and Jean were given crafted Japanese bone fans. Ian and John each received an Australian boomerang. Although Ian spent hours trying, he was doomed to suffer the same frustration as the comedian Charlie Drake: 'My boomerang won't come back!' Ian became close to Robert only years later when he returned from the sea.

Ian sometimes became aware that Robert regarded him as an outsider, by the occasional unthinking remark. When this happened Brady said, 'I winced in silence and pretended I hadn't overheard or understood.'

Ian was eight in January 1946. The Sloans went on holiday in the summer. It proved to be the setting of a profound spiritual experience, leaving its mark on Brady for the rest of his life. He described it in a letter to me: 'All of us went to Loch Lomond by bus, calling at Balloch on the southern tip of the loch. We strolled along the west-shore road that skirted it. I remembered particularly the deciduous trees on the slopes that reached down to the edge of the loch. Leaving the family to their own pleasures, I clambered up through the dense trees for a better view of the loch and the mountains in the distance.

'I was shattered by the sense of vastness. It was as though I had suddenly stepped through an invisible barrier and had arrived in a different dimension. I was dizzy and breathless, gulping for air, as though I was trying to breathe underwater. My body felt light, as if something was supporting me while my mind swam ahead of me into space. This new sense of reality and freedom was intoxicating. I was encountering the naked essence of life itself. This was the earth in cinemascope.

'In my reverie I could hear Ma calling me back down from the hill. I reluctantly obeyed the call. I was still excited and full of the experience when I joined the family again. I jabbered on and on about it and was heard by uncomprehending ears. Not that this troubled me. The feral, atavistic vision had marked me indelibly deep within. Years into the future, I was to have countless days like this.

'I had a very different, contrasting experience later on the same day. Robert could afford to hire a rowing boat for an hour on the loch. All of us climbed into it and Robert claimed the man's job of taking the oars. The sun had been blazing hot all day and I was surprised that the water was freezing cold when I dipped my hand into it. The water was calm and crystal clear in the centre of the loch as I looked down into its depths. The sight terrified me. I was experiencing the duplicity of Loch Lomond's brooding presence. There, far below me, was the tip of an underwater mountain in the ice-cold blackness.

'Robert laughed and rocked the boat when he saw my mood had changed to fear. In spite of my terror, I sensed instinctively that this too was part of the day's apotheosis. I couldn't be spared the dark side. That too was nakedly real and indifferent to the squeamish whims of human beings. In a moment, my fear changed to wonder again as I gazed at the mountains of Ben Lomond, snow-tipped on the far horizon. This was my first experience of the wildernesses of Scotland. I was to know many more.'

Years later, when he was reading Colin Wilson's *The Outsider* for the first time, Ian Brady realised that Friedrich Nietzsche too experienced a similar 'indescribable sense of well being . . . without confusions of intellect' on Leutsch hilltop. Nietzsche writes to his friend von Gersdorff:

Yesterday an oppressive storm hung over the sky and I hurried to the top of a nearby hill . . . At the summit I found a hut, where a man was killing a kid, while his son watched him. The storm broke with tremendous force, gusting and hailing, and I had an indescribable sense of well being and zest, and realised that we actually understand nature only when we must fly to her to escape our cares and afflictions. Lightning and tempest are different worlds, free powers, without morality. Pure will, without confusions of intellect – how happy, how free!

The annual fortnight's holiday of the Sloans became a pattern in the post-war years. Brady later came to wonder how Ma and Da could possibly have saved the money to pay for holidays which in successive years included Rothesay on the Firth of Clyde, Wemyss Bay on the west coast, Troon and finally St Monans. Ian had the strongest feelings for their stay at St Monans, some fourteen miles south of St Andrews. He returned there with Myra Hindley in the 1960s and recalled it in his first letter to her in Holloway immediately after their trial.

Peggy sometimes took Ian on a holiday that involved only the two of them, although May Sloan went with them on one occasion. One year

Peggy took him to Tobermory, taking the night train from Glasgow to Oban on the west coast and from there by the steamship. Brady had this holiday in mind when he once warned me about the ever-present drizzle when I told him about my plans to visit Oban.

It was at Tobermory that he had another encounter with the Scottish wilderness: 'My exhilaration experienced at Loch Lomond was transcended at Tobermory.' One morning Ian had left his mother to wander up the nearby slopes. On the way up he saw a Scottish wildcat. At the summit he was taken aback by the view of the wild terrain: 'The sight took my breath away. I was a world away from the mundane locomotions of space and time in the Gorbals. As far as I could see, there were hills of bright yellow gorse and purple heather. It was five miles or more to the horizon and there was no sign of human life to spoil the view. It was a moment of magic and benign enchantment.

'I was experiencing the intensity of pure willpower expanding my heart and mind. I knew then that this was the real world. This was real power. The moral and legal restrictions of conventional reality were discarded like a ridiculously small item of clothing that has been outgrown.

'This was what it meant to savour absolute freedom: to see through the classifications projected by the mind on to the real world, a world that cares nothing for humanity's concerns for its own importance. I was deranged with delight, my senses devouring everything with heedless wantonness. The atmosphere was redolent with the deep drones of bumblebees gorging themselves in the heather. I laughed with joy at the luxurious beauty of the world. My whole being searched frantically for more and more, not knowing of what, but possessed by the passionate certainty that there were numberless experiences to discover. All I needed was the will to do so. It was not until I reached the black ravine that the cold hand of caution reappeared and held me back.'

When I had returned from my own holiday, Brady wanted to know whether he had been right about the drizzle. He had! I told him about a day's visit to Tobermory by boat via the Isle of Mull. Brady said that he remembered the particular scent in the air of Tobermory. It was something he couldn't define, 'But on mild days, exercising in the prison yard or gazing out of my window, the smell of the town drifted in through the bars to me, whether real or imaginary. I was back in Tobermory again, and remembering those happy times, now long gone.'

By late July 1946, Myra Hindley had celebrated her fourth birthday. A few weeks later she had a sister, Maureen, who was destined to play her own part in the fate of Ian Brady. With the new arrival, her mother's small house – in Gorton, Manchester – was too crowded. Myra moved around the corner to live with her grandmother, Mrs Ellen Maybury.

Ian Brady knew very little about his real mother's family. Becoming pregnant with Ian put Peggy in disgrace with them: 'But I remember one occasion when Peggy took me to a prosperous tenement just beyond the territory of the Gorbals. She introduced me to a large, heavily built man, who was naked to the waist. He was shaving and looking at himself into a small cracked mirror. I learned later that this man was Peggy's brother, Murdoch. Peggy's mother was sitting there. I can't picture her face now. I just have a memory of a scowl on her face. She looked at me sternly with tight-lipped severity. As young as I was, I knew that I was not welcome in that place. I took the hint and moved away from the three adults, leaving them to their conversation. I explored the room and discovered what I thought was a clothesbasket. I soon realized that there was an old, scraggy Scottish terrier lying on top of a small pile of clothes. It growled menacingly. I was not welcome in the dog's corner either.'

Peggy took Ian more regularly to another of her relatives, Auntie Jessie, who lived in a tenement in Crown Street. He remembers her as mild mannered with brown hair in a bun. Ian was ten years old in January 1948 and halfway through the worst winter on record. He was soon to see less of his relations. There was news that the Sloans were to move from the Gorbals into a new council house on an estate being built in Pollok on the outskirts of Glasgow. Ian couldn't, and didn't want to imagine, any other kind of life than the one he had known with his friends, the one he was about to lose.

The song, 'The Days of Pearly Spencer', by David MacWilliams, with its theme of a childhood in tenement slums, 'triggered' Ian Brady's memories of the first ten years of his life in the Gorbals. He gave me two taped versions of the song but preferred the later 1992 Marc Almond rendition because of its evocative backing sounds. When he mentioned the song to me, he cupped his hands to form a trumpet and imitated the atmospheric 'wowing' effects of Marc Almond's track and the reference to old eyes in a small child's face.

Brady recalls that it was common to see children running through the streets barefoot when he was growing up in Glasgow. During their time in the Gorbals, Ma and Da Sloan were poor but their children were never without shoes, or rather the black rubber 'wellies' that were in season at any time in the year; the tops were bent down in pirate style during the summer. Through the annual fortnight's holidays with the Sloans, Ian learned that residents at seaside resorts could always spot children from the Gorbals by the circles of chafed skin on their legs, caused by the 'wellies'.

Brady also recalled the ever-present threat of violence on the streets, particularly from youths carrying knives and cutthroat razors. After police purges – they had 'stop and search' powers – the youths resorted to sharpened steel combs. One judge started to sentence them to a year for every stitch in the victim's face.

Older men were subtler than their teenage sons. Brady told me about one night when Da Sloan was injured: 'As he walked out of a pub a man accidentally bumped into him. The peak or "skip" of the man's flat cap caught Da's forehead. There was no harm done, or so it seemed. As Da walked home he felt blood trickling down his face. The peak of the man's cap had a row of razor blades embedded in it. Da was left with a permanent scar.'

The Gorbals days were rapidly drawing to a close, along with the friendships that had filled Ian's days. Commenting on what Ian was leaving behind, Emlyn Williams mistakenly reports, 'He had no pals.' The young Ian Brady was facing an unknown future, as were many hundreds of others in the Glasgow slums. Part of that future would reveal that a day after Ian's tenth birthday, Edward Evans, the final Moors victim, was born in Manchester. Just six days later, David Smith, the main prosecution witness in the Moors trial, was born in the same city.

CHAPTER THREE

WHY DOES IT FEEL GOOD
TO FEEL BAD?

At the first opportunity all the Sloan family travelled by bus to look over the new house, six miles away in Pollok. Many of the houses on the council estate were only partly constructed. Number 21 Templeland Road was semi-detached and on the brow of a hill. The façade had pebble-dashed walls and a front garden that sloped upward to a height of ten feet above pavement level. The family were surprised by the mod cons in the kitchen, taken for granted now but a luxury compared to what they had known in the Camden Street tenement.

The Sloans moved in after a few weeks and the bedrooms were allocated. Da and Ma occupied the largest back bedroom; John and Ian the other. May and Jean Sloan slept in the front bedroom. The absence of the sounds of the Gorbals was the weirdest feature of their first night in Pollok – no noise from streets and backyards, or from people moving up and down the stone stairs of the tenement.

When more families moved into the estate Ian made new friends and emerged the leader of a gang of six. Bressie was well built with a curly mop of black hair. Willie T was a redhead with freckles and a permanent laugh. Frankie Fraser was a straw-blond. The remaining two boys were brothers: John and Tam. Most of the gang's activities were in or on the banks of the nearby river Cart.

Ian reached puberty early. He acquired his first girlfriend at eleven: 'Sylvia'. I shall use this name to guard her anonymity. Later, he still recalled her features – long straw-blonde hair, high cheekbones and the feature he

47

looked for first in all the female friends he had in his life – almond-shaped eyes. In most boy-girl relationships of those times it was a matter of trial and error in sexual matters. Ian discovered the joys of kissing violently so that both mouths bled. This pleasure would last until he was imprisoned.

The summer holidays were over and Ian was allocated to a new school to continue his primary education: Househillwood, some miles away. He was reminded of his time there when he was in Gartree Prison in the early 1980s. Just before Christmas, the daughter of one of his classmates sent him a class group photograph in which he was standing near to her father. Ian felt like Scrooge looking at the shadows of Christmas past. He wrote, 'I doubt that there is anyone, no matter how cynical or sophisticated they have become with time, who cannot be pierced by such surprising or accidental evidence of childhood innocence.'

His stay at Househillwood School had been a short-term measure and he was transferred to Carnwadric School, five miles from home. He was soon attracted to a girl who sat in front of him in the mixed classes: Evelyn Grant. Emlyn Williams made a few references to Evelyn, and her innocent part in Ian's childhood, in *Beyond Belief*. After a few days he was tugging at her pigtails. He remembered her lithe and pert figure, honey-blonde hair, high cheekbones and the obligatory almond-shaped eyes. Ian enjoyed the wild glint in Evelyn's grey eyes: 'I was probably seeing a reflection of myself in the promise of devilment. Her understated craziness was as appealing to me as her taut nubile curves. Once, during some horseplay, I gave her a bite as a barbaric token for a ring.'

Ian and Evelyn both achieved top grade passes in the school examinations, as they were known in Scotland, and were allocated to Shawlands Academy, a four-mile journey into the city. The school was established in 1894. Boys and girls were segregated for their lessons during Ian's time there, but he and Evelyn saw each other regularly during the day and in the evenings.

Years later, Brady told me from time to time that he had a pantheistic attachment to material objects and added that it dated back to the time he joined Shawlands Academy: 'I began more and more to invest inanimate objects with personality and sentience – perhaps because they didn't change as people do and were more reliable. I even regarded the moods of the sky above the tenements as personal spiritual responses to my inner fears, conflicts and doubts.' He gave me odd items over the years – typewriters, video recorders – and usually commented on the pantheistic associations he had for them.

Ian caught a bus into the Gorbals as often as he could to meet his old gang. He visited Peggy too who, by this time, had moved from Caledonia Road into a two-room flat on the top floor of a tenement in Kidson Street. Her front window looked down on Camden Street School and the back room looked directly on to Govan Iron Works.

Peggy left Glasgow in May 1950 to marry Patrick Brady, who lived in Manchester. Ian had never met him though he was to adopt this man's name in due course. But for the present, his pals knew him as 'Sloany' and the school register had him down as 'Stewart'.

Ian was leading a double life between Pollok and the Gorbals. His relationships with his friends at Shawlands Academy underwent a subtle change. In what Brady later called a sinister escalation of his leadership and power, he was attracting the bored discontents at school, who were looking for excitement. He was about to provide it. But there was a problem: the Pollok and Gorbals gangs just wouldn't mix. The Gorbals boys were contemptuous of Ian's more respectable Pollok friends. The Pollok boys were afraid of the wilder Gorbals gang, who reacted violently towards just about everything that crossed their path. Ian wanted to remain friends with both groups.

This was the beginning of a trend that would dominate so much of his later years – compartmentalising the different lives he led. It had been present in embryo in his happy immersion to an equal degree in the starkly contrasting worlds of the Glasgow slums and the wildernesses of the Scottish countryside.

Ian was beginning to lose interest in classroom studies. At night he looked through Peggy's back window on to the flames of the Govan Works furnaces and realised something more than iron was being moulded inside him. At first it was relatively harmless. Ian and his friends kept the dinner money meant for the teacher's drawer and spent it on cigarettes. They stole food from bakers' shops. Ian was slowly becoming aware of swift mood changes that in later years would swerve erratically and violently without warning. In captivity Brady reflected on these early subtle changes. Why did it feel good to feel bad? As he noted: 'And so from a tiny seed, nurtured in so oblique a manner, a vine of scarlet and black would take deep root and unobtrusively thrive in the shadows until, in the slow turn of the years, it grew to hideous proportions, letting the priceless blooms of humanity shrivel in its shade.'

Ian abandoned all efforts to put the Pollok and Gorbals gangs on speaking terms. He had more success in linking his friends from the Pollok estate and those of the Academy, although he still saw his pals in the Gorbals and felt more relaxed with the arrangement since they no longer relied on him to plan the night's mischief. However, Ian's Pollok friends faced him with their most pressing problem – lack of money to enjoy the forbidden pleasures of the city. With no means of disposing of stolen property, they had to steal cash. Ian shared what little experience he had.

In the early 1990s he described his first break-in to me. It was in the Gorbals when he was nine years old; a ground floor tenement apartment. As he moved silently through the two rooms he realised it was the home of a sailor. Ian opened a sideboard drawer full of packets of foreign cigarettes and shut it. He stole nothing and left the apartment.

Brady told me that his early break-ins were done for excitement and out of resentment. The Pollok gang, however, were usually in it strictly for cash: 'First of all, we needed tools for the job. We helped ourselves to bags of workmen's tools that had been stored in half-constructed houses on the estate. We secreted the tools near the river. Everything was ready and we sat there in the twilight discussing our opening night. I remember watching a water hen sweeping through the lilies and reeds towards its hidden nest.'

Sometimes the gang broke into premises simply to add variety to their nightly escapades: 'I remember one night in particular. We broke into a school purely on whim. We had no intention of stealing anything. Once we were inside we behaved like characters on the stage, lit as it was by the reflection of street lamps. I sat myself on the teacher's high chair, smoking and flicking ash into the inkwell. It was pure entertainment. Nothing more.

'We were often comedians rather than thieves. When I remember the bright faces of all my childhood friends, each of them is smiling or laughing.'

Da Sloan enlisted Ian's help in clearing the rubble from the front and back gardens of number 21. Ian was allowed to have a small area for the rabbit hutch he built. He caught the bus into the city and bought a Dutch in the pet section of Lewis's. He called it Smokey. Within a short time he acquired two more: a large grey called Jenny and an even bigger black, Harry. In one of the earliest letters I received from Ian Brady, I learned that the next pet to arrive at Templeland Road precipitated what he called 'the first major change in me': 'A dog joined my rabbits in the Sloan family. It was initially for May, who named it Sheila. It was a pedigree tan-and-white cocker spaniel: a placid dog, easily excited by the fuss everyone made of her. She was dead in less than a year.

'I went out one evening and caught a bus to the cinema. I had wrapped Sheila in woollens and put her by the fire in Da's chair before I left. She had distemper. A dark cloud hung over the family.

'I left the cinema alone and walked to the bus stop. I could think of nothing else but Sheila and kept looking up at the sky. Atavistically I whispered desperate prayers, promising everything I could think of, if Sheila were allowed to live. Like countless millions before me I turned to the illusory when all else fails. I was crying as I walked and was grateful for the darkness. As I approached the bus stop I sheltered in a doorway and tried to remove all trace of tears.

'I entered through the back door at home. Ma was at the sink and gave me a glance. I could tell that she had been crying. Her eyes were red-rimmed. Nothing was said. I walked through the kitchen and into the living room, looking only at Da's chair, where I had left her. Vacant. I glanced around the room. No sign of Sheila. I looked at May's face and knew the truth. I said nothing and walked into the street through the front door. I walked the empty streets without direction or purpose. I lost all sense of time and cried till I could cry no more.

'A change was taking place in me. My lips began to curl with contempt. I could sense cold fury in my stomach. I shouted obscenities into the night. All my venom was focused on whatever "Thing" might be lurking in the black sky, what malignant being. I was consumed by a foaming, mad fury. I was grinding my teeth. I clenched my fists till they ached. I wanted to rip the "Thing" to shreds with my teeth and taste its vile, malevolent life-force, whatever the merciless power gave it its being.

'I have no idea how long this spell lasted but my fury had taken its cathartic effect. I felt empty but calmer now. I was even smiling. It was my first taste of nihilism. It was succulent. There was an energy and power I had never known before, a spiritual ecstasy, as though I were breathing in the very essence of the life force of the universe.

'I was intoxicated. I felt omnipotent. I sensed the barriers crumble, the sweeping away of man-made barricades. I was aware of my consciousness evolving at uncontrolled speed. Was this madness? Was this a revelation of something beyond life? If it was, I wanted to embrace it, immerse myself in it and succumb to its intoxicating new vistas. This death was better than life. It was realer than real. It was how life essentially is and should be conscious that it is so. This was authentic freedom. But what made it so? What brought it into being? It was pure contempt. Contempt, pure and simple. That was what had moulded the key to the realm of total possibility. I had been a fool for not knowing it before. I was free, unrestricted by false beliefs, and was now looking beyond small-minded laws and localized, transient moral codes.

'I felt weightless with my new contempt! It was stupid of me to believe in such self-evident nonsense from the very first. Clarity. Everything fell into place once you realised that God was a projection, a human fantasy in the brain when we cannot face the horrific prospect of a meaningless, purposeless universe. There are no absolutes and there never have been any. There never will be any final, divine retribution. It is futile to harbour such illusions. There is no rhyme or reason for anything under the sun, just as there is nothing new under it.

'Sheila was dead. Everything in the world would die. Even the firmest of wooden floors to stand on would eventually turn into maggots. My grief was mollified now that I knew I too would die like Sheila. There were no limits now. Outrage no longer had a threshold. There were no restraints on contempt. I walked back towards Templeland Road reborn.'

After reading this account from Brady, I replied that a boy in his early teens could never have put the experience in this way. He agreed, but insisted that this was how it 'felt'. He admitted that he could only have written about it in this way after reading Dostoevsky when he was eighteen years old and also Nietzsche some time after that. I also commented that the depth of his anger at that 'Thing' in the dark sky relied for its force on the theologically naïve assumption that there was some 'Thing' *up* there to be in revolt against. Brady admitted this too and said that it was a paradoxical protest. Later, he described the same kind of paradoxical reaction when, after putting the last bit of earth over a victim on Saddleworth Moor, he raised his fist to another dark sky and shouted, 'Take that, you bastard!'

Meanwhile, on the Pollok estate, everything was coming up roses for the small band of burglars, who now carried out three break-ins most evenings. They had money to spend. Ian was seeing more of Evelyn Grant and spending most of his share on her. She never knew where the money came from, but forty years later Brady remembered one particular gift – a rabbit's-foot brooch. He took her home to number 21 and played the piano for her, as he would later for Myra Hindley.

Evelyn's parents were strict and insisted that she could only venture out in the evenings if her friend went with her. (Brady remembered her chaperone was a girl, plump with dark hair, but had forgotten her name.) He was frustrated and realised for the first time that three is a crowd.

Da and Ma Sloan knew nothing of Ian's nocturnal burglaries or the change in him after the death of Sheila. The only signs of family discord at this time emerged when Ma and Da insisted that Ian attend Sunday school and join the Boy's Brigade or the Scouts. The Sunday school was held in an unheated prefabricated hut 'as cold as the subject itself'. He attended for the first week or so but walked round the frosty estate for an hour rather than be subjected to 'saintly tosh'. Ma and Da never knew about his non-attendance, but Ian was openly defiant in his refusal to join the uniformed organisations with their 'puerile regimentation'.

As time went on, Ian began to wonder whether the gossip about his double life in the playground of Shawlands Academy had reached Evelyn's ears. Not that he cared: 'Her ears were shell-like, small and pink. My only interest in them was that I wanted to bite them.'

On leave from the Royal Navy, Robert Sloan brought home a revolver. The butt-plates were missing but it was in perfect working order. Ian had found a rifle in the Gorbals but the revolver, simply as an object he could hold in his hand, intrigued him. There were heavy penalties for possession of unlawful firearms after the war and Brady later assumed that this one was thrown into the Clyde. Much later he would have two revolvers during most of his time in the company of Myra Hindley.

Ian was beginning to be aware of changes in his mind and body that none of his friends seemed to be affected by: 'Looking back, my mind often encounters grey areas in which transitions were taking place without my conscious knowledge. I felt frightened by it at times. I wanted only complete awareness. I didn't admit to anyone that blank patches were beginning to occur. My friends looked to me as the intelligent one who was always in control. What would happen if my friends found out that I was sometimes spinning along erratically with no conscious control for sporadic short periods?'

In my conversations with Brady, he sometimes made the point that the 'blank periods' gave him delightful insight into experiences which are not allowed by what Aldous Huxley called the 'measly trickle' of ordinary consciousness. For Brady it was an 'inner state of serendipity, beyond conventional norms, or exploring intuitive leaps over mental barriers. I had experienced such moments of spontaneous delight or insight. A kind of understanding beyond the normal limitations of the mind, a spiritual lightness rising to supreme heights; an atavistic intoxication.' Brady sometimes quoted Goethe to me: 'The moment one definitely commits oneself, then providence moves too. Whatever you can do or dream, you can begin it. Boldness has genius, power and magic in it. Begin it now.'

When Sheila died, May Sloan was as devastated as Ian. Ma and Da bought her another dog, a pedigree, 'a beautiful silver and black German Alsatian bitch, about six months old.' May called her Una.

Ian and his gang of thieves had a particularly lucrative run but were stopped in their tracks when a pupil at the Academy informed on them. The police arrived at number 21, but Ian's real fear was the likely reaction of Ma and Da.

The young gangleader appeared with the others in the Children's Court that was then peculiar to Scotland and had no equivalent in English law. He was thought to be the prime mover. None of the gang had any previous convictions, and since all of their families were of 'good character', they were officially 'admonished' and sternly warned never to appear before the court again. The court knew nothing of the actual number of undetected burglaries.

Ian discovered the identity of the police informer relatively easily but decided to let him 'cook' for the moment. In this, as in almost every other case in his later life, his revenge would be served cold. He let the offending one suffer the uncertainty and, in Brady's words – quoting the Prayer Book – 'Let them perish through their imagination.' Years later, he gave me an example of just how cold his revenge could be served: 'Someone shopped me and my friends for breaking and entering when I was fifteen in Glasgow. I waited ten years for revenge. I found his address and went up the stairs of his block in order to knock on the door and shoot him in the head. As I approached his door a woman came out of another door on the same landing to beat a carpet on the stair rail. I remember she was using a clover-leafed shaped beating cane. I had to turn away and walk back down the stairs. On such little things people's lives depend.'

As fate would have it, the informer at the Academy was attacked a few weeks later by a group of boys unconnected with Ian and his pals. The small-time burglars decided that enough was enough.

Looking back on this time, Brady usually made the point that any lucidity he had as an adult shouldn't be confused with any perceptive fluency at the actual time of the events: 'The world was as confusing to me, sometimes, as it was to those around my age. I was learning to swim by instinct.'

If there was any doubt before, it was crystal clear now that, for the young Ian Brady, puberty had arrived. In a later chapter, I shall attempt to describe what he understood by the 'Napoleonic complex'. Of this stage in his life he spoke with hindsight about an 'Alexander complex' – the conquest not only of one sex, of only half a world, but both sexes: the love that could and could not speak its name. The young Ian Brady was bisexual.

He was beginning to notice how even the roughest of boys succumbed to their feminine side under the slightest suggestion, oblivious to the subliminal forces over which they no longer had control. It was a girl, however, who did not attend the Academy, who most attracted Ian. I shall refer to her as Bridie. She had long black hair, a lithe body, understated beauty – and almond-shaped eyes. The attraction was mutual. She was quick-witted and streetwise in a way that made the Academy girls feel threatened.

Other boys thought that Bridie was 'easy' but Ian put this down to their feelings of inadequacy: 'We indulged in the forbidden pleasure with that wild energy only the youthful can experience. Coitus interruptus might have been an ancient Latin manuscript for all we knew. We didn't need to know what it was. We practised it instinctively, knowing that to delay the final enjoyment was an even greater delight.'

Occasionally, Bridie and Ian would mutually seduce a boy or a girl, to deepen an intrigue that began when they confided to each other their early forbidden longings for irregular sex. Ian was still seeing Evelyn Grant regularly: 'Uncharacteristically for me, I wanted the relationship to remain platonic, even though I knew I could take her at any time. Her fresh-soap aroma had become sacrosanct to me. This may have been from a lingering penchant for purity or, more likely, the piquancy of complementary contrast – an indulgence that would fascinate me in the years to come in every compartment of my life.'

After a suitable lapse of time the Pollok gang resumed their nightly burglaries, although one of the boys was still under a curfew at home. The gang became more secretive and moved their activities to an area farther away, a residential district called Corker Hill. Ian hid his share of the takings in a biscuit tin under the rabbit hutch.

Ian was still in touch with his mother in Manchester and she invited him down south for a fortnight's holiday. He relished the prospect of the train journey. As an adult he would spend time at large railway stations and simply sit on a platform bench to imbibe the atmosphere: 'I loved railway stations; the smell of coal smoke and soot, the hissing of escaping steam, the tooting of trains departing, the scurry of passengers arriving late, the piercing sound of the guard's whistle and porters running to slam doors.' Myra Hindley learned not to probe too deeply or expect to share this solitary fascination of her lover.

The year was 1951. May and Jean Sloan bought platform tickets to make sure that Ian, still only thirteen years of age, caught his train. He had never been south of Glasgow and spent the journey at a corridor window taking in nicotine and the passing scene. He noticed a mountainous landscape he knew only later as the Lake District on his travels with Myra. After six hours the view changed to miles of redbrick houses with featureless roofs. It was dark. Decades later, Ian Brady quoted the Ewan MacColl song about the (now City of) Salford area of Manchester, 'Dirty Old Town', Manchester – Ian Brady's Nemesis.

Peggy was waiting the other side of the ticket barrier with a genial-looking man of stocky build – Patrick Brady. He had black hair parted in the middle and looked about forty. On the way home, after calling in a pub for a drink, they passed through the fruit market where Pat worked as a porter. An eerie silence pervaded the walkways of the lines of stalls covered with canvas hangings.

The exit from the market came out into Ancoats Lane, dominated by the *Daily Express* buildings. The noise of the presses could be heard in the street, presses which would print many stories about the Moors Murderers: 'One of the men on the catwalk waved to me and I waved back.' Peggy and Pat's house was in Grammar Street, number 9. It was a small house with sagging ceilings. Ian was given a camp bed.

Pat left money on the kitchen table for Ian before leaving for the fruit market at 4 a.m. Peggy took Ian to see Pat at work and Ian breathed in the exotic and earthy smell. They walked out of the market into Shude Hill and the Pollok mastermind was in qualified raptures at the sights to left and right. On the right side of the road was a firm of safe makers with displays of open safes in the window. Just a few yards down, on the left, was a gunsmiths, Stensby's, with racks of rifles and handguns on show. Fifteen years later Myra Hindley would look in Stensby's window, walk into the shop and buy a rifle for Ian Brady.

Ian had dinner with Peggy at Grammar Street and walked alone to Piccadilly in the city centre. He was surprised to find that there were so many large department stores with branches in Glasgow. He walked into Lewis's to keep out of the glaring sun and wandered into the music section, where he bought two 78 rpm records – both songs were to have strong associations for him throughout his life. The first was by the father of the film director John Huston, the old actor Walter Huston. 'September Song' became a hit through the combination of Huston's gravelly voice and its haunting melody. Brady reflected on the song in middle age: 'This song seductively evoked autumn in my mind, particularly as the years slowly turned to reveal the destructive course of my life. The unobtrusive change from late summer to autumn was always accompanied by a change in me. It was, unfailingly, a change for the worse. When the leaves began to turn to gold and wither on the branch, the fall matched the Fall within me, in the biblical sense. At first I was unaware of the transformation. I merely felt empty and deeply depressed. Then I slowly became forgetful to the degree that some days, even a whole week, would be a complete blank.

'At first I thought that everyone felt like this at some point. I slowly realized that it was not so. I was determined to hide this seasonal change in me rather than disclose my lack of control. Paradoxically, it was my good memory that helped me to keep the blank periods hidden.'

When I saw Brady in the autumn months, I noticed the change but put it down to a rhythm caused by the pattern of medication given to him. In a letter to me in autumn 1994 he voluntarily raised the subject of what he called the 'autumn fugue': 'My accent becomes more pronounced, my language and general manner roughens, I become more expansive and my handwriting changes. Who is to say I've not already entered it? As I said, both states are equally real to me. It is essentially a question of degree, both in action and words. Would you notice anything different, do you think?'

On another occasion he wrote about the conclusions of two consultant psychiatrists who discovered the significance of autumn for him. They diagnosed Ian Brady as 'an autumnal killer', subject to 'autumnal madness'. I asked him whether the intensity of the fugue showed any pattern of change during autumn. He replied: 'It reached its peak in December. If I ever wrote my Ode to Autumn it would be about nothing but its baleful influence on me. Keats might well ask, "Where are the songs of Spring?" I felt a profound, pervasive emptiness that would sometimes derange my senses.'

The second record was the soundtrack music from one of the most successful of British films: *The Third Man*. Brady gave me his video copy of the film at the end of a visit in the early 1990s. Ten years later he asked whether the film was still available. The soundtrack for the film was the haunting refrain played on the zither by Anton Karas. I located a video version of *The Third Man* that had a special introduction with Karas performing on the zither. Orson Welles, playing the anti-hero Harry Lime, composed the classically cynical sentiments himself and Brady quoted them to me from time to time: 'In Italy, for thirty years under the Borgias, they had warfare, terror, murder and bloodshed but they produced Michelangelo, Leonardo da Vinci and the Renaissance. In Switzerland they had brotherly love, and five hundred years of democracy and peace. And what did that produce? The cuckoo-clock!'

A few authors have made a great deal of the influence that *The Third Man* had on Brady. There is some truth in this but it had nothing like the significance of 'September Song' or even James Stewart's, *It's a Wonderful Life*. Brady asked me to search for a copy of Stewart's classic and I eventually found one with an introduction describing the making of the film. It was clear that the film had made a huge impact on Brady, though he never explained to me in what way.

I asked him just what was the importance of *The Third Man* for him. He replied that it was the 'first lesson in cinematic moral relativism'.

Ian stepped out of Lewis's and bought a slice of watermelon from a barrow boy. He sat on a wall and watched the life of Piccadilly pass before his eyes, as he would a decade later: 'an absorbing pastime, which Myra and I grew addicted to as we tried to deduce a person's life from their appearance'.

He walked back to Peggy in Grammar Street and satisfied his thirst with Manchester's creamy sterilised milk that he had begun to drink by the bottle. He scanned the entertainments pages of the *Manchester Evening News*. Peggy, Pat and Ian went out to the cinema to see *The Quiet Man*. As they walked home in the dusk, eating fish and chips, the men slaving over the presses of the *Daily Express* recognised Ian and waved.

The following day Peggy and Ian went to an amusement park in Belle Vue that included a zoo among its attractions. Brady remembered the visit because of a performing seal, but even more for a 'criss-cross' that occurred. He used this term numerous times to me in conversations and letters – it was his translation of C G Jung's 'synchronicity', a word the great psychologist used for coincidences of events in space and time that seemed to mean more than mere chance. Brady used to insist that they were there to be enjoyed, not understood. Ian persuaded Peggy to pay for a ride on the roller coaster: 'It crawled slowly upward like a steel centipede on silver rails, taking me skyward. I gazed across the grey canopy of Manchester's skyline, at the sagging rooftops of huddled dwellings, grimy factory chimneys and the spires of ramshackle churches pointing nowhere except up to the overcast sky. It was my first view of Manchester's sprawl, its industrial blackened brick piles and grid of cramped streets, with matchstick, ant-like people walking through them. I glanced to the left as the roller coaster climbed to look in the direction of a district I knew much later to be Gorton.

'Did my eyes fall on one particular dead-end street in that district, far away and indistinguishable from the other streets in which it nestled? Is it possible that I glimpsed any of the tiny inhabitants of that street, Bannock Street, as the roller coaster made the summit and before it plunged into the drop below? Is it possible that any of the distant inhabitants of that narrow Gorton street looked up for a few seconds as the screams from Belle Vue drifted across the Gorton rooftops?

'Ten years into the future I visited Bannock Street regularly myself and sometimes looked up to see the roller coaster on the horizon when I heard the screams. After this fleeting distraction I tapped on the door of number seven. Myra Hindley opened the door and said, "Zzzeee! I thought it was you."'

A few days later Ian was walking the streets alone and wandered into Moss Side with its West Indian population in evidence everywhere: 'I found it exotic and exciting, stimulated by their easy-going, exuberant lifestyle. It was all new to me, as Glasgow at that time had no coloured district. Moss Side became one of my favourite haunts at a future date, particularly after dark. Decades later I was to exchange stories with the Yorkshire Ripper, Peter Sutcliffe, who also knew the area well, it being rich in prostitutes, two of whom he murdered.'

One morning Peggy asked Ian if he would like to meet the boy downstairs. He was about three years older than Ian but had the use of two bikes. The boys spent the day together riding around in the hot sunshine. They rode up the Oldham Road and met up with a group of teenagers outside a block of flats. The girls were particularly taken by Ian's Scottish accent. He was flattered by the attention but soon grew tired of having to repeat himself. From that day, he carefully enunciated his words whenever he found himself south of the Scottish border: 'I lost my strong Scottish accent after living for a couple of years in Manchester, except when I lost my temper. But whenever I returned to see my friends in Scotland they said I sounded "Englified"!'

On Saturday morning Peggy said that she was going to shop at a large open market on the outskirts of the city. Ian decided to go with her and sowed a seed for another set of criss-cross years from then: 'We took a bus trip to the market; the name of the place meant nothing to me and I soon forgot it. As Peggy moved around the stalls searching for bargains, I wandered off on my own, arranging to meet her later. I rifled through the

second-hand books before walking down a narrow side street parallel to
the market. I found a small bookshop and bought a science fiction
magazine. I could remember nothing else about the day.

'Eleven years later I was riding out of Manchester on my bike and
rediscovered the market. I had no ominous feelings when I recognized the
place, but simply rode around it, slowly jogging my boyhood memories.
At least I now knew the name of the place was Ashton-under-Lyne. I could
not have known that, at a time not far into the future, late on a November
Saturday afternoon, as the fog descended like a shroud on the market,
Myra Hindley and I would provide a corpse for the shroud and take a
stranger with us to the high barren wilderness of Saddleworth Moor.'

On the eve of his return to Glasgow, Ian strolled alone around the city
in the mild summer dusk, a ritual he would perform many times in the
future. Peggy waved him off in the morning from Victoria station. He
reflected on his first visit to England as the train moved slowly through the
outskirts of Glasgow. Brady had fourteen years of freedom left before
being imprisoned within England's borders for the remainder of his life.
For the moment, however, he sensed a recharge of energy as he felt
Glasgow pavements beneath his feet – the ritual of return.

Back at Shawlands Academy, autumn was approaching: 'I sensed the
ubiquitous ache that there was something I was compelled to do. But what
was it? The first victim of my autumnal enthralment was the police
informer.'

The two of them found themselves alone together purely by chance in the
school gymnasium. Ian had forged Ma Sloan's handwriting in a letter to
excuse himself from a session of what was then called 'PT'. The last few
stragglers from the previous lesson left the changing room and the informer
struggled to get dressed. Ian was sitting out his class's session impassively,
having lit up a cigarette. After a minute or so the boy began to cry.

School gossip had long identified him as the informer. Was he waiting
for the retribution to descend so that the agony would be over? Were they
tears of self-pity? Were they tears of regret? The informer's sense of
helplessness no doubt seemed endless to him but it fanned the young Ian
Brady's instincts and imagination. No word was exchanged between the
two of them as the informer 'melted before me like a girl as I lowered him
to the dirty floor and had him roughly, devoid of feeling or affection.'

After this encounter, Ian never felt that there was any question of a quid
pro quo. The informer had sought him out. He would not be spared. But
Ian hadn't anticipated the boy's understated audacity. He begged for secret

meetings. Ian complied and arranged to meet him at the foot of the same tree where he continued to frolic with Bridie. By this time he had conjured up a pseudonym from letters in the informer's name and called him Jasmin. He made his clandestine lover use Bridie's lipstick.

Ian gazed at the leafless branches, thin against the white sky, and felt the mood of absurdity and emptiness that would always overcome him as autumn deepened. As an adult he knew that there was nothing he could do to prevent this seasonal change in him. In his childhood he sought escape from it by being feverishly busy, but sensed nothing but futility and banal routine that defeated any amount of immersion in frenetic activity: 'I would lie on my bed and allow inertia to envelop me and stare at familiar objects where I had thrown them. They looked like fragments of a stranger's life; remnants left behind by someone deceased. When I became conscious of my torpor I became angry and paced up and down in my room. I would see an arrogant and morose face staring back at me from the mirror and, for a split second, I was a stranger to myself.

'That sudden reflection would often make me laugh at the ridiculous, pretentious image. I would feel refreshed and less serious, more at home with the world. But not every time.

'Often I would feel that nothing was impossible and that all abstract limits were mere conventions decided by a show of hands. Gestures of gratuitous execration would sometimes give vent to the autumnal change. Half of me would look in animadversion at the antics of the other half.'

I asked Brady if he could remember any particular occasions when this occurred. He replied in a letter: 'I was talking to some friends outside the gates of Shawlands Academy. An old, plump woman came up to me and asked if I had the right time. I said, "Yes. Have you got a watch?"

'My pals laughed at my sarcastic reply. I expected and wanted a mouthful in reply but she just nodded and walked on. I felt ashamed as she ambled away with short steps. I wanted to chase after her and apologise, to explain that it was only a joke. But before I could act, I resented that she had made me feel ashamed. I just laughed loudly to add to her humiliation. Just as quickly, I felt guilty about that also.

'On another occasion I travelled into the Gorbals to look for some pals but none of them were to be seen. I killed time waiting for them by sitting on a wall in the back of a tenement and watched the passing scene.

'Tramps and meths drinkers were a common sight and they often hung around the backs hoping to pick up pennies thrown down to them from tenement windows.

'I could hear someone singing. A tramp appeared in a long tattered coat and holding his cap to his heart as he murdered the old song, "Darling, I am growing older" before doing the same to "I'll take you home again, Kathleen". He stooped twice to pick up what he thought were coins. He was about seventy and had a dirty battered face. As he raked through the dirt for a penny he seemed to have a serenity and dignity that disturbed my feelings of superiority. I felt angry and made sure he could hear the distinctive sounds of silver coins I was jingling in my pocket. I felt petty for doing it. I wanted to wound him verbally or physically for making me react in this way. Instead, as though I was a detached stranger, I watched my right hand leave my pocket and hand him a silver half-crown, rather than throw it for him to scrape for in the filth and dust of the backs.'

I responded to this with the comment by the French religious philosopher Simone Weil on the subject of disinterested goodness. She observed that if anyone gives a beggar money, however small the amount, they are in the beggar's debt forever, if for a single, brief moment they reflect on their generosity. She added: 'You can only do good unintentionally.' Brady took the point and replied: 'Who would deny that we are all a changeable blend of absurd conceits and self-deceits? I am, but endeavour not to be. Yet I am capable of doing good or ill in equal measure and equal pleasure. Sometimes I feel empathy and sympathy. At other times I am severe and full of malevolence. I can pity a tiny insect one minute, and yet despise the whole human race the next.' This response reminded me of something Brady wrote to sign off at the end of a letter in June 1993: 'Here's a little exercise. Can you think of a thought or action not attributable to vanity?'

One evening, at midnight, Ma Sloan woke Ian from his slumbers. The police were waiting for him downstairs in the living room. Ma, in her Chinese dressing gown, sat down to hear the worst. The gang's latest recruit had taken a stolen crafted cutthroat razor – his share of the loot – and had simply hidden it under the cushion of a chair in his bedroom. His father found it and handed him over to the police. He confessed everything and implicated the other members.

All of them appeared before the Sheriff's Court and Ian, pinpointed as the evil genius of the gang, was given two years' probation. The informer could only wait in dread for retribution from his former pals.

A curfew descended on number 21 Templeland Road. Ian suffered it for a short time before running away from home and taking three of the group with him. They slept in a barn of hay at a farm on the top of Corker Hill, where Ian usually bought straw for his rabbits. At first light they moved down to the estate and helped themselves to bags of crusty rolls and bottles of milk from doorsteps.

Eventually they found their way into Glasgow city centre, after tea and toast in a café on the Paisley Road. They kept warm by going into the large department stores and stealing the occasional item. After closing time, they went into a cinema and saw Humphrey Bogart and James Cagney in *The Roaring Twenties*, a film about the Prohibition era. It was now too frosty for another night in the hay and the four drifted home to face the music.

After the due period of punishment, the gang persuaded their parents that they had stayed out of trouble, although they had simply changed their field of operations. Ian and four friends were allowed to go on a camping holiday to Dunoon.

They smoked and drank as the paddle steamer *Waverley* moved across the Firth of Clyde. Still two inches below his eventual six feet, Ian was the tallest and bought the drinks at the bar. He performed the same duty on the return journey as they looked through portholes across the Clyde. Years later, Ian Brady and Myra Hindley had the same view and the same seats as they steamed back to Glasgow from Tighnabruaich. As the small group of stragglers made their way down the gangplank and on to the dimly lit wharf, Ian looked back and felt another small sense of dying.

Thirteen years would pass before he would board the *Waverley* again for a final voyage 'doon the water'.

Ian knew an older boy, who had left school and worked at a butcher's shop. Through him he was taken on as a Saturday morning delivery boy covering the Shawlands district near the Academy. Apart from the pocket money, Ian saw the job as a way of gathering information on vulnerable houses in this highly residential neighbourhood. Once the basket on the front of the bicycle was loaded, he was a free agent and the customers invariably gave him a tip.

One delivery was fortuitous. A boy at the Academy had enlisted Ian to convey his tame overtures to a striking, lithe and well-proportioned girl with large dark eyes and long black hair. I shall call her 'Margo'. She opened the door and Ian forgot any sense of obligation to the wimp at school. They arranged to meet that night at Shawlands Cross and went into the city to see James Mason starring as Rommel in *The Desert Fox*.

The young Ian Brady explored Margo on the back row and felt that the night was not yet over. On the way home, he guided her towards Queen's

Park. The gates were closed but Ian knew of a loose railing in the fence. They sat on a bench looking at the black pool of water. Ian had his arm around Margo and could feel her trembling in the cold night. He was trembling himself, but not from the cold. He undid her silk blouse and she trembled even more as her breasts were exposed to the night air. They slid from the bench on to the pathway near the pool and were momentarily startled when one of the resident swans glided across to investigate this contribution to the nightlife in the park.

Margo and he met regularly in the shadows of Queen's Park for sex. They made love on her living room carpet in front of the fire whenever her parents were out. She knew that Ian was still seeing Evelyn Grant. Margo's admirer at the Academy continued to give Ian puerile notes of affection to pass on to her; occasions for hysteria. Brady still had recollections years later of having toyed with the idea of 'having' the admirer as well as Margo. He couldn't remember whether he was too lazy or too busy.

Evelyn was still the forbidden apple, 'rosy and fresh, to be enjoyed in the mind apart from tender caresses', but Ian had heard rumours that another boy was interested in her. The gang's bush telegraph discovered that he was a policeman's son. His every move was noted in case Evelyn had innocently passed on incriminating information about them.

From the time Ian first attended Shawlands Academy he found the diet of studies as tasteless as forced fruit. Emlyn Williams writes that the novels of Walter Scott 'caught his fancy' with their luridly romantic themes of 'castle and gorge and battle and dungeon'. The truth is that Brady loathed Walter Scott and dismissed his books as 'stodge' and 'cold porridge', compared with the 'lightning' of Shakespeare, who was not on the curriculum. Brady wrote in a letter; 'I saw Olivier's "Hamlet" when I was ten, and this led me to Shakespeare's works.'

Brady would sometimes illustrate his points to me by quoting long passages of Shakespeare from memory. In one letter he looked back to this time in his school years as one when he was devouring Shakespeare as a 'human god': 'The psychological dilemma of Macbeth, and his eventual rejection of all moral restraints; the reckless, ruthlessness of Richard III; the controlled, self-mastery of Henry V; the arrogant Coriolanus inflicting self-defeat upon himself; the nihilistic machinations of Iago; the pathos in Lear's betrayal. All of these taught me principles I could clothe with the flesh of the real world when their time came. I was contemptuous of the sausage-machine education at the Academy: the ceaseless preparation for something that never happens. I would be self-educated. I would make my own use of relativist and eclectic means. My priorities would be my own priorities.'

The falling leaves ushered in another dying season for Ian. He planned to meet it halfway. Ian found a length of black hosepipe and made a cosh by filling it with lead. He also bought a sheath knife to be better equipped to cope with the 'slings and arrows of outrageous autumn'.

Out of the blue, boys at the Academy were given the chance to go potato picking for two weeks near Dingwall in the north of Scotland. Ian and his group signed up right away when they were told that the boys would be paid. May Sloan had promised to feed and water Ian's rabbits while he was away. When he returned, he found that the big grey Jenny and the small Dutch Smokey had died. The big black Harry was dying. May had forgotten to pull the cover down over the front of the hutch on a night of sharp frost. Ian wasn't bitter but simply accepted May's oversight. When Harry died, he put him in a box with an inscription on the lid and launched it on to the river Cart. Brady was later to say that this was one of his early experiences of the democracy of death. He destroyed the hutch.

Ian contemplated the few remaining months of his school days and the thought of 'sitting at a school desk grappling with the irrelevances of trigonometry and algebra'. In a last fling, he ran away from home again with an older boy and three of his friends in search of the 'fifty caves of Arrochar'. Arrochar was on the northern tip of Loch Long, separated from Loch Lomond by a four-mile isthmus.

The caves proved to be elusive and a disappointment when they were discovered. Nevertheless, years later Ian Brady returned to the caves with Myra Hindley. Loch Long also came to feature in Brady's admissions to murders that were not part of the original Moors investigations; a subject for future chapters.

It was around this time that Ian first experienced what he would later call 'black light'. In a letter of July 1995 he spoke of his experience of 'heightened perception': 'In times of danger and test of will, all my senses would become supranormal, everything outlined as though by needle-sharp electricity.' He recalled the event: 'I can't remember now whether I had the lead cosh with me for any sinister reason but, in hindsight, I was glad to be carrying it. I hadn't used it before.

'I was walking with two friends, making my way towards Govan through the gas-lit alleys of the Gorbals, well outside our own home territory.

'A group of boys were hanging around the entrance to a tenement. They began larking around as we approached them. I had almost passed them when one of the gang bumped into one of my friends, who reacted by pushing the boy and swearing at him. We could easily have been outnumbered within a matter of seconds. It was their territory. It was too late to avoid trouble. A fight erupted.

'The cosh was tucked down the back of my belt. I retrieved it and held it out of sight, waiting for the inevitable. One of their gang moved close to me in a threatening manner and I smacked him across the face with it. He held his face as blood seeped through his fingers. I can still remember how black and oily the blood looked in the dimmed light. Suddenly my vision was transformed. Everything was immediately vivid and sharp, as though illuminated by liquid electricity.

'Everyone seemed to be moving in slow motion. It was pure exhilaration for me. As my blows landed there was a sound like that of hitting a hollow tree trunk. Half of me found the cartoon sound effect hilarious. The other half was fully alert and taking the necessary steps of self-preservation in the midst of the fray. I instinctively swiped my way into the relative protection of a tenement entrance and a route to make the escape with my pals.

'In my bedroom, later that night, I reflected on how my vision had changed in the fracas. Could it have been just an optical illusion? What brought about such a change? Although my hyper altered state was experienced at the vortex of a violent encounter, it had excited and fascinated me. How could I recapture the sensation? I wanted to experience it again.

'What if it were a freak experience, a phantasmagoria? Perhaps I had been hit on the head and been unaware of it in the midst of the fray.

'There was no tender swelling or mark on my head. Nothing hurt. In fact, it had given me an unbidden fluid muscular dexterity. It had enhanced my hearing power. I didn't know it then, but in the not too distant future the whole experience would make sense when seen in a wider context.'

Ian's last days at Shawlands Academy were marked by a series of 'happenings' that led to his final break with Evelyn Grant. These events have long since been dwarfed by Brady's actions at a later time, but he always regretted his own part in the ending of their friendship. The details need not detain us here except to mention what was the last straw for Evelyn. She had apparently taken a roundabout route to the shops on the estate that would take her past number 21 Templeland Road. Ian was with his friends on the corner when one of them, Tam, threw a stone that bounced on the pavement and hit Evelyn's ankle. She looked at the group for the culprit. Ian's was just one of half a dozen faces staring blankly back: 'I shall never forget her reproachful look. I remember it with shame.'

Ian Brady's childhood was drawing to a close. He felt that spontaneity was giving way to conformity. Yet he still felt that he had the edge and the chance of 'one final, defiant fling against mediocrity': 'What the others might think was now only of transient concern to me. If they were timid enough to succumb to the dull future that social conditioning had seduced them to accept, then so be it.

'Life was a brief show in which you either mimed the part of someone else's script, or both wrote and performed your own. There were no rehearsals in that fundamental drama. You either capitulate to the system, the status quo, or you find your own path, follow your own way in the black forest. I had already made my choice subconsciously – the only level that ultimately matters.'

CHAPTER FOUR

RAIN IN THE AFTERNOON ON THE PAISLEY ROAD

Early in January 1953, at the age of fifteen, Ian Brady left Shawlands Academy without regrets. From the beginning, he had no wish to work for a living but was regularly reminded by Da Sloan to learn a 'trade'. An apprenticeship lasting five years, for a weekly pittance, was Ian's idea of slavery. Having left school, he couldn't expect to live off Ma and Da and was forced to take a job on the railways, cleaning the grease from steam engines. This meant an early start out of doors in winter frosts. The railways didn't employ anyone with a criminal record and Ian was relieved to be sacked after a few weeks, once enquiries had been made.

A week or so later, Ian obtained a job as a butcher's delivery boy. Again, he was able to observe closely houses that were likely targets for burgling. Some of the books on the Moors Murders have hyped the job to that of a slaughterhouse worker. Emlyn Williams confuses the sequence of Brady's occupations and comments that his job with the butchers gave him his first sight and smell of blood: 'Every day a butcher's assistant does get more and more used to the mechanics of carnage. Used to the innocent eyes one moment liquid with life, the next – at the flash of the axe – glazed with sudden disbelief, the blood spouting red and smelling warm, the thud of the carcass: used to swift expert dismemberment, the rhythmic crunch of bone and parting of tissue to the accompaniment of a jaunty whistle.'

As Brady remarked to me once: 'I could never have brought myself to kill sheep or cattle,' adding, 'The idea of killing people had never bothered me in the least.'

Ian met several girls in the course of his deliveries, but remembered one in particular. To preserve her anonymity, I shall refer to her as 'Betty'. She combined the characteristics of Sylvia and Evelyn Grant – high cheekbones, almond-shaped eyes and blonde hair. Ian was particularly attracted by her deep laugh, which was accompanied by sidelong glances and elaborate gestures. She went with Ian to cinemas in that area. His habit of keeping areas of life in fixed compartments was well established by now. None of his friends knew that Betty existed. Ian and Betty made full use of her bedroom when her parents were out.

The young Brady was still looking for jobs that were better paid. In the course of this search something happened that would change his life forever. I questioned him several times about this event and describe it below in Ian Brady's own words.

Ian had a job interview with a firm on a large industrial estate near Paisley Road. One afternoon he set off on his bicycle in the Glasgow drizzle, beneath a sky almost black with clouds. In later years he had no recollection of the interview or the nature of the job, except that it would be handy for meeting Betty. The vivid luminosity of what was about to happen next wiped out most of the more mundane memories of that day. Because of its seminal importance in his life, Brady had written down a brief description of the event years before I met him. He had changed small details from time to time and the following is the form of it when he eventually handed it to me. He commented on different features of the experience during visits: 'It was raining heavily as I cycled home. As I approached the Paisley Road I felt a strange change coming over me. My body felt light and I felt a little dizzy. My bicycle appeared to be moving with a will of its own. I was becoming enveloped by some kind of bright radiance. The buildings, vehicles and people around me seemed not to belong to my world any more. I felt removed from them. I had never experienced anything like this before, but I succumbed to it and became completely passive to what was about to happen to me.

'I had never imagined such a thing was possible. I had never heard anyone speak about this. Was it a secret known only to the elect? Was I showing any unconscious resistance to what it appeared to want to do to me? I sensed I was in the process of some initiation whose significance depended upon there being no anticipation of its appearance. Was it to be a revelation of biblical proportions? St Paul was on the Damascus road. I was on the Paisley Road. I was drawing from a vital, tremendous power source. I felt dizzy still. Was I in danger?'

'I managed to stop the bike on its own course at the corner of Paisley Road and slumped against a newsagent's shop window, and then moved into the dry shelter of the shop's entrance.

'It was dim in these early stages. Then it slowly grew more intense. Years later, when I had the ability and maturity to do so, I wrote down what I could remember of this strange event. I read the account again before writing the account here. There was a green radiation, beautiful and warm, making what Dickens would describe as mere phantoms of passing individuals and the road traffic, making both insignificant. I entered willingly into the green manifestation, immersing my whole being in the swirling, warm cloud.

'There was something waiting within it, as yet indistinct, seen in brief glimpses through the green mist as a more substantial fluctuating formation. Sounds were coming from its centre as though from a great distance or depth, hollow and not yet identifiable as a familiar language. Features formed slowly in the shimmering green radiance. Was it male or female or hermaphroditic? They were sounds rather than words. Were they coming from my subconscious?

'And then came the realization. I was in the presence of death itself. I was witnessing it and hearing its sounds.

'I felt helpless. I experienced total panic. Rereading the account written all those years ago, I have realised again the impact of this event in my life. I wrote; "Was I dying or already dead?" The voice assured me I was neither. I had not spoken a word: "Death" had read my thoughts and answered immediately. My excitement began to temper fear. Was I insane? No. What did it want? I would learn. Would it help or harm me? It would help. Why me? I would know. How? I would see.

'The shadows of the old world were taking the shape of people once more. I was disorientated as I looked into the faces of passers-by to see whether they showed any awareness of what had happened. Had they experienced the revelation? I was surprised to see that everything seemed normal and unchanged. I stood in the doorway for quite some time, gathering my thoughts and adapting to the new reality.

'I was looking at a radically changed world, a world vibrant and charged with internal contradictions, a world in which moral and ethical interpretations of life seemed absolutely stultifying and irrelevant, as I had believed for years.'

Hearing voices in the head is, apparently, one of the classic signs of schizophrenia. In the first conversation I had with Ian Brady, he told me that a psychiatrist had asked him whether he heard voices: 'I told him "No, I'm agnostic."' Many thousands of people, without being thought of as insane, have claimed down the centuries to hear voices in religious experiences.

It was dark when Ian arrived at Templeland Road. None of the family had arrived home from work and Ma was preparing the meal. He looked to see whether there were any signs that she had noticed any change in him. Nothing. Ian wanted to be cautious but couldn't help mentioning the dizziness and the warm attractive green as Ma was laying the table. She seemed worried and asked questions. Ian gave vague answers and said nothing about the vision of Death. Ian was concerned: 'Why did Ma seem so troubled? Was there something amiss with me? Were visions of Death a warning? Were they hostile or friendly? Was mine a common experience? Would I recognise their familiarity with it in their eyes? Would they see it in mine? If they did, how would they react? If I did, what would I do and say? Did I have to defend the vision of Death? Would I receive help and guidance?'

Ian Brady, in fact, later compared his experience with that of religious converts. A sensation of power, privilege and inspiration coursed through him in much the same way: 'Death would be my omnipresent guide and friend. People fear the manner and uncertainty of the transition from life to death. Each breath is a step towards the waiting arms of death. I wanted to meet death halfway, choosing the manner and time of departure, rather than shuffling my way towards senility.'

Fifty years later, Brady was still breathing and approaching the enfeebled state he dreaded most of all.

In a letter to me in April 1992, he wrote, as he did at other times, of the 'new dimension of heightened being' that he entered at fifteen years of age: 'An astonishing revelation or esoteric visitation that would motivate all my actions for the remainder of my life.'

I asked Brady about Fred Harrison's book on the Moors Murders in which there are some brief references to the 'green face of Death' experience. Brady dismissed Fred Harrison's simplistic interpretation, in his book *Brady and Hindley*, when he implied that the murders were sacrifices in Brady's private auto-soteric cult: one that provides its own salvation. Brady rejected this as journalistic licence. During Peter Topping's reopening of the Moors case in 1986, Myra Hindley was asked whether she knew anything about the 'green face of Death'. She said she knew nothing. I shall attempt to put Ian Brady's Paisley Road experience in a wider context in a later chapter.

Ian eventually began work as an apprentice in the huge Harland and Wolff shipyard on the Clyde, a job that pleased Da Sloan. Brady enjoyed the rough company of the workers but couldn't stand the cacophony of the working shipyard, or the prospect of monotonous years as an apprentice. There would be fifty years of waiting for the daily blast of the siren signalling the end of the day, followed by three hours of drinking to compensate for the living time that had been lost.

After work, in the 'daily mindless tumult' of the shipyard, Ian joined his friends in the heady excitement of housebreaking: 'a balm to be breathed in deeply whilst viewing the infinite dark sky.' When he was alone, he had time to think about the change that was taking place deep within him. When Brady was speaking to me about this time in his life, during a visit, he gave me the following on a sheet of paper. He thought he might adapt it for use some time: 'In tandem a darkness was being nurtured within me each time I went back to the Gorbals and walked through the familiar gas lit alleys I had grown to love. This was my real element, the peace at the centre of the cyclone. In this place, even inanimate objects were sentient to my touch and spoke their own greeting in return. Those blackened tenement walls knew me better than I knew myself. The iron lampposts seemed to nod and bow their flickering greeting as they illuminated my way. The curled up granny cats, on ground-floor windowsills, purred their welcome. I could laugh in this world.'

Ian and his pals increased their nocturnal criminal activities. He returned to the Gorbals more and more. He was surprised that he was drawing out his lock-back knife in a reflex action in disputes with other boys. Ian pierced a boy's shoulder one evening, outside the Kidson Street Necropolis, and began to worry about being reckless of consequences. He was happy just the same for having a charmed life: 'I had entered a period of mental farrago; a manic medley of events became just a blur in my mind. I saw dark alleys, anonymous faces struck by weapons; swearing and shouting from disembodied voices; blooded hands; parlours in ransacked houses; a startling glimpse of myself in a cracked mirror; sounds of shoes on wet cobbles; smells of rotting animals in gas lit alleys; the rasping breath and the rapid beat of the heart; sweat cold on the brow; the sudden luminosity of vision within an enveloping green radiance.

'Inevitably, it came to an end, but the long run of good fortune I had in such chaotic circumstances only served to reaffirm my trust in Death the divinity.'

Brady's luck did indeed run out, at the hands of another informer. The police held him in custody on nine counts of burglary. The year was 1953, and because he was still only fifteen years old, he was put in a remand home with another member of the gang. The older boys were kept in Barlinnie Prison. Ian was taken in handcuffs to the remand home in St Vincent Street in an affluent residential area of the city. The boys were set menial cleaning chores and attended education classes; one of them in religious instruction that ended in chaos – the boys guffawing at the teacher, whose words were drowned out by their laughter.

On the second evening, May Sloan came to visit Ian with Peggy, who had travelled north from Manchester. He was released the following morning when Peggy arrived to collect him.

The prospect of appearing before Glasgow's Sheriff Court evoked Ian's sensation of *black light*. In future, it would be triggered by situations of danger, excitement and tests of will: 'All my senses would become supranormal.' On the first occasion Brady described the *black light* to me, he asked me if I remembered the kind of mapping pens that could be bought from post offices. This was going back to a lost age, but I could remember. He explained: 'Imagine the needle-sharp nib of the pen dipped into a container of liquid electricity. The pen thinly delineates both buildings and people, making everything finely etched by an electric radiance. Holding up a colour negative to the light can produce a small semblance of the effect.

'Wrapped in the enchantment of *black light*, I was free from any sense of legal or moral inhibition. It was as though the "on" switch not only enabled me to see in the dark but also through the conventional norms of society and reality. Yet despite this amoral transfiguration, there was an exhilarating feeling of oneness, a unity with the organic and inanimate, completely oblivious to the sense of superiority habitually claimed by humans. Everything would pass and all was vanity. It might be compared to a religious experience, but in my case the merry, merry pipes of Pan would be ringing. It had a spiritual certainty beyond the banal, predictably dull, one dimensional institutional religions.

'Another visual effect was that, if I gazed at any specific object, it appeared to grow before your eyes revealing grain and texture. My hearing greatly improved in volume and tone. It picked up all sounds, far away or close at hand. You could compare it to the clarity a parabolic microphone has.'

Ian Brady was gripped by the overwhelming desire to feel everything intensely, to capture and maintain these sensations: 'I sank into deep depression when I returned to "normal", everyday consciousness. I loathed this. I found myself driven to experiment.

'I realised that danger was the confederate of delight. Another factor was an extreme act of will. The ingredient of conscious choice, the act of willing a dangerous confrontation into being, engendered transfiguration more rapidly than anything else could. I now had the keys to open two doors that contained the *black light*. Unfortunately, I made little headway on how to hold on to the experience. I was disappointed by the final answer to this question.

'Power over fear simply meant outlasting the enemy by seconds or minutes and, when the danger passed, so did the *black light*. Conversely, if the will wilted under the threat of danger, then so did the *black light*.

'For example, I had used the lock-back knife during an incident in Glasgow, but the man facing me was still moving towards me with a piece of steel piping. Blood had run down the blade of the knife and on to my fingers and palm, making it difficult for me to grip the handle. My confidence disappeared with my powerlessness to hold it. It drained away as the *black light* was eclipsed.'

As the date of his court appearance approached, in mid-December 1954, Ian became convinced that he faced captivity rather than another period of probation. He sought consolation in the gentle caresses and laughter of Betty, his girlfriend from Paisley. She knew nothing of his life of crime. Anticipating his impending loss of freedom, he warned her that he might be spending some time in England in the near future. He didn't foresee at the time how this lie would become a simple statement of the truth.

After seeing a film together in the city, Ian took Betty over the river to introduce her to the Gorbals. She was scared but excited. After this visit, the highest honour Ian Brady could bestow on anyone he cared for was to share the Gorbals with him or her. The last girl to be given the honour was Myra Hindley.

The day arrived and Ian thought of Death, his faithful friend: 'Death still held sway. I had trapped myself. I couldn't expect it to intervene in trivial matters while protecting me from greater dangers. Discretion would not bend me to accept the third-hand opinions of others, nor to adapt my beliefs to satisfy whoever I dealt with. It would suit my purposes to dissemble, but I was not yet mature enough to do so in deeper, more fundamental matters. I cut life down to the bone and saw nothing more than animated skeletons devoid of muscle, flesh and blood. One singular thing counted for me. I had being through my will to act.'

Peggy, Ma and May Sloan accompanied Ian to Glasgow's Sheriff Court. In later years, he often drew attention to the undeserved help he received on such occasions when any writer suggested that his upbringing was to blame for his part in the Moors Murders. Ian dressed conservatively for his court appearance after having a crew cut hairstyle at Fusco's, a fashionable but expensive barber in the city.

Against all expectations, the court gave Ian another term of probation on the condition that he left Glasgow and moved south to Manchester to live with his real mother and stepfather. He couldn't find words to express his relief as the party travelled back to Pollok. It was only a day or so later, when he talked with his friends, that he realised the cost of his freedom – separation from everything he held dear. For the remainder of his life, he would try to defy the old advice of a parent to a child: 'Take what thou wilt – and pay for it.'

The enforced separation had sown seeds of resentment that would bear fruit with the passing of the years: 'I watched the family with an increasing sense of imminent loss. I had never, and would never, lose that conviction of belonging.' He made a solitary journey around the Gorbals, pressing his brow against tenement walls, his inner voice penetrating the stone and whispering its farewell. As Brady said to me: 'If Prince Charles can talk to trees, I can talk to stone walls.' He would revisit the labyrinthine Gorbals many times.

Peggy returned to Manchester to prepare for Ian's arrival. His pals joked about him being 'deported': 'I joked, when I felt able to, to give an air of flippancy to hide the depression. I felt the city and people I had so much affection for were rejecting me. My insides were being eaten away. Laughter sounded hollow even to me. I felt like a monk about to enter a monastery and take life-vows of holy poverty and isolation that would cut him off forever from all he held precious.

'My awareness of imminent departure gave me a new sense of immediacy. A passing cloud or a blade of grass was more mysterious now. Glasgow's air was intoxicating as it had never been before. I shunned company and vacuous prattle.'

In the days leading to his departure, blanks in Ian's memory were more frequent but no one remarked on any change in him. He wanted to go to Glasgow Central Station alone when the day arrived.

After a time of excruciating small talk in the living room, he picked up his suitcase and walked into Templeland Road; 'I shall never forget that moment.'

It was only after he turned the corner that he wiped his eyes and felt the killing rage. He found an empty compartment and chain-smoked until the buffet car opened. Ian Brady drank whisky as the train took him south to Manchester and catastrophe.

CHAPTER FIVE

NEW YEAR'S EVE IN STRANGEWAYS

Languorous on whisky, Ian Brady gazed through the window of the compartment and recalled the journey he had made two years before. Those two weeks on holiday in Manchester had been a tonic. The prospect of two years' exile from Glasgow, family and friends was another matter. The train dropped speed as the redbrick suburban sprawl of Manchester appeared through the approaching dusk. He shrugged off the gloom of being dealt a bad hand and whispered, 'Richard's himself again.'

The train drew in half an hour late. Ian saw Peggy and Pat Brady waving at the ticket barrier. As the three of them walked towards a taxi, Ian felt the stirrings of excitement and the pervasive sense of licence he would always feel when he was anonymous in a strange city. Peggy's house had been in Ancoats when Ian first visited her but she was now living with Pat in a two-room-and-kitchen flat in Denmark Road in Moss Side.

Ian had explored and been excited by this exotic West Indian district of Manchester during his holiday two years before. A divan bed had been set up in the back room for him. Lying on the bed and working his way through a packet of cigarettes given to him by Pat, he reflected on the love and generosity which had been showered on him since his arrival. He would never forget it.

Brady slept the sleep of the dead after the two hundred-mile journey south from Glasgow. He dreamt the omnipotent dreams of a sixteen-year-old. Two miles away, across the sagging rooftops, a young girl was dreaming about her new secondary school. She slept in a tiny squalid bedroom in Bannock Street, a grimy cul-de-sac in Gorton. It would be only seven years before these dreamers met. Meanwhile, Myra Hindley and Ian Brady had other things gentle and not so gentle on their mind.

Pat Brady worked at Smithfield Market and found Ian a job there. Peggy and Pat, however, thought that Ian needed a week of freedom to settle in Manchester before he started work. Ian walked around the open market near Denmark Road and hovered over a stall that sold second-hand books. Just behind the market he came across a small café that was a launch pad for local teenagers in the evenings for pub-crawls across the city. He tagged along and appreciated the bitter beers while listening to the drink speak through others, 'especially the obviously downtrodden who suddenly became possessed with courage to speak the truth and harangue all and sundry. Transient words without action.'

Brady started work at the market and soon learned the knack of moving heavy packages with relative ease. He dropped Peggy's surname of Stewart and adopted the name of Brady to cut out the possibilities of the police tracing his criminal record. It made no difference. After Ian's first arrest in Manchester, Peggy told the whole story of his background to the police. She was 'constitutionally honest'. Glasgow police listed him as Ian Stewart alias Brady; the English police as Brady alias Stewart. When I travelled to see him, I signed in to see 'Ian Stewart-Brady'. As I waited with rows of other visitors in the reception area, the girl at the desk shouted 'Ian Brady!' More often, an older female at the desk simply said, 'ISB'.

Ian had adjusted to the demands of work in the market after a few weeks. His shift began in the dark early mornings but he was finished by noon. He soon discovered that almost everyone was 'on the fiddle' to supplement their wages. Ian appreciated the mid-morning break, which was spent in Kitty's Café just a street away. As a Glaswegian he was, inevitably, always referred to as 'Jock' by his workmates.

He was mildly surprised at the higher rates of pay in England compared with the wages earned by workers on the Clyde. He made friends in the market with Chas, a Londoner who was on the run. He proved to be a reliable friend even though he was easily provoked into violence. Chas enters Brady's life from time to time as this story unfolds.

Brady made friends at what he referred to simply as the Jukebox Café in Moss Side. The customers were lively and wild and dominated by Pete, a pleasant West Indian half-caste. They had two main interests, both of which suited Ian: girls and drink. He joined the gang on their nightly pub-crawls across Manchester. They usually called him Mack, which became

Mack the Knife when Louie Armstrong's record of the same name was released.

Ian was less happy with the expanded nickname because it alerted strangers to the fact that he was carrying a lock-back knife. This eliminated the element of surprise and gave the enemy an advantage. Brady was almost fanatical about this principle in later years, as I discovered myself on more than one occasion. As we shall see, Myra Hindley received Ian Brady's fist in her face when she momentarily violated this sacred tenet on Saddleworth Moor, when both of them were in the process of committing murder.

Brady's Scottish accent was beginning to fade. He became bored with having to repeat himself and consciously spoke his words carefully. Years later, in my conversations with him, his words were perfectly understandable until he lost his temper over some grievance. The broad Glaswegian accent would take over and become even more incomprehensible if he was asked to repeat himself. Eventually, I recorded all of our telephone conversations and deciphered them later in the calm that followed the storm.

Brady was looking at the world through the bottom of a glass. Because the market pubs opened early, he could drink mid-morning as well as during the afternoon and evening. Like the character Grigory Petrov in Chekhov's short story *Grief*, his mind was permanently dulled in the fog of alcohol that only daytime drinkers know. The pubs along the Rochdale Road – the Balmoral, the Old Loom, the Milan and the Derby – provided midnight oblivion. Later, he recalled the pub-crawls: 'The pubs all seemed cloned and predictable, filled with smoke and crowded bodies. There were the inevitable peroxide, glit-lipstick look-a-likes of the singer Kathy Kirby mewling boozy, tone-deaf pleas to "Let Me Go, Lover". Anytime, I thought. One evening we were in a pub in the slum area of Salford when an argument erupted between our group and another at the next table. I've no idea why. My eyes were fixed on one of them; I detested everything about him. He stood up and went to the gents. Everything around me was suddenly electric-sharp and all my senses were heightened with *black light*.

'I was on my feet, gliding effortlessly between tables circled by drinkers as though they weren't there. Yet I seemed to be watching it all from a distance. I walked through the doorway and into a dingy corridor that led to the toilet. I grabbed a large empty bottle from a pile of crates and broke it on his head. He ran out as someone else was walking in. I raised my hand with the broken neck of the bottle to attack one of his friends. It was only an old drunk. I let the glass drop to the floor and felt a stinging sensation in my cheek. Blood. I looked in the mirror to see a glass splinter. I dabbed the cut with a wet handkerchief and saw I had a small wound in the shape of a V.'

The other group had left by the time Ian returned to his friends. He was told one of them was clutching a bleeding head. Ian's friends found the whole thing hilarious but he was uneasy at his own stupidity. The pub was full of witnesses; fingerprints on the weapon as well as on bottles and glasses on the gang's table: 'Death had enticed me into pointless danger. It could have led me to self-destruction. A breach of faith? Or faith put to the test? My mind was full of questions the whole evening − until the balm of alcohol had run its course. In future, I would be forewarned of the avoidable perils of nights such as these. Forewarned and alert.'

Brady's only permanent memento of the evening was the faint V-shaped scar on his cheek that showed itself only when he stretched the skin with his hand.

Ian had looked forward to his two-week holiday in Glasgow and reunion with the Sloan family he was still devoted to. He had saved enough to buy a tailor-made three-piece black pinstripe suit. It wasn't fashionable but that meant nothing to him. In clothes − as in everything else − he was his own man. He bought an expensive camera for the occasion. This was the beginning of his passion to record everything pictorially, a passion that would imprison him for life.

Brady's train journey back was uneventful apart from sharing a compartment with a girl about the same age. When the buffet car opened he treated her to a few drinks. She got out at Carlisle and Ian was alone as the train trundled through the familiar outskirts of Glasgow with its tenements and wide streets. He felt the surge of energy through the pavements as he walked to Morrison's Bar in the dock area. Before taking a taxi to Pollok he savoured Glasgow's whisky and listened to its accents.

At number 21 Templeland Road Ian wanted to try out his camera on the family right away, and took the first photograph of Ma Sloan just as she said, 'I can smell whisky on yer breath!' He wanted to take impromptu snaps of everybody, just as he would when he eventually took Myra Hindley to see his family.

He caught up on the gossip with his pals and learned that the informer had been dealt with. There was someone else Ian Brady was determined to get; but not during this holiday. He would wait eight years before attempting to kill him.

Ian was up early next morning and went 'doon toon' with a few friends. After a drink in a bar in Sauchiehall Street, he persuaded them to cross over the Clyde and into the Gorbals: 'We drank in a few pubs unmistakably characteristic of the Gorbals – sawdust on the floors and all the fittings necessary in a place for serious drinkers: heavy furniture of dark wood and a foot-rail at the bar. Women were excluded, leaving men at liberty to use heavily accented, coarse, strong language of the Gorbals. The topics of the customers' conversation were usually about their work in the docks and shipyards, illicit gambling places, the factors with their "key money" and the police – the word sounding like "polis" in the Gorbals accent. The talkers looked work-weary and strapped for cash in their flat caps, or "bunnets". In the ten years of freedom that remained for me I returned again and again to places like these, to be a silent listener. When the workmen moved in to demolish the tenements it grieved me to see them reduced to huge piles of broken stone. The faded wallpaper, flapping in the wind, simply added to the pathos. Was it waving farewell? Those tenements had been like living beings to me, each with their own idiosyncratic personality.'

After the pubs closed in the afternoon, the group went to the Bedford cinema to see *Marty*, the film that became a classic and attracted several Oscar awards. There was another pub-crawl before their return to Pollok. The following day was the dreaded Sunday and Ian compensated by going alone to see Betty. Since all the pubs were closed, they travelled out of the city and persuaded the barman at a 'residents only' hotel to serve them drinks. They returned to the city after making love in a bluebell wood.

The weather was fine the following day. All of his friends were working, so Ian took the opportunity to travel out to Loch Lomond. He walked along the west-shore road from Balloch at the northern tip looking for the hill of transfiguration of his childhood holidays. Ian couldn't find it but the day was saved when he heard the Glasgow accents of two girls looking across the loch. They were 'wee herries': Glaswegian for streetwise teenagers.

Ian felt overdressed for them but struck up a conversation by offering them cigarettes. He discovered that they were from Govan and was surprised when they said he sounded English. He was particularly attracted to one of them: a blonde with the requisite high cheekbones and almond-shaped eyes. They went to a nearby pub and Ian brought the drinks out to them. Glasgow tradition excluded women from the bar even there. After the goodbyes he walked back along the loch road and caught a bus to Glasgow.

Years later, he visited Balloch with Myra Hindley. As they wrote postcards in the car they overheard a group of 'wee herries' on the pavement. Myra had never heard the term before. It made her laugh.

Ian glanced in the mirror and was surprised to discover that the day out to Loch Lomond had given him a suntan. The weather was fine a few days later, when he decided to travel alone by coach to see Rannoch Moor and Glencoe again.

Glencoe has a notorious historical significance. In 1692, men of the Campbell clan slaughtered the families of the MacDonald clan as they slept. On his way into the glen, Ian cooled a bottle of his favourite Cypriot wine in the River Coe. Ian Brady was to spend his life with Myra Hindley cooling bottles of wine in cold streams. He told me once that he and Myra drank at least a bottle of wine a day in the period they were together.

As he walked into Glencoe, Ian was aware of it as the scene of the bloody massacre and sensed the greenness beneath the towering mountains of the Three Sisters; 'solemn crags as befit the dead'. The warm 'green vision' of the face of Death began to swirl. A chill stole over Brady as the shadows drifted across the hills. He put his jacket on. He leaned against a rock and threw the bottle away after drinking the dregs. Lighting a cigarette he drank in the greenness. He was stirred and thought of the 'green one' as he hummed to himself – 'I love to go a-wandering, along the mountain track . . . fal-da-ree . . . fal-da-ra . . .'

Brady told me he was fascinated by the thought that things he discarded casually when he was free – wine and beer bottles, matchsticks, cigarette stubs – could still be lying where he had thrown them. He was intrigued too by the thought that the moon he saw through his cell bars, was shining down on scenes he had once been part of when he was free.

The day after Brady's trip to Glencoe, Jean Sloan was off work and went with him to see a young Diana Dors in *A Kid for Two Farthings* at the Odeon cinema. In the late afternoon, they went for drinks at the Trocadero bar and Jean worried about what Ma would say about drinking in the afternoon. Ian felt the urge to visit the Gorbals but hesitated to expose Jean to danger. In later years, he would only take Myra Hindley there in daylight and when they were both armed.

It was the weekend. Ian was halfway through his holiday. He went into the city with a few friends and they eventually found themselves in a flat with three or four girls. Drink, cigarettes and records playing – 'Wheel of Fortune', 'Jezebel', 'Singing the Blues'. Brady drifted into a bedroom with a faun-like girl and drifted out half an hour later to drink more whisky and light a cigarette. Then . . . a blank.

Ian woke up on a hard bed in a police cell. He felt his pockets for cigarettes and lighter, wallet and lock-back knife. Nothing. He looked at his hands and clothes for blood. Nothing, apart from grazed knuckles. He felt a swelling on his cheek. The light was too dim for him to see his reflection in the water of the toilet bowl. Brady pressed a button on the cell wall. Slamming steel doors, jangling keys and echoing footsteps. A policeman appeared at the door with a pint mug of tea and said that he could pick up his possessions at the desk.

There was no hint that any of his friends were in the other cells. Ian reclaimed his cigarettes, lighter, wallet and tie but there was no mention of a lock-back knife. He learned that he had been arrested for fighting in the street but had no recollection of it. The police picked up the name Brady from his wallet and so failed to connect him with a criminal record under Stewart or Sloan.

Immediately after being released, he examined his face in a shop window and found that his right eye and cheek were bruised. Later, Ian's friends told him that he left the flat to buy cigarettes but never returned. He scanned the Sunday newspapers for any reports that could be connected with him but drew a blank. On the following Monday he appeared before the court and had to pay a small fine. The mystery of the disappearing lock-back knife has remained so.

A few days later Ian went alone on a coach trip to Loch Ness that took him past Loch Lomond, through Glen Falloch and past Rannoch Moor. There was a half-hour stop at Fort William where he had a few drinks. Ian left the coach at Glen Urquhart and dipped his hand in the waters of Loch Ness. He killed the freezing sensation with a few swigs from a half-bottle of Bell's whisky.

In the prison years, Ian Brady spent hours looking at ordnance survey maps of Scotland: 'It's like reading *War and Peace*.'

The fortnight's holiday was almost over. Ian took Betty to the city and the Trocadero. He sought out Bridie and was taken with the way her beauty had bloomed in his absence: 'She was as sly and witty as ever. She made me laugh just as she used to and I loved her for it. We talked about the times we used to meet in secret under our special tree in the meadow. She was strikingly beautiful now and I felt sad that I would probably never see her again. I shall never forget her laughter. It was a moment of unsullied joy in my life – whatever happened to me in later years.'

Late one evening Ian took a circuitous route home and stood smoking near Evelyn Grant's house. He wondered whether she was still seeing the dull creep of a policeman's son. He was never to know. Evelyn lived only in his memories.

Ian's stay was up. He planned to travel to Manchester by train on Sunday and wanted to make the most of Saturday night with some friends. As they walked through St Enoch's Square, Ian noticed the sports shop where he had bought a sheath knife when he was fourteen. He saw a stainless steel lock-back in the window display and couldn't resist the temptation. He still had it when, ten years into the future, his eyes caught a last glimpse of it as he was surprised in bed by the police at the final arrest. It was not an exhibit at the trial as there were no traces of blood on it. He never saw it again and assumed that a policeman had kept it as a memento.

Ian and his pals walked along the Gallowgate to the oldest pub in Glasgow, the Saracen's Head, to begin the farewell binge. They ended the night at Morrison's bar down by the docks. Ian glanced at the clock just before closing time and asked the barman to sell him half a bottle of whisky.

He wanted to walk the streets of the Gorbals alone and, clutching the bottle wrapped in tissue paper, he made an excuse and left. He bought fish and chips in Crown Street and walked to see the old Sloan tenement in Camden Street. The guttering gas-mantel lit his way to the stone stairs. There was a different name on the brass nameplate on the door once so familiar and regularly polished. He stared at it for a time and descended back into Camden Street. He was watched only by the granny-cats on windowsills as he walked to find a taxi back to Pollok in the small hours.

The following day, Sunday, Ian woke with a thumping hangover and after packing his suitcase said his goodbyes while he waited for the taxi. Events were on a course that would change his life forever. As he reflected in captivity: 'I was about to make a trivial mistake and the English legal system a grave one that would haunt them for decades. In the words of Shakespeare's Richard III: they were destined to set my life upon a cast and they would stand the hazard of the die.'

Back in Manchester, Ian slipped back into his hedonistic routine of drinking morning, noon and night. At midnight, after a pub-crawl, he found himself with his friends in a house in Moss Side. There were four or

five girls in the room and Ian started to chat to one of them – I shall refer
to her as 'Alison', the sister of a man named Kenny, who was part of the
hard drinking group. Alison had black silky hair and dark searching eyes.

Ian began seeing her two or three times a week and made full use of her
bed when the house was free. This didn't stop him from seeing other girls
at the same time. One of these was a girl from the Rochdale Road area. He
ditched her after a month or so. She believed in marriage.

A few weeks after the premature romance, Ian's drinking group became
involved with a few youths outside a pub. One of them flung a bottle and
beer splashed on to Ian's shoes. He felt the *black light* begin to operate and
grabbed a steel dustbin lid for protection. He withdrew his lock-back knife
and, as the youth grappled with the lid, he swiped him twice with the blade.
The blood looked black under the street lighting. The *black light* began to
fade. He replaced the lid.

One evening, Ian was alone and found himself in an alleyway with no
idea what had brought him there. He eventually swallowed his pride and
asked a passer-by the name of the district. Ian was in Manchester's
Openshaw district. He was a little shaken by the event and decided to stay
at home for a period, listening to the radio in his bedroom, subsisting on
Forest Brown ale with chasers from a bottle of Tio Pepe sherry.

Outside, the nights were autumnal and Ian felt the seasonal foreboding.
But he would remember this particular autumn till his dying day. It would
– eventually – enter his name indelibly into the annals of murder.

The day began promisingly enough with Indian summer sunshine. Ian
Brady, a loads man and stall-hand for Howarth's Fruiterers in the market,
was in the process of killing the mindless hours till midday and the first
pint.

A Howarth's lorry driver told Ian that there was a sack of lead seals
lying discarded in the warehouse. He asked Ian to load the sack on to his
lorry so that he could sell it as scrap. Lorry drivers had fewer opportunities
than the other employees to make money on the side, so Ian obliged
without giving it another thought.

The driver pulled into the yard of a local scrap merchant and offered the
lead for cash. The name of Howarth's Fruiterers was painted on the side of
the lorry and the dealer made a note of it. His suspicions were aroused
when he saw the sack's contents and contacted the police.

Later, during the same morning, two detectives called in at the market
and took Brady in for questioning. He was locked into a white-tiled cell
with just a bed-board for furniture: 'The autumn sun found its way through

a porthole of a window near the ceiling of my cell. I walked from wall to wall in the confined space wondering why I had been arrested.

'Sunlight takes on a strange purity to prisoners, a quality unknown to those who have never known captivity. It assumes the quality of a reassuring spiritual entity that connects us with the world outside despite the bars and shares its radiance so that you can almost taste freedom in its stream of light. It mocked the clinical white tiles that enclosed me in an alien hole: a mortuary reeking with carbolic or pine disinfectant and body odour. I smelt blood in whatever was possessing me.'

A detective entered Brady's cell with papers detailing his crimes, by courtesy of the Glasgow police. Peggy – as honest as the day is long – had let the cat out of the bag and given them his real name.

Ian shrugged when the bare facts of the driver's statement were read out to him. He didn't attempt to defend his own neutral part in the events, assuming that he would be released there and then and given the chance later to set the record straight. But he was in for a shock. He would be held in custody overnight and appear in front of a magistrate in the morning. By the time the detective had shut the cell door behind him, Ian was boiling with rage and already thinking about arranging for someone to give the scrap dealer a call.

At the Chester trial ten years later, the Attorney General would trace the origins of the Moors Murders to the writings of the Marquis de Sade. In one sense, the truth is much more prosaic. We need only to picture the young Ian Brady in the tiled cell that evening and Peggy being consoled by Pat Brady in their tiny home in Denmark Street: 'Have I done the right thing?' Ian Brady would have many years to reflect on his mother's question: 'The wheels of retribution had began to turn on their resolute course. An almost worthless base metal – lead – was pre-ordained to claim more than its weight in cataclysmic, bloody chaos. It was the alchemic process in reverse. It would create an unbending resolve within my consciousness and be the psychic catalysis, the element which would transmute of all my future thoughts and actions. I lay awake for most of the night in my white tiled mausoleum.

'I was in a more sanguine mood when the light of day found its way into my temporary tomb. I was sure that I'd be released before midday. At midmorning, I was herded with other prisoners into a single cage with some of the thickest prison bars I would ever see. A grimy narrow staircase led up to the dock. The lorry driver was not in custody. I couldn't see him around. I climbed up to the dock when my name was eventually called.

'The lorry driver was standing in the court when I emerged from the depths. He diverted his eyes away as I looked around the courtroom. A few insignificant men were leafing through papers below me and a small box of world-weary journalists had their pens poised for yet another banal bit of copy for their editors. The clerk read out the charges and we were asked how did we plead. I simply wanted to get out of that place and into the street. I pleaded guilty.

'We were asked whether we wished to be tried there and then or at the quarter sessions. I opted for the latter, expecting nothing more than a fine. The magistrates muttered among themselves. The lorry driver, a man in his mid-thirties, was given a fine because he had to support his family. I would be held in custody till the quarter sessions next met. The driver looked relieved as he walked away a free man. I didn't realise that I would not be free for a long time as I was escorted back down the stairs to the cells.'

Ian Brady's head was reeling. Two fellow prisoners, well versed in the system, explained his plight while they were waiting at the foot of the stairs. The quarter sessions had sat a few days before. Brady would be held in prison till the next session in three months' time. Since he had pleaded guilty he would be treated as a convicted prisoner awaiting sentence. If he had pleaded not guilty, he would have received remand privileges.

When the court concluded its business, Brady and the other prisoners were handcuffed two by two and taken in the Black Maria to prison: 'Strangeways was a Victorian, blackened, redbrick pile. I was processed through the reception procedure, fingerprinted, washed and handed ill-fitting prison uniforms before being moved to the main prison block. This was an echoing four-storey sepulchre of iron stairs, clanking keys and banging metal doors. At its core was a huge iron grill set into the floor, from which all the wings branched off. I was escorted to C2 landing for young prisoners – YPs. Beneath us were the PDs – Preventive Detention – and above us the CTs – Corrective Training. The latter were first-time offenders called "Stars". The whole place stank of urine in a sewer. It was a semi-human version of the latter. The whole place was rank with stale sweat.

'My cell was furnished with a low bed, a wooden table, a chair and a metal chamber pot. I stood on the chair to get a view outside. The exercise yard was floodlit. I could see the lights of the city to the horizon.

'During my years of freedom I remembered this first day when, one night, in a car parked near Strangeways I drank wine with Myra Hindley as we looked up at the many tiny squares of yellow light. Each one had a story to tell. The spectacle heightened our sense of freedom, making the wine taste like nectar, as I relished how different my life was now.'

Near midnight, Brady reflected on the events of this first day – the senselessness of it all. Through an act of generosity, he was in prison and the driver was free. A police informer yet again. Brady rested his chin on folded arms, surveying his situation. It was time to get serious. Really serious. No more little games. He stood on the chair again and tried to take a deep breath of the night air. Manchester was asleep as far as the eye could see.

The morning bell woke the prisoners at seven. After breakfast Brady was given a job in the boiler house shovelling coke into the furnaces underneath Strangeways' towering chimneystack. Within a few minutes, he discovered that one of the prisoners on the team came from Glasgow and was in the next cell. He made a note of the name – Wallace – a potential contact for the future, the first of many he met in Strangeways.

Across the wall, behind the coke pile, it was possible to see the top two rows of windows of the women's cells. This, to Ian's surprise, provided the mid-morning entertainment. A prisoner at work on the coke pile shouted, 'Christ! They're flashing their tits!' A prison officer told the men to keep shovelling. A female's voice from nowhere shouted, 'Tell that prickless wonder to piss off!' This light relief lasted until dinnertime.

After evening tea, 'association' was allowed on the landings, which meant that YPs could mix with the Stars. Ian Brady lost no time in picking the brains of fences, safecrackers and the like and played darts with killers who had recently been reprieved from the death cell. One of these, Nuttal, had his grave dug ready and waiting by the side of the wall and covered with planks.

Brady grasped the opportunity provided by his incarceration to study accountancy. He wanted to know how to handle money once he had acquired it. He also took up a tool-making course.

The weekly allowance in Strangeways was ten and a half pence – enough to buy tobacco, a packet of papers and a box of matches. There were ways to economise on matches. A tinder-box could be made by getting a shoe-polish tin and burning a piece of cloth in it, then ignite it by using a flint sparked by a razorblade. I was fascinated to hear about an alternative to this. The prisoner removed the light bulb in the cell and twisted a piece of toilet paper around a length of lead from a pencil. When this was put into the electrical socket, the circuit would be completed, the lead would glow red-hot and the paper would ignite. This invariably fused all the cell lights on the landing. The desperate inmates smoked dry tea leaves wrapped in thin pages torn from hymn books during the compulsory Sunday church service.

Ian Brady quietly persevered with his accumulation of information for future use. He had the names of contacts in several cities, together with their addresses. He obliquely discovered how much money they would be prepared to kill for. He noted names of those with grudges against society. He sorted the doers from the talkers. All of this information was blended into the notebooks he used for the permitted and regular studies. Over-estimating the opposition, as we shall see, was one of the life-long absolutes for the man who denied all absolutes.

Strangeways gave Brady the time to conceptualise feelings and beliefs that had been, until then, only matters of intuition and instinct. In Strangeways he realised how much he didn't know: 'Prison shook my confidence in ignorance, you might say.'

His autumnal madness arrived on cue and, as in years past, reached its climax in December: 'Strangeways, the cold, dilapidated Victorian pile that it was, deepened my autumnal fugue. One day, I was working in the gloomy twilight of the poorly lit boiler house, immersed in the seasonal thrall. A yammering voice of one of the workers was irritating me. Without warning the *black light* transformed my senses.

'The screw told us the shift was over and I threw the shovel into the wheelbarrow and arrived at the boiler house before the rest. Inside, I stepped to one side of the doorway and raised the shovel above my head, waiting to inflict the blow. As the youth with the irritating voice walked in, I struck him on the head with it. There was a cacophonous twanging sound as the shovel vibrated.

'I couldn't stop myself laughing at the farce of it all. The victim stood there completely bewildered. We became friends afterwards. He had a sore head for a day or two and the lump disappeared.'

For three years, since he was fourteen, Brady had read Charles Dickens' *A Christmas Carol* in the days that led up to Christmas, pacing himself to read the final stave on Christmas Eve. His interest was sparked by the 1951 black-and-white film *Scrooge* starring Alastair Sim. Part of Brady's fascination was a scene in the book where the Ghost of Christmas Present takes Scrooge to the house of the childhood sweetheart whom he lost through his own greed. Scrooge looks on and sees her now happily married and surrounded by her loving children and reflects with remorse on what might have been.

Brady always associated this scene with one of his earliest lost loves: Evelyn Grant. He always read the book alone so that no one could see him weep at the pathos and laugh at Scrooge's antics and the joy at his final salvation. Among the items he bequeathed to me was a copy of *A Christmas Carol* with his name and prison number inside. He had scored many passages with lines and exclamation marks.

Most people will be incredulous at the thought of Ian Brady being capable of such human emotions. Nevertheless, he always maintained his claim of the grip the story had on him, its magical charm and power of good upon him. He didn't believe in absolutes and admitted that it was paradoxical of him to talk of any power of good in his life. The flaw lay deep within him, and the knowledge that he could not change. 'It was an ineradicable part of my character; a varicose vein running through every dimension of my being. When I thought of it, I was overwhelmed with sadness. For this reason I shall die a fool.'

It was Christmas 1954 in Strangeways. He managed to find a copy of *A Christmas Carol* and keep up his annual ritual. He was aware this time of the irony that Dickens had written the book's plot while staying in Manchester at the Midland Hotel in October 1843. A few faded Christmas decorations were draped on the dreary brown and green peeling paintwork inside Strangeways. It served only to mock the festival and remind the inmates that there was seasonal festivity everywhere but that place. A few of them wondered whether the judge would be moved to clemency by the season of goodwill in the quarter sessions, which were just days away.

Brady thought of the two gentlemen who tried to get a donation from Scrooge on Christmas Eve: 'It is more than usually desirable that we should make some slight provision for the poor and destitute, who suffer greatly at the present time . . .' 'Are there no prisons?' asked Scrooge. Ian Brady pondered: 'Would I have welcomed a small act of redemption? Perhaps. The lives of many people would have been different.'

The morning arrived: a bitterly cold one beneath an overcast Manchester sky. With others Brady was taken in handcuffs in the Black Maria to court. As he climbed the stairs when his case was called, he could see the gallery packed with sixth-form schoolgirls in green uniforms with striped ties and white blouses. In Brady's own eyes, he had already served three months in prison for a trivial offence – 'petty larceny as a servant' – that was merely an act of generosity for a lorry driver.

Later, in prison, he often thought of the lives that would have been spared, had the quarter sessions judge been more lenient. But the truth is that Ian Brady virtually condemned himself to the sentence he received. He offered no plea of mitigation and, when questioned, refused even to utter a few words of contrition that could have saved him. He was indifferent to the proceedings and shared his gaze between the sixth-formers and the ceiling. He was sentenced to two years of Borstal Training. Brady regarded the old judge with indifference: 'He was of no consequence now. The reckoning had already begun.'

The Black Maria travelled down Oxford Road on its return to Strangeways. As it passed the Odeon cinema, Ian saw that it was showing Alastair Sim in *Scrooge*. Brady looked back on this time of his life many years later: 'The coin of my future was still spinning in the air, and with it the fate of others yet to be met.'

Ian was waiting for his transfer to Borstal. It was New Year's Eve in Strangeways, the most sacred day in the Scottish calendar. Most of the inmates stayed awake to hear the bells of nearby churches ringing in the New Year. A little Scot with something of a singing voice, who occupied a cell on Ian's wing, responded to anonymous requests shouted into the night. Ian, as young as he was, had lived in Scotland long enough to surrender to the mysticism of the moments before midnight; falling asleep in the wee small hours to the haunting sounds of 'Skye Boat Song', 'Love is a Many Splendoured Thing' and the ironically fitting 'River of No Return'.

I was talking with Ian Brady in Ashworth Hospital, one New Year's Eve in the 1990s, when the strains of the song 'I Belong To Glasgow' drifted in from a television set in a room across the corridor. He stopped mid-sentence and listened in silence to a verse or two of the song. With a look that penetrated the haze of smoke he said, 'I belong to Glasgow, but Manchester belongs to me!' It seemed pointless to say that it didn't. A decade later, in a letter to me in which he reminisced about New Year's Eve, he wrote; 'Naturally I was subjected to the traditional Scottish, pagan revival of hope brought in by the midnight chimes when I was free. Now the only chimes I hear at midnight are those of Zarathustra.'

Two hours into 1955 the young Ian Brady succumbed to sleep. The little Scot on the same wing was still singing.

The morning of the New Year dawned. The die had been cast and Brady had already recovered from the verdict. He felt full of purpose, power and energy. The authorities had pronounced and would provide his element for the foreseeable future. He was already beginning to feel at home in it. Perhaps the *black light* was within permanent reach and could be experienced by the sheer force of will. It was as though his brain was on the verge of igniting and burning out. Ian Brady knew for the first time just how near the boundary of insanity lay.

He was still in Strangeways on 2 January 1955, his seventeenth birthday. Brady claimed that he never gave the event a second thought. He had just ten years of freedom to enjoy, during which Manchester would be reaping the whirlwind of the seeds sown by a white-haired judge at the quarter sessions of December 1954. He wrote to me in a letter of November 1992 about a 'watershed' in his life: 'When I was sentenced to Borstal at the age of seventeen, I vowed vengeance and that I would never again take risks for anything trivial.'

During a visit Brady recalled writing those words and added: 'My natural relativism became logical relativism in Strangeways. I said to myself that if they wanted me to be a criminal, I'll be a *proper* one!' He quoted the philosopher Alfred North Whitehead: 'How the past perishes is how the future becomes.'

CHAPTER SIX

WHISKY IN THE WALLS
& DOSTOEVSKY

Early on a bright morning in January 1955, Ian Brady was part of a group handcuffed in pairs and herded into a bus destined for the south of England. The first stop was London and Wormwood Scrubs Prison – 'another infested Victorian redbrick pile'. A few prisoners were left there and the bus continued south. Twenty years later, Brady would see Wormwood Scrubs again, handcuffed to two officers in a Black Maria and an escort of police cars.

Darkness had fallen by the time the bus arrived at its destination. It looked like a concentration camp with its floodlights and high fences topped with barbed wire. It was Latchmere House, a former prisoner of war camp for Germans. The new arrivals felt the night frost as they stripped for reception and changed into Borstal uniform.

The next day, the 'receptions' as they were called were given an introductory talk by a man he described as 'small and ridiculous'. In the evening, they were allowed to mix with the other inmates in the gym hall. Brady spotted Chas right away, the man who had been on the run when he worked with him in Smithfield Market. Chas, whom Ian described as 'a loner with a restless manner', passed on the local knowledge needed to survive and exploit their present circumstances.

It was back to the cells for everybody at eight o'clock and Ian used the time to write letters to the Sloans in Glasgow and Peggy in Manchester.

The following morning began with all inmates doing physical jerks in the dark on the freezing parade ground before breakfast. Later they were divided into work parties. Ian and Chas were both in the group shovelling coke. In the afternoon, Chas ruthlessly battered another youth in an argument. Ian admired Chas's relentless style and made a note of his name as a possible accomplice.

Brady adapted to the routine of Borstal and spent his leisure time reading whatever books he could find: 'I was exhilarated by the acquisition of knowledge and intoxicated by its latent power. I danced a jig to celebrate whenever I discovered something that resonated with my imagination or plans. I felt like an explorer on an adventurous quest for treasure. I felt no need for psychopomp, no fustian incursions. My own strong stream of enquiry sped me along, absorbing new and forceful tributaries as I glided past, heedless of all but my progressive course. I wanted nothing of utopian principles and ceaseless provisos gravitating to equivocation and indecision. I would pillage at will.'

Ian appeared before an assessment panel to determine the future course of his training. He was asked to give his preference between a 'closed' and an 'open' Borstal. The former was identical to prison and the latter had no walls or fences. Ian explained that he wanted quietness for his studies and would prefer the closed variety. The assessment panel decided otherwise. He was marked down for Hatfield in the north; an open Borstal for those of above average intelligence.

Their decision was a small matter for Ian Brady. He was by now beyond society's spheres of influence: 'I was more concerned about the life in my hours rather than the hours in my life.'

It was dark when the bus arrived at Hatfield Borstal, in the countryside a few miles from Doncaster in Yorkshire. I had lived in Doncaster for a time in the 1970s and could relate to Brady's recollections of his two years in Hatfield. After the handcuffs were removed and the reception procedure completed, he was assigned to a barrack dormitory. Boys were lounging around in pyjamas and piped music was playing. He was the centre of attention for an hour or so while the inmates were giving him the score.

After lights out, and his eyes had adjusted to the darkness, Ian stared through the window and made out trees and open fields. He could walk out to freedom any time. But for what purpose? Most of the contacts he had made would be in prison for some time. The thing now was to wait; plan and wait.

In the cold light of day, Ian could see that it was an ex-army camp. Each 'house' was made up of three barrack dormitories. The total population of the inmates was 120. Wooden buildings were set in a square around a central parade ground; these included the canteen, the hospital and the gym. Larger buildings housed the workshops and the staff lived in prefabricated dwellings near the main entrance. The governor greeted the newcomers: 'He had a stocky physique of man in his forties. He had a generous, genial manner and I warmed to him immediately.'

That evening in the dormitory Ian sat on his bed listening to three or four seasoned residents and noticed, for the first time, a boy in a bed almost facing him. He was slim with straw-blond hair, high cheekbones and almond-shaped eyes and reminded Ian of one of his early girlfriends, Sylvia. The boy was studying Ian with averted eyes. Ian Brady slept soundly on that second evening in the camp.

His first work assignment was – predictably – shovelling coke with Chas. After some weeks, Ian was allocated the less tedious job of working in the canteen. The weekly allowance in Borstal was six shillings. Inmates supplemented this with money sent in from outside, secreted in toothpaste and Brylcream containers. In the kitchens, Ian was able to exploit a profitable scheme of making and selling illicit booze: 'The powerful concoction was popular and soon demand outstripped supply. I strengthened it with white surgical spirits supplied by the hospital orderly. This even more potent brew went up in price. In no time I had accumulated so much cash that I had to persuade other boys to carry it for me in case I was searched without warning. With the profits I began running a book on dog and horse racing. I made provision also for card gambling.

'Short, sharp action was taken against informers – one was gang-banged in a dark field and fled from the camp the same night. A few weeks later I fought with a youth who reneged on a gambling debt. The *black light* was in operation. Without effort, I located his carotid artery in seconds and he blacked out. All told, things ran smoothly without aggro. Most of the inmates welcomed the illicit diversions which relieved the tedium of Borstal life. I was motivated more by the thrill and challenge than the profits.'

Ian Brady became adept at locating the carotid artery to disable a victim and sometimes kill them. This is a subject for future chapters.

A minor revolution was erupting in the world outside and the inmates of Hatfield Borstal heard it through the piped radio in the dormitories. 'Rock Around the Clock' by Bill Haley and his Comets marked the arrival of rock and roll. Teenagers danced in cinema aisles to the theme music of the film *The Blackboard Jungle*. Elsewhere, on the international political scene, Egypt seized control of the Suez Canal and was invaded by Great Britain, France and Israel.

Summer arrived and with it the annual holiday laid on for all the inmates. Groups of a dozen were taken in turn on a camping trip for five days with two staff members supervising. The place chosen was Gilling, a small village about fifty miles from Hatfield. Ian and the straw-blond youth from the same dormitory were together in one of the groups. The blond boy chose a place in the tent next to Ian on their first night there. The ground was hard and Ian lay awake chain-smoking.

One of the compulsory activities was to do a good turn for the locals. Ian's group had the task of weeding the car park of the village pub. Ian's group walked to the pub. With the weeding in progress, the landlord's attractive daughter went out to the workers with five pints of beer on a tray.

Shortly afterwards, a youth dressed in expensive riding gear cantered into the yard on a chestnut horse, dismounted and walked up to a boy in the weeding gang. Without saying a word, the rider pressed the reins into his right hand and a sixpence into his left and strode into the pub. One of the gang shouted, 'Who the fuck was that?'

The landlord's daughter came to replenish the supply of beer shortly afterwards and she told the gang that the rider was a student from the nearby Ampleforth College, an exclusive private school for Roman Catholics. The Borstal boys felt insulted by the 'upper-class bloody twit' and plotted their response. The most popular option was to gang-bang him in a neighbouring field, but first they slapped the horse's rump and watched it gallop out of the yard. The rider never appeared.

The next day, the boys saw Ampleforth College itself, a Gothic building on a hill, and Ian Brady made a mental note of its setting for a future time.

While Ian was telling me this story, I interrupted him to say that a teacher had just arrived at my own college in the Midlands on a promotion from Ampleforth. This prompted him to tell me about the time when he and Myra Hindley approached the grounds of Ampleforth College with German binoculars and a rifle, to balance the account with the rider who had slighted the boys years before. I made the obvious remark that the student would have long since left the college. Brady brushed this aside and said that it was what the youth represented that made any member of Ampleforth College a legitimate target.

I asked what happened. 'Nothing,' he replied. 'On the day, Myra and I felt too exposed in the open fields which led up to the perimeters of Ampleforth. We decided to make a different approach to the college in future. As it turned out, we never had the chance to return.'

Summer faded into autumn and Ian Brady prepared for Christmas in Hatfield Borstal, 1955. Boys who were approaching their leaving date were put on a discharge list and allowed to go to Doncaster every Saturday, unsupervised and in their own clothes. Ian gave some of them money to buy bottles of whisky and wine in the town and put them in a hedge to be retrieved later. But where could he store the bottles? Brady came up with a solution – in the walls.

A friend of Ian's, who worked in the carpentry shop, cut out panels in the wooden walls above Brady's bed. The panels could be fitted back easily once the bottles had been inserted in the gap between the inner and outer walls. A picture covered any signs of the replaceable panels. Brady later hid caches of whisky behind the wall panels in the Quiet room and under the floorboards in the Switchboard room.

Ian was still in touch with Peggy and Pat Brady. They had bought a house in Manchester's Openshaw district, but lost hundreds of pounds and the house through a lawyer's bungling in the conveyancing. Another name for Ian Brady's notebook.

On Christmas Eve, some of the boys went to midnight mass while Ian shared out his supply of whisky. There was a piano in the next dormitory and he played boozy versions of 'Frankie and Johnny', 'As Time Goes By' and 'My Blue Heaven'. The boys let the drink talk after lights out. In the darkness, Ian was content with slowly tracing his fingers over the straw-blond's lips that parted for exploration.

The New Year of 1956 was just two hours old when Brady poured himself a cup of whisky, lit a cigarette and walked into the dark fields to look at the stars. Myra Hindley, now thirteen, was awake and in a small room filled with her relations in Bannock Street, Gorton in Manchester.

Ian had served almost eighteen months of his prison sentence and was on the discharge list and would be free in three months. He could go into Doncaster every Saturday in his own lighter clothes, travelling on the bus into town with his friends and walked around until the pubs opened, keeping clear of the policemen, who seemed to be everywhere.

Brady said that whenever he and Myra travelled through Doncaster to meet contacts on the east coast, there were as many policemen on the streets as there were during the hours of his Saturday jaunts from Borstal.

On Brady's first Saturday excursion into Doncaster from Hatfield, he and his friends saw the film *The Rainmaker*, which bored them. After a long session in a pub they bought peppermints in a futile attempt to mask the smell of alcohol. In Hatfield Borstal, the smell of peppermints on the breath was a more lethal sign of alcohol than the smell of alcohol itself.

He was just weeks away from freedom and was told that there were a few routine preliminary conditions to be met. One was having his photograph taken in his own clothes at Wakefield Police Headquarters. He was happy to oblige. Another condition left him speechless. He was expected to do National Service in the army for two years.

Ian travelled by train to Sheffield for an army medical examination with another boy, Fab, who was 'dull and monosyllabic'. They had to go through a medical examination and an interview. Brady passed the medical easily – A1 – as it was called in those days. The interview was pure Ian Brady. He gave me a long account of it. Put briefly, he said that he had been in Borstal for two years and, faced with another two years in the forces, he would simply walk out of an Army camp at the first opportunity.

A few weeks after the interview, Brady was sent to see a psychiatrist in Doncaster. During a visit to Ashworth, we talked about Doncaster and discovered that we both knew the Bear Pub he used on the day. He had killed time by watching a film. He received a letter excusing him from the call-up with the proviso that he could be called upon to dig trenches in the event of an atomic war. He told me that if he had been compelled to serve in the Armed Forces he would have passed information to his friends on the whereabouts of weapons and ammunition.

Borstal boys were given five days' 'home leave' near the end of their sentences, to help them to adjust to civilian life and, perhaps, find a job. When his time came, Brady caught the train to Manchester. He smuggled out the notebooks containing the names and addresses of criminal contacts he had gathered from Strangeways and Hatfield.

On his arrival in Manchester, Ian knew that he had a few hours to kill until early evening when Peggy and Pat Brady would be home from work. Ian walked down a narrow side street in the city centre to Liston's, off Market Street, a basement bar and a haunt for the criminal underworld. It was open but empty. After a few drinks, he left the bar with all the chairs still upended on the tables. It was too early in the day for crime. While speaking to me about this during his captivity Brady commented that Liston's bar was now a chic eaterie owned by The Rolling Stones' Bill Wyman.

Ian looked around for a cinema and found one showing Gregory Peck in *Moby Dick*, a film mentioned in an earlier chapter. Ian had read Herman Melville's classic before he saw the film. He spoke to me about its theme of a madman pursuing a creature as unknowable as the sea itself and the novel's indirect commentary on America in its pursuit of expansion and power. As a film-buff of fifty years' standing, he explained to me how the director, John Huston, processed the film to give it the quality of an old whaling print. On first viewing, it was an enjoyable film of a literary masterpiece. It had filled an afternoon.

Peggy and Pat Brady had moved house and Ian located their new address in Cuttell Street. After a meal, he went out to Moss Side to look up his old friends. The songs on the jukebox were the same as those he had recently heard piped into the dormitories – Elvis Presley's 'Heartbreak Hotel' and 'Freight Train' by the Chas McDevitt Skiffle Group and Nancy Whiskey. But his friends were locked in a time warp with monotonous moronic chat about only two things: girls and booze. Ian realised that this was how he would have been if it hadn't been for his narrow escape to prison and Borstal. He nodded and smiled in approval as the dead-heads planned the evening pub-crawl, but knew full well that he wouldn't be there: 'Poverty and drink had lobotomised them of the desire for higher things. I never met any of them again.'

Ian's possessions had been stored in boxes by Peggy since his arrest. He searched through them until he found his sheath knife and the stainless steel lock-back.

When the five days of freedom were up, he caught the train back to Doncaster. The truck that should have been waiting to take the discharge list boys back to Hatfield wasn't there. They had walked halfway along the ten-mile route to Borstal when the governor appeared in a van to drive them the rest of the journey.

After a few weeks, a new governor arrived at Hatfield. He was a former submarine commander and deputy governor of Dartmoor Prison. He was a flamboyant man, small and stocky with a swashbuckling style. His name was Steinhausen. All of this was academic for Brady, who had only to coast through the last few weeks to freedom.

It was time for the annual camp holiday for the Hatfield boys. The place chosen was Hornsea on the north-east coast, a few miles north of Hull. Within hours of arriving, they were told they they would be unsupervised for most of the time. There was just one absolutely binding rule – they must not visit the Alexandria pub, where the staff would drink.

Ian and his pals set out to explore Hornsea and look at the sea. The boys bought bottles of ale and Ian had enough cash for a half-bottle of whisky. His eye was caught by the striking façade of a small cinema showing *The*

Fastest Gun Alive, starring Glen Ford. Ian didn't try to persuade the rest to watch it but instead went with them to the amusement arcade.

The local youths resented the Borstal boys invading their territory. By contrast, the resident girls seemed to come alive at the prospect of a deviation from the routine. There was a confrontation in the arcade and the back of Ian Brady's hand accidentally hit one of the girls. She began to cry as the Borstal boys retreated. Ian knew that there would be no opportunity now to apologise and took the first of many swigs from his whisky bottle.

After a time his mind became a blank. It was more than a year later, when he met some of the boys who were there that night, that he learned what had happened.

Ian and his pals were lurching back to their tent when they happened upon the Alexandria pub. They entered the forbidden zone and were noticed by two of the Borstal staff. The boys left without incident and crossed a railway line on the way back to the tent. Ian insisted on walking along the rails and was dragged back to the camp by his friends. He was still drunk when the two staff members returned. Ian came to blows with one of them. Someone contacted Governor Steinhausen.

The following morning, Brady woke up with a hangover in a two-cell block at Hatfield Borstal and knew nothing about it until he looked through the cell window. Steinhausen visited later and told Brady that he been drunk and abusive.

Ian suffered the boredom and heat of the day until early evening when Steinhausen and an assistant came to put him in handcuffs. Steinhausen then drove Ian back north to Hull Prison, part of which had been adapted as a Borstal. It was late evening when they arrived and within a few minutes he was given the job of scrubbing the stone floor of the punish-ment block. He had kissed goodbye to his release date.

After serving his time in the punishment block, Ian was set to work with a party breaking bricks to rubble. He had been at Hull for a few weeks when he caught sight of two cells, one above the other, which were bricked up. They were the execution cells, where people were hanged when the buildings were part of the prison. The windows of the two cells were still intact on their outside walls. With boys in the working party keeping lookout, Ian climbed a drainpipe to look into the cells: 'Two halves of a trapdoor, each about six feet by four. Two planks across the open trap, for the screws to stand on while holding the prisoner between them. A beam in the ceiling with a ring-bolt for the rope. In the corner the trap lever, like the clutch lever on a bus. Dust and stones – thrown to break windows. All pretty unimpressive.'

Brady had often talked about capital punishment in conversations and letters to me. He usually raised the subject when the media reported debates on the reintroduction of hanging. He wrote to me in August 1992: 'As for those who say that Myra and I just escaped the gallows; not so. The Abolition Bill had still not gone through the House of Lords at the time of our trial. And, quite frankly, we couldn't have cared less. As I think I told you, and described, I saw the execution cells at Hull Prison when I was eighteen. It didn't impress me at all; just a sense of idle curiosity at the crude contraption and the speculation as to how many people had dropped through the trap. I climbed down and continued with my plans.

'Further, it is often overlooked that the known murders committed by Myra and I in the Moors series took place while people were still being hanged – which is why we carried two revolvers and a rifle. A final thought. Don't people realise that hanging can be an incentive in prison? A perfect mode of suicide combined with the satisfaction of taking some enemy with you, or perhaps several.'

Brady showed me his responses to a questionnaire he had received from a researcher for Esther Rantzen's BBC television programme on the question of whether the British are becoming obsessed with crime. Brady wrote that not only would he advocate the return of capital punishment but also the introduction of euthanasia for all patients in Special Hospitals: 'I would be the first volunteer in either case.' As he was describing to me his replies to the questionnaire, he said, 'The simple truth is that people are fascinated by crime because their own lives are so boring.'

On the subject of murderers' 'fame', Brady added to Esther Rantzen's questionnaire that, 'Criminals don't *become* celebrities, the media makes them celebrities for financial gain.'

Ironically, in October 1994, Esther Rantzen decided that the time had come to execute Myra Hindley and Ian Brady, nearly thirty years after they were convicted. Writing in the *Daily Telegraph*, Auberon Waugh commented: 'It will add a certain something to the daily lives of all long-term prisoners if they know that they can be taken out and hanged at any time – even after 30 years – if an important television presenter like Esther Rantzen suddenly changes her mind about a case.'

In *The Gates of Janus*, Ian Brady comments, 'By all means punish or execute transgressors, but do not bore them to death with concepts based entirely on social engineering flatteringly disguised as divine wisdom.'

Brady and I were discussing Fred and Rosemary West's part in the notorious Cromwell Street murders in Gloucester. By the time I returned home Fred West had hanged himself in Winson Green Prison in Birmingham. A week or so later Brady commented that West's death had robbed the media of all the juicy facts. They screamed for the return of hanging and condemned Fred West for taking the easy way out – by hanging himself!

After a few weeks in Hull Borstal, Brady settled into a routine of study in the hours after work. He was eighteen when he experienced one of the most seminal events in his life: 'My discovery of Dostoevsky was imminent. In several of his writings he refers to the occasion when he was arrested and sentenced to death for writing radical and subversive pamphlets. He was taken to a yard where the firing squad was waiting for their next victim. He was seconds away from death and resigning himself to the inevitable, when he was reprieved. And informed that it was merely an execrable charade to teach him a lesson. It astonished me that, in the years of life left to him, he was nostalgic about his terrifying ordeal. In the very seconds before the rifle bullets were to rip through his body, Dostoevsky said that he was overwhelmed by the wonder he felt at the beauty and richness of existence. The imminence of death had given him a more intense immediacy about life than anything before or since.

'The great paradox in all of this is that Dostoevsky created two of the most vivid and memorable characters in all literature, both of whom were driven by the demonic.

'The first was Stavrogin in *The Devils* with his nihilism and zeal for travel and action. I shared all three of these characteristics of Stavrogin. The second was the supercilious, poverty stricken student Raskolnikov in *Crime and Punishment*, whose Napoleonic hypothesis found an echo in my own deepest held beliefs.

'Had either Stavrogin or Raskolnikov faced a firing squad they would have spat in the face of the squad's commanding officer and plotted vengeance.'

Brady eventually read all of Dostoevsky's books many times over. The psychological depth of the novels fascinated him: 'You learn more from his books than a mountain of arid textbooks on psychology could ever teach.' He added: 'He rips the soul bare. The characters are full of paradox, non-conformity and unpredictability – they are alive, they don't care about consistency. Consistency is for bureaucrats, zombies and the superficial.' Brady had time to read many hundreds of books in captivity, but he valued Dostoevsky's *The Brothers Karamazov* more than any other.

Ian Brady's own collection of Dostoevsky's novels – including his personal copy of *Crime and Punishment* – were among the items of his property I received. I have used his marked passages and margin notes in *Crime and Punishment* as a guide in the following paragraphs for describing the book's power over him. Brady's written comments, in purple ink, still evoke the sheer force of the book's impact on him: 'Marvellous psychological insight' . . . 'Stupendous observation of human nature!' . . . 'The human interaction is pure genius!' . . . 'Chaotic humanity!' . . . 'Stupendous chapter!' . . . 'Another Dickensian touch' . . . 'Not British!'

In one letter to me Brady was discussing *Crime and Punishment* and commented that Dostoevsky had 'spilled the beans in a persuasive and brilliant way. Anyone could absorb its meaning.'

The story is set in St Petersburg. The city is a powerful presence in the life of its central character, Raskolnikov, in the way Glasgow and the Gorbals were for Brady. George Panichas's comment on *Crime and Punishment* applies equally to Brady: 'The streets are Raskolnikov's contact with life. The real city is also a city of the mind in the way that its atmosphere answers Raskolnikov's spiritual condition and almost symbolizes it.'

I mentioned Panichas's observation to Brady and he responded: 'The Gorbals and Petersburg? I liked the "slums" and dock districts of all cities; the natural heart, not the plastic and chrome façade.'

Ian Brady was entranced from the moment he read the opening paragraphs of *Crime and Punishment*: 'The sheer drama of the style, the spasmodic breathless dialogue, the frenzied pace, the cruel absurdities of reality, all brilliantly blended together to create a scintillating enduring tension and interplay between action and reaction, making the reader's mind delirious with exhilarating laughter and excited recognition. Dostoevsky's literary genius is comparable to Shakespeare, a genius in a related medium. Like his execution which never was, Dostoevsky could survive devastating self-analysis and stare, unblinking, at naked reality and eternity.'

Before he read *Crime and Punishment*, he was familiar with Shakespeare's *Hamlet*, the study of a man contemplating murder and suicide but who is made indecisive by inner conflict: 'Conscience doth make cowards of us all.' But in *Crime and Punishment*, its anti-hero,

Raskolnikov, pushes conscience aside, overestimating his own ruthless-ness and strength of will.

Living in wretched conditions of poverty, the student Raskolnikov is forced to cut short his studies. He lies alone in his room, lethargic, feverish and guilt-ridden about the sacrifices his sister and mother have made for him to finish his studies at university. His self-loathing paradoxically fills him with energy and ferocious power: the will to act on his darkest beliefs. He plans to rob and murder a rapacious old moneylender, a worthless parasite of no use to anyone. Her death will not only benefit himself, his sister and his mother but also the world in general since the money will enable him to complete his studies and become a valued member of society.

Raskolnikov murders the old moneylender with an axe and steals some money and a few trinkets. He also kills her sister, who interrupts him in the act. He hides the money and the trinkets and almost forgets all about them, then heedlessly gives most of the money away to people he feels sympathy for. Afterwards he realises that money was not the real motive for his crimes, but that the crimes themselves were existential tests of personal will.

As we saw earlier, Brady used the phrase 'existential exercises' to describe his own murders. He used the same words to describe Raskolnikov's crimes. Brady meant that they – both Raskolnikov's and his own – were an inner challenge to convert his theories and beliefs into action. In later chapters, we shall see that Brady distinguishes between the Moors Murders he admits to – three of which he was tried for – and other murders he was not charged with. He calls the former existential murders and the latter 'happenings'.

Raskolnikov reasons to himself: 'No more delusions, no more imaginary terrors, no more phantom visions! There is such a thing as life! Life is real! Haven't I lived just now? My life hasn't come to an end with the death of the old woman! . . . Now begins the reign of reason and light . . . And of will and strength . . . And we'll see now! We'll try our strength now! . . . And to think that I practically made up my mind to live in a square yard of space!'

As the events unfold, Raskolnikov realises that the examining magistrate, Porfiry, suspects him. Porfiry raises questions about an article by Raskolnikov that had appeared in a periodical. Raskolnikov responds: 'As far as I remember, I dealt with the psychology of a criminal during the whole course of the crime.' Porfiry replies: 'Yes, and you insist that the perpetration of the crime is always accompanied by illness. Very, very original, but as a matter of fact it wasn't that part of the article that interested me so much. What I was interested in was an idea you suggest at the end of the article, but which, I'm sorry to say, you merely hint at without explaining it clearly enough. If you remember, you just hint at the existence of certain people who can – no, I'm sorry, not can, but actually have a perfect right to commit all sorts of enormities and crimes and that they are, as it were, above the law . . . All people seem to be divided into ordinary and extraordinary. The ordinary people must lead a life of strict obedience and have no right to transgress the law because, you see, they are ordinary. Whereas the extraordinary have a right to commit any crime they like and transgress the law in any way just because they happen to be extraordinary. I'm right, am I not?'

Brady describes this as the first glimpse of what he calls Raskolnikov's Napoleonic complex. The plan to murder the moneylender had at first been for utilitarian purposes but had become an expression of a higher state of being. Raskolnikov confesses to his lover, Sonia: 'Listen. I wanted to become a Napoleon . . . You see, what happened was that one day I asked myself this question: what if Napoleon, for instance, had been in my place and if he had not had a Toulon or an Egypt or the crossing of Mont Blanc to start his career with, but instead of all these splendid and monumental things, there had simply been some ridiculous old woman . . . To get money from her box . . . Well, would he have made up his mind to do it if there were no other way? Would he too have felt disgusted to do it because it was far from monumental . . . and wicked, too? . . . Well, so I, too, hesitated no longer and – and murdered her – following the example of my authority . . . I wanted to dare . . . I had to find out then, and as quickly as possible, whether I was a louse like the rest or a man . . . Was it the old hag I killed? No, I killed myself, and not the old hag. I did away with myself at one blow and for good.' Ian Brady used an axe to kill his final victim. He would be very aware that his anti-hero, Raskolnikov, used the same weapon to commit murder.

Raskolnikov eventually confesses to the police and is sent to a penal colony. In later years, Brady argued that Raskolnikov's remorse was slight and fleeting and that the regret he felt was because he had not properly thought through the crime and its consequences. Raskolnikov's repentance was forced upon Dostoevsky by the Russian censorship of that period. Raskolnikov must not only be seen to be punished for the murders but also must be seen to repent. He regarded Dostoevsky's hints in the final paragraphs – that Raskolnikov is undergoing a spiritual transformation – as derisory. In a letter to me he reflected on the impact *Crime and Punishment* had on him in Hull Borstal: 'I was elated, at first, thrilled that I had chanced upon a kindred spirit. After the sheer force of my discovery became more familiar to me I began to resent the fact that convictions were by no means unique to me. I resented too that Dostoevsky had made them public property. After a time, I realised that most of his readers would stop reading the novel before they progressed as far as Raskolnikov's thesis. This was consolation enough. Even if they did they would probably not realise its radical significance, or be capable of the will and imagination to convert the ideas into action.'

Despite his indebtedness to Dostoevsky, Brady said that the seeds of the revelation were already within him: 'It reflected precisely what I had always believed.' As Boyce Gibson notes in *The Religion of Dostoevsky*, 'Raskolnikov', in Russian, means 'Loner and Dissenter'. *Crime and Punishment* provided fertile soil for the ideas to grow. This is an aspect of Brady's rejection of all forms of censorship. If individuals claim to be the victims of corruption, they were corrupt already, before they met the person, read the book or saw the film.

In conversations with Brady, I commented on Dostoevsky's ironical place in the complicated fabric of the Moors Murders. Dostoevsky accepted responsibility for his dead brother's children and wrote *Crime and Punishment* to pay for their survival. An act of compassion in 1866 – the year of the first instalment of the book – is a significant factor leading to a series of child murders for which the perpetrators were tried exactly a century later in 1966.

A book that saves children's lives in the nineteenth century contributes to the murder of children in the twentieth. Further, Dostoevsky wrote that the worst conceivable crime on earth was crime against children. I asked Brady whether Myra Hindley was Sonia to his Raskolnikov. Silence for a minute. Then, 'No.'

In the early 1970s, living in Doncaster, I travelled up to Hull University from time to time. I knew something of the area and could relate to Brady's memories of his time there. He was allocated to the farm party two months after his arrival at Hull Borstal.

The early evenings were warm in Gorton, Manchester in June 1957. It was steaming on 14 June and Michael Higgins, aged thirteen, from Taylor Street and a pupil of the Catholic school of Gorton Lane, called round after school on his friend, Myra Hindley. She attended Ryder Brow

Secondary School and was looking forward to her fifteenth birthday in a few weeks' time.

Michael asked Myra to go swimming with him in the Station Road reservoir – the 'Rezz' – a mile and a half away behind Melland Playing Field. Myra was a good and enthusiastic swimmer but was too hot and bothered to accept the invitation. She went instead with her friend Pat Jepson to visit someone in Reddish. Later in the evening, Sally Cheadle from Taylor Street ran round to Bannock Street to tell Myra that Michael Higgins was missing in the 'Rezz'. They both went to the reservoir only to find about thirty people gathered round his body. Myra was beside herself with grief and guilt. Eighteen months later she took communion for the first time in the Roman Catholic Church.

Ian Brady was given his second release date – 14 November 1957. He spent his final weeks at Hull working with the farm party. He avoided trouble and fed carrots to the big carthorses in the stables. The most popular song being piped on the tannoy into the dormitories was portentous for him – Jerry Lee Lewis' 'Whole Lotta Shakin' Goin On'.

CHAPTER SEVEN

SATURDAY NIGHT REVOLVERS & THE HOLY GRAIL

Ian Brady, nineteen years old, walked free from Borstal and breathed in the soot-filled air of Hull station as he boarded the Manchester train. He sampled the whisky as he waited for the Manchester skyline to appear. The chimneystack of Strangeways was unmistakable. His only item of luggage was a canvas bag containing a cheap suit of clothes issued to all inmates on their release from Borstal. He was given three pounds for it in the first pawnshop he saw and spent some of it in Liston's Bar on his way back home to Peggy and Pat Brady.

Ian reported to a probation officer after a few days. The officer arranged for him to attend a series of job interviews. He had no intention of being appointed to what he regarded as a dead-end job and sabotaged the probation officer's best intentions by a couldn't-care-less attitude during the interviews. Besides, Brady had looked up contacts whose names he had written in his notebooks during his detention in Strangeways and Borstal. His days were spent observing money being transported from banks to factories. He rose early to check and recheck routes, times, changes of routes, police foot and car patrols. He studied getaway routes that avoided traffic lights and looked for parking spots with no overlooking windows where cars could be dumped or changed.

In the evenings, Brady observed the use of night safes outside banks in the centre of Manchester, looking particularly for deposits from large department stores and again checking escape routes. On Saturdays, he concentrated on electricity and gas showrooms used by people to pay their monthly bills. Brady was, in fact, working night and day for six days a week. It was repetitive and tedious. It was also impossible to plan for the human factor on the day of a robbery. An individual carrying the money could react violently and passers-by might fight in his defence.

Ian Brady's plans took him beyond the confines of Manchester. Even though he liked, and often preferred, doing jobs in other cities, he never completely trusted his contacts' planning and assessments and usually took the precaution of checking the situation himself. He enjoyed the travel from city to city and invariably returned to Manchester the same night: 'I was always on the lookout for the Holy Grail, the one big job which would free me of the chore of working for a living. I was permanently in search of cash. Apart from money to live on, it was expensive to set up a job. In pursuit of contacts I regularly took a train to another city only to find that the individual was no longer at the address or was back in captivity. My pressing need for capital to get more capital made more acute the nagging anxiety of being imprisoned for a trivial offence.

'There was nothing inevitable about the arrival of the Holy Grail. Jobs in other cities seemed to offer less risk. In any case those jobs infused me with extra energy. They gave me the time and space for innovation. Finding my way about in unfamiliar cities exhilarated me. It was an added bonus if they had an architectural heritage. I even went into churches to absorb the tranquillity, to look at stained glass and breathe in the smell of ancient wood. Given the choice I preferred to travel between places by train and was paranoid about being driven in stolen cars, particularly over long distances. They were a metal trap that could snap shut any second. Besides, not being a driver, I had to depend on a driver who, if stopped or pursued, would not be prepared to go to the extreme I would go.

'One of the drivers used to lift cars from the dark street alongside the old Hippodrome Theatre in Manchester where the patrons parked them. He took a two-seat convertible black Jaguar one night for a job we had in Bradford. I became nervous when I saw opera glasses on the dashboard. The owner might nip out from the Hippodrome to fetch them and report the car missing. Next, the driver stalled the car at the traffic lights, where a PC Plod was bending his knees, before we were out of the city. He didn't give a passing glance.'

After a few weeks of planning, one job was particularly lucrative. It was a money-snatch involving Brady and two of his contacts: I shall refer to them as 'Alex' and 'Mike'. Brady's share was £250. A prison officer's weekly wage was £10. Because of his activities, he had little chance to spend the money. His social life consisted of occasional visits with his friends to pubs, always choosing a table near the back exit for a quick getaway if necessary.

Brady had a few hours to spare one evening and went to the Cinephone, a cinema in Manchester specialising in foreign films. The main feature that night was a documentary on the rise and fall of Hitler. The film had subtitles, so he didn't have to call on his smattering of German. For decades, much has been made of the part played by Nazism in the Moors Murders. It is part of the received wisdom that Brady was obsessed with Nazism from his earliest days in school. Brady himself claims that he had only seen snatches of Hitler on newsreels, just as millions of others would who went to the cinema.

Writing in answer to a question of mine in September 1993, Brady said: 'Hitler is the only politician I've seen who could roar and be believed. His passionate conviction communicated itself to the crowd. I've seen cinema and television audiences who don't know a word of German mesmerised by this quality alone.' Speaking about that night in the Cinephone, he wrote in a letter: 'It's not necessary to speak Italian in order to applaud Caruso's voice. Hitler's passionate orations were hypnotic, striking some receptive, atavistic appetite in the subconscious. His audience were compelled to attend to the authoritative verbal stream of boldness and energy.

'Watching and listening, you slowly realised that here was a rare case of a politician who actually believed every syllable he uttered. It was impossible to doubt it. Conviction rang through every word.

'This riveting oratory was enhanced by its setting: by the astounding spectacle of the political rallies, with thousands bearing banners and standards in phalanxes of ordered ranks. The night rallies in particular exuded a stunning, audacious sense of the mystical, with the vertical skyward searchlights producing a magnificent cathedral-like dome, and the smoke from thousands of flaming torches evoking an atmospheric pagan gathering. If you want to see what I mean, I can send you a video to copy and return – Riefenstahl's *Triumph of the Will* – if you don't already have it. The mystical audacity of the spectacle – darkness and flame – is reminiscent of Hieronymous Bosch. Mesmerising.'

In all of my conversations with Ian Brady he showed hardly any interest in Nazism as an ideology underlying the spectacle. Assuming that he was fascinated by it, over the years correspondents have sent him books on the subject. They were largely unread. He gave me a copy of Charles Bracelen

Flood's massive *Hitler – The Path to Power* that had been sent in to him. He had never turned a page of it.

Brady stressed that his interest in the Third Reich was purely aesthetic. If we are to believe him, the attraction for him was that of pure theatre and was on a par with his enjoyment of Hollywood epics such as *Ben Hur*, *Quo Vadis*, *The Robe* and *The Greatest Story Ever Told*. In Ian Brady's *The Gates of Janus* there is a brief comment on Hitler's power to mesmerise: 'The spoken word can possess a psychic penetration far beyond the reason of the written – as exemplified by the hypnotic oratory of Adolf Hitler and other great manipulators of primal emotion whose vocal delivery takes on the mystical power and sway of music.'

I discussed the Holocaust from time to time with a colleague, a teacher who was herself a Jew. We shared the revulsion of the Nazi atrocities that almost everyone feels today, but, to my surprise, she actually quite liked Hitler's style and his genius for creating an atmosphere. We live and learn.

Whatever we make of it, Brady claims that commentators on the Moors Murders have chosen a predictably superficial – and false – explanation for his own and Myra Hindley's motives by searching for it in Nazism. Whenever I raised the subject with him, Brady invariably said that he was being used as a national folk devil on which millions of people were projecting their guilt for their own fascination and obsession with Nazism, Hitler and crime in general. Brady commented; 'I crystallise their dark side.'

Television programmes on crime – factual or fictional – are available at any time during the day somewhere. Brady quipped on one occasion: 'What a uniquely high threshold of boredom the UK possesses.' I am writing this page on Easter Sunday, on an April day in England in 2003. The television schedules available to British audiences today show that one channel alone is broadcasting nothing else but a selection of programmes on Hitler and Nazism, continuously, from 7 o'clock this morning until one hour after midnight.

Ian Brady and his friend Alex planned a money-snatch and involved Gil Deare, a contact he had made in Borstal. He gave me an account of the robbery to illustrate how the best-laid plans can easily be thrown into chaos by the unpredictable human factor: 'A woman with an open umbrella unintentionally impeded me as I ran towards the car. I lost vital seconds as I swept her out of the way. Gil was already in the back of the car clutching the case of money. I heard shouts behind me. I held on to the open back door of the car as it moved slowly to allow me to jump in. A man grabbed the back of my coat collar.'

'Gil was hitting out at whoever was holding me and Alex, in the driving seat, was shouting, "Hit the bastard!" Some of Gil's blows were hitting me. I whirled round to see who was holding me. Then I saw that the moving car door was about to hit a lamppost and trap me.

'I drew back from the car. My hand was free to swing the lead-filled hose at the man restraining me. I rained down blows with abnormal force born of fear and fury, reacting to him as nothing more than an obstacle threatening my freedom.

'He released my jacket to protect his head. By now the getaway car was lost to me in the traffic. I jumped on a passing bus to throw off the people chasing me. I jumped off it when I spotted the car and threw myself into it alongside Gil, only to find that we were stuck with the traffic lights against us and a car in front. Alex drove on to the pavement and turned left into a long straight road.

'I relaxed now, sprawling on the back seat, attempting to piece together the shambolic series of events. I gave up the attempt when I collapsed into uncontrollable laughter at the farce.'

Gil Deare has a place in the story of the Moors Murders and it is worth hearing Brady's thoughts at this time: 'The combination of Gil, Alex and myself was to become a dream team, although I was unaware of it at the time. The ruthlessness we shared bound us together. We knew we could depend on each other whatever the circumstances.

'Gil was a dead-ringer for Alec Guinness, the film actor. He was very mildly spoken and even compliant on first meeting. Below the surface, however, he was both lethal and calm. Alex was more happy-go-lucky, but – again – his ferocity was below surface. If he was driving and someone blocked our escape route, he would give them a simple choice. Get killed or crippled, or move out of the way.

'The only problem was that Alex and Gil didn't relate very well to each other socially. Fortunately, this made no difference when we were on a job.'

The three of them reflected on their recent fiasco and concluded that they needed guns to insure themselves from capture. That said, guns were significantly absent from the criminal scene in England at that time. The general public reacted to axes and knives, but not to guns. Brady said, 'The psychology wasn't right for guns in the fifties and sixties. If you put a gun in someone's face in England they would just look at it and wonder what it was – a dinky toy from Woolworth's?' He mulled over the problem but had other things on his mind, the chief of which was to return to Scotland, however briefly: 'I drank in the cool, fresh air as I walked through

Manchester's empty streets to Victoria Station. It was after midnight. I bought a ticket for the 1 a.m. train to Glasgow. I was carrying a black leather zip-up briefcase, containing half a bottle of Bell's whisky, packs of Camels cigarettes and chocolate bars.

'I had an impulsive, irresistible urge to visit Glasgow again. I was happy with the thought that I could still act spontaneously on such desires.

'The station was empty at that time of night, apart from a solitary policeman and some people asleep in the waiting room. I was the only one awake in the room and warmed myself by the coal fire. The waiting train was empty. I found a conducive compartment and sat by the open window to inhale the sooty tang, which revived many memories of past journeys. The driver and fireman passed my window and we were soon moving, leaving Manchester to sleep through the darkness.'

At home in Manchester, Ian Brady was under pressure from the probation officer to get a job. Brady told me that his idea of a decent job was that of a contract killer. When inmates were released from Borstal, they were still on licence and had to report their movements and obtain a legitimate job. The alternative was a recall to Borstal.

Early in January 1958 he was forced to take a job in a gasworks as a steel-erector. He was bored and cold from handling icy lengths of tube on frosty mornings. To Brady's relief, he was made redundant after a few weeks. In March he moved with Peggy and Pat Brady and the dog, Bruce, to a new address, number 18 Westmoreland Street, a five-room terrace house in Longsight, off the Stockport Road.

Late in April, Ian Brady started work as a bottle washer in Boddington's Breweries, situated beneath the towering chimneystack of Strangeways Prison. Employees were allowed free beer and this eased some of the pain. The daytime quota wasn't always sufficient, however, and on 9 June 1958 he was fined for being drunk and disorderly.

Early in October, Boddington's Breweries made him redundant. Brady wondered whether firms had a charitable arrangement with the probation service to help ex-prisoners find their feet. After a few days of unemployment, he felt an overwhelming urge to return to Glasgow for a spiritual recharge among its tenements.

He boarded the night train from Manchester Victoria. It was virtually empty when it left at 1.00 a.m. He spent the journey staring into the dark landscape with whisky and strong tobacco evoking happy memories. The train trundled into Glasgow at 7.00 a.m. in time for a breakfast of ham and eggs.

Brady made his way to the Eastern Necropolis on a hill overlooking the city. He sat on a bench and recalled that the graveyard had provided the setting for many of his childhood adventures. The 'green vision' swam at the back of his mind but didn't disturb his reverie. In a letter to me in November 1994 he wrote: 'Victorian graveyards are very atmospheric monuments. A favourite panoramic view of Glasgow can be seen atop the hill of the Eastern Necropolis. In the summer, I used to see the sun glinting on this hill above the city and wondered what was causing it. I was about ten, and discovered it was caused by bell jars covering flowers on graves. In later years I used to go up there when visiting Glasgow, and sit peacefully watching the city below. Nothing morbid in mind, in fact I invariably swigged whisky from the bottle in my briefcase.'

To return to our story, Brady walked back down into the city and had a bath, shave and shoeshine at Glasgow Central Station. He went to the buffet and bought a coffee that he surreptitiously laced with whisky before taking a taxi to Pollok. He walked the last half-mile and by a circuitous route arrived at the entrance of a block of flats from where he could see the family house in Templeland Road.

He had no intention of letting the family know he was back. This was at least partly because of the shame. In any case, everybody would be out at work apart from Ma Sloan, who would be knitting by the front window. As Brady watched, the front door opened and a dog walked out. It was Una. He followed her to a piece of waste ground and whispered her name. The dog reacted momentarily but moved away without showing any signs of recognition.

Brady caught a bus back to the city. After a few drinks in a Gorbals pub he had chips and black pudding for dinner and crossed over the river into Glasgow Green. He offered a cigarette to a teenage girl who was gazing at the river. Decades later he could still remember details about the encounter. The girl had dark eyes and jet-black hair and was wearing a woolly hat topped with two pom-poms. She came from Govan and was wearing an engagement ring. He lapsed into Glaswegian slang when she thought he was English. He poured whisky into the coffees as they sat in Ross's cafeteria and noticed that the manageress was watching. 'Purely medicinal!' he told her.

They said their goodbyes outside the station. He took the train back to Manchester.

In Gorton, Myra Hindley had left school by now and had obtained her first job as a junior clerk with Lawrence Scott and Electrometers in Louisa

Street. As the winter of 1958 approached, she began instruction in the Catholic faith with Father Theodore of the Monastery of St Francis. She was given the name 'Veronica' and took part in her first communion on 16 November 1958. Myra had been encouraged to adopt the faith by her Auntie Kath, a Catholic, who was married to her mother's brother, Bert Maybury. Kath and Bert presented Myra with a white prayer book, suitably inscribed with their names and 'Souvenir of your first Holy Communion'.

The prayer book would later feature in the investigations of the Moors Murders. At a ceremony in the Monastery, Myra became godmother to Anthony John, the nephew of Michael Higgins, whose death by drowning had so traumatised her. The Higgins family were grateful for Myra's support over Michael's death and wanted her to be linked with his memory.

A few weeks after his return from Glasgow, Ian Brady claimed to have stabbed a man in Manchester. He would say nothing about it afterwards, except, 'There was a reason. I felt justified. I was still far short of the "Great Contempt" that Nietzschean delight in unrestrained aspiration and exercise of will. Killings of rage were of no account. They did not test the will. They were mere "happenings" which, for a few red seconds, attained transitory importance and brief afterthought.'

The stabbing was almost certainly not a fatal attack. The first of the 'happenings' probably took place some time later. After the stabbing incident, Brady went to the Oxford cinema to see *Ben Hur*. He wept at the end as the credits rolled on the screen. More than thirty years later, in August 1992, he asked me to track down a video version of the film for him and relived the evening.

Ian Brady was 21 years old on 2 January 1959, but didn't give it a second thought. The probation officer was snapping at his heels and hindering what he regarded as his real career. But a return to Borstal was unthinkable. He decided to compromise by taking a job that was the nearest to no work at all – a nine-to-five job in an office: 'If I hadn't been so forced I wouldn't have ended up with Myra Hindley as my typist and been brought down by existential folly. Before that, all my objectives were mercenary.'

There was a post advertised in a Manchester evening paper. Brady sorted through the notes he had made in Borstal on accountancy and bookkeeping and applied for the job. Within a few days, he was invited to an interview in the Gorton area of Manchester and found himself looking at a sign:

Millwards Merchandise Limited
Levenshulme Road Works
Gorton Manchester 18.
Chemicals & Oils of all descriptions – Gums, Resin, Turpentine,
Waxes, etc. for all Industrial purposes.

Tom Craig, the manager, gave Brady the job and introduced him to the foreman, Bert Matthews. He started work on the following Monday, 16 February 1959. He recalls: 'I had made another step closer to catastrophe. In a short time, a matter of months, Myra Hindley would walk into my life and, at the same time, into criminal history forever. There were no omens, no sudden voices from heaven or the underworld, or shooting stars or earth tremors to augur that I had made a fateful move towards a banal, provincial meeting – in Gorton of all places – that would make nonsense of all my plans, entice me on to the path of pure existentialism and lead to the ultimate, sensational slide into captivity till death.'

Millwards was the Lancashire distributor for the massive ICI company, Imperial Chemical Industries. Brady was in the stock control department, which maintained and ordered stocks of chemicals in the Manchester railway stations, and supervised deliveries from the stations and warehouse to customers. Most of his time was spent in dictating orders and letters.

His colleagues were pleasant and sociable. None of the girls in the department caught his attention, apart from the switchboard operator, Lily, who was happily married. She was German and had been in the Hitler Youth. Brady tried out his German with her. Many years later in captivity, he wrote to me to say, 'It's just occurred to me that, although I controlled orders and deliveries of chemicals in six railway stations and several warehouses, I never set eyes on the stocks or people I dealt with by phone daily – even those at the ICI.'

Forty years later, in *The Gates of Janus*, Ian Brady reflected on these times and the small world of ceaseless routine in the office at Millwards: 'The serial killer . . . daily observes people throwing their entire lives away on repetitive jobs, territorial obsessions, promotions to a particular desk, key to the executive toilets . . . To his eyes this is insanity. He craves excitement. Vibrant meaning. Purpose. But it never seems to come.'

Early evenings were used to watch deposits at busy night safes before he visited a pub or a city cinema to relax. At weekends he had more time to tour target areas. In the office, he felt like a tourist just passing through.

His criminal contacts had his office telephone number. Brady was thinking about this time in his life when he wrote in *The Gates of Janus*: 'I can state with authority that, contrary to popular belief, much crime is tedious and repetitive work, wearing on the nerves and an anti-climax. In the words of the song by Peggy Lee, after the completion of each successive, escalating crime, the criminal is left spiritually asking himself: "Is That All There Is?" '

In Bannock Street, not far from Millwards, Myra Hindley was learning about love on the dole. Just before Christmas 1958, she started seeing a Gorton boy, Ronnie Sinclair. He lived in Dalkeith Street and was a tea blender at the local Co-op. Myra was made redundant at about the same time that Ian Brady started at Millwards. She found a new job at Clydesdale Furniture Shop on Ashton Old Road, a short bus ride from home. It was common in those times for girls to buy things for the 'bottom drawer': pots and pans and the rudiments of married life.

Myra, like many working-class girls at the time, saved money in 'clubs' and bought items from catalogues run by friends. Ronnie Sinclair had saved enough to buy a ring with three diamonds and they were engaged on 23 July 1959, Myra's seventeenth birthday. On 18 December 1995, writing more than three decades later in the *Guardian*, Myra Hindley drew on her memories:

I didn't have a grudge against society or a chip on my shoulder. The things I wanted in life were not unusual. I got engaged at 17 to a boy I first met when I was 11 and pulled the ribbon out of my hair at the pictures.

But when I began to witness many of my friends and neighbours, some of whom "had to get married", having baby after baby, almost tied to the kitchen sink and struggling to make ends meet while their husbands went out every night drinking and betting away their wages just as my father had done, I began to feel uncomfortable and restless.

I wanted a career, to better myself, to travel and struggle to break free of the confines of what was expected of me. Although so much was unattainable, I still dreamed and made plans and kept everything to myself. I didn't want to leave home, because I loved my family, but I wanted more scope and space, and they would think I was 'getting above myself' if I confided in them.

In another part of Manchester, Ian Brady had discovered his 'Holy Grail'. During one of my earliest visits to him, Brady gave me a detailed description of the occasion.

It was about four in the afternoon on a damp November day. He was on the top deck of a bus travelling into the city, idly looking down at people boarding at a stop outside a bank. He could see into the bank and was mesmerised by the sight – a pile of banknotes stacked a few feet high. Although the bus had started to move, he ran downstairs and jumped off.

It was Thursday. Security vans would have delivered that day in preparation for the payroll collections the following day. The front wooden doors were locked but he noticed a smaller side entrance. Brady, chain-smoking in the drizzle, was taking in the scene. The *black light* was beginning to operate. He took note of windows overlooking the bank and the presence of police in the vicinity. After a time, the street started to fill with factory and office workers hurrying home and he blended in with the passing crowd, moving his vantage point from time to time to avert suspicion.

Just before six o'clock, two women stepped into the street through the bank's front entrance and opened their umbrellas in the rain. Three men followed them, one of whom turned off the lights and locked the double doors. Brady deduced that this was the manager. The five of them said their goodbyes and went their separate ways. During a visit he told me what happened next: 'The manager walked to the end of a small queue at the bus stop where I had stepped off the bus a couple of hours before. I walked over and stood behind him. He was about five feet ten and in his mid-forties. I was staring at the back of his neck like a hangman calculating what drop to give the condemned.

'When his bus arrived and he took a seat downstairs, I sat a few seats behind him. He got off and joined the crowds at Piccadilly in the city centre. I was just behind. He stepped on to a bus already waiting at the terminus. I waited for the bus to move and jumped on again, sitting behind him. As the bus travelled through the city, I made notes.

'He left the bus in a residential, middle-class district. I stepped off after the bus was moving. He walked along an avenue of tidy, semi-detached houses; he unlatched a garden gate. There were lights on in the downstairs rooms. He let himself in the house and disappeared. The trail had ended. I had all the information I needed for now. I made my way back into the city by bus.

'I ordered a double whisky in a nearby empty pub and sat by the fire to warm up after the cold drizzle. I needed to find out the bank manager's name and those of his family. I heard no dog bark at his master's return, but there could be one in the house.' In a later chapter, we shall see how Ian Brady used the same method of surveillance with murder in mind.

After sleeping on his discovery, Brady decided to take the morning off from work to observe staff arrivals and the opening of doors. He stayed on to watch the various payroll collections to obtain the full picture. It was then that he discovered his second 'Holy Grail'. A large grey car drew up outside the bank. Leaving a man at the wheel, three men walked into the bank. A few minutes later two of the men reappeared, carrying between them a long sausage-shaped leather bag with handles at each end. The third man followed them out, holding two smaller leather bags. All three bags were put into the boot. The car moved away and almost immediately turned into a narrow side street.

Brady moved quickly to see the car turn left again into an even narrower street and then drive on to a main road. He walked the lengths of the two side streets and could see that none of the battered houses were occupied. A plan for a robbery was already forming in his mind. Two cars would be needed. Once the payroll car had entered one of the side streets, the robbers' cars could block the entrance and the exit. A few months of planning, checking getaway routes that avoid traffic lights, police patrols, etc.: 'Relying on luck was not a weakness of mine.' But the basic idea seemed perfect.

Brady called in at the nearest pub to order a glass of Drambuie to celebrate. He could call Gil and Alex to Manchester for the payroll snatch, but he needed one more accomplice for the four-man team. Brady met his two friends and outlined his plan, leaving out the exact location – cautious as ever. They decided that a mutual friend, Frank, would be the fourth man.

A few weeks later, Brady bumped into his friend Bruce in the Robin Hood pub. He was a fellow Scot, who had met him in Borstal. Bruce was now a pimp and had three girls on the game. He was capable of casual spontaneous violence and had one of his hands in plaster on the night that Brady met him. The two of them talked till midnight then ate hot-dogs at a stall in Piccadilly with one of Bruce's prostitutes. She was a pretty eighteen-year-old blonde girl named 'Tina' for the purposes of this book and Brady told her that he would never have guessed her trade.

Tina lived in Longsight and invited him to stay the night. They went out together for a time but Brady didn't like to see the streetwise, cold look she had in her green eyes sometimes. He tried to make her laugh to dispel it.

Ian Brady described several robberies he was involved in at this period of his life. Not all of them were successful and some of them involved railway yards with their freight wagons of cigarettes and alcohol. One bitterly cold November evening, railway police gave chase after spotting Ian and his gang trying to locate a particular freight wagon after a tip-off. They scrambled over the railway tracks and ran to climb in their getaway van. It was nowhere to be seen. The gang split in all directions. Brady ran along empty streets and took refuge in a derelict pub: 'The place still had its Victorian furniture, bars, settles, staircases, pale with dust in the dim streetlight; ghosts of many past carousals and drunken choruses adding sadness to the dereliction.

'Suddenly, a peripheral movement in the corner of my eye startled me. I swung round and was face-to-face with a stranger. I froze and stared at him. He returned the stare. It was my own reflection in a large mirror behind the bar; in ghostly parody and reflected shadows. I was shaken. I sat down and lit a cigarette.

'I stayed there for a couple of hours until the coast was clear. I toyed with the vain thought that there might be some comforting booze left in the cellar, but was sufficiently unconvinced not to venture. I found my way through empty streets to the main road.'

After one successful money-snatch, one of Brady's accomplices accused him of excessive violence. Brady, Gil and Alex gave him a nickname – 'Jittery Ed'. Ed changed his tune when he found that the bag contained more than expected. This was the third lucrative job in a matter of weeks. Alex had a girlfriend in Amsterdam and suggested to Brady that they spend some of the takings on a short trip to Holland.

Brady was still under licence from Borstal and needed permission to leave the country. Alex had illegal passports requiring merely a change of photographs. Brady enjoyed his first trip abroad and explored Amsterdam on his own when Alex was with his girlfriend. He discovered the sleazy parts and had some 'special fun'.

Sometime later, during August, Brady and Alex travelled south from Manchester by train and crossed to France. Carlyle's *The French Revolution* was one of Brady's favourite books and he was looking forward to stepping on to French soil: 'I had an interesting night encounter in the quarries of the Catacombs in Paris, mixing with after-midnight revellers dancing by candle and firelight.'

Brady returned again and again to what he called his favourite fantasy: 'Exploring the secondary roads of France on foot, discovering the little villages, taking field work where offered, living in a tent and sampling the local cheese. I could live on cheese alone and taste the wines, the world of crime gone and forgotten. A pity for all concerned that such modest ambition only blossomed when it was too late.'

On the boat back to England, Alex complained to Brady about the danger 'Jittery Ed' posed to both of them. They could both lose their freedom if he caved in on a job. Leaning on the side of the boat, smoking and watching the white cliffs drawing nearer, Brady said calmly, 'Get rid of him.' Just as calmly, Alex asked, 'The River Ouse?' Brady agreed, but warned Alex to make sure the river was in full flood after heavy rain.

Before the boat docked they discussed the possibilities of smuggling revolvers through English Customs. Handguns were easily bought in Belgium, but Brady was still haunted by the spectre of being arrested for a trivial offence.

Ian Brady's trips abroad all took place before he met Myra Hindley. To describe them here would be too much of a distraction from our story. It's enough to say that apart from Holland and France he claimed to have visited Germany, Austria and Belgium, and – at Alex's suggestion – the United States. In a letter Brady wrote: 'I owed the opportunities to contacts made in Strangeways – I should've stayed in the US, but my doctored documents were short-term. Still being on licence my travels had to be concealed. Thinking back, I was too cautious and should've taken the minor risk of staying afterwards.'

He had destroyed the first illegal passport, but he had a friend who ran a travel agency and supplied him with the necessary documents for free movement. He visited New York, Alabama, and saw a big steamer in New Orleans that reminded him of the *Waverley* on the River Clyde: 'In New Orleans a low night mist from the river left the heads of the lamp-posts peering up into the night decapitated on a pearl cushion of light.' In a letter written in the 1990s, he said that New York was very much like Glasgow in structure and spirit. It had the same brownstone tenements, wide streets and wide pavements: 'The spiritual affinity was harder to define, except in terms of unpredictable violence.'

Brady saw the outskirts of Chicago on the way to Lake Huron, before briefly crossing to Canada. The visit to the United States was 'mercenary' according to him. In 1994 he asked me to track down *Most Wanted – A History of the FBI's Ten Most Wanted List* by Mark Sabljak and Martin Greenberg. The book describes the evolution of the 'wanted' lists issued by the FBI since 1950 and has mug shots on almost every page. I found a copy and was intrigued by the front cover – a black-and-white close-up of the top half of Ian Brady's first, notorious, security photograph.

I posted the book to him without asking the question that begged to be asked, supposing that there lay a mystery. Years later I dropped the question casually into a conversation. Brady said that he had no idea why they used his photograph. He remembered the half-hour stopovers in the night on long-distance bus journeys, calling in diners for a drink and walking down Main Street to share the early hours with dogs and cats.

In May 2002 we were discussing the American 'Beat Zen' author Jack Kerouac, who had recently featured in a television film about the hippy phenomenon in the 1960s. Talk of Kerouac's book *On The Road* reminded me of a comment by Ian Brady that I had heard him make more than once: 'We are never more truly ourselves than when we are briefly someone else – travelling free of the normal surroundings.' In the same context he acknowledged his affinity with a character in a Dostoevsky novel, as I mentioned earlier: 'People have compared me to the main character in *The Possessed*, a satire on the revolutionary mind – Stavrogin – as he also liked travel and organising, and a sense of the absurd – the one shared characteristic of humanity that relegates all others, exemplifying them as performing fleas in a circus. If only we could have a rewind and a replay, what a fascinating experience that would be. I'd spend my life travelling – which is what I wanted to do anyway, without having to keep breaking off for financial goals. Always came more alive on the move, shedding stale conditioning and breathing new air and experiences. Travel regenerates everyone; it's the dullness and repetition of ordinary life that creates neurosis and destructive impulse. Life has become too safe and predictable and that's why we have to dramatise trivia and magnify minute risk.'

Brady visited Glasgow again before Christmas, without telling anyone. Back in Manchester he arranged for a wine shop to send a gift crate to the Sloans after he had tied personal tags to the necks of the bottles of whisky and Drambuie. As usual, he read *A Christmas Carol* and went out with Tina over the Christmas break. He never told her that his home in Westmoreland Street was just a few streets away from her flat. He used railway stations for meeting contacts from other cities rather than give them his Longsight address.

In the New Year, Brady travelled by train to Edinburgh to meet a contact, Mel, at the station. Mel wanted to take him home to discuss the job, but he was anxious about showing his face to Mel's family. The two of them talked in the station buffet but Brady's heart wasn't in it. More spiritual matters distracted him. He realised that his personality changed on the sacred soil. He was thinking of the prospect of a reunion with the family in Glasgow.

He pulled out of the deal with the excuse that Scottish banknotes would be difficult to exchange in England and softened the blow by asking Mel to be part of a job south of the border. They parted amicably and Brady sent a telegram to Ma Sloan to expect him at Templeland Road in the evening.

He killed time waiting for the Glasgow train by stocking up with whisky, rum, port and cigarettes for the family. I asked Ian Brady once, why – if he loved Scotland so much – he hadn't gone back to live there after the Borstal licence period had expired. He replied that as well as the problem of exchanging Scottish banknotes, there was the fact that most of his contacts were in England.

As he walked up the path of number 21, he saw Ma get up from her chair by the side of the window and put her knitting on the table: 'Ma opened the front door. She seemed older and frailer than I remembered her. I was smiling at the pleasure of seeing her again and she returned my smile. "You've come back at last. No' before time. Staying away this long! Imagine! You must be occupied doon south in England."

' "Not busy really. Just the odd thing or two from time to time," I lied. I put the package on the table. "I'd forgotten how long it's been." Ma was busy in the kitchen. The rest of the family were all at work. I took a serious swig of whisky behind Ma's back.

'I looked at the objects in the living room that had once formed an unnoticed background when I had lived there: the chest-of-drawers with the eccentrically shaped mirror, the piano, Da's bookcase, and the ornamental marble clock that even now didn't work. Ma said that Eric, May's husband, had wallpapered the living room.

'Ma, now almost stone deaf, read my lips when I asked her if she wanted a glass of port. She shook her head and said she would be asleep in no time. She said she would have nothing to do with the bad habits I had picked up from the English.

'I laced my tea with whisky and sat back, basking in the joy of simply being there. I was thinking of my time as a boy in Pollok. I had no hidden agendas in that domestic setting. I was surprised to find myself smiling – I probably looked goofy. When I realised this, I smiled all the more. What of it? I could have cried with happiness.'

John was the first to arrive home from work. He was now as tall as Ian and heavier. When Ian saw him last, he was still at school. Da was next and shouted, 'What a sight for sore eyes!' while he washed himself in the kitchen. Jean was the last to walk in. Ian had time to see that she was rosy-cheeked as usual before she welcomed him with, 'Look what the cat's dragged in!' Everyone sat round the table for tea and took turns to ask Ian why he had stayed away for so long.

May had a home of her own with her husband Eric and was not expected for tea. Years later, Ian revealed to May Sloan that he had returned to Glasgow many times without telling anyone, and how he had observed number 21 Templeland Road from a distance.

When the washing-up had been done Ian persuaded everyone to have a stronger drink than tea. He could see neighbours and friends through the front window, but he didn't want to meet them. It would take up too much of his fleeting visit. In the evening, he took John into the city for a drink in the Trocadero. John had only been five when the Sloans moved from the Gorbals and he could remember little of the place. Ian decided to jog his memory.

They walked through the city streets and crossed the River Clyde carrying bottles of beer. Ian drew on his store of memories as they wandered through the gas-lit streets and tenements. John remembered nothing and was nervous about the Gorbals' notorious reputation. Ian was completely at home: 'I don't think John noticed the way I kept touching the walls of the tenements for spiritual recharge.' At midnight the two of them caught the last bus back to Pollok.

Da Sloan was the only one still up when the two of them returned to Templeland Road. John went up to bed almost immediately. Ian recalls a conversation in the small hours: 'There were bottles of Lamb's rum and whisky standing between Da and me as we faced each other across the kitchen table. We talked through the night. I had never spoken with him so intimately before, or at such length. He was a man to me that night – not just my foster father. I dominated the conversation, expounding my relativist views and general philosophy.

'I was relentless. I was unremitting and he seemed overwhelmed. He was an uncomplicated, honest man. This is why I had admired him so much. Even the little he seemed to understand shocked him. I had never before told him of my convictions or tried to explain my way of looking at things.

'I didn't know it that night, but Da had not long to live. Only after his death did I realise that our conversation in the wee small hours was the last chance I had to bare my soul to him.'

At lunchtime the following day, Robert Sloan arrived by car to take Da and John to see a soccer match. Robert was surprised to see Ian at number 21 and invited him along. Ian accepted the invitation although he had no interest in football. He met his old school friend Ian Campbell at the ground, and was relieved to talk about old times rather than watch the match.

After a time, Ian looked around to see where Da was and realised at once that something was wrong. Da was sitting alone on the concrete steps of the terraces showing no interest in the game. He was miles away. Ian sat down beside him and said a few words but Da showed no signs of hearing: 'Robert saw us and came over. There was something in his soft tones in which he spoke to Da that told me that this had happened before.'

After the match, Ian travelled to see May and her husband Eric in their house at Barlanark. May's eyes bulged with surprise when she saw Ian. Why had he stayed away so long? As usual, she spoke her mind. When Eric returned home, all three of them went to see the offbeat western *One-Eyed Jacks* starring Marlon Brando, an actor Ian had always admired.

The following evening Ian went out with Bridie, the girl he had spent so much time with in the meadows near Pollok. Bridie hadn't changed; she was still lively and beautiful as before. They had a drink at the Trocadero then walked across the street to the Odeon cinema. Ian spent the night with her and returned to Pollok at dawn to pack his suitcase for the train journey back to Manchester.

Brady was uneasy about the tension that had developed between Gil and Alex. It was eroding the exclusive bond of trust the three of them had formed. Alex and Gil exchanged petty slights and bickered when they were together. The antagonism was deeply rooted and Brady's efforts to heal the rift failed. At the same time, he was juggling several balls in the air, travelling from city to city to keep his contacts alive. He enjoyed the travel. Information about jobs more than offset the cost of train fares. Closer to home, Gil talked to Ian about the potential for making money in Gil's home town of Bradford, Yorkshire.

The woollen mills in and around Bradford were employing Asian labour and landlords were renting beds and rooms to them on an eight-hour shift system, while paying tax on one rent. Gil and Ian researched the market of potential properties in Bradford. Ian often commented on the irony of the suspicion by police that he had murdered Gil, a friend whom he had liked and trusted.

Ian Brady at this time was searching constantly for a safe and plentiful supply of guns and bullets. Shotguns were easy to obtain and saw down.

He and his friends had acquired some 'Saturday night' revolvers, kept for common use in a safe house. Ammunition was the real problem. Brady was also looking in particular for a pump-action shotgun, holding five cartridges for maximum security and insurance. Most suppliers would sell or trade clients to the police and, consequently, Brady kept himself in the background. Out of the blue, however, he found that his needs could be met on his own doorstep.

George Clitheroe, the foreman in the warehouse at Millwards, was a member of the Cheadle Rifle Club and something of a marksman. Brady nurtured his friendship and, showing some interest in his expertise with guns, discovered the rules of entry into the club. An applicant had to be first sponsored by a member. Secondly, they had to be vetted by the police, who checked whether the applicant had a criminal record. This ruled out Ian Brady: 'I was unaware of it, but fate was bringing my ideal partner closer and closer, in the form of a girl as calculating and merciless as I was. Unfortunately, psychologically speaking, she appeared on the scene at an inauspicious time. Several of my contacts were in police hands or were on the run. It was a time when I was literally becoming almost deranged with my frustrated plans.

'It was the moment to embrace pure existentialism, a relativist delirium of total possibility. The time to exercise supreme will, the final challenge. It was the moment in which to mock all divinities but my own – *Death* itself. If only Myra had appeared earlier. It would have changed everything.'

In London Alex stole a black Mercedes and drove to Manchester with his friend Nev, a large and pleasant man who turned out to be too compassionate for Brady's taste. Brady would accompany them to Newcastle in the dark early hours to meet three other men for a robbery. On a Thursday evening, they met Brady around nine in Manchester's Piccadilly Station and all three drove for a drink at the Mersey, a large hotel on the borders of Manchester.

There was a holdall under the back seat containing two shotguns, two pairs of overalls, two woolly hats with eyeholes cut in them and two pairs of surgical gloves. Brady and Alex were also carrying revolvers. Brady was tired after clearing a lot of work at Millwards, knowing that he would be absent the following day. The Mersey closed at midnight and the three of them drove to another hotel, where the owner was the father of a friend, and drank through the early hours until it was time to set out for the north-east.

They arrived in Newcastle just as people were going to work. They parked in a quiet road beside an office block as prearranged and walked a mile or so with the holdall to Pat's flat: 'Pat was becoming the nigger-in-the-woodpile. He was a disturbing element in the developing personality clashes, which were growing more rapidly than any of us could handle. We were becoming distracted from the big picture. Pat was messing up everything. He was a liability.

'Knowledge usually emerges from conflict rather than brain dead compliance. Unfortunately, Pat had an imagination like cement: wet and set. He sounded off ad nauseam in his own superficial style, and took offence if challenged. He was confident that he had that certain something. It was invisible to everyone else. He was blind to glances Alex and I shared. His days were numbered. He could be used as a dispensable before being eliminated.

'Nev, Alex and I were on a job and picked up a stolen car from an old lock-up garage. Pat and his friends had stolen a van and parked it nearby. It wasn't necessary to fire the guns and the robbery went smoothly. The stolen vehicles were ditched and the takings were divided in Pat's flat. My share was £300, which was less than I anticipated. We left the cheques for Pat to dispose of.'

Ian Brady was tired but on a high from lack of sleep and suggested to Alex that they drive the hundred or so miles to Glasgow since they were virtually on the Scottish border. Everyone agreed. Brady, Alex and Nev travelled in the stolen Mercedes with false number plates. The shotguns and the holdall containing the woolly hats and overalls were hidden under the back seat.

Brady looked like a city gent in his three-piece suit and tie. He had a revolver in a holster under his arm. They bought whisky and beer in Newcastle and headed for the Great North Road, followed by Pat and his two friends in his own car.

Brady slept in the back of the car until they drove through the outskirts of Glasgow. The gang stopped for a meal in a Ross's self-service cafeteria in the city centre and Pat changed a fiver to see what Scottish banknotes looked like. Alex had heard so much about the Gorbals from Brady that he wanted to see it for himself. The Mercedes led the way down Rutherglen Road and turned into Camden Street, stopping at number 56: 'A few ragamuffin Gorbals children playing near the site, shades of my own childhood there. We dropped small change into their eager palms to keep watch over our cars, before walking through the close into the backs. My partners in crime could never share the happy visions these familiar surroundings evoked for me. Pat put it laconically; "It's a fucking dump!"

'I remembered how hot the summers seemed in those far distant days and it was hot that day. I undid my tie and was suddenly conscious of my exposed gun and holster. It was out of place and time as I shielded my eyes from the sun to look up to the back window where Ma had thrown down "pieces" of bread and jam to me. My fellow criminals were like intruders that day, aliens trespassing on a few square yards which were sacred to me.

'The urchins were still putting on a well-rehearsed show of protecting our cars. The others gave more coins to them. I put on a Glasgow accent and tried to banter with them but it had zero effect. It was mannered and hollow to their ears. But I spoke their language when I gave each of them a banknote, their eyes wide at the prospect undreamt of fun it gave them. They wouldn't remember me, only the fun the money bought. I was content with that, knowing how I would have felt if a stranger to the Gorbals had done the same for me and the gang, all those lost years ago.'

The two-car convoy drove out of the Gorbals and headed for Loch Lomond. Pat and his pals wanted a drink and called in a pub in Balloch at the southern tip of the loch while Alex, Brady and Nev travelled along the western shore before cutting left at Tarbet to Arrochar at the northern tip of Loch Long, the scene of one of Ian's runaway adventures. They filled the empty beer bottles with ice-cold water from a roadside stream to cool down in the sun.

Brady told them something about the place as they walked along the western shore of the sea-loch until they were strolling in the twilight. Back at Balloch, Pat's car followed the Mercedes into Glasgow and Brady left the group.

The next days were Saturday and Sunday and Brady spent the weekend with some girlfriends. He avoided Pollok and the Sloan family, and he caught the Sunday night train back to Manchester.

In Gorton, Myra Hindley's engagement to Ronnie Sinclair was over after only six months. He was too immature for Myra's tastes. She worked for the engineering company Bratby and Hinchliffe but was sacked for absenteeism. Looking through the *Manchester Evening News* she saw a vacancy for a typist at Millwards Merchandising in Levenshulme Road, Gorton. The advert said that the job had 'excellent prospects'. The real 'prospects' would have been beyond the wildest imaginations of the person who drafted the advert.

CHAPTER EIGHT

NIGHT TRAIN TO GLASGOW & THE TYPIST WITH PEROXIDE HAIR

Ian Brady looked up from his desk when Tom Craig guided a girl into the office. Shirley Gain had left Millwards to be married and Ian assumed that the new face was her replacement. Tom told Ian and his colleague, Bert, that Myra was the new typist and that she would be starting work next Monday.

Brady recalled his first impression. She looked around twenty. She was fairly tall and had peroxide blonde hair. She looked cool but not enough to stop him from attending to his paperwork right away, after giving the new arrival a nod and a sideward smile. In fact, he thought that Tom had said that the girl was named 'Endley'. It brought *Wuthering Heights* to his mind.

He thought nothing more of it and was more occupied with the horses he would place bets on when he slipped out to the bookies at lunchtime. It was just another banal moment in the routine day of Ian Brady, a Millwards clerk. There was no hint to augur the catastrophic, ghastly nightmare that would result from that morning's monosyllabic exchange of words between two people who were destined to rank among the most hated murderers in the long catalogue of British crime.

It all began on a chilly January morning in a featureless road in working-class Gorton. Myra's school was located in the same road. She had walked past it on her way to the interview at Millwards. As she walked back home, past her old school, she may well have looked wistfully across the playing field and recalled the days when she was a star in the netball team: 'Those were the happiest days!' They were.

Some weeks later Brady received a telephone call from Gil saying he wanted to see him urgently. Brady met his train and they ordered drinks in the station buffet.

Gil was uncharacteristically nervous, gulping down the whisky and chasing it with a long swig of beer. He wiped the foam from his lips and came to the point: 'That bastard Ed has grassed me up. I don't know why. It was all so fucking petty.' He was chain-smoking and stubbing the cigarettes out viciously in the ashtray. 'You know how mad he is on cars. Well, he kept the black Jaguar, the hardtop convertible. Can you imagine the mentality? He held on to it and was using it for months with false number plates!'

A few months before, Ed and Gil had brought the stolen Jaguar from Bradford to Manchester to do a job with Ian Brady. The Jaguar had only a bucket seat in the back, making it difficult to get into at speed. Brady wanted to remove the hardtop to make jumping in easier, but they arrived late and time was short. They drove straight into the city centre. It was after six with poor light. Brady and Gil got out and left Ed to park in a side street and wait as planned. The job was to rob two men, who would be carrying money to deposit in a bank night safe.

Gil and Brady separated to converge on the men from opposite directions. Brady would attack from behind and Gil would snatch the bags. Ed was to drive up to them for a fast getaway. Fortuitously, the men chose a different route to the bank that night and the robbery was aborted. The three of them sat in the Jaguar fuming with frustration. Ed wanted to rob a petrol station to salvage what was left of the evening. Brady convinced him of the stupidity of the suggestion.

Before returning to Bradford, Ed asked if he could keep the car radio. Brady agreed but stressed that the car must be dumped as soon as possible. As Brady listened to Gil in the buffet, he was incredulous and concerned. Why did Ed inform on Gil over something so trivial? Why did he keep the car? Why hadn't he informed on him as well?

In fact, he could have informed on Brady over more serious matters. Had Ed thought he would escape retribution? He must have known Brady's inevitable response to informers. Gil and Brady were of one mind. It was simply a matter of when and how. As their conversation drew to a close, Brady said, 'Alex will give him swimming lessons, in a sack!'

They said their farewells and Gil walked out of the buffet. Brady was never to see him again, despite his efforts to trace him.

Ian Brady had received letters from the Sloans telling him that Da Sloan was in hospital. When he returned home from Millwards one evening he found a telegram to say that Da was dead. Without showing it to Peggy and Pat, Brady was devastated. He thought of the two of them sitting at the table drinking and talking to the early hours. How could he be dead? He was only in his mid-fifties.

Brady changed into a dark suit and caught the night train to Glasgow. He had packs of American cigarettes, rum and whisky in his black briefcase. He had no thoughts other than his life with the Sloans. He had a café meal and went for a drink before going home to Pollok. He had always looked forward to his visits but he dreaded this one. Conversation in the house was strained and one by one the family walked upstairs, resigned to a night of fitful sleep.

Finding himself alone at midnight, Brady put the whisky into his pocket and walked aimlessly along deserted streets. He had walked the same streets on the night Sheila died: 'Weeping over goodness transforms itself into rage. I had always felt this instinctively, as a child, without knowing why. I knew now.'

In the morning, cars came to take the family to the funeral in Govan. Ma Sloan stayed at home. Brady saw relatives he had not seen for years: 'Da lay in an open coffin in the funeral parlour. He was large in spirit in life, as I had known him. Now he looked small and frail; an empty shell of the generous man he had been. There was only a shadow of him in the coffin.

'The sight was too much for May, who broke down in tears, wailing the loss that everyone there felt. The funeral cortege travelled to the cemetery along Paisley Road – the place of revelation for me in the distant past. The religious service meant nothing to me. The parson dutifully intoned the platitudes of disposal; "I am the Resurrection and the Life, saith the Lord. Whosoever believeth in me, though he die . . ."

'I stared at the coffin as it slipped, slowly and silently from this veil of tears to the oven and an eternity of oblivion.'

Back at Templeland Road, Jean and Ma had set out the tables with food and drink for the mourners. Ian Brady was in no mood to eat or chat but gazed through the front window.

He had always thought of Robert Sloan as remote and self-contained, but his eyes were red from crying. Robert offered to drive Jean back home and Ian joined them to avoid seeing Ma grieving. They all drank rum and whisky at Jean's house, Robert clearly needing it. Robert and Jean drove Ian to the station in the evening and said their farewells.

As Ian Brady waited for the train to move out he reflected that during the day he had become closer to Robert, who was now much mellowed. He could see the genuine loss and grief Ian shared with him and, probably for the first time, realised how much being part of the family had meant to him.

Robert had made the most of his humble origins as a Gorbals child. After being demobbed from the Royal Navy, he joined the large animal feed manufacturing conglomerate BOCM and studied hard at night school. He became an executive in the company but paid for his success with a stroke in his mid-forties. He was made redundant. Robert and his wife, Jean, joined their son in Canada. Before Robert could start work there, he was found to have cancer. Jean moved back to Scotland after his death.

Brady reflected on May's uncontrolled grief as her father lay dead before her. Her later fortunes reflected those of her brother Robert, though without the tragic outcome. She left the printing firm to become a nurse, as she had always planned. Nurses in those days were expected to buy their own wristwatches. Da bought her one with what he could afford. Before she could begin her training she was found to have a spot on her lung. Her hopes of being a nurse were extinguished when a doctor told her the results of her X-ray. Brady remembered visiting her in Bellshill Sanatorium with the Sloans. May recovered in due course, married and had two children.

Ian stood smoking by an open window in the corridor as the Manchester train moved through the suburbs of Glasgow: 'My mood changed. I felt angry and ruthless in my helplessness. A raging, malignant energy boiled inside me. It sought an outlet. I wept as the wrath exploded. I pulled out my lock-back knife, stabbing and tearing the upholstery. Each slash jarred with a vehemence that made my wrist ache. I could see nothing but crimson blood. The eviscerated compartment seemed drenched in blood. Death's due paid in arrears. Ghost-like shadows of living and dead antagonists flitted before the hacking knife.

'I couldn't account for the time that had passed. I glanced around me at the disembowelled compartment as though I was waking from a drug-induced nightmare. I stared at the knife in my hand. I was shivering with the cold. The outside door of the compartment was open and banging in the wind. I reached out to shut it. My clothes were plastered with shreds and lint of upholstery. I removed the light bulbs and tossed them out of the window before stepping into the corridor to find the toilet where I could lock myself in. I carefully removed and brushed all trace of lint from my jacket, trousers and hair, then moved to another compartment.

'My rage had been cathartic. I felt relaxed after a few serious swigs of whisky. My wrist sore, a reminder of what had been, and a prelude of what was soon to come. Balancing of accounts. Everything had a price.

'Through all of this, England had passed in darkness.'

CHAPTER NINE

THE NIGHT MANCHESTER DIED

Myra Hindley reported for work at Millwards on 16 January 1961. Within five years she was destined to become an infamous part of the folk memory of the 'swinging sixties' and the most hated woman in the country. As Nicci Gerrard commented in the *Observer* (17 November 2002) after Myra's death, she was 'as much part of the Sixties as the Beatles and the Pill. She was the end of innocence.'

All of this for £8 per week.

On the international scene, 1961 would be memorable for many reasons. At the height of the Cold War, the Russians won the race to put the first man into space. It was the year that the Berlin Wall was built. It was also the year when the youngest American president would be inaugurated. John F Kennedy was assassinated the night before Myra Hindley helped to murder her second victim.

The late 1950s and the early 1960s was the era of the 'Angry Young Man' in the theatre and in films. *Saturday Night and Sunday Morning*, *The Loneliness of the Long Distance Runner* and *Look Back In Anger* still have the power to evoke the raw moods in those black-and-white years.

When discussing the Moors Murders with sixth-formers, I used to try to create what Ian Brady would call the 'gestalt' of the story by showing them a large coloured film poster of *Rebel Without A Cause*: James Dean, with brooding and sulky good looks in the style of another contemporary icon, Elvis Presley. Their British counterparts were charismatic rebels whose mystique was enhanced by being knee-deep in the kitchen-sink frustrations and ugliness of working-class life: angry young milk-bar messiahs.

A teenage girl with any imagination would find the youths on offer at the local dance halls parodies of the real thing. This partly explains Myra Hindley's rejection of Ronnie Sinclair and her later infatuation with Brady. Ronnie simply wasn't old enough, didn't know enough, to rival Brady's effortless, mysterious presence. Ian Brady looked as though he had lived. But how, when and where?

Ian Brady actually looks like James Dean in some of the photographs from that time. Ronnie Sinclair wasn't even a starter in the brooding, romantic stakes. Brady told me how much Myra loved to watch Elvis Presley's films. He didn't share her taste although he did like some of Presley's songs. With the hindsight that thirty years of prison gave her, Myra wrote about this period of her life in the *Guardian*, December 1995:

> My only 'fatal weaknesses' when I met Ian Brady were that I was emotionally immature, relatively unsophisticated and sexually inexperienced – I was still a virgin and intended to be so until I got married.
>
> Before I met Ian, and when I applied for a job as a shorthand typist, a friend who worked in the same small typing pool suggested I phoned Millwards, as a vacancy there had been advertised, and she had worked there herself in the recent past.
>
> She told me something about the firm and mentioned some of the people I'd be working with if I got the job.
>
> She told me about Ian, describing him as tall and good looking, very quiet and shy; an 'intriguing man' who had appealed to her. When I was given the job after an interview, I was introduced to the others in the office, and before his name was mentioned, I already knew it was him. I can only describe my reaction as an immediate and fatal attraction, although I had no inkling then of just how fatal it would turn out to be.

In a letter to me Ian Brady also reflected on life in Millwards thirty years later: 'Myra had been working in the office for several months, but she was simply the new typist as far as I was concerned. I paid no more attention to her than I did the rest of the females on the staff – that is to say, very little. She worked in a small room close to mine. She typed the letters I dictated to her. I can't recall having any memorable conversations with her. It was just standard, routine office dialogue. I didn't go for her peroxide hairstyle. She had obviously been standing or sitting too close to the fire at home – she had heat marks on her calves.

'A couple of colleagues told me that Myra had been asking questions about me. She was intrigued to know why I lowered my voice when I answered the phone to certain callers. Who were they? After hearing about this, I was careful about what I said and kept an eye on her. Her curiosity made me curter with her. Much later, I was told that she had written down her feelings for me in her shorthand notebook. It was only puerile romantic tosh.'

Myra Hindley, in fact, had kept a diary for seven months, safely locked in one of her desk drawers. Her first entry was, 'Ian looked at me today.' Myra's agony was not helped by having to listen to The Temperance Seven's hit 'You're Driving Me Crazy', an ironic reflection of her own frustrated state over Brady, which was in the charts for sixteen weeks in 1961. She wrote down any little fact she had gleaned about him. She discovered that he drank Boddington's beer and gambled on horses. Most of the entries, however, reflect the self-inflicted mental torture of being in love with Ian Brady. Romantic tosh:

'July 23rd 1961. Wonder if Ian is courting. Still feel the same.

'July 25th. Haven't spoken to him yet.

'July 27th. Spoken to him. He smiles as though embarrassed. I'm going to change; you'll notice that in the way I write.

'August 1st. Ian's taking sly looks at me at work.

'August 13th. Wonder what Misery will be like tomorrow?

'August 14th. I love Ian all over again. He has a cold and I would love to mother him.

'August 24th. I am in a bad mood because he hasn't spoken to me today.

'August 29th. I hope he loves me and will marry me some day.'

I asked Ian Brady why it took a year for them to get together. He replied that he was simply too busy on jobs. A run of successful robberies brought in enough money to buy what were luxuries in working-class Manchester in those times. The first item on his list was a brand new Triumph motorbike with a fitted fibreglass fairing. He paid cash for a sophisticated camera, a large tape recorder and a VHF radio receiver that picked up police communications. He also spent the money on clothes – tailor-made three-piece suits as usual, sweaters, raincoats, overcoats and several pairs of black kid gloves.

Brady had no premonition then that he would have virtually no income at all for most of the years that remained for him. In fact, forty years into the future, he would ask me to find him clothes from jumble sales and charity shops, when he had very few things to put on his back.

In her 'confessions' to Inspector Peter Topping, twenty years after she was sentenced to life imprisonment, Myra Hindley said that Ian Brady was 'always cloaked in an aura of mystery and secrecy' that she could never penetrate. This was what fascinated her and made him so attractive to her.

Brady was aware that his unavailability simply stoked the fires of Myra's passion. Impossible loves were the only loves worth having. He offered no relief for Myra's emotional agony. In this, as in most other matters, he frankly didn't give a damn, my dear.

Myra's emotions and thoughts at this time of her life were not merely the dreamy, romantic projections of a lovesick teenager. There was a power there, however demonic, to compel her attentions and her total surrender. Myra Hindley was not the only person to have described Ian Brady's attractive, enigmatic presence. Lord Longford visited him over a long period and commented that at the time Myra met him, Brady would have been, 'powerfully, almost hypnotically attractive'. Professor Malcolm MacCulloch, Brady's psychiatrist for some years, spoke in similar terms on a television programme: 'Brady is intelligent, tall, charismatic, engaging, interesting to talk to, widely knowledgeable about certain areas of life and extremely self-controlled. He is able to dangle you on a string if he knows that you want to know something about him and he doesn't want you to know – you won't learn what it is you want to know.'

The summer of 1961 had faded. Wind began to whip rain against the office windows and sing through the piles of empty chemical drums out in the yard. The dreaded season of autumn had arrived. In his own copy of E. M. Cioran's *Anathemas and Admirations*, Brady has highlighted a passage which reflected his mood in such a time. 'The last leaves dance, as they fall. It takes a big dose of insensitivity to confront autumn'. Myra Hindley knew nothing then about Ian Brady's fugues but her diary entries record his rapid mood swings and coarser language, which she would come to know as signs of his descent into autumnal madness: 'October 25th, Ian and Tommy had a row. Ian nearly hit Tommy. Ian swearing. He is uncouth. I thought he was going to hit Nellie.' Nellie was Mrs Egerton, the cleaner, who usually received a bottle of port from Brady at Christmas.

The entries continued: 'November 1st, Months now since Ian and I spoke. November 6th, Ian still not speaking. I called him a bigheaded pig. November 28th, I've given up with Ian. He goes out of his way to annoy me, he insults me and deliberately walks in front of me. I have seen the other side of him and that convinces me that he is no good. December 2nd, I hate Ian, he has killed all the love I had for him.'

In her *Guardian* article of December 1995, Myra looked back on her first year in the office at Millwards:

> For almost a year, during which I broke off my engagement, he took virtually no notice of me. It was a year of emotional torture which I'd never experienced before. I went from loving him to hating him, and loving and hating him at the same time. When he smiled at or was nice to me, I felt blessed and floated on air.
>
> I often took my baby cousin out in his pram, and when I discovered where Ian lived, I began taking Michael down the long street he lived in hoping I'd see him and he'd stop to talk to me, but I never did.
>
> I asked one of my friends to come with me to the pub on the corner of his street in the hope that he might be there, but he never was. I'd become utterly obsessed with him, though tried desperately not to show it.

A month before Christmas 1961, Alex and Brady went by car to London. Brady wanted to look over the offices of The Lord's Day Observance Society and its president in order to take revenge for all the miserable Sundays he had suffered in childhood. He intended simply to walk into the office and shoot the man in the head. However, he was diverted from his plan – nurtured for years – when he called in with Alex on a mutual friend. They stayed for two days, devoted almost entirely to sex and alcohol with short bouts of sleep in easy chairs, while the Lord's Day president survived to preside over another miserable Sunday.

Jittery Ed was taken care of by Alex and Brady assumed that Gil would surface again now that he was safe. Gil didn't appear and Brady travelled to Bradford, to his parents' home, to seek him out. They knew nothing of his whereabouts.

It was Christmas. On the day before Christmas Eve Millwards went through the annual ritual of the office party. The staff spent a few hours at the Haxby pub nearby and returned to the office for more drinks. Ian Brady describes the fateful event: 'A couple of typists were dancing in the accounts office and I joined in. I picked up a director's homburg and put it on my head at a jaunty angle. Myra heard the laughter and walked in the office. I had been kissing all the other typists and kissed her too as she walked through the doorway. She snatched the handkerchief from my breast pocket and wiped off lipstick she had planted on my face a few seconds before. For the first time, I realised how large and enticing her eyes were.

'As the staff drifted one by one from the office and into the bitterly cold darkness of the Gorton evening, Myra and I stepped out together. She chatted alongside me as I wheeled my bike into Levenshulme Road. As we walked, the months of abrupt and tense exchanges were suddenly forgotten. I had planned for nothing that evening and asked her out for a drink. She seemed pleased by the invitation and we agreed on details for meeting a few hours later.'

In another letter, Brady compares their meeting to 'the arc of electricity between two electrodes – shades of Frankenstein.' It was the night Manchester died. 'Myra Hindley, do now what you nearly did. Emigrate,' urged Emlyn Williams in *Beyond Belief*.

Ian and Myra met at the Three Arrows pub at the corner of Hyde Road and Church Lane. After a drink they went to the Deansgate cinema and bought tickets for the front circle. The books on the Moors Murders heighten the horror by saying that the first film they saw together was *Judgement at Nuremberg*. It was actually *King of Kings*, about the life of Christ. Brady remembers that they saw Marlon Brando in *The Young Lions* and *The Best Things in Life are Free* at the Deansgate later in their relationship.

As we saw in an earlier chapter, when I described Ian's reaction to *Ben Hur*, his atheism didn't prevent him from enjoying religious epics. During the crucifixion scene in *King of Kings*, Myra nudged Ian to show him that the woman next to her was weeping. Myra had overheard Ian's arguments with a Methodist in the office and wanted to ingratiate herself with Ian on their first date.

They had drinks at the Thatched House after the film before walking back to Gorton. They stopped at the end of Myra's street and Ian noticed its name, Bannock Street. He told her that in Scotland a 'bannock' is an oatcake. He told her too about the Scottish victory over the English at the Battle of Bannockburn. He was also something of an authority on female underwear. They were kissing and his hands were everywhere. Myra was wearing a girdle. Ian told her that they accumulated stale sweat. She never wore one again.

The following evening was Christmas Eve and Ian took Myra to see another film, *El Cid*. It was the second epic in two days. They had drinks before walking back to Gorton. As they approached Bannock Street they heard church bells ringing. Myra told Ian it was Midnight Mass. He was cynical but curious. They followed the sound of the bells and entered a church.

The church was empty apart from three rows of people at the front. Ian and Myra sat in the empty pews at the back. A bottle of whisky in Ian's pocket clanked against the wooden pews and a few of the regulars turned their heads. He felt both anger and pity for the sparse congregation. He was surprised by his empathy for what the Old Testament would call the 'saving remnant', in Gorton of all places! Nietzsche described churches as the tombstones of God. Ian Brady should have felt vindicated.

The priest climbed into the pulpit and intoned his seasonal clichés. After a few sentences, Ian relaxed back into his contempt for organised religion and whispered, 'Richard's himself again.'

As they were leaving the church, Ian called to Myra, 'Hang on!' He was urinating against the church wall. This was *his* sacrament: the outward and visible sign of his own inward and spiritual contempt. Myra couldn't have realised that night just what that contempt would mean. The day before she had written, 'Eureka! Today we have our first date. We are going to the cinema.'

Ian Brady rearranged his dress and walked with Myra Hindley up Gorton Lane to her home in Bannock Street. He described to me what happened next: 'We chatted for a minute or two on the doorstep of number 7 and then Myra asked me in. There was just Myra's grandmother, Mrs Maybury, asleep upstairs. I was accepted on the spot by a ginger-brown dog, Lassie, who gave us both an excited welcome as we stepped into the living room through the front door. I made a fuss of the dog and Myra looked slightly jealous.

'Myra and I sat by the fire chatting and drinking our way through two bottles of wine. With the heady wine and the flush of a possible romance, we were sexually inventive through the small hours.

'It was nearly eight in the morning when I put my clothes on, feeling invigorated in every sense as I invariably did after a night of acrobatic fornication. Our farewells seemed tame and casual in the light of what had happened between us through the night. We were both sexually replete by morning. I stepped into the Christmas early morning air, drawing Gorton into my lungs. It was sheer pleasure to walk the three miles across the city. All was right with the world.

'At home in Westmoreland Street, Peggy and Pat were still in bed so I made a huge fry-up – eggs, bacon and fried bread, all swallowed down by a jug of my preferred sweet, black tea. After consuming everything with relish I dropped on to my bed for a long sleep. It was early evening before I woke up. After a wash and brush up, I told Peggy and Pat that I would see them at breakfast next morning. I went on a pub-crawl around Manchester with a few friends. This was to become a regular weekend ritual for me.'

Myra and Ian arranged the next date for New Year's Eve. They saw a film in the city and, after drinks in a pub, joined the crowds in Albert Square as the midnight chimes welcomed the New Year – 1962.

Ian bought bottles of German wine and whisky for the celebrations in Myra's house in Bannock Street. Shortly after they had walked into number 7, Myra's father, mother, uncle, and aunt joined them. Ian felt that he had been set up for inspection as marriage fodder. It was suffocating. He wanted to breathe Gorton's fresh air.

Myra was sheep-eyed as she listened to Ian telling her father about the thoughts of G K Chesterton. In her diary she wrote: 'Dad and Ian spoke as if they'd known each other for years. Ian is so gentle, he makes me want to cry.'

Thirty years later, I walked through Gorton to see what was left of the streets that had formed the innocent backdrop to that New Year's Eve party. Myra's primary school in Peacock Street and the monastery church of St Francis were still there. I called in the Steelworks Tavern in Gorton Lane and leaned on the same bar where Myra's father drank every day. I ordered a pint of lager and thought of his first encounter with Ian Brady, the new man in his daughter's life. Bob Hindley had been disabled by an accident at work. During the war he had been a paratrooper with the Loyal North Lancashire regiment.

Myra had the Steelworks Tavern in mind when she wrote in prison about her childhood in Gorton: 'Pub closing times were dreaded, because we all knew what would happen. Women ran out into the street, trying to escape from being beaten. All the kids used to jump out of bed and rush outside to try to stop our fathers hurting our mothers, and we were often turned on too.

'My own father – described by Lord Dean of Beswick as being known as "a hard man" – went off to the pub every night, and being a taciturn, bad-tempered man almost always got into a fight (he'd been a boxer in the Army) and staggered home bruised and bleeding.

'I was often sent to the pub to retrieve his jacket, which he'd taken off before fighting; it was the only "good" one he had. When my mother berated him for the state he was in, he began knocking her about, and when I tried to prevent him, I was hit too.

'I disliked him intensely for his violence, drunkenness and the tyrannical way he dominated the household. We were in almost constant conflict, and with hindsight I can see that my sense of family values and relationships were seriously undermined by his influence on me as a child. I have never sought to blame him for anything I did when I was older (it devastated him that his daughter could possibly have done the things I did, and he disowned me) but he was far from being a good role model.

'Through witnessing and being on the receiving end of so much violence within my own family, I was given many lessons in dominance and control, which was probably the foundation stone on which I built my own personality' (*Guardian*, 18 December 1995).

Myra Hindley was about to learn more lessons in dominance and control from someone who made her father look like a mere dabbler. The holidays were over and it was back to the office routine at Millwards. In conversation with me thirty years later, Ian Brady recalled his Christmas fling with the peroxide blonde by drawing from his bottomless pit of quotations: 'The natural rhythm of human life is routine punctuated by orgies.'

Myra, still only nineteen, was a world away from this in her naïve diary entry for 1 January 1962: 'I have been at Millwards for 12 months and only just gone out with him. I hope Ian and I love each other all our lives and get married and are happy ever after.' Writing in the *Guardian* more than thirty years later, Myra reflected on these first few days of her relationship with Ian Brady: 'My whole self became almost totally subsumed. Almost totally, for I secretly didn't believe or agree with everything he said. To confront him with anything, resulted in "silences".'

Ian Brady had different feelings about his first day back: 'I behaved as though nothing had occurred between us. This wasn't difficult. From my point of view, nothing had. Myra should accept that fact or find some loser in pastures new. She could do whatever she wanted; I intended to. There was no chance of my walking blindly into the death trap of marriage and respectability. I had other things on my mind. I was too busy to bother. I made the real money at night. My job at Millwards was a necessary inconvenience.'

Brady was referring to criminal matters: 'Our ambitious plans were still being delayed and threatened by some of the brain-dead among my partners in crime. I was supposed to be everywhere at once. Why couldn't they use their own initiative occasionally and get things done, as they should be, swiftly and efficiently? I was beginning to take too many risks by unconsidered haste to get things going.'

CHAPTER TEN

FIVE-FINGER EXERCISES OVER LAGER & LIME

The year 1962 saw a young David Frost front a new late-night television show *That Was The Week That Was* – an instant success with its biting satire on the high and mighty. It caught the mood of the country and was an iconoclastic breeze in the winds of change that were to characterise the sixties. Teenagers tuned in to the pirate ship Radio Caroline, which broadcast non-stop pop music from its anchorage in the North Sea. New groups were being formed by the week and two of these were to dominate rock music for years – The Beatles and Ian Brady's favourite group, The Rolling Stones.

Brady bought photographic equipment to develop his own films, prints and slides. He was using his small Minolta camera to photograph the movement of money, routes and couriers. He also acquired a small tape recorder for what he called 'sensitive' conversations. Photographs and tapes were easily destroyed. This, at least, was the theory. He could not have been more mistaken.

It was in these early days of his relationship with Myra that Ian Brady discovered Saddleworth Moor, 1,600 feet above sea level and 24 miles across. It occupies some 400 square miles of land between Manchester and Huddersfield. I asked him whether the discovery was accidental. He replied in a letter of February 1993: 'Yes, pure serendipity. Many mornings, in the summer, I'd walk out of the house into the warm sunshine and say, "Bugger the office!" I'd then let the motorbike take me wherever it wished. One such morning I ended up on Saddleworth.'

Brady left his home in Westmoreland Street and drove straight through Ashton-under-Lyne, forgetting that he had visited the market there at thirteen when he was on holiday with Peggy. The road took him through Staleybridge then Mossley. The air was becoming fresher as the houses were thinning out. There was a sign for Greenfield. A few houses to his left nestled in a deep valley. He reached a fork where the road ahead had a sharp gradient, disappearing upward through a green arch of trees. He changed gears, opened the throttle and began the steady rise.

The ascent seemed endless. There were rocky, ragged slopes on the left and a pine forest on the right. Beyond that there was a lake far below. Brady passed a farmhouse and suddenly the whole landscape opened up. Across a deep valley a dark precipice rose to the horizon and the panoramic sweep of the terrain ahead was stark and cold.

The road was still curving upward as he sensed the silence. There were no birds to be heard or trees for them to perch in. As he neared the brow of the hill he passed a rocky knoll on the left, a skyline he and Myra Hindley would come to be identified with forever. He was now on the plateau and could see what the hill had led him to.

There was desolation as far as the eye could see: 'Vast sullen-green low hills and plains, with exposed black and brown earth spots everywhere, undulated under a pallid canopy of brooding silence. I scanned the scene for some sign of human life, but there was nothing to contaminate the sense of utter barrenness. Not a single ship on this sea of wilderness. No trace of gorse, heather or single wild flower to diminish the sense of desolation which pervaded everything.'

Ian Brady drove deeper into this barren landscape and turned off the engine. He was awed by the stillness. His eyes slowly adjusted to the vista and began to recognise its recondite beauty. He could see streams and valleys. He sat astride his Triumph motorbike and lit a cigarette. This was the real world: primeval, fetid, dark. Barbaric beauty.

As the cigarette smoke met the chilled air he had a sense of déjà vu. Brady explained in a letter of February 1993: 'From my childhood on, I've known many moors – Rannoch; Tobermory on the Isle of Mull; the wildernesses of Inverness and Sutherland; and even the other many moors in the north of England. They are all seas of land. And, like seas and mountaintops, are a source of spiritual regeneration. They put the world in perspective – "Regard the world as from the edge of a far star." At first we feel awe and personal insignificance, then gradually the spirit expands in tune with the great vastness and becomes at one with the gestalt, and the rare sense of omnipotence enters the being. We see with the eyes of gods. The more times we act as gods, the more we become as gods are. Nothing religious. Pantheistic and atavistic – or pagan, if you prefer. Would you find this a dangerous doctrine to teach students? I believe everyone experiences such feelings at some time. The unique part is how they interpret and respond to them as individuals. One can laugh with pure delight, or weep in gratitude, or even do both simultaneously.'

Brady stared into the void for some minutes before stepping off his motorbike. He lit another cigarette and walked on to the moor. The earth was moist and acidulous as it yielded underfoot. He knelt down and scooped a handful. He would become familiar with its texture and aroma as he dug into the peat a few feet from a corpse with dead eyes staring at the dark sky.

Brady walked back to his motorbike – 'I descended from the wilderness, from Saddleworth Moor. I felt transformed by its barbaric beauty as I left it behind and glided through the city streets. Life would never be the same.' The words of Milton's *Paradise Lost* drifted through his mind – 'Receive thy new possessor; one who brings a mind not to be changed by place or time' – Satan's words on entering Hell after being banished from Heaven. Perhaps others would have thought of the descent of Satan in W B Yeats' *The Second Coming*:

> Things fall apart; the centre cannot hold
> Mere anarchy is loosed upon the world.

And what rough beast, its hour comes round at last, slouches towards Manchester to be born?

In the plot of Russell T Davies' television play *The Second Coming*, broadcast in the United Kingdom in 2003, a video shop worker believes he is the Son of God and spends his forty days of temptations on Saddleworth Moor.

Writing in *Moving Targets* thirty years after Brady's discovery of Saddleworth Moor, Helen Birch commented; 'Situated on a psychic boundary between civilization and wilderness, the moors, as the locus of murder, are themselves suggestive of the horror and the otherworldly metaphors which the case continues to invoke.'

*   *   *   *   *

Ian and Myra kept a matter-of-fact distance in the office. Brady commented: 'No one in the office knew how involved we were with each other: that we were virtually living together. It wasn't just another romance: another Winter's Tale. I had experienced those before. It wasn't merely that we could rely on each other now. Something beyond that was growing. I hadn't planned it this way, but was happy to let things evolve as they would. It meant that I now had another person I could trust and speak frankly with.'

The Waggon and Horses pub was the setting for their early meetings. They avoided the crowded bar and were usually alone in the snug room at the back. A church steeple looked down on them through the window, giving the tiny room the atmosphere of a confessional. A shaft of sunlight would slant through the window of the snug on summer evenings, casting the steeple into shadowed relief and causing diamonds to dance in their drinks.

I asked Ian Brady if this was the backdrop for the 'brainwashing' of Myra Hindley: 'No, it was more a process of mutual-osmosis, but I had a head start as it were. It wasn't master and slave. It was more like teacher and student. Bit by bit we were moving towards an almost telepathic relationship. I was never conscious of having to exert myself to coerce Myra into accepting my belief in relativist morality. I aired my views for open discussion, nothing more. They were on the table to be rejected or accepted. The universe is boundless. Why shouldn't the individual be the same?'

The above was part of a letter from Brady in January 1993. He repeated the same story to me face to face: 'Myra was surprisingly in tune with me from the very beginning. She was as ruthless as I was. I had no need to force her intellectually, and she didn't have to pretend she was being forced.'

One evening in the snug, as he doodled with beer on the tabletop, Brady put a question to Myra: 'How many people do you really care about and would miss if they died?' She sipped her lager and lime before replying: 'I've never really thought about it. It's hard to say – Gran, my sister Mo, I suppose. Oh, and Mam, of course.' Brady nodded his approval: 'It's the old five-finger exercise. Some people are struggling for names even to reach five, and that speaks for itself. They are fishing for more names because they think they ought to, not because they care. It just looks good that way. Of course there are the fortunate few who can almost reach ten fingers right away.'

'The self-deluded ones come next. They claim to love everybody on the planet! They dilute their milk of human kindness so much that it's like drinking tap water. Try counting your enemies now. There are not enough fingers on your hand!'

They both laughed, eyes bright with shared delight.

The Waggon and Horses was quiet that night and they carried their drinks to the piano in the lounge bar. Brady played a few tunes from his repertoire before the regulars walked in.

Back in the snug, Myra asked Ian what it was like in prison: 'Captivity was useless and boring for most of the inmates without a brain to use or a goal to aim for. Prison wasn't as theatrical as it appears in the movies. But it opened my mind and eyes in a way the powers that be never intended or dreamed of in their wildest nightmares. The whole Borstal period was exciting for me. It was a pure gift. I was never so mentally active – I felt inspired.'

He asked Myra why she gave up religion: 'No special reason particularly. I woke up one morning and I realised I just didn't believe it all any more. I looked around me and none of it made any sense – a heavenly Father up there and the Devil down below. It was all tosh. We are all just grains on the sand. Of no significance whatsoever. And that priest was a bloody pest and a bore. He kept creeping to the house to ask mother, gran and me why we didn't go to confession, why we didn't go to mass any more. I used to dodge out of the way when I saw him coming.'

Ian murmured his approval and joked: 'The heavenly Father *always* answers prayers. He always says *No*!

'When you know it has no meaning, life's much more interesting. I've always distrusted anyone who preaches and tries to convert.' It was dark in the snug by now, but Ian Brady didn't want to switch on the light as he waited for Myra's response. Like secrets, he thrived in the dark.

Myra was silent for a time. She gave Ian a sidelong glance and an enigmatic half-smile before she responded: 'It depresses me to think about the future. My friends will marry and become dreary housewives, pegging away for nothing and ending up in that prison called being a mother. It's a big deal if they are allowed out for a drink and a laugh occasionally. They lose their looks, become overweight and gawk at the telly every night like sacks in front of it. We're all stuck with it: there's no escape.'

Ian replied: 'Not everybody. This is my whole point. We are all free to make a decision. Bovine subservience isn't inevitable. Mediocrity isn't the only realistic goal. Not to decide, is to decide anyway.' He recalled the conversation years later: 'My senses became ultra sensitive. An inner energy flowed freely from me like a mountain stream. The furniture in the snug was etched with liquid electricity. I felt the room inside of me and sensed its texture, the weight of its wood and stone. I had a sensation of being out of myself: mercurial and lighter than air. Words just came to me spontaneously, like words of a dream.'

He continued to expound his creed against ritualistic servility. Myra hung on every word: 'Is it preferable to live for a few moments as a tiger or forever as a sheep? You *are* what you *believe*. The need to be self-aware, to be self-analytical, is fundamental if we want to make our own world, our own microcosm, with its rules, morals and defences against threats from any hostile macrocosm. We are limited only by our imagination. Life's a game, and it's the *natural* laws that count, not the conventional and the artificial.'

For Myra, it was as though Ian's words were etched in tablets of stone and handed down from Sinai to be read in the Waggon and Horses. Brady reflected later: 'When we were together, there was a third entity; something intangible that possessed a power beyond both of us. We were both conscious of the joint momentum developing into an intoxicating, unified force.'

Conversations such as the one just described were clearly in Myra Hindley's mind when, more than a decade later, she reflected on this early period in their relationship: 'Within months he had convinced me that there was no God at all: he could have told me that the earth was flat, the moon was made of green cheese and that the sun rose in the west, and I would have believed him, such was his power of persuasion, his softly convincing means of speech that intrigued me. I could never fully under-stand. I could only grasp the meaning of the odd sentence here and there, believing it to be gospel truth. He became my god, my idol, my object of worship and I worshipped him blindly. I just couldn't say no to him.'

They became more relaxed with each other. Ian's favourite nickname for Myra was Kiddo. He never called her Hessie or Myra Hess, as Jean Ritchie and many other authors have claimed. Myra called him Neddie after the character in the manic radio programme *The Goon Show*. Ian sometimes called her Minnie, after another character in the same show. (I found tapes that Brady had made of *The Goon Show* in the property I inherited from him.)

In the Waggon and Horses, there was a hubbub coming from the lounge bar as Ian said, 'Home, Kiddo?'

They walked back to Bannock street through the redbrick streets and alleys of Gorton and, according to Brady, 'kept kissing so violently that our teeth clashed and blood flowed from our lips to mingle'.

Myra gave a different picture of their love life to Peter Topping: 'He didn't even know how to kiss properly.' She said to someone else that Brady bit her lip in his first few attempts at kissing. Myra didn't know that Ian Brady had mixed saliva and blood through years of kissing his lovers. Jean Ritchie, in her book on Myra Hindley, suggests that he had probably never had a lover with whom to develop a sexual relationship.

In a letter of September 1994, Ian Brady gave me some hints of what he would later relate to me about this stage in his relationship: 'Find me a person who denies that their mind isn't littered with the bodies of their enemies and I'll show you a liar or a lunatic. They doubtless transpose the faces of their enemies on to other people's victims, and thoroughly enjoy the experience.'

By the time they reached number 7 Bannock Street, Myra's gran was upstairs in bed. Ian opened a bottle of red wine. He lit another cigarette from the one he was smoking and, staring into Myra's eyes said, 'Tell me, Kiddo. You, like everybody else, have a special enemy, someone you'd like to eliminate. Who's yours?'

Myra sipped her wine and said, 'Ronnie Sinclair.'

Ian put down his cigarette: 'OK. If he were killed in an accident, you wouldn't suffer any remorse, or would you? You would be elated, wouldn't you? But if someone volunteered to remove him for good, and you complied, how would you feel about your role in his death?'

Myra replied instantly, 'I'd feel nothing. I'd be relieved.'

'Good,' said Ian, 'we're talking about fundamentals now. The average person is on a slow conveyor-belt from complete obscurity to total oblivion. With a bit of luck, they might have one opportunity to step off it. You are at that point. In itself, the crime is nothing to be perturbed about, only the sentence and the odds of being arrested. Some of the cards are on the table. How do you feel now, Kiddo? Are you still in the game or do you want to fold?'

'Include me in! You dare or rot.'

'Excellento! Now I want you to do something for me. Tomorrow night I want you to see a film – *Tunes of Glory* – and retain the ticket stub. Remember what's shown on Pathé newsreel and anything else that's on the bill. Tell me if anything unusual occurs – an incident in the audience or a break in the film, any exception to the routine. I'll meet you outside the cinema when it's finished to collect the ticket stub.'

Myra asked no questions – it would be pointless. She said, 'OK. Will do, Neddie.'

The Tornados were playing 'Telstar' as the man of secrets descended to the rug with Myra Hindley.

CHAPTER ELEVEN

BLACK MUSHROOMS WITH MYRA HINDLEY

I asked Ian Brady whether he thought it was fate that he had met Myra. He said it was pointless to think in that way: 'We did meet!'

I then asked whether they were in love. I half expected him to dismiss the idea as 'romantic tosh', just as he had when talking about Myra's diary entries. What he actually said was, 'Of course we were in love. We wanted to go down together at the trial.'

The socialite Janie Jones, writing about her life in Holloway Prison, put the same questions to Myra and included her answers in *The Devil and Miss Jones*: 'She told me that, oh, he was fantastic-looking, he had confidence, there was something about him that was different from other men and, in her own words, her feeling for him "soon became an obsession".'

Reflecting upon these early days as Brady's girlfriend, Myra wrote: 'Although I saw him almost every day at work and every Saturday, with just on occasional week-night thrown in at first, for most of my free time he just wasn't available. He didn't volunteer much information about his private life. Because our relationship was new and very unsure, I was afraid to do or say anything which might jeopardise it, so I stifled my curiosity and accepted what little information he volunteered.'

But things were about to change. Ian's relationship with Myra was intruding upon his other career of planning robberies and maintaining contacts in other cities. Ian commented on this in a letter to me: 'Among the various separate compartments of my life; the one Myra occupied was encroaching on the time I had, in the past, assigned to others. Black mushrooms were growing and flourishing in my mind in Myra's company which filled most of the waking hours. Dark preoccupations, luring me to take the path of pure existentialism, in which the will to dare all, and suffer the consequences, was becoming all-important rather than the acquisition of cash from my evening criminal exploits.

'Was I mad already? If so, it was catching – Myra was a soul mate. We were pushing the limits. I had no need to coerce her intellectually, and she didn't have to pretend she was being driven. You either form an eclectic philosophy of your own making or are tyrannized by the less permissive tastes of others. The path beyond good and evil provides its own integrity and rationale.

'I made sure that Myra understood that we were both still individuals, free to indulge as we wished. Extra-sexual activity wouldn't sap the strength of our personal relationship, no more than would the whimsical preference for a different kind of wine. We laughed together as we exchanged details of our excursions into irregular sex.'

Several writers have claimed that Myra was the victim of the condition known as *folie à deux* – 'the madness of two'. That is, Brady's madness was contagious and Myra Hindley caught the disease. The passage I have just quoted could be regarded as firm evidence for a case of *folie à deux*. However, Brady always dismissed this diagnosis out of hand whenever I raised the subject. He acknowledged that, in a very obvious and weak sense, '*folie à deux* occurs in most normal love affairs, where two individuals unconsciously begin to share and combine their tastes and beliefs and gradually behave as one entity, an almost telepathetic communion of minds taking place between them.'

It may be true to say that, from a perspective based on years of hindsight, there was a philosophical and spiritual form of *folie à deux* when the two worlds of Ian Brady and Myra Hindley melted into each other, in the Polish writer Stanislaw Lec's sense: 'Our separate fictions add up to joint reality.'

When Myra Hindley lodged her parole appeal to the then Home Secretary Jack Straw in 1997, Brady wrote a letter to the BBC to 'clarify certain points': 'First accept the determinant. Myra Hindley and I once loved each other. We were a unified force, not two conflicting entities. The relationship was not based on the delusional concept of *folie à deux*, but on a conscious/subconscious emotional and psychological affinity . . . Apart our futures would have taken radically divergent courses.'

Writing to Janie Jones from prison, Myra recalled her early days with Brady and spoke of 'a pleasant sense of permanency' that had settled into their relationship. If the weather was mild they went for motorbike rides through the empty streets in the early hours as Manchester slept. If it was cold or wet they stayed in Myra's house in Bannock Street, drinking wine and listening to music in front of the coal fire. Chubby Checker's hit 'Let's Twist Again' was on the radio all the time. It entered the charts and re-entered three more times over a year, although it never became number one. It was re-released more than ten years later and evoked memories in at least two prison cells.

Myra bought a tape recorder. Anyone who possessed one at that time would know that it was a bulky item of furniture. It was just like Ian's. Myra's education in classical music could now begin. Ian Brady introduced her to Berlioz, Stravinsky, Wagner and Tchaikovsky. They both enjoyed Berlioz's *Symphonie Fantastique* and Wagner's *Twilight of the Gods*. Brady explained to Myra that music, played in the mind at moments of stress, could induce demonical energy – as in the inexorable *Agnus Dei* motif or *Carmina Burana*.

Early in January 1993, the video of the film *The Silence of the Lambs* was released and I sent a copy to Ian Brady. He wrote back to me, giving his reflections. However, it wasn't until a conversation a few weeks later that he mentioned the scene in the film when Dr Hannibal Lecter pauses before escaping from his cage to conduct with his hands the classical music coming from a small tape recorder. Brady said, 'A psychopath would never do that. He would be alert to the immediate threat of capture.'

Ian Brady also introduced Myra to the world of books. He recommended the existentialists first of all: Camus and Sartre. Dostoevsky was his favourite, but she had trouble with the patronymics of Russian literature. He took her to see the film version of *Richard III* starring Olivier. Myra had little interest in Dickens but was aroused by the pantheism of Wordsworth's poetry. She sent the complete works of Wordsworth to Brady after they had been in prison for a year.

Myra also responded to the books of Machiavelli, de Sade and Nietzsche. Colin Wilson's *The Outsider* was required reading with its treatment of modern and classical literature. Colin Wilson appears later in our story.

If Ian Brady is to be believed, he and Myra were voracious readers. They had tickets to four public libraries, including the massive Manchester Central.

Brady and Myra Hindley were drawing ever closer, bound together by their nihilism. As Brady put it: 'We had a motto – "Live fast, die young".

We accepted gladly the indifference of the universe.' They agreed that, by virtue of birth and upbringing, the only power the less fortunate could aspire to rested upon their personal will, and that morals were something only the rich could afford. But Ian Brady did have a virtue that transcended all circumstances – keeping one's word to those one trusted. Myra was left in no doubt about it. If the trusted party broke their word, they should be destroyed by every available means. He added weight to his point by telling Myra the Parable of Mektoub, a Turkish master wrestler.

Mektoub taught a student three hundred holds with which to defeat an opponent. In the course of time, the student became arrogantly confident and challenged Mektoub to a bout. Mektoub easily defeated the student with a particular hold. The student complained angrily, 'You never taught me that hold!' Mektoub solemnly replied. 'Just because I loved and trusted you, did you take me for a complete fool?'

I asked Brady whether Myra knew that he had a move in reserve: 'She did, but she didn't think I would use it. In fact, I had many moves in store.' He reflected later: 'If caught, it is only human for the pupil to blame the master for his criminal conduct. Should the criminal enterprises succeed, believe me, from wide personal experience, the pupil's enthusiasm and devotion to criminal activities can outdo that of the master like that of a convert.'

Ian Brady raised the question of Ronnie Sinclair with Myra: 'Do you still want to see him dead?

'I do,' said Myra. 'I gave him his ring back.' Myra's reply made Ian wonder why she still bore so much malice. He asked her whether she wanted to be there when Sinclair was murdered. 'Yes! But I want to watch him being humiliated before he dies.' Ian asked if she had anything particular in mind.

Myra giggled and said, 'I'd love to see him treated like a woman. Believe me, Neddie! Now that would be compulsive viewing.' Ian said, 'Spell it out, Kiddo. Don't mince your words.'

Myra made the high-pitched, excited 'Zzzeee!' sound that she always made when she realised that Ian was pulling her leg or to show her approval. Ian asked her whether she would like to finish him off herself. Myra said she wouldn't mind but would prefer to watch and savour the scene.

Brady told me that the subtle cruelty of Myra's requests on this occasion surprised him, and that it wasn't to be the last time. He picked up his German binoculars and walked with Myra out of number 7 Bannock Street on to the nearby playing field. He trained the binoculars towards Dalkeith

Street where Ronnie Sinclair lived. It was a mild, beautiful evening and Ian said they would go out for a run on the bike while the sun lasted. He knew where they were going.

They left Manchester's streets behind and followed the route that would become so familiar, through Staleybridge, Mossley and Greenfield. They dropped into lower gear for the long ascent through the arch of trees to the plateau before switching off the engine. The sun was setting and the air became cooler. A thin mist was developing on Saddleworth Moor.

The only sound was the ticking of the engine as it cooled. Ian lit a cigarette while Myra took in the brooding vastness: 'It's powerful, Neddie. Beautiful but spooky.' Ian revved the engine and said, 'Do you think Ronnie would like to spend eternity here?' Myra, on the pillion, put her arms around Ian's waist and replied, 'We agree on everything these days, Neddie.'

Brady told me that as they dropped down through the mists towards civilization, he was singing a few verses of Cole Porter's 'Anything Goes'. The lyrics could hardly be more appropriate.

Myra was trying to make herself heard through Ian's crash helmet: 'Neddie, I want him to be terrified, to know he's going to die.'

Ian shouted into the wind. 'What do you mean?' Myra shouted in reply, 'I want him to know that he's going to die just before he's murdered.' Ian shouted back, 'No! No chance!'

Myra asked why. Ian shouted, 'Forget why!' and broke into song again: 'Hi-ho hi-ho, it's down to work we go!' Myra said, 'Neddie! Call me Snow White! "Some day my prince will come" . . .' Ian shouted back, 'You can count on it, Kiddo! Several times tonight!' In no time they were riding through the bright lights of the city.

Beyond Manchester, the eyes of the world were focused on Cuba. John F Kennedy had blockaded Cuba and ordered Khrushchev to withdraw Russian missiles from the island. Russian ships were heading for Cuba and millions held their breath. Nuclear war ceased to be an abstraction. Ian Brady looked forward to seeing the end of the world in glorious black and white: 'I was detached from the whole thing. I was merely curious. I sat in front of the television with several packets of cigarettes and a bottle of Drambuie. Who cares if a nuclear war erupts? The common man could have no part in the scenario – apart from being a powerless victim of it. He could only sit back and enjoy the fireworks of the seemingly inevitable apocalypse. Only the rich and mighty would be in dread at the prospect of seeing their chattels of wealth, immunity and power going skywards in a mushroom cloud. I actually relished the spectre of the whole planet having to start again from scratch. The new game-rules – the fittest survive – held no terrors for me.

'Every man for himself. I was restless for the denouement to commence. But it all turned out to be a damp squib. The whole saga had been a bore. Endless words and posturing for nothing.'

Ian Brady took Myra back to Saddleworth Moor: 'The sunlight on the moors gave the whole landscape a pearl-like, blue, eerie lustre. The evening was at the mid-point, the fleeting moment between the fading day and approaching darkness. The human world cast no light or shadows on this primordial domain, which seemed to welcome the rising of dreary, nebulous phenomena from the sodden, dark moor. Malevolence incarnate was stalking us, drawing ever closer as it drifted imperceptively through the concealed undulations of its feral habitat, stalking us. It's there! But it was ourselves we saw swaying towards us.'

As usual, Brady took the precaution of discussing criminal matters out of doors or in a room with the radio on. Walls have ears. In the cool air of the moors he told Myra that the murder of Ronnie Sinclair would have to look like an accident, unless a third party did it. As the new love in Myra's life, Ian would become an obvious suspect who may have acted out of retrospective jealousy. In any case, he had a criminal record. Eliminating any connecting thread with the victim was an elementary principle of his criminal psychology.

During their walk on the moors, Brady drilled into Myra something we have heard before – always overestimate the opposition. As their footsteps on the gravel broke the silence, Ian mentioned the Brontë novels, *Wuthering Heights* and *Jane Eyre*, inspired by the barbaric landscape of the moors around Haworth. He told Myra about being taken by Peggy to see Laurence Olivier and Merle Oberon in the film version of *Wuthering Heights*. He broke off the conversation and told Myra he wanted to get an early night to be up in the morning and take a closer look at Ronnie Sinclair. Myra showed her approval with a 'Zzzeee!'

As I mentioned earlier in this book, Brady told me in detail, during my first visit to him, how he planned the murder of Ronnie Sinclair. He added to his account over the years. What follows is a distillation of what I learned.

The alarm clock roused Ian Brady from his fitful slumbers in Longsight at 5 a.m. It was still dark. He gulped down his usual breakfast of raw eggs in milk. He tried not to wake up Peggy as he closed the front door and stepped into the deserted street: 'I climbed the iron railings into the dark playing field. Down the embankment, across the rails and up the other side to the fence made of sleepers. I had arrived well before the time Sinclair normally left for work. I had a view of the street through a convenient gap. I smoked my way through half a packet of cigarettes while I waited for some sign of movement. I heard the sound of a door opening. I listened to hear the door shut and saw Ronnie Sinclair step into the street. He was a shadow under the dim street lighting at the far end of the street. Ronnie took a left turn. There was no one else about. I vaulted the fence and followed him, keeping my distance.

'At the end of this long street he turned left towards Hyde Road and walked over to a bus stop right outside the Lake Hotel. I kept myself inconspicuous in the vicinity and cupped my lighter under my coat to light another cigarette. He stepped on to a bus and I followed him upstairs. We travelled into the centre of Manchester and out again. I sat behind him. He was weedy and a couple of inches shorter than my six foot. He had dark hair and looked to be in his early twenties.

'We were somewhere in the Cheetham area when he left the bus with me a dozen paces behind. He crossed the road and walked into a side street. At the end of it he crossed a broad expanse of waste ground surrounded by streetlights. He opened the door of a building and slipped inside. I ended my stalking in the centre of the waste ground and could see that the houses surrounding it were too distant from where I was standing to present a threat. I turned round and saw a row of pre-fabricated concrete lock-up garages. This open ground would be an ideal place to commit murder.

'I made a note of the street names that had led me there as I retraced my steps to the bus stop before catching a bus which took me back into the city centre.'

Ian went back to Peggy and Pat Brady's house in Westmoreland Street rather than to Myra in Bannock Street. Peggy and Pat had left for work and, with a cup of coffee and a cigarette, Ian thought through the plan to murder Ronnie Sinclair: 'I felt no hatred towards him. He was simply the target in an exercise, a problem to be solved.' Ian Brady wasn't planning premeditated cruelty, killing him slowly, as he might with a police informer.

It was a job for Alex. A stolen car without lights could drive at speed on to the waste area from between the lock-up garages and hit Sinclair from behind before he was aware of any danger. To divert any suspicion, Ian Brady would make sure that he was at work in the office at Millwards. He gulped down another couple of raw eggs in a pint of milk and left for work.

By mid-morning Brady had cleared the day's mail and had finished dictating letters to Myra. He took her into the small typing office and gave her a brief account of what he had learned about Ronnie Sinclair's movements and a possible plan for his murder. Ian made no mention of Alex's possible contribution. Myra didn't belong to that compartment of his life. Brady told me that his life at this period was divided into five compartments: the Sloan family in Glasgow; his family in Manchester; work at the office; life with Myra and his life with fellow criminals.

Brady reasoned that in loving someone you might be arming a future enemy. He was actually beginning to feel sorry for Ronnie Sinclair, who was 'blind to the unforeseen perils of love turned sour, and of solicitous Death hovering above his head, waiting to slaughter a charming delusion by an inexorable truth.'

The evening was mild. Ian and Myra were at a loose end with nothing to do and decided to drive up to an inn on the moors, little knowing that Death would issue them with a gentle reminder of their own mortality on their return. The inn was well into the moors before the road dropped into Holmfirth, where the long-running television series *The Last of the Summer Wine* was filmed. It had an open fire surrounded by horse-brasses and copper ornaments: 'There was a St Bernard dog as big as a lion, lying full length on the carpet in front of the fire. The lounge was empty. The poor dog had to suffer our attention, with Myra and me stroking it.' More than twenty years later, in the course of the reopening of the Moors Murders investigation, Ian Brady reminisced about the evening and was upset when Inspector Topping told him that the stone-built inn had been destroyed.

After a few drinks, Ian and Myra climbed on the motorbike and headed back to Manchester. They were cruising along Hyde Road well within the speed limit and began to overtake a bus. The bus suddenly started to turn right and Ian was forced to turn across the road to avoid a collision. The bike missed the oncoming traffic, mounted the pavement and ran into the fence that circled the Bell Vue car park. It came to rest at the feet of two uniformed policemen.

Ian was unconscious for a few seconds before righting the bike and declining the policemen's offer of help. He wanted to leave the scene as quickly as possible. He wasn't drunk, but the police may have thought so from the alcohol on his breath. Ian thought he had escaped injury but one

of the policemen pointed to the blood streaming from his right leg. The
other policeman had already phoned for an ambulance.

Until she climbed into the ambulance with him, Ian hadn't realised that
he had hit a woman. His goggles were in pieces and the right side of his
crash helmet was torn. He had a V-shaped cut under his nose and received
five stitches in his knee. Myra didn't have a scratch on her. Ian had
contravened two laws – he was a learner driver without 'L' plates and was
carrying a pillion passenger.

Back in Bannock Street, Ian and Myra celebrated their escape from
serious injury with sex on the rug as Mrs Maybury slept soundly upstairs.
The plaster on Ian's leg caused him to limp for a few weeks with curious
side-effects. During that period he was approached by no fewer than four
girls, all complete strangers. The limp obviously evoked their motherly
instincts. In successive weeks he took each one out for a drink in the
Cheshire Cheese, a pub at the rear of the black glass *Daily Express*
building in Ancoats Lane.

Autumn had descended on Manchester and seeped into the subconscious of Ian Brady: 'I was drifting into a fugue without being conscious
of it. It was a prolonged period in which I would live a life within a life,
one completely discontinuous with my day-to-day, ordinary existence.
While in the fugue, I had no memory of the familiar patterns and my usual
haunts. Whenever I emerged from this state, I could remember nothing of
what had happened while I had been in it. I had no idea whether I had been
Jekyll or Hyde. Occasionally, perturbing images would drift through my
normal waking mind and dismay me by their vividness.

'One of my recollections before succumbing to the fugue was standing
in a courtroom charged with a driving offence. I paid a small fine. I
passed my driving test soon afterwards and tore up the "L" plates there
and then.

'As strange as it may seem, I later regarded this trivial action as a
symbolic, ritualistic entrance into a new stage in my life where I felt
justifiably arrogant in my use of what knowledge I had gained. I was
intoxicated and felt inspired whenever I had a sudden, original insight
into the familiar. The *black light* suffused omnipotence through my
being until I saw my skin glow in the dark. I was delirious with joy when
– in the rapture of the *black light* – I gazed in silence at my skin,
luminous in the darkness.

'Was I mad? Who wants to live a life as sober as a judge? What a bore!
Why long for your soul to be saved when you can spend it? William Blake

knew it: "Energy is Eternal delight" [*The Marriage of Heaven and Hell*].'
Brady's colleagues at Millwards were to catch a glimpse of the effects of
the autumnal fugue.

He was enraged by something a clerk had said and had faced up to him
in front of colleagues in the invoice department. After a string of
expletives, Ian grabbed him by the throat and dug his fingers into the
man's carotid artery. The clerk's eyes began to lose focus and his face
turned purple. They fell to the floor with Ian still strangling him. A
pushbike, which happened to be leaning against the office wall, toppled on
top of the two of them. The farce of the situation snapped Ian out of his
insane trance and he burst into laughter. He helped the terrified man to his
feet and treated him to a drink after work.

Brady discovered that he had visited Bradford and Leeds without
knowing why or what he had done there. As usual, he concealed the fact
that he had no recollection and asked oblique questions about his visits.
Brady had also been to Glasgow again without letting the family know. He
had a vague recollection that he had been to his favourite high point, the
Eastern Necropolis, to look down over the river Clyde and the city. As far
as he could recall, he had been in a peaceful state of mind. This was far
from the case with another incident that occurred during the fugue.

This incident was, if we are to believe him, the first of the 'happenings'
– murders, as we have already acknowledged, committed in a rage rather
than the five known Moors Murders that, to Brady, tested the will. He
claimed to have a vivid vision of having bodily picked up a woman and
thrown her over the parapet wall into the Rochdale canal in Sackville
Street, near the Rembrandt pub in Manchester.

He had been drinking heavily. Brady first mentioned this killing, one of
five 'happenings', to Peter Topping during the reopening of investigations
into the Moors Murders that began in 1985. Brady claimed that much later,
having no sense of passing time, he ran a check on the incident and
discovered that a woman had been found dead in a canal with a bruise on
her head. The coroner pronounced it as suicide, despite the fact that there
was no suicide note. Brady wrote 'cover up' in the margin of his copy of
Topping's book on the Moors case.

Brady told Topping that he was in a relationship with Myra at the time
of the killing. Topping looked into the alleged incident and confirmed that
a body had been found but that this had happened two months *before*
Brady started going out with Myra Hindley. Topping himself concluded
that Brady's claims about the extra murders were explained by his mental

condition or by his attempts to engineer visits to Saddleworth Moor and Scotland, places that held especially potent memories for him.

Ian Brady was slowly finding his equilibrium. His mental state at this time was a form of what American psychiatrists describe as a 'dissociative fugue', an inability to remember one's recent past: 'Gradually emerging from a fugue can be weird and disturbing when you realize that some part of your life has taken place without leaving clear memories of it in the conscious mind. At a later time, the unconscious sometimes releases transient, phantom images of what has occurred in the blank period.

'Some of these fleeting images eventually made me realise that I had been evading and neglecting Myra for some time. I'd been completely ignoring her existence, as though she had no part in my world.

'I didn't intend to admit to her that I had been through a period of memory loss. In this case, as with the times when it had happened before, I found a way of asking oblique questions to elicit responses from people in which they assumed they were only saying things I was already aware of. I used this tactic to resurrect and nurture the intimate relationship I shared with Myra before the latest fugue.

'I chose what I thought to be the right moment and picked her up from Bannock Street. I drove out to a small pub we had visited a few times before. It was just beyond Whitefield golf course. It was packed when we arrived. I rode farther on and turned the engine off some distance away. It was very dark and I left the bike's headlight on. Myra and I talked for some time and I eventually came to the real question. Did she want us to carry on together, as we had been some months before? She said she did. I said, "Fine, Kiddo. We carry on. Richard's himself again!" Myra said she was glad I was!

'From this inconsequential exchange of words the seeds of catastrophic ignominy were sown. Later the same evening, we had a drink in a favourite pub and went back to number 7 Bannock Street as though there had been no glitch in our relationship.'

'We made up for lost time. The office was empty at lunchtime and I made love to Myra on her desk, my own desk and then the director's; in that order.'

Myra Hindley told Inspector Topping about her conversation with Ian Brady near Whitefield golf course. About nine months before she broke off contact with him in captivity, Myra received a letter from him in which he said that he sensed she was drifting away from him. In the letter, Brady asked Myra if she remembered the question he put to her, when – after a week of not speaking to each other – he had given her a note asking her to meet him that night. He was now asking the question again. According to Myra, he threatened to kill himself if she decided to break with him.

I put this to Ian Brady and he replied, as I suspected he would: 'She flatters herself.'

Myra realised that this was emotional blackmail, but wrote back to say that she wanted to continue. She told Topping that she felt sorry for Ian because he had no one else in the world, whereas she had friends who were giving her their quiet support.

Ian Brady's contacts in other cities were puzzled that they had not heard from him for some months and assumed that he had been arrested. When he did make contact he did not, of course, mention the fugue but simply said that he had been busy. He re-established contact with Alex and the two of them travelled south to Birmingham to do a job. Brady, however, was still obsessed with his second 'Holy Grail', the wages car with a boot full of money. He feared that he might bungle the robbery and worried over the prospect that someone might get there first. He needed it as a goal to work for: the big prize that would free him from the drudgery of the office. He observed the bank from time to time to check whether procedures were unchanged. Meanwhile, his mind turned to alternative ways of making money.

The early 1960s were still the days of strict censorship and pornography was a lucrative racket. Brady realised that there were ways of offering totally innocent material to suckers, who paid money thinking that they were getting the real thing. They would hardly complain to the police that they were expecting obscene photographs for their money. Genuine pornography sold for a much higher price, but the risk of detection was correspondingly higher.

Brady took his photographic equipment round to Myra's house in Bannock Street and waited for her grandmother to go to bed. He covered the furniture with white sheets to prevent identification and set up floodlights. He and Myra stripped and wore only white hoods with eye-slits. Brady put the camera on a tripod and set the delayed timer. There were thirty photographs in all. Thirteen of them show Brady and Myra in the normal sex act. Myra appears in various poses on twelve of the prints. In some she is kneeling, in others she is lighting a cigarette. One shows her face down with lines on her buttocks.

Part of a knotted whip appears in one picture and was presumably there to show that it had been used to make the marks. Brady appears alone on the remaining five photographs and seems to be urinating against a curtain on one of them. A page from a picture newspaper has been inadvertently caught in the frame on one print and, with a magnifying glass, can be dated to some time in May 1963.

Before taking the photographs, Ian Brady had established outlets in two bookshops, both of which, he claims, were paying protection money to the police. In the course of his research, he was amazed to discover the money that could be made by outlets loaning banned books for short periods. Supplies were bought from the Olympia Press in Paris and smuggled into Britain at the bottom of crates filled with harmless books. The unexpurgated edition of the Marquis de Sade's *Justine* was in several volumes and loaned in their plain green covers for five pounds each.

Virtually all writers on the Moors Murders, as I implied earlier, swallow the dogma that the writings of the Marquis de Sade had a decisive, catastrophic influence on Ian Brady. From the beginning, this idea was at the core of the holy writ on the case, as though de Sade's writings in some way precipitated the murders. When the subject arose in our conversations, Brady always dismissed this view as 'nonsense'. On one occasion, he mentioned that the prosecuting Attorney General argued that the Marquis de Sade was a major influence in the murders. He added: 'He was talking nonsense like all of the others. By implication, he could just as readily have blamed Shakespeare's *Richard III* – a book I read at school!' The Marquis de Sade was a nihilist as far as life's purpose and meaning is concerned; but so are thousands of philosophers, scientists and intellectuals of all varieties, not to mention the person sipping lager and lime in the pub on the corner.

In the same breath that Ian Brady ruled out the significance of the Marquis de Sade for the Moors Murders, he said that practically all the great authors had read de Sade, particularly the existentialists – Dostoevsky, Camus and Sartre. In a letter to me, Brady commented on de Sade: 'Few people had heard of him in the early sixties. Even fewer realised that the term "sadism" had its derivation from de Sade's name and teachings. This was all changed in the wake of our trial at Chester in 1966, when the prosecuting Attorney General, Sir Elwyn Jones, in attacking us, unintentionally made de Sade a household name and generated an international regeneration of his works in books and films. Geoffrey Rush played de Sade in the latest film interpretation, *Quills*.

'It is not the repetitive, turgid pornography in de Sade's books that are believed to be dangerous and corrupting by the censors and rulers of the status quo. Rather, it was his ideas, pushing existentialism, nihilism and relativism to that tightrope between sanity and madness. His writings have been perennial since the eighteenth century for this reason. As for his pornography itself, I was bored rigid by it.'

As I sorted through Ian Brady's property, I came across two volumes by the Marquis de Sade. One was the complete American edition of *Juliette* and the other, a composite book, *Justine, Philosophy in the Bedroom, and Other Writings*. The signatures and dedications in the front of the books show that Colin Wilson had sent them to Ian Brady.

In her conversations with Peter Topping, Myra Hindley distanced herself from the 'pornography' Brady and David Smith read. Ian Brady said to me that, on the contrary, she bought some pornographic books herself from a porn dealer.

Pamela Hansford Johnson attended the Moors trial and made much of the pornographic dimension to the case in her book *On Iniquity*. She claimed to be discussing censorship with the gloves off and saw the Moors case not as an isolated incident, 'but like a septic wound that burst in the entire body of our society'.

Brady's photographs of his victims and their graves put him clearly in the realm of hard pornography of the most depraved kind. The photographs he took of himself and Myra in number 7 Bannock Street are weak tea by contemporary standards. Much stronger material can be bought at the corner shop, and explicit sexual acts are piped by the hour into living rooms on television channels.

Myra Hindley talked to Topping about the photographic session in Bannock Street. As we should expect, her version is very different from Ian Brady's. She said that Brady came round to her house one night with a Cinzano bottle filled with his own home-brewed wine. Myra claimed to have got very drunk and to have been reduced to semiconsciousness. She could recall only flashing lights and pain before she woke up the following morning feeling quite ill.

According to Myra, Brady saw her the following evening and admitted that he had drugged her by putting a couple of her grandmother's sleeping pills in the wine. He said that his dog, Bruce, was old and going blind and that he wanted to put it to sleep himself with sleeping capsules. He had tried them out first on Myra to test their strength, knowing that they could not possibly kill her.

Myra went on to tell Topping that she only realised that Brady had been taking photographs of her a few weeks later when he told her he wanted her assistance in committing the 'perfect murder'. She said she was appalled but Brady had produced pornographic photographs of her, threatening to show them to her family and staff in Millwards office if she didn't help him. She then realised what the flashing lights were.

Topping was sceptical and thought that Myra was attempting to excuse her subsequent behaviour by blaming it on Brady's attempt to blackmail her. The detective kept his suspicions to himself. Myra's account is certainly at odds with what I learned from Ian Brady. He dismissed her version as fanciful. After all, the photographs would condemn him as much as Myra.

In September 1998, Ian Brady sent me a copy of the four-page letter he had written to Home Secretary Jack Straw in response to one of Myra Hindley's bids for release. In the letter Brady wrote that the 'whip marks' in the photographs that Myra claimed were proof of the beatings he had given her were actually drawn with lipstick.

In her interviews with Inspector Topping, Myra said that she wanted to tell him about two incidents that had happened at about the same time of year as the photographic session. They both concerned her grandmother. In the first, Brady had threatened Myra that he would push her grand-mother downstairs and told her that people would assume it was an accident because of her age. Myra said that her grandmother was the person to whom she felt closest to in the world.

The second incident happened one morning when she took her grandmother a cup of tea in bed and was unable to wake her. Myra fetched her mother from nearby and she couldn't wake her either. A doctor was called and diagnosed a double dose of sleeping pills. Myra claimed that Brady later admitted he had put the double dose in her grandmother's bedtime drink. Myra believed that he was capable of doing worse to her grandmother if she didn't help with his plans.

Ian Brady denied all of this in conversations with me. In response, he mentioned a letter that had survived and shows how Myra was at least involved in the criminal side of his life. It was a letter that was found in one of the suitcases recovered from Manchester railway station after their arrest and was an exhibit at the trial. It is addressed to Miss M Hindley and dated 16 April 1963. This places it just before the photographic session: 'I have sprained my ankle . . . Let's capitalize on the situation. I shall grasp this opportunity to view the investment establishment situated at Stockport Road next Friday. I will contact you before then to give other details.'

This clearly refers to the intention to commit a robbery and fits into a pattern of criminality that has been traced through the pages of this book. Under cross-examination at the trial he claimed that the letter was part of an innocent plan to buy a second-hand car. Brady admitted to me that he was lying and that the whole court could see that he was.

Sometime during Brady's neglect of her during his fugue, Myra had applied for a job in the NAFFI in Germany. She had seen an advertisement for cafeteria and clerical workers. Her application was taken up after Brady had emerged from his fugue, but she decided to travel to London for an interview anyway. Myra was offered a two-year contract, provided she had some dental work done. She would have to be available to fly out in a couple of weeks.

When she arrived back in Manchester she could see Brady waiting on the station platform. They went back to Bannock Street, where her grand-mother, sister and mother were waiting for her, even though it was late. They were upset when they realised Myra was all set to go to Germany. But it wasn't to be. In her conversations with Topping, Myra said that although she wanted to get away from Brady, she couldn't bear to leave her family. She turned down the job. Brady simply said to me that her application came to nothing.

The prospect of a new job for Myra gave Ian Brady pause for thought. Myra could apply to join the police: 'She had no criminal record and could pass the Neanderthal entrance examination with ease. We discussed the possibilities for access to inside information which could be useful to us; movement of money, for example. But my intuition intervened and I had second thoughts about the idea. Myra had an interview with a police-woman, who recognised Myra when we were eventually arrested.'

It was June 1963. Myra's sister Maureen joined the office staff at Millwards as a filing clerk. She would stay there for a year. June was also the month that Ian Brady moved into Myra's house virtually full time.

One Saturday, Myra and Ian drove across the Pennines to Bradford in another attempt to locate the missing Gil Deare. The wind almost blew the motorbike off the road as they travelled over the moors. Ian didn't want to draw attention to himself in case Gil's disappearance had been reported to the police. Myra went to his house to make enquiries and posed as a former girlfriend. His family had no idea of his whereabouts. Ian and Myra made the most of a bright day by sunbathing in a meadow as they watched a lark circling above them.

If we are to believe Rena Duffy, Myra had a different view on that visit to Bradford and the fate of Gil Deare. Duffy's story appeared in the *People* on 23 November 1986 after she had been released from Cookham Wood, Kent. Myra told her that when she called on Deare's parents they referred her to his sister, who lived nearby. Myra gave her the Bannock Street address in case she heard anything about her absent brother.

Gil's sister sent Myra a letter a fortnight later saying that there was no news. After reading the letter she resealed it and the same night gave it to Brady in a cinema. He took it to the toilet and returned in a furious mood, accusing her of opening the letter. Myra admitted that she had read it and Brady didn't speak to her for a week. Brady told me that he had done nothing of the kind.

Myra is alleged to have said to Rena Duffy, 'I think, now, that he had already murdered that boy, and he just wanted to know the family's reaction.' Ian Brady told me that this was nonsense and that Gil Deare had been killed and found in a reservoir near Sheffield some time after the Moors trial.

In her book *Myra Hindley – Inside the Mind of a Murderess*, Jean Ritchie claims that Deare had continued his life of crime in London and died there an alcoholic. She doesn't say how she knows this. Brady had read Ritchie's book and said to me, 'The word was that Gil had become an alcoholic. Alex had a penchant for using water as a clean method of disposal. He would have viewed loose, drunken talk as a danger to his liberty. Too bad. I really liked and trusted Gil, but we choose the ideals which suit us.'

A few weeks after visiting Bradford, Brady went alone to see Alex to discuss the elimination of Ronnie Sinclair. He didn't offer a reason for the murder. Alex was puzzled. He hadn't heard Brady mention the victim's name before. Alex was told there was no urgency and that the job could be done at his own convenience.

Ian and Myra were driving into the country more often now. They relaxed and cooled bottles of wine in streams and waterfalls. Brady comments: 'The callous power and indifference of the moors and sea put life in perspective, blowing away the shabby tinsel of civilisation. Innocence is lack of self-consciousness. The gregarious seek to hide from themselves in the clamour of the crowds, the sweaty comfort of mediocrity. The mob is humanity at its worst.'

Having introduced Myra to classical music and the great books, Ian Brady now concentrated upon her appearance. To quote one of Brady's common sayings: 'Elegance springs from simplicity, a designed indifference.' He tactfully commented to Myra that her peroxide hair didn't do justice to her complexion. In fact, he detested her brash hairstyle. Apart from anything else, it made her too conspicuous for their future activities. By drawing attention to herself, she attracted attention to Brady himself.

Brady diplomatically suggested she try an urchin style in honey-blonde. Myra took the hint and her hairdresser told her that a new colour would have to be done in stages. After the first stage, Myra emerged from Maison Laurette in Taylor Street, Gorton with a pink rinse, duly cut in urchin style.

Myra didn't like the result and made sure that her crash helmet was already on when Brady called to pick her up later the same evening. After much persuasion, she revealed the 'new Myra' to her relieved lover. Brady liked it. He commented that they had the wildest sex they had ever had in Bannock Street after their night out: 'A woman should change her hairstyle occasionally to seduce her partner into thinking that he is being unfaithful or committing adultery.'

The following day Ian and Myra went to Bollington and soaked up the sun in a lush meadow. Ian wanted some photographs of Myra and her new hairstyle. She was lying with her eyes closed, listening to The Beatles singing 'From Me to You' on the transistor radio. As the shutter clicked, she opened one eye. She then took a shot of Ian balancing a beer mug on his head. A few cows gazed at the pair of them. By 2003 the *Daily Mirror* was offering this particular photograph for sale at ten pounds a print on the Internet. He didn't like being photographed, for pragmatic reasons. After his arrest, the police commented that there were few photographs of him after the age of sixteen.

Ian suggested to Myra that it was time she had driving lessons and bought a car. Myra responded with a 'Zzzeee!' A few days later she booked a course of lessons and bought a black van from a friend in Gorton.

At about the same time, Brady was involved in burgling a large department store. A pea-souper fog, a close confederate of crime, induced him to take part. The gang gained access through a skylight on the roof that Brady had smashed impulsively with his elbow after one of his friends made little headway with a glass-cutter. The robbery collapsed into a Marx Brothers' nightmare. They escaped to the safety of the driver's flat with a few cases of loot and examined the haul while they drank whisky.

They each took some item that they fancied and the driver would fence the rest. Brady chose a small gold watch for Myra's birthday, just a few weeks away. The gang slept overnight at the flat and the money was divided after the takings were fenced. On the way home Brady bought a bottle of Drambuie to celebrate the windfall.

In the wider world, Britain had witnessed the Profumo affair and would soon hear the news of the resignation of Prime Minister Harold Macmillan in its wake. In the United States the charismatic President John F Kennedy had only five months to live.

Ian Brady wrote a memo in his appointments diary, 'Gns and Bulls?' – Guns and Bullets. As I mentioned earlier, the warehouse foreman at Millwards, George Clitheroe, was president of the Cheadle Rifle Club. Ian and Myra had discussed how she could win his unsuspecting confidence to gain entry into the club. They decided on a mixture of interest and flattery, as Brady had employed before Myra appeared on the scene. Ian outlined his second 'Holy Grail' robbery to Myra and her response was the same as Gil Deare's had been: 'Why not just shoot the driver?'

As Brady commented to me: 'I had never been opposed to this on moral grounds, simply pragmatic. Death was insidiously reinforcing and repeating practical advice already given. Might is Right. Destroy all obstacles to ambition.' Things were looking up for Ian and Myra. They would soon have access to guns and ammunition.

CHAPTER TWELVE

DO WHAT YOU WILL, KIDDO

Do What You Will was the title of one of Aldous Huxley's earliest books. The epigraph of the book was a quotation from William Blake, Ian Brady's favourite poet:

> Do what you will, this world's a fiction and is
> made up of contradiction.

St Augustine had said, 'Love God, and do what you will', and this was possibly in the mind of Blake when he wrote those words. Augustine obviously meant that a true lover of God would not commit an evil act.

Huxley's book was first published in 1936. Twenty years later, Brady had been transformed by reading Dostoevsky. Aldous Huxley had reacted very differently to Brady's favourite author. In a chapter on Baudelaire included in *Do What You Will*, Huxley asserts the absolutes that had dissolved in the mind of Ian Brady: 'The horrors that darken *The Possessed* and the other novels of Dostoevsky are tragedies of mental licentiousness. All Dostoevsky's characters (and Dostoevsky himself, one suspects, was rather like them) have licentious minds, utterly unrestrained by their bodies. They are all emotional onanists, wildly indulging themselves in the void of imagination. Occasionally they grow tired of their masturbations and try to make contact with the world. But they have lost all sense or reality, all knowledge of human values. All their attempts to realize their onanistic dreaming in practice result in catastrophe. It is inevitable. But however agonizing they may be (and Dostoevsky spares us nothing), these tragedies, I repeat, are fundamentally ludicrous and idiotic.

171

They are the absurdly unnecessary tragedies of self-made madmen. We suffer in sympathy, but against our will; afterwards we must laugh. For these tragedies are nothing but stupid farces that have been carried too far.'

Aldous Huxley died on the same day that President John F Kennedy was assassinated, the night before Ian Brady and Myra Hindley murdered their second victim – John Kilbride.

In conversations with Ian Brady, I discovered that he had used Tarot cards before four of the five Moors Murders. I was surprised to hear this. I had taught courses on the Tarot for some years in the context of offbeat spiritual and philosophical traditions that belong to the penumbra of the mainline religious traditions. Like all things religious, the Tarot can be understood in a literalist sense as a means of predicting the future. Adverts in tabloid newspapers depend on this.

The girlfriend of one of Brady's contacts had presented him with a sealed pack of Tarot cards. The cards can be used simply to randomise the intellect by presenting an array of pictures that evoke a projection from the user, rather like a Rorschach blot. In a letter, Ian Brady spoke about his own use of the cards: 'I used them from a psychological viewpoint, not occult. The combination of intricate designs and colours, plus the multi-interpretational relationship of meanings, made the cards not only a meditative but also a psychological conduit, providing a conduit to the subconscious, reflecting inner doubts or confidence in some immediate project in hand.'

For some years, I had known Ian Brady's views of the forensic psychiatrists in the academic world – they shamelessly pursued, through self-publicity, a profitable media career on the basis of one success out of a hundred stabs in the dark, on the back of the film *The Silence of the Lambs*. In *The Gates of Janus*, Brady comments on the forensic experts: 'Based on a study of such self-serving amateurs, I do not hesitate to state that one could achieve a higher percentage of success with a Tarot pack.'

Myra decided to learn German. For Ian, this meant that the two of them would be able to communicate covertly in public with a quick exchange of words. They already had a rudimentary secret code of words and body gestures. For example, a 'Groucho' – raising the eyebrows quickly twice – meant 'follow the direction of my eyes'. When either of them saw a sexually attractive or provocative male or female desirable to either or both of them, they said, 'DC' – 'delicious creature'. This private language they shared belonged to what Brady called their telepathic ability to home in on the same object of desire.

Maureen Hindley – Mo or Moby – asked her sister Myra whether Ian would take a few photographs of her to give to David Smith, her boyfriend of the time. Brady described Mo as 'a coltish seventeen-year-old, with dark hair in a beehive style and black eye make-up. Attractive.'

Ian reflected that Mo's boyfriend could be useful to his plans if he wanted money. Ian quizzed Mo about David Smith with incidental questions during a photo session at Myra's.

Ian Brady told me that he was attracted to Maureen and that he had openly flirted with her throughout the session as Myra looked on, fuming in silence. As Mo was about to leave Myra's house, Ian added the final touch to Myra's evening of jealousy. Glancing sideways to Myra, he nodded a 'Groucho' towards Mo and muttered his approval with his smattering of German: '*DC, nicht wahr?*' Myra knew enough German to reply. Her sister was very pretty but not available: '*Sehr, aber nicht frei.* See you tomorrow night, our Mo.'

After Maureen had left, Myra and Ian drank what was left of the wine. Myra wondered aloud whether David Smith could be useful. Ian told her that there was no rush and to ask around about him. Myra said, 'I've just remembered something Mo mentioned. Dave Smith was seen with another girl. She lives next door to him in Wiles Street. A right dump,' as she waved towards the playing fields. 'Her name's Pauline Reade.'

Ian asked whether Myra knew her. Myra said that she only knew her to speak to and that she was about sixteen. He told Myra to pump her about Smith in an oblique way. In a letter, Ian Brady was laconic: 'Without our knowing, and in this relaxed manner, the fateful machinations of carnage slowly ground into motion towards depravity and disaster.'

Myra Hindley was near-sighted but too vain to wear glasses while driving. As though to prove the point, her van hit police bollards just outside Ashton-under-Lyne as she and Ian were out for a spin to Saddleworth on a fine sunny evening. The bollards were protecting the scene of a road accident. As a policeman walked towards the van, Ian told Myra to relax, smile at him and apologise. The policeman shook his head and waved Myra on. She simply hadn't seen the bollards.

In her confessions, Myra claimed that Brady followed the van on his motorbike when he gave her signals to pick up the first victim. Brady told me that without her glasses she would never have seen him through her rear-view mirror. He told me about the incident with the bollards to undermine her story.

Alex arranged to meet Brady in Manchester and, as usual, they talked business over a drink in the station buffet. Alex was worried about the disappearance of Gil Deare but Brady tried to reassure him by saying that Gil would never grass on the two of them. Alex also wanted to know about the big payroll job, the second 'Holy Grail'. Someone had to replace Gil. Brady told him that he knew a possible replacement, but didn't tell him that he had Myra in mind as a second driver. Alex knew nothing of Myra. If she were involved in the robbery, she and Ian would share between them fifty per cent of the haul. Myra knew all about Brady's second 'Holy Grail' and was as captivated as he was.

Before Alex caught his train, Brady cheered him up with the news that – without giving names – they would probably have a new source of guns and ammunition in a few months' time.

Hettie, Myra's mother, didn't like the idea of her daughter living with Ian Brady without any prospect of marriage. Ian liked Hettie in spite of this. She was a nervous woman and was in a particularly agitated state when she came round to Bannock Street to ask Myra if she had seen Maureen. David Smith had been hanging around for Maureen and Hettie had chased him away. She couldn't stand the thought of Mo having anything to do with what she called 'the dirty bugger'.

Myra put her coat on and told her mother that she would find Mo and sort out Smith. Ian put on his own coat and followed Myra out of the door. Myra was worried about what Ian might do: 'Don't get involved, Neddie, the little toad isn't worth it.' Ian assured Myra that he just wanted to look at him.

Myra and Ian saw Smith – long hair with hands in pockets, standing in the entrance to an alley, his back against the wall. Smith wore drainpipe jeans, a jacket and was just under Ian's six foot. He was thirty yards away in fading light as Myra approached him. Ian told her to hide her hostility in case he was still of some use to them: 'If he isn't, we can put an end to all his troubles. How would you like him as a present?' Myra hissed, 'Zzzeee!'

Years later, Brady spoke to me about the first time he saw David Smith: 'He didn't look promising on first viewing. It's a pity I didn't heed my own first impressions. I would still be a free man.'

'Mo wants to marry Smith!' Myra screamed when she returned to Ian. Ian calmed her down: 'Find out what Mo wants before we decide what to do. If Smith married Mo, we could exploit the relationship.' Myra couldn't see how. Ian explained: 'A blood relationship would be a safeguard against grassing, Kiddo, if we decided to use him. If we don't, and you don't want

Mo to marry him, you can have him gift-wrapped.' There was a gleam in Myra's eye. In the living room of number 7 Bannock Street, for weeks now, the radio had been playing The Beatles' number one hit 'From Me To You': 'If there's anything that you want . . .'

Ian was feeling trapped in the office and longed for action: 'I was frustrated in every direction. The time I was wasting at Millwards galled me. I was longing for action but small, important details were impeding me, leading to ever more resentment. Not to decide is to decide. The desire to take radical action and break free from oppressive routine, to be an individual, to put my will to the test and experience the *black light*, was mocking my caution.

'Was there a subconscious, parasitic defect gnawing at the roots of my will, or was it stunted from lack of action? The anxiety of staking everything on one wild throw of the dice was making me contemptuous of myself. If I did not act consistently on my convictions, I would be an absurdity to myself and to others. I felt the wrath slowly intensifying against the complete awareness of the possibility of my plans falling to ruin and tipping my personal scales of karma.'

Ian Brady lay on his stomach in the living room of number 7. Myra was stroking the back of his neck to relieve his headache. After a few minutes Ian asked her if she had seen Maureen. Myra said that she had and that Maureen still wanted to marry Smith. Ian digested the news in silence for a few minutes and reminded Myra again that the marriage would be advantageous. Ian said he could use him and, sensing Myra's anxiety for her sister, added that Maureen would be kept out of any criminal activity.

Myra continued to stroke Ian's neck until he was almost asleep and entering what he later called 'collection time' – the fleeting moments when a crack occurs in the barrier separating the conscious mind from the subconscious.

Ian was still in this state when Myra said something. Ian asked her to repeat it. She said that Ronnie Sinclair had been reprieved and now so had Dave Smith. Ian accepted this as criticism. Was he becoming soft?

He was fully awake now. Myra's remarks had been the trigger he needed. The dark agenda, which had simmered deep in his subconscious for years, had broken the surface. The *black light* began to operate: 'So you want excitement? You want to make things happen, Kiddo? The mysterious adventure is about to begin!' The warm 'green face' of Death swirled contentedly, humming Scottish ballads last heard in the chalky classrooms of Ian Brady's childhood.

176 IAN BRADY — THE UNTOLD STORY OF THE MOORS MURDERS

First things first. There must be a written plan. The two of them sat surrounded by hand-written sheets on the living room floor. It was a warm evening and they kept cool by mixing cold water with the wine. Mrs Maybury's dog, Lassie, was excited by the unusual activity. In this Gorton back street, Myra Hindley and Ian Brady plotted carnage and scribbled their lives away. Ian had, of course, written lists before and discussed them with Myra over a long period. By the end of the evening they had produced the master list. Brady wrote out a brief summary of the list for me: 'The first principle was absolutely fundamental. There must be no thread connecting our starting point with our destination, and vice versa. All surfaces had to be free of tyre and footmarks, hairs, fibres and fingerprints.'

There must be duplicates of all clothing including shoes. The set used on the day would be burned and the ashes thrown into a river. Buttons should be carefully counted and cleaned. The vehicle used must be thoroughly cleaned and polished before and after the event.

Both the inner workings and outer surfaces of guns must be free of fingerprints. Bullet heads must be scored to turn them into a shapeless mass, destroying all ballistic markings on impact. Disposable plastic sheets must cover the interior of the vehicle.

The house had to be cleared of anything that might arouse police suspicions. These items would be placed into left-luggage at a railway station. In the target area itself, the vehicle must not be parked where it could be spotted through overlooking windows. False number plates must be used. All weapons, guns excepted, must be broken up and disposed of over a wide area after use.

Alibis must be established and remain valid for fourteen days. Then it would be relegated to 'vague' status. Few people can remember where they were a fortnight before, unless there was something special about the day. Normal, daily routine behaviour must be adhered to, on or after the day in question. Verifiable records would show no break in the regular schedule.

The master list would apply to any criminal activity, ranging from theft to murder. There were very detailed cross-references, modifications, sub-procedures and divisions, and footnotes for each category of crime; making up a comprehensive list of detailed procedures to select from. Red and green colours were used to pinpoint cross-references and details germane to a particular activity.

When everything was transferred to the columns in thirty pages of foolscap, all other sheets were torn up and burned, as well any blank pages that might have served as pressure copies. The complete master list was finally put into a large brown envelope with other items such as lists of contacts, maps of projects and photographs, address books, tapes and other incriminating material. A working list for each particular crime would be written by drawing from the master list. After all their hard work they uncorked another bottle of wine.

The following day they hid the envelope among piles of redundant files in a locked room in the warehouse at Millwards. When the pair were arrested two-and-a-half years later, the police seized a hastily written working list and wrongly deciphered two abbreviations – WH and REC – to mean Woodhead and Reconnaissance.

The police never did discover that they really stood for 'Warehouse' and 'Records'. Myra was arrested five days after Ian and in the interval managed to destroy all of the warehouse material as planned.

The gambit for Myra's entry into the rifle club was on course. Apart from a rifle, Ian wanted two revolvers – a .45 and a .38 snub-nose. Automatics were not reliable.

One evening, Ian and Myra were at home drinking warmed German wine. A heavily pregnant Lassie slept beside them. Myra was worried about the reliability of David Smith. Ian said that he was worth a try. He could be treated as expendable. Ian told Myra to tell Smith that they wanted no connecting threads. He would have to keep his distance and be picked up at a point outside the area. Ian asked Myra to check obliquely that Maureen knew nothing of the arrangement with Smith and added, 'If there's any problem, he's yours. When the time comes we'll give them a treat as a wedding present. You've been to the Lake District often and enjoyed it – we'll take them there.'

David Smith would marry a pregnant Maureen in just over a year's time. He was six years younger than Myra and eighteen months younger than Maureen. David was the child of Joyce Hull, who disappeared when he was two years old. His father was Jack Smith, who worked as a travelling maintenance fitter and rarely saw his son. Jack Smith's parents, Annie and John Smith, legally adopted David and made a home for him in their house in Ardwick, Manchester.

His real father, Jack, eventually took him away from Annie to live with him in his lodgings at number 13 Wiles Street, Gorton, round the corner from Myra's house and next door but one to Pauline Reade's house at number 9.

In the vernacular of the late 1950s, David Smith had become a juvenile delinquent. He fought with his father and was sent to Rose Hill Remand

Home. On his release he was accepted at Stanley Grove School, Longsight. His aggression was channelled there constructively and he excelled in the school's boxing championships. However, he lost control and struck his headmaster, Mr Silver, in a dispute about school uniform. David liked his trousers skin-tight and went to work on them himself with needle and thread. He was expelled.

David Smith now looked for his fights on the streets of Gorton, where he earned the nickname 'Smogger'. He joined All Saint's School in Gorton Lane and was expelled again. David used a cricket bat to break the fingers of a boy who had called him 'a bastard'. He had been charged with wounding and assault at the ages of eleven and fifteen.

On 8 July 1963, he appeared before magistrates and was given three years' probation for house breaking. Pauline Reade had four days to live.

It was early evening when Ian Brady rode towards Myra's house and stopped to buy a bottle of wine. He turned a corner in the Gorton back streets and saw Maureen standing with a group of teenagers outside a shop. David Smith was in the middle of them and stared back at Ian. Maureen waved as he swerved into Bannock Street.

Lassie gave him an excited welcome as he tossed the bottle to Myra and asked for glasses. He lifted her off the ground as she squealed 'Zzzeee!' 'Are you mad, Neddie, or is something going on?' she asked. Ian poured the wine and replied, 'What's wrong with both? You little twisted girl!' He explained just what was going on: 'We'll begin tomorrow. I'll clear my house of anything that could be incriminating. You do likewise here. We put the suitcases into left-luggage tomorrow night. I'll take the master list from the warehouse and put it back when we have worked out a working list from it. Then we'll gather the items we need.

'It's the *hunt*, the *game*, *death* made real. Pick up anyone you choose – it's of no consequence to me. An existential exercise of sheer will power. A sacrifice. One slip-up and it's beer money for the hangman – if we're caught alive. If trapped, we use the revolvers to the limit to fight our way out. If it's obvious we won't make it, we turn them on ourselves. No trial. No prison. Oblivion. Perfect. Better to live and die by choice rather than vegetate. We've talked it through often enough, Kiddo. Now we throw the dice for maximum stakes. It's "hide and seek". The game's begun.

'Are you hungry for it? Did you think that it was all an academic exercise? Look into my eyes, Kiddo! Seeing is believing. The idea is flesh and blood now. It's breathing. The blood's pumping. Can you feel it? Are you up for it? Remember the biblical ultimatum? "He who is not for me is against me." It's your decision. Top up your wine glass, Kiddo?'

Myra topped up the glasses and said, 'Of course I'm with you! I knew it wasn't all talk – I was just waiting for the word "go".' Ian was pleased to hear it: 'We shall see, won't we? You know my side of the deal. You can indulge whatever you like. Do what you will, Kiddo.' Myra looked down, her face a little flushed. She lifted her head and sipped the wine: 'You'll see, Neddie. Just you wait and see!'

In a letter to a journalist, after she had served more than thirty years of her life sentence, Myra wrote: 'I knew then and still know that there must be a callous streak in my nature, a cruel streak even: there must have been. And I still don't know what it was rooted in, or where it came from. Sometimes I've thought I'd drive myself insane trying to discover what it was.'

The rear of 56 Camden Street, Glasgow. The Sloans' window is the second up on the far left.
Manchester Evening News

ABOVE: Ian Brady's first school – Camden Street Infants – two minutes' walk from home.
Manchester Evening News

RIGHT: Brady aged eight.
Manchester Evening News

LEFT: The Sloans' second home – 21 Templeland Road, Pollok.

BELOW: Brady's secondary school – Shawlands Academy, Glasgow.

Ian Brady's mother, Peggy.
Manchester Evening News

BELOW: Myra Hindley at Ryder Brow School – third from the left on the third row.
Mirrorpix

Brady's own copy of *Crime & Punishment* with his marginal comments.
Author's private collection

BELOW LEFT: 3 Westmoreland Street – Brady's home in Manchester.
Manchester Evening News

BELOW RIGHT: Brady at Millwards Merchandising.
Manchester Evening News

ABOVE LEFT: Brady and Hindley hid their murder records in this warehouse at Millwards. MIRRORPIX

ABOVE RIGHT: Gorton Lane, showing the left turn into Froxmer Street where Pauline Reade was enticed into Hindley's van. Author's private collection

BELOW LEFT: Keith Bennett. **BELOW RIGHT:** Pauline Reade. PA Photos

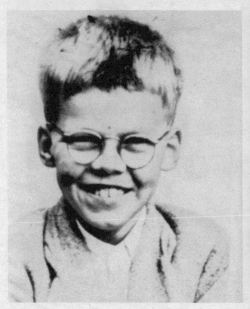

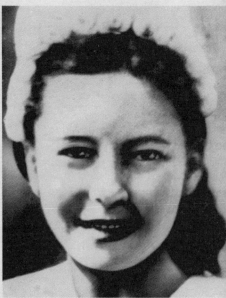

an Brady on Saddleworth Moor with Myra Hindley's van in
he background. Manchester Evening News

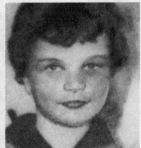

Ann Downey searches for her daughter, Lesley. _{Manchester Evening News}

BELOW: Three anxious mothers: From the left, Sheila Kilbride, Ann Downey and Winnie Johnson, the mother of Keith Bennett. _{Mirrorpix}

LEFT: David and Maureen Smith.
Mirrorpix

ABOVE: Edward Evans.
Rex/MGG

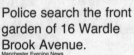

Police search the front garden of 16 Wardle Brook Avenue.
Manchester Evening News

The living room of 16 Wardle Brook Avenue, where Edward Evans was murdered.
Rex/David Magnus

RIGHT: Myra Hindley's vehicle outside her home on the morning of Brady's arrest.
Manchester Evening News

BELOW: Hindley's mother seeks news of her daughter after the arrest.
Manchester Evening News

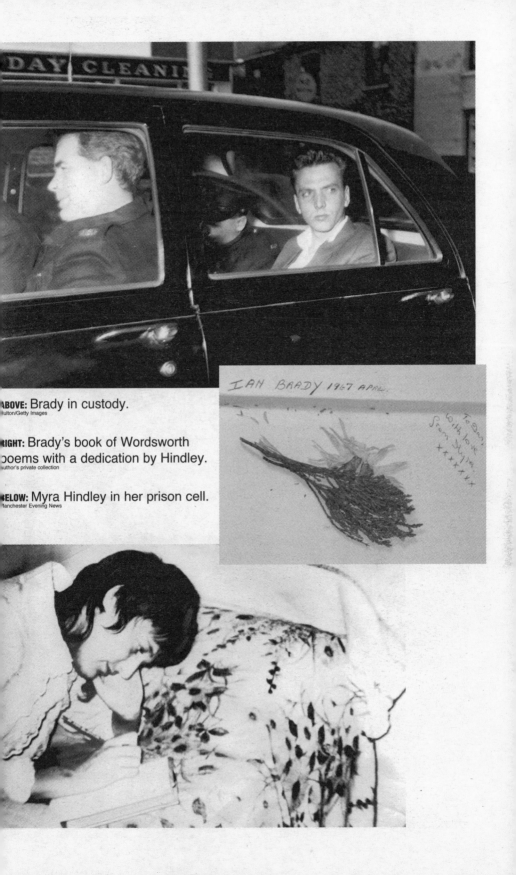

ABOVE: Brady in custody.
Hulton/Getty Images

RIGHT: Brady's book of Wordsworth poems with a dedication by Hindley.
author's private collection

BELOW: Myra Hindley in her prison cell.
Manchester Evening News

IAN BRADY 1967 APRIL

To Ian
With love
from Myra
xxxxxx

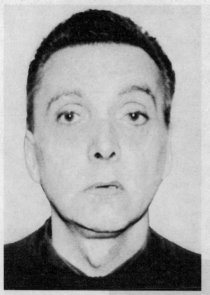

A prison security photograph of Ian Brady in later years.
Mirrorpix

BELOW: The certificate for a correspondence course in psychology completed by Brady in Wormwood Scrubs prison.
Author's private collection

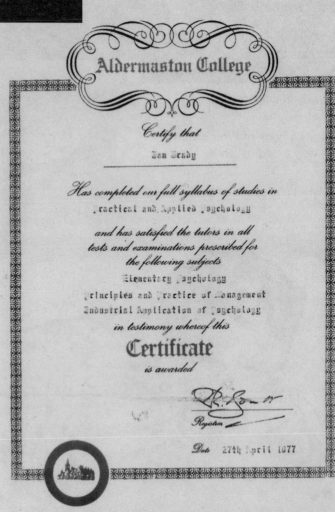

Aldermaston College

Certify that

Ian Brady

Has completed our full syllabus of studies in
Practical and Applied Psychology

and has satisfied the tutors in all
tests and examinations prescribed for
the following subjects
Elementary Psychology
Principles and Practice of Management
Industrial Application of Psychology
in testimony whereof this

Certificate

is awarded

Registrar

Date 27th April 1977

ABOVE: Brady – in overcoat and dark glasses – with police on Saddleworth Moor search-ing for Keith Bennett's grave.
Manchester Evening News

RIGHT: Brady's written comments in the margins of his own copy of *Topping*.
Author's private collection

realized at this point that Brady's solicitor was taking detailed notes of the interview; because of the conditions they had imposed on me, however, I had no back-up to take notes on my behalf. Mr Birnberg said there was nothing sinister in it, and although I did feel uneasy that a one-sided record was being made I agreed to continue when they accepted that, if necessary, I could call on them for a copy of the notes. By refusing to have another police officer present, I realized in retrospect, Brady was trying to establish his dominance.

I told him again that I thought he could help us accurately pinpoint the two graves, thus relieving the great anguish of the children's families, and that this would clear up, once and for all, the mysteries of the case. He was still very sceptical about the confession until I outlined the story of Pauline Reade's abduction. As he heard the details he was visibly shocked and his mannerisms became agitated. He has a facial twitch, which he blames on the medication he is given, and this became more noticeable. But he didn't throw up his arms and ask me to leave; he was calm enough to talk, and he continued to be polite.

He told me that he was prepared to confess provided it could be on his own terms. He said he would make a written confession on condition that afterwards he was immediately given the means to kill himself. He believed this would be the ideal solution to the whole problem.

I explained, and so did his solicitor, that this was not possible. I told him that he was an intelligent man and must therefore have known that this was an unrealistic condition when he imposed it. We talked for hours, going round and round the possibility of a confession but always ending with the same ultimatum: 'I'll tell you as long as you help me to end it all afterwards.' In his eyes he was putting the ball into my court: he was in control. He had not refused to co-operate – it was me who was refusing to meet his condition. He had known all along that his condition was preposterous, but it allowed him to feel that he was making a reasonable offer and that I was the one who was being unreasonable.

158

Winnie Johnson digs on Saddleworth Moor for her son, Keith, after police abandoned their search.

Peter Timms in discussion with students (the author is on the right).
Author's private collection

BELOW: Alan and Ann West with the author and three students. Stourbridge News

OPPOSITE: A sample of Ian Brady's abbreviated notes on his crimes.
Author's private collection

RIGHT: Ian Brady as he appeared during the period of the author's visits.
Expresspictures.com

BELOW: Brady personalised all of his possessions. These are some items in his smoking kit, with reading glasses.
Author's private collection

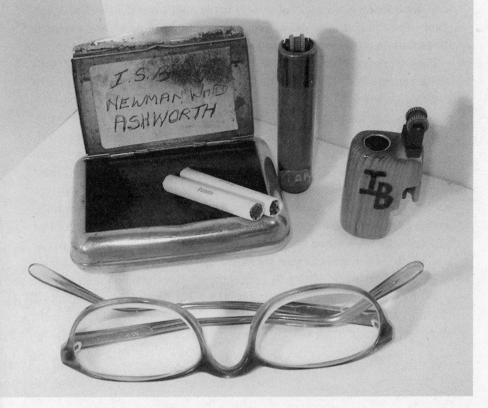

CHAPTER THIRTEEN

DEATH IN NEW STILETTOS

The sun was hot and bright in the Manchester skies. The bike swept under the trees and made the steady rise to Saddleworth Moor. Ian and Myra walked into the moor and used dried-up streams as pavements to find a pool. Ian sank a bottle of wine to cool. They were looking for a spot where a parked car wouldn't attract attention. The Beatles were singing 'Love Me Do' when Myra switched on the transistor radio. Ian had noticed a horseshoe scoop in the rocks at a curve in the road when they had made the climb. They pulled in at the scoop on their way back down and explored the terrain on foot. Del Shannon was singing 'Swiss Maid'.

They were invisible from the road after thirty paces. In front of them was a barren plain where any intruder could be spotted a mile away. By standing on a knoll of rock, approaching traffic could be seen from both directions. Looking back into the moor they saw a deathscape. Ian whispered 'Perfect' to himself. Myra overheard and murmured her approval. They drove back down to the city with the sun low on the horizon.

After a meal they deposited two suitcases in left-luggage at Manchester Central Station. The ticket was pushed into the spine of Myra's prayer book, which was then placed openly on the sideboard. The pair wrote out a working list from the master list. They knew that the destination would be Saddleworth, but needed to choose a target area by studying a map of the city. Myra favoured the Gorton area itself. Ian was sceptical. After the incident, the police would obviously concentrate their efforts on the local area.

He had second thoughts, however. He wasn't an official resident of Gorton and, in any case, the police wouldn't be looking for a female abductor. Gorton it would be. They needed a pick-up point with no overlooking windows and where a parked car would not attract curiosity. Froxmer Street was chosen. It had the Beyer Peacock factory wall on the left and the blank wall of a building on the right. The Vulcan pub stood on the corner. From Myra's house it was a left turn off Gorton Lane: 'After the van had been parked, Myra would use her discretion in selecting a target. If no one had been chosen by 8 p.m., the plan would be aborted for that evening. The deadline time was vital. I would stay at home in Westmoreland Street till 7.45 p.m. to establish an alibi, and then ride over to Gorton. If Myra's van were neither at her house nor Froxmer Street, I would know that she had picked up a target and travelled to Saddleworth Moor. I would follow on my bike.'

The person selected had to be at least sixteen. The police treat teenagers of that age as missing persons, thousands of which are recorded every year. Myra chose the bait – a few 78-rpm records. The chosen person would be asked to help stop the records from sliding off the seat and breaking. The reason for going to Saddleworth Moor was to look for an expensive glove Myra had dropped during a walk on the moor. A spade was hidden in readiness on the moor.

If Myra had the least suspicion that she had been seen with the pick-up, she was to stop the operation there and then with a prepared excuse.

Ian Brady admitted that all this was clinical and cold. He commented, 'That was only one side. The other was vibrantly transformed by the *black light*, making the world an infinitely fascinating spectacle.'

On the eve of their first crime together, Brady felt the call of Glasgow and his roots. Was his subconscious warning him of the perils of the immediate future? Ian and Myra had no such worries and chose to travel by motorbike to make the best of the warm weather. A petrol attendant filled the tank until it overflowed on to the hot engine.

Myra had the radio tuned to Radio Caroline as they swept on to the A6 road northwards. They stopped on the steep descent of Shap Fell to light cigarettes and absorb the wild panorama. A wasp stung Ian as they rested. The weather turned to rain when they crossed the border.

They were wet and cold when they booked into the Crescent Hotel in Glasgow. After a change of clothes they warmed themselves with a few whiskies in the bar and went out to eat black pudding and chips at Joe's Chip Bar. Afterwards, they walked past Queen's Park to Ian's old school, Shawlands Academy. He looked into the dark playground and remembered childhood friends who had gone forever. Back in the Crescent Hotel he made wild love with Myra.

The next morning Ian went to Pollok to visit the family and left Myra in the city to entertain herself. He took John Sloan to the Trocodero in the evening, before a ritual walk through the Gorbals. Ian wanted to take Myra for a trip on the paddle steamer *Waverley* to recall his boyhood journeys and on the following day they travelled down the river and out into the Firth of Clyde, passing Holy Loch and Dunoon on their right, then into the Kyles of Bute to Tighnabruaich. The weather was cold on the journey back, so Ian and Myra sat in the red-leather comfort of the lounge bar below decks. The paddles hardly caused a ripple as the *Waverley* stole along the river into Glasgow. The great rusting hulks of the gigantic cranes in the shipyards were what Dickens would have called mere spectres. Ian took an atmospheric photograph of Myra at the bow before the boat berthed.

He remembered the day in his childhood when he returned home with his friends on the *Waverley* after a camping holiday in Dunoon. A small pipe band had played 'Will Ye No Come Back Again?' on the pier before they left. He had come back again in very different circumstances. In captivity Ian Brady remembered his day 'doon the water' with Myra Hindley when he gave me a tape recording of another Scottish song that reminded him of a long lost world. The song was 'Home to the Kyles' or, as he usually referred to it, 'Tighnabruaich'.

The morning after their day out to Tighnabruaich, Ian and Myra headed back to Manchester to secure their immortality in the history of murder.

More than twenty years later, Myra informed Topping that Brady had said to her on 12 July 1963 that he wanted to commit the 'perfect murder' – implying that it was news for her out of the blue on that day. She added that Brady often spoke to her about *Compulsion*, a book giving the account of the 1924 murder of a twelve-year-old boy by Leopold and Loeb in Chicago. The two killers had allegedly been influenced by the writings of Nietzsche, as Brady was.

Brady denied speaking to Myra about a 'perfect murder', arguing that in her comments about *Compulsion* she was simply mouthing another 'myth' about the Moors case. I asked Brady about the book. He replied in a letter of October 1992: 'I was not impressed by the novel *Compulsion*, nor the film. Leopold and Loeb sought a triviality – "the perfect crime" – an irrelevance best left to writers of detective fiction.

'If you were to put this letter down; get up from your chair; choose an implement of murder; catch a train to a random city; find a dark street; wait for an individual; strike the fatal blow; catch the next train home – you will have committed the "perfect crime" with ridiculous ease, with only your conscience and subconscious to fear. If people knew how easy it was to commit murder, the murder rate would double.

'One spokesman for the Manson "family" said, "Anyone can be killed, even the President." '

*   *   *   *   *

Pauline Catherine Reade lived in a terraced house with her parents, Joan and Amos, and her brother Paul in Wiles Street, Gorton. She was sixteen and worked with her father as a trainee confectioner at the local Sharples bakery. Pauline had attended the same primary school as Myra Hindley in Peacock Street. She later went to the same school as Maureen Hindley and David Smith. Pauline was raised a Catholic and attended mass every Sunday.

As I have implied, I have drawn on a variety of sources to describe the murders that follow: remembered conversations with Ian Brady; notes made after visits to him; letters from him; telephone conversations and notes that he gave to me. Brady used his own abbreviations in these notes and it has taken some effort to decipher them, helped – of course – by his conversations about them during visits. I have also used Ian Brady's own copy of *Topping* – an item in his property – which is virtually a transcript of Myra Hindley's confessions to Peter Topping, made twenty years after the original Moors Murders trial.

Brady made notes in the margins of *Topping* for his personal use, never supposing that another person would read them. These notes are particularly significant for that very reason. They represent his own, private and spontaneous reactions to Myra Hindley's version of the murders.

It was Friday, 12 July 1963, and Pauline wanted to go to a dance at the Railway Workers' Social Club in Chapman Street, just ten minutes' walk away from her home in Wiles Street. She had been twice before but didn't particularly want to go alone. Pauline had called on her friends, Linda Bradshaw and Pat Garvey, to go with her, but both of their mothers refused to let them go because alcohol would be served at the club. Speaking thirty years later, Pauline's mother recalled the final moments she spent with her daughter: 'Pauline was looking forward to this dance. A friend was going with her and then, for some reason, her friend couldn't go. Pauline was very upset. I didn't want her to go on her own.

' "Get yourself ready and go round to your other friends and see if they'll go."

' "Mam, Sandra and Pam said they may be going and they will see me, so I'll be all right."

'With that, she convinced me and I let her go; otherwise I wouldn't have let her go on her own.

'I got her ready before she went out. Done her hair and everything. She looked beautiful. Even her father commented on it, how beautiful she looked.

'Before she went out of the door, I put my necklace round her neck.'

' "Oh, Mam! That's your favourite necklace." '

' "Well, you're my favourite girl aren't you?" '

' "I will look after it."

'I went out with her and I stood at the top of the road. I watched her disappear and waved to her as she went round the corner.'

As she set out at 7.45 p.m., Pauline was wearing a black blouse, a pink and gold Lurex skirt, a hand-knitted cardigan and a powder blue woollen coat belted at the waist. She had on a new pair of white stiletto heeled shoes, with an ankle strap, which she had bought that day.

In her book on Myra Hindley, Jean Ritchie curiously – and incorrectly – states that Pauline walked past the end of Westmoreland Street where Ian Brady lived. Brady's house was in Longsight – at least three miles away from the short walk to the social club, which would take up only a few minutes of Pauline's time.

Pauline actually walked from her home in Wiles Street into Charmers Street, then Benster Street, Taylor Street and Eaton Street, and then took a short cut across a patch of open land behind the Shakespeare pub – the Shakie – into Gorton Lane. Ian Brady wouldn't miss the irony of his beloved Shakespeare's symbolic presence in the midst of these grimy back streets of Gorton as one of its young inhabitants was about to be murdered in cold blood.

Pauline walked down Gorton Lane as far as the Vulcan pub and turned left into Froxmer Street.

She saw that the street was deserted apart from a parked black van. It was a warm and brilliantly sunny evening. The driver of the van had the windows down and could hear the clicking sounds of stiletto heels getting louder and louder. Had the balmy Gorton evening offered up its prize?

Myra attracted Pauline's attention as she was passing the van. She told her story of the glove lost on Saddleworth Moor and pointed to the 78-rpm records on the passenger seat. Pauline could have them if she helped Myra to search for the glove.

Pauline was too early for the dance and a trip out with Myra would fill in the time before the Social Club jive got into a swing. She took the bait. Myra did a three-point turn, headed for Saddleworth Moor and wondered whether Ian Brady would be pleased with her catch.

Across the city, in his bedroom at home in Westmoreland Street, he put a two-inch broad elasticised band on his right wrist and slipped a knife under it, handle towards the hand, a button-clasp holding the knife in the oiled sheath. He put on surgical gloves and covered them with a leather pair. The camera and binoculars were already hidden in Myra's van. At 7.45 p.m. he went downstairs to Peggy and Pat Brady, who were watching television. To establish an alibi, he deliberately asked them if the clock was right. The clock *was* right. He said that he would be off and would see them tomorrow.

Brady rode his bike to Gorton and dropped speed as he glided past Bannock Street. There was no black van there. He took a right turn into Gorton Lane and rode past the Shakespeare pub. He held his breath as he turned left into Froxmer Street.

No vehicle. It was on.

Brady switched off the engine in Froxmer Street. He lit a cigarette and looked ahead of him towards the railway line. The Railway Workers' Social Club was just the other side of a bridge over the line. He turned his head to stare back to Gorton Lane and the Vulcan pub. He thought momentarily of the time he heard music coming from the Vulcan. He had raised himself to look into the pub over the frosted glass. Someone was singing Chubby Checker's hit 'Let's Twist Again'. But there was no music tonight. Froxmer Street was quiet and deserted; touched by sunlight.

Ian Brady lit another cigarette and thought about his feelings as he had driven there across the city: 'No one who saw me ride past them on my way to Gorton could have guessed what I was about to do. It was enfolding before their eyes, but how could they know? They would know many years later, but wouldn't remember that I rode past them that night. For me it was the beginning of an existential exercise beyond good and evil. The streets of Manchester were the backdrops for Scene I.

'This was the one far-off event to which my destiny had been taking me all these years. I recoiled at the idea but, at the same time, I was impatient for its fruition. The passing throng could not know it. They were cut off from me forever. Something irrevocable was about to happen, which would affect the lives of thousands for decades into the future and soon reduce my life to the status of a ghost on the human stage.

'I felt a strange sense of nostalgia for the world I was about to abandon as though an irreversible, final parting was taking place. Was I about to step through the final doorway to madness? Or had I already entered it long ago?

'In my years of captivity I always thought of my ride across Manchester on this particular warm, sunny evening when I read John Milton's verse from *Paradise Lost*:

> Farewell happy fields
> Where joy forever dwells: Hail horrors, hail
> Infernal world, and thou profoundest Hell
> Receive thy new possessor: one who brings
> A mind not to be changed by place or time . . .

Brady stubbed out his cigarette as the dark mood lifted and the *black light* gleamed. He laughed at his self-doubt, straightened and laughed again at the hesitation: 'Richard's himself again!' He kicked the Triumph bike into life and swept through Manchester's dusty, dingy streets towards Saddleworth Moor, where Death was waiting.

The bike took him under the now-familiar overhanging trees and up towards the summit. Who would be waiting with Myra? A boy or a girl? Would it be one of her friends who trusted her? She had mentioned Pat Jepson and another named Cummings among others.

Ian Brady observed later; 'If words were deeds, the death rate of Myra's "friends" would go through the roof. Her enemies? Myra hadn't read Machiavelli's *The Prince*: "If a person betrays a friend to seek advantage with you, do not trust him, for he will also be capable of betraying you with equal ease." It is harder to wound an adversary than a friend. Your opponent will exact revenge with no concern for sacrificing your non-existent affection.'

He broke through the trees into bright sunlight and passed the last sign of civilisation, a farmhouse on the right, before pulling in at the horseshoe scoop beside Myra's black van.

Pauline was sitting with Myra, smoking a cigarette between her index and second finger. Ian pushed his goggles on to his forehead and gathered his thoughts as he balanced the bike on its stand. Without thinking, he began to take off his leather gloves before realising he would reveal the surgical gloves beneath. He pulled his gloves back on and opened the van door. Myra said they thought he was never coming.

Pauline nodded silently. Brady muttered that he had been held up by traffic.

Ian Brady later recalled that Pauline had a delicate beauty unspoiled by too much make-up. She pushed along the seat towards Myra as Brady climbed into the van and lit a cigarette. The two girls chatted and left him to his thoughts: 'So here it was at last: the place where my whole life had been leading. The radical exercise in pure existentialism, and the genesis of the hidden agenda. Faith is faith in any theological currency. Yet there was a sense of unreality about it all, a detachment, an innate distancing.'

Myra said they had better search for the glove as the sun was fading. Brady related to me what happened next. It is a very different account of events from the versions Myra Hindley gave to Peter Timms and Peter Topping: 'I pinched the life out of my cigarette and pushed the stub into my pocket. I strode as casually as possible up the slope of the moor that led to the knoll at the top. I was about five yards ahead of Myra and the girl.

'Cars passed by on the road, windows down for the passengers to enjoy the mild evening, oblivious to the unfolding drama. As I approached the knoll I walked further into the moor. Myra and I knew exactly where we were heading for. We had rehearsed it. It was a place on the moor where we would be out of sight from the road.

'The *black light* began to illuminate my vision. I dawdled and pretended I was scrutinising the grass closely, to allow the girl and Myra to walk past me. Pauline's eyes were also focused on the ground. Myra furtively glanced back in my direction. I nodded a 'Groucho' and immediately moved forward to grasp the girl's neck in a Japanese stranglehold.

'She collapsed on to the ground and stared up at me. I knelt down and said, "Don't make a noise and you'll be all right. It's pointless."

'She turned to plead with Myra, who was standing looking down; "Myra, tell him to stop!"

'I looked up at Myra. Her lips formed a smile, but her eyes had other intentions. Her expression was taunting and pitiless. Myra snapped, "Just keep quiet!"

' "But Myra, tell him I'm ill. I'm unwell."

'Myra translated girls' talk for my benefit: "She means it's her time of month," Myra was looking down scornfully at the girl, who justifiably thought she was about to be raped.

'Myra knelt on the grass to unbutton the girl's coat, disregarding her pleas. I was standing by this time and looked for any movement on the moor. The sun had slipped below the horizon, the reflected light bathing Saddleworth Moor in a cold, portentous luminosity. The ghostly cry of a curlew sounded across the wilderness.

'Myra forced the girl to sit up before easing off her coat and unzipping her dress at the back. She then slipped her dress and a slip down to the waist. She released the chain of a bronze medallion and put it on the grass beside her. Myra was trying to unfasten the bra at the back when the girl clutched the front of her bra to stop her exposure.

' "Myra! Please don't! Please don't!" The girl averted her eyes and blushed as Myra pulled the bra from her grasp. Myra gently fondled the girl's breasts while whispering sexual words in her ear. I was aroused by the lesbian seduction. The girl lay, passively accepting the violation and her humiliation with half-closed eyes. I leaned towards her and kissed her left breast.'

Ian Brady detected a jealous look from Myra as he kissed Pauline. Brady and Myra both carried out sexual acts on the girl. Daylight was fading rapidly. Ian stood up and told Pauline to get dressed. She put all her clothes on in order and finally reached for the bronze medallion. Myra snatched it from her and snapped, 'You won't be needing that where you're going!' Brady was alarmed: 'Impulsively – from long experience – my arm swung sideways and my hand swiped Myra hard across the face. Had I overestimated my own heartlessness, or was it simply fury at Myra for exposing both of us to danger by her pointless remark? Strike quickly – without warning – had always been my way. To warn the victim beforehand with a fatuously, gratuitous remark broke an absolute with me – the man who has no absolutes.'

Myra told Brady later that she made the remark because she had a feeling that he was going to let the girl go, and was making sure he didn't as it would have led to disaster. Brady, in fact, had no intention of taking such a risk and the remark had been pointless. He continued his description: 'The uncomprehending look of terror in the girl's eyes – as her fate dawned upon her – has haunted me every day to this day. Myra was staring at me in silence. Then she broke the silence on the moor with a thunderbolt: "She's Pauline Reade." I didn't understand at first, absorbed as I was with the next task. There were suddenly fireworks in my head as the name came back to me – Maureen, Smith, and Pauline Reade. Jesus! So that's it!'

Ian thought that Myra had used the situation to rid her beloved Mo of a rival. He looked at the girl with new alarm. The 'no connecting thread' principle had been breached. He wondered what other idiotic risks Myra had taken to trap this girl. What could be done to limit the possible damage and unforeseen dangers? It was Catch 22 – peril loomed from both directions.

Brady was silent for a minute or two and said that he would go and fetch the necessary from the van – the binoculars and camera. Myra had trained in Judo and could handle Pauline on her own. Pauline pleaded not to be left alone with Myra and said that she would not tell anyone: 'I pushed aside her plea abruptly, "Don't worry," as though she had brought this calamity on herself. I vented my anger on Myra and shouted, "Keep alert!" Then I walked quickly down the slope, trying to beat the oncoming darkness and appear casual to anyone peering out of the windows of passing cars.

'It was almost dark when I returned to the knoll and found Myra only after some anxious moments. I could make out some frenetic movements in the darkness. I walked faster, thinking that the girl was making a fight of it. Myra was astride the girl's head, pressing down on her face.

' "What's wrong?" Myra looked over her shoulder when she heard me and shouted, "Quick, Neddie!"

'I saw the glint of the steel kitchen knife on the grass. Myra had attempted to stab the girl's chest but the knife didn't penetrate her. The blade was bent.

'Myra had punched the girl's head and face. Blood was streaming from her nose and had soaked the front of her dress. Her eyes were closed now. She gasped for breath.

'I instantaneously withdrew the sheath knife from my wrist, knelt towards the girl to cut her throat. My first attempt was not deep enough to sever the carotid artery. My second attempt was. Blood gushed from her throat. She was dead within seconds.

'I pushed her coat collar into the wound to stem the flow. Saddleworth Moor was silent. There were no sounds after the last trickle of blood.'

Brady pushed the sheath knife into the ground several times, put it into his pocket and handed the kitchen knife to Myra. He told her to take it with the camera back to the van and return with the spade. It was too dark to photograph the site by now. Without telling Brady, Myra moved the van nearer the site. Ian scanned the wilderness with binoculars looking for a silhouette. There was nothing. He sat down and lit a cigarette. His eyes fell on Pauline Reade: 'I reflected on the chain of events that had led her to this high barren wilderness on a sunny evening. Innocence is a birthright we relinquish with each tick of the clock, without knowing it. But the innocence in others festers and bewitches us, perplexing both ourselves and those we dispossess.

'As I waited for Myra to return, I chain-smoked, taking the precaution to put the butts in my pocket. When she appeared Myra handed me the spade and held on to the binoculars. I told her to scan Saddleworth for the least sign of movement.

'The peat was soft and I was able to dig out a burial spot to a depth of four or five feet in just a few minutes. I held the shoulders and Myra grasped the legs as we lowered the body into the grave. I shovelled in the peat as Myra pulled up clods of grass by the roots from the surrounding area. Both of us stamped the clods into the surface of the grave so that the plot would show no signs of recent disturbance.

'Both of us counted our strides back to the knoll so that we could locate the grave and photograph it periodically to check that there had been no change to the surface of the peat to arouse suspicion.

'Then, a bolt from the blue. The sight of it horrified me. I ducked and tried to assimilate the shock. Suddenly I whispered frantically to Myra: "There's a vehicle parked on the side of the road!"

'Myra had ducked when she saw me crouching. She raised her head slowly, paused for breath and said sheepishly: "It's ours, Neddie."'

The evening had descended into farce. Ian asked Myra why she didn't just hang up a sign. He told her to take her shoes off and drive the van back to the parking place while he buried the spade. At the horseshoe scoop they changed into fresh clothes. Myra drove the van and Ian followed on the bike at the speed of a funeral procession.

Almost forty years later, the pathologist who performed the autopsy on Pauline when her body was discovered in 1987, published a photograph of Pauline's foot and white stiletto shoe, uncovered in the peat of Saddleworth Moor.

In some newspaper reports, Myra claims that she saw Mrs Reade looking for Pauline after they returned home. Brady denies this. The journalist Robert Wilson reports, in his book *Return To Hell*, that Pauline's brother Paul saw Myra Hindley in Charmers Street at 9.45 p.m. as he returned home from a night at the cinema. He went to bed in his home in Wiles Street but was woken up by his mother Joan after midnight. Pauline hadn't come home. He dressed and went out with her to retrace Pauline's steps to the social club.

There were a few stewards still cleaning up at the club but no one had seen Pauline that evening. Pauline's father Amos got out of bed to join the search. At 2.30 a.m. Joan Reade eventually telephoned the police from a callbox.

Back in Bannock Street, Ian and Myra were tearing up their used clothes and burning them – a 'tedious chore' that took them till three in the morning. The blade of the kitchen knife and the ashes of its wooden handle would be thrown into the River Irwell the next day, after the bike and the van had been meticulously cleaned. Ian and Myra unwound with a bottle of wine. He asked her if she was sure that no one saw her pick up Pauline. Myra was positive.

As they dozed before the fire, Brady reflected on the unanswered questions about the manner and motive of Pauline's abduction, but they would keep till daylight. He didn't know it then, but Myra had another unpleasant surprise for him.

They cleaned the van and bike, bagged the ashes and were all set to drive to the river Irwell when Myra touched Brady's shoulder and, looking shamefaced, bleated: 'You won't be angry, Neddie, if I tell you something?' Turning round to face her, and bracing himself for calamitous news, he snapped, 'What?'

Without Brady's knowledge, Myra had held on to Pauline's bronze medallion. It was the very thing that had provoked him to strike Myra in front of Pauline on the moor. The 'no connecting thread' principle had been breached. Pauline's talisman seemed to have followed the pair of them back to Bannock Street to exact revenge.

Brady was fuming in silence as he grabbed his cigarette packet, puffing three cigarettes in a minute, snatching them from his lips and stubbing them out half-used.

The tiny front room was filled with dense, strong cigarette smoke. Then Myra – speaking quietly through the cloud – made Brady even more furious: 'I picked up these four half-crowns when they fell from Pauline's pocket. I'd forgotten I had kept them, Neddie – I didn't mean to.'

Brady broke his silence: 'Say that to the bloody judge! Theft in the course of murder guarantees you a date with the hangman! We leave now to spend the coins. Then we bury the medallion without trace.'

Many years later, I mentioned to Brady that Myra had told Peter Topping that she had never seen Pauline's medallion. Brady said, 'She's lying. What would I want with it?'

Ian stopped the bike at the first shop and Myra bought chocolate and cigarettes with the half-crowns. They threw the ashes into the river Irwell and buried the medallion in Alt Hill. Brady breathed a sigh of relief. They decided to go to the cinema and went to the Odeon in Oldham to see a double feature, *The Legion's Last Patrol* and *The Day of the Triffids*.

The soundtrack of the former was a poignant trumpet-solo with a featured piece by the Ken Thorne Orchestra entitled 'Theme from the Legion's Last Patrol'. It became a hit in its own right and Ian and Myra always associated it with Pauline Reade. Twenty-three years later Ian used it to trap Myra with what he called 'spectacular success'. Brady told Inspector Topping to mention the track to Myra. According to Brady, it led her to believe that if he had revealed such an intimate detail about the murder, he must have confessed to much more.

Whenever Ian or Myra hummed the trumpet theme of *The Legion's Last Patrol*, it recalled only one event. Brady gave me a tape recording of the record when I commented that I had never heard of it.

Police were everywhere in Gorton when Ian and Myra arrived home from the cinema. Ian Brady reflected: 'The police were looking for a murderer and not a missing person. This was bad news for Myra and me. It was the very scenario we had planned to avoid. I wanted Myra's reassurance that no one could have seen Pauline Reade get into the van in Froxmer Street. She was sure that she hadn't been seen. I was still not satisfied. I suspected Myra was hiding something from me.

'I learned that her sister Mo and David Smith had been fighting outside on the pavement in Wiles Street on the night of Pauline's disappearance and that Smith had struck her. What had they been fighting over? Myra had shrugged her shoulders; "Search me, Neddie. They're always fighting."

' "Is that why they are talking about marriage?" Myra laughed too hysterically at this. I forced a smile; "Well, Kiddo . . . " and then grabbed her throat with both hands. "Which of them sent her to you? Smith or Maureen? Which one?"

'Myra was suddenly cowed by my rage. She bleated that nobody had. I looked into her eyes, "If I find out different, it's fucking both of them . . . !" '

Brady wanted to question Maureen and David Smith but that would only attract attention. The police would be searching house-to-house, and Myra accepted that it would be safer for Ian to keep out of Gorton until things cooled down. They could discuss any new developments in the office.

More than thirty years later, Myra reflected on the first murder that put her and Brady beyond the pale: 'After the first murder he told me that if I'd shown any signs of backing out I would have ended up in the same grave as Pauline Reade. I felt doubly doomed: first by the crime itself and also because I believed it was impossible to envisage or hope for any other kind of existence.

'As Mr Mars-Jones [the prosecutor at the trial of Brady and Hindley] further said, the horrible secret we later shared bound us together more closely than any ties of affection possibly could. There was no going back, and what Ian said shortly after our arrest, that it was he and I against the world, felt very much the case for as long as our relationship lasted.'

In conversations with me, Ian Brady denied that he had made any such threats to Myra.

The police investigation was underway. They interviewed Pauline's friends, issued posters and dragged the canal in Cornwall Street. There were rumours that she had run away from home with a fairground worker or because she was pregnant. The *Manchester Evening News* reported her disappearance under a small headline: 'GIRL, 16, VANISHES ON WAY TO JIVE CLUB'.

Myra told Topping that Ian tried to strangle her when she broke down some days later after seeing an entry in the same newspaper from Joan and Amos Reade: 'Please come home, we're heartbroken.' When I put this to Ian Brady he dismissed Myra's version as nonsense. In several conversations, over a long period, he vehemently ridiculed virtually every detail of Myra's account of the death of Pauline.

Over the years, to friends and correspondents, Myra shared some of her memories of conversations with Brady in the aftermath of Pauline's murder. She repeated one of those conversations to several of her friends. Myra claimed that Brady was pleased when, one evening, she admitted that she had crossed the Rubicon through her involvement in Pauline's death. She recalled that they were watching television as they were speaking. Scenes of a packed football stadium appeared on the screen during a late night news programme. Brady pointed to the screen and asked, 'Would anyone miss one person – even two or three – out of all the millions in this country?'

Hindley admits that she didn't reply that their family would miss them. She commented to her friends that such a reply would have been pointless. Such a consideration would never have entered Brady's head. Predictably, his reaction to Myra's version was suitably unprintable, when I raised the matter with him.

In my first conversation with him about the murder, I asked about Myra's story that he was riding behind her van, flashing his headlight as a signal for her to stop and pick up Pauline Reade when he saw her walking ahead of them in Froxmer Street. Brady simply said to me, 'I wasn't there.'

Myra had, in fact, claimed that Brady had flashed his headlight for her to pick up a girl in Gorton Lane, before the left turn into Froxmer Street. She said that she had to explain to Brady that the girl was Marie Ruck, who lived only two doors from Myra's mother. It would invite danger to abduct her.

Myra's version of what happened to Pauline on Saddleworth Moor, repeated to Topping, is also at odds with the account Ian Brady gave to me. There is no space here to go into all the discrepancies but the fundamental differences between the two versions can be stated simply.

Myra claimed that Ian and Pauline walked on to the moor alone. Ian returned to Myra after half an hour and took her to the dying Pauline. Myra said that Pauline was gurgling from a massive throat wound. Ian told Myra that she would end up in the same grave if she attempted to run away. She was told to stay and wait for Ian to return with a spade. He came back and told her to go to the van, where she found that Ian had removed the ignition key.

In her confessions, Myra said that she seriously thought of driving away to contact the police after Ian and Pauline left her to walk on the moors. She didn't do so because she feared Ian's vengeance if he had not, in fact, harmed Pauline. She was afraid for her family as well as herself.

All of this flies in the face not only of Brady's account, but her own comments to police after the arrest, some of which were used as evidence at the trial. Under interrogation by Inspector Tyrrell she said, 'I made all my own decisions. People go through several stages in their life. After discussions they change their mind. Ian never made me do anything I didn't want to do. All that about killing is bloody rubbish.'

For a few months, I re-read *Topping* before each visit to Ian Brady. I recorded most of the contentious details about the case on audiocassette and listened to them on my drive up to Liverpool so that they would be fresh in my mind. You had to get up very early in the morning to be prepared for any encounter with Brady. He found it fatuous, for example, to say, as Myra did, that they went back to the moors to scatter four half-crowns on Pauline's grave. Why should they deliberately leave evidence in that wilderness which could lead to the discovery of a body?

Myra told Topping that Ian Brady gave her a record at the time of each murder they committed. When I asked him about this, he simply said, 'Crap!' He did agree, however, that they associated a song with each murder, as was the case with the killing of Pauline Reade, as we have seen.

As in most murder cases, there are minor mysteries in the death of Pauline Reade. When I first read about the case I realised that the site of Pauline's grave, and also that of Lesley Ann Downey killed eighteen months later, was variously named as Hollin Brow Knoll and Hollin Brown Knoll. Ordnance Survey maps show it as Hollin Brown Knoll.

There are also conflicting accounts of what Pauline Reade was wearing when she was murdered. Several authors say that she was wearing a pink party dress. In Ian Brady's account, Myra unzipped a *dress*. My earlier description of what Pauline was wearing when she set out from home was based on what was discovered at the autopsy after Pauline's body was found on 1 July 1987. Dr Geoffrey Garrett performed the autopsy and described the findings in his book, *Cause of Death*.

Pauline was found with her body facing the main A635 road and lying on her left side. Her right arm lay by her side and her left was folded across her body, with her hand resting on her right shoulder. Her knees were bent and her heels were tucked up near her buttocks. Pauline's underslip and skirt had been pulled up above her waist. She was wearing stockings and suspenders, but the knickers and suspender belt she had on when she left home were missing.

She had two parallel knife wounds across the front of the throat, the deepest one of which severed the spinal cord. Pauline's right hand became detached from her wrist soon after her body was removed from her grave of peat. Her left hand became detached soon afterwards in the mortuary.

Pauline's skin had turned into the texture of leather by the acidic peat after 24 years in her shallow grave. Her body needed to be immersed in a liquid for almost a week to prevent it drying and cracking. Polyethylene glycol was used to preserve the wood when Henry VIII's flagship, the *Mary Rose*, was recovered from its watery grave after it sank off Portsmouth 447 years previously. A similar liquid, a variation of anti-freeze, was used for Pauline's body.

Pauline's gold coloured chain had been cut through and the missing fragment of it was found in the wound. Her coat collar had been pushed into her severed throat. She had a swelling on her forehead, a haematoma caused by blunt force – a fist or an instrument. The swelling was the diameter of a kitchen mug. This was, in fact, part of Myra Hindley's contribution to the murder. It wasn't part of Brady's killing style. Pauline's body had deteriorated too far for there to be any signs of the sexual assault she suffered. However, Brady told me that he had raped her.

Pauline's brother, Paul was convinced for years that his sister had been disposed of in the Gorton area. Robert Wilson describes Paul's theory in his book *Return to Hell*. Like many of the books and articles on the Moors Murders, its contents have been superseded by subsequent events and revelations.

Some years ago I watched a television studio debate prompted by tabloid stories and pictures of Myra Hindley receiving her Open University degree. Paul Reade took part in the programme and was clearly obsessed by the question of what exactly had happened to his sister, as any sensitive person naturally would be. If the pages of this book can be believed, they answer Paul's question.

From my own perspective on the case, of all the many people harmed in the drama of the Moors Murders, Pauline's mother, Mrs Joan Reade, is one of the most outstanding characters, with her transparent wisdom and restrained grief. She embodied the sheer spiritual power that can be found in so-called ordinary people. Like her son Paul, she was severely traumatised by her Pauline's disappearance. She was eventually admitted into Springfield Mental Hospital, Manchester. Mrs Reade recalled the impact of the terrible nightmare of loss in her life: 'It was just one living in hope, all the time, thinking she'd come home. I was sat with my coat on for about three months, waiting for daylight to come, to run out to see if I could find her. I was just crying and crying and thinking about what had happened, in my mind. And I kept thinking about it, it built up and built up and I think that's what caused it – my nervous breakdown.

'I always had a living hope that she was about somewhere. I never thought she was dead, or anything happened to her, in any way. I had a hope that she was alive and walking about somewhere. I was always looking. I even did an Avon job, going from house to house, thinking I'd find her in one of the houses. I went miles on my own, travelling on buses and everything, thinking I'd seen her on a bus and I'd be running after that bus.

'I never thought that Myra Hindley and Ian Brady was to do with it all, because her sister was a near neighbour, lived next door but one – Maureen. She went visiting there. Myra Hindley was talking to me normally and saying she was sorry about Pauline – knowing she had done that. I didn't think till after. It all came back to me, what was what.'

Eleven days after the murder, on 23 July 1963, Myra Hindley celebrated her 21st birthday. In captivity, over thirty years after Pauline's murder, Myra said, 'Three people died that night – Pauline Reade, myself and God.'

CHAPTER FOURTEEN

TWO CRIES IN THE ROARING SILENCE

Ian Brady reflected, decades later, on the significance of a serial killer's first murder: 'The first killing experience will not only hold the strongest element of existential novelty and curiosity, but also the greatest element of danger and trepidation conjured by the unknown. Usually the incipient serial killer is too immersed in the psychological and legal challenges of the initial homicide to form a detached appreciation of the traumatic complexities bombarding his senses.

'He is killing his long-accepted self as well as the victim, and simultaneously giving birth to a new persona, decisively cutting the umbilical connection between himself and ordinary mankind.'

After several weeks, the police seemed to have no leads on Pauline Reade's disappearance. Ian and Myra began to relax. Myra committed a minor traffic offence and was chatted up by a policeman. She began a casual relationship with him and later assured Peter Topping that Brady knew nothing of it. The policeman left by the back door in Bannock Street when they heard Brady's motorbike arrive at the front.

In a later version of this story, Myra said that she fell in love with a policeman, who had called at her house about a van she had offered for sale.

Ian Brady told me that, in fact, he encouraged the relationship as a possible source of inside information. Topping knew that the policeman involved came forward to be eliminated from police enquiries after Myra was arrested.

Brady remained suspicious that he had been used by David Smith or Maureen and contemplated getting outside help to deal with them if necessary. He began to feel a change within himself: 'My habitual outward appearance of flippancy had always allowed me to enjoy a kaleidoscope of characters. I was losing the power to be this way. I was troubled by something sweetly corrupt in my subconscious. Something both repulsive and inviting. The look of fatalistic terror in Pauline Reade's eyes haunted my waking hours. I responded brutally with well-practised cynicism. My mind was fragmenting. The self-contempt phenomenon grew stronger by the day, increasing my contempt for everyone who breathed. The stronger it became, the more I felt all-powerful.

'A shock was waiting for us when we eventually returned to Saddleworth Moor. North Sea Gas had dug a trench for a pipeline across the knoll. They had narrowly missed the buried spade. If the trench had been dug on the other side of the knoll, they would have uncovered Pauline Reade's body. A commercial intrusion in such a prehistoric landscape was, to put it mildly, untimely for us, and never a prospect we considered for one moment. It was an ominous reminder that nothing was foolproof. The shadow of the unexpected intruded into all our preparations from then on.

'I photographed the burial site on our next visit. There was always some seasonal movement of peat on Saddleworth but it had brought no trace of Pauline's grave to the surface.

'On the ride home I swept round a bend in the narrow road and was forced to brake dangerously when a young girl walked into my path – "Jesus Christ! What the . . . !" Before I could spit out the expletives, the girl shouted, "Sorry! God bless!" The words stunned me. I ached from head to foot as I watched her run away. I was overcome by sadness. I revved the engine in senseless rage – "The stupid little . . ." – as I tried to ignore the cold hand of repentance that was creeping over me as I rode home.'

Ian Brady recalled this apparently insignificant incident years later: 'I was often puzzled why innocence could so easily infuriate me. I may have feared it, or its power to disarm and potentially injure. It costs nothing to be kind if you believe in a rewarding God. The belief then makes such acts selfish. The real trick lies in being capable of being kind while believing in a god that offers only oblivion, without recompense and the consolations of a future life.'

Three months after the murder of Pauline Reade, Ian Brady met David Smith for the first time. In October 1963 Smith was waiting outside

Millwards near close of work. He had heard that a man had made a pass at Mo and proposed to 'sort him out'. She had been working there for a few months. Myra and Brady saw Smith as they were leaving Millwards and offered him a lift.

Myra passed her driving test a few weeks later. She had been having lessons with a local man, Harold Rainger, and passed at her fourth attempt on 7 November 1963, sixteen days before the murder of John Kilbride. One of the incontrovertible facts at the Moors trial was that Ian Brady couldn't drive, Myra Hindley could.

As planned, Myra had gained the confidence of George Clitheroe at Millwards by flattery, asking him to demonstrate his skills as a marksman. He put a matchstick on a sack in Millwards warehouse and ignited it from a distance with a single shot.

In mid-summer 1963, Myra paid John Boland, a member of the club, eight pounds for a 0.45 Webley revolver and twenty rounds of ammunition. In September 1963, Alan Cottam, another member, sold her a 0.38 Smith and Wesson revolver for five pounds, without ammunition. Myra would buy a rifle in 1964 from Stensby's in Manchester, a shop Ian Brady had noticed a few years before when he had visited Peggy for a two-week holiday.

Autumn had arrived in Gorton, and brought with it the annual transformation of Ian Brady. Myra and Ian were having a night in at Bannock Street: 'We sat in front of Myra's glowing fire, drinking cherry wine.

' Myra was half-awake as she said, "Neddie. When's the next, one?"

' "*Another* one? Are you *that* hungry? You surprise me!" ' I grabbed her and we dropped to the floor, wrestling. I bit her shoulder and whispered, "Just stroke my neck for now. We'll see, Kiddo." Outside the dying season was tightening its lugubrious grip. Leaves, now turned to flame, dropped into wind currents as they swept in barren whispers along the pavements of Gorton. The air was mordant with decay.'

Ian surfaced from the green mist clouding his mind and reached for the cherry wine. Chris Barber's Jazz Band was playing 'Petite Fleur' on the radio. Myra said, 'So you're awake, Neddie.' Ian asked her what time it was. It was just after midnight. Ian opened the front door and looked up and down Bannock Street. It was quiet and deserted, a dry, clear night. He said, 'Let's go for a trip out and see what there is to see.' Almost without thinking, he added: 'We'll retrieve the master list from the warehouse tomorrow.' Myra responded with 'Zzzeee!' Ian said, 'You've got it in one, Kiddo!'

They roared out of Bannock Street on the bike with Ian singing a song from his childhood, 'When whippoorwills call, and evening is nigh, I hurry to my blue heaven.'

But where was that particular heaven? They would soon find out.

The following night they spread a map of Manchester on the table, pushing the wine and cigarettes aside. The police were probably assuming that Pauline Reade had met her fate with someone she knew or encountered in Gorton. Myra said that they couldn't risk picking up the second victim from the same vicinity. Ian nodded in agreement and thought aloud: 'We could choose another city, Huddersfield or Leeds, say, but then the Manchester police would probably not link the two disappearances and continue to concentrate on Gorton. And, in any case, the farther we have to travel with the selected target, the more chance of being seen by an eye-witness.'

Myra said that wouldn't be a problem if they picked another burial ground nearer the target district. Ian replied: 'We've learned our lesson from the gas pipeline. We shall have to check out any new burial ground, however remote.'

They exchanged more suggestions while staring at the map and eventually agreed on an option that had been staring them in the face all evening: choose an area both distant from Gorton and nearer Saddleworth Moor. Ian's eye fell on Ashton-under-Lyne. It was six miles from Saddleworth and five miles from Gorton.

Ian picked up his jacket: 'Let's take a look at it. What do you know about it?' 'Nowt,' Myra replied. At the trial, she would deny that she knew anything about Ashton market. Her sister Maureen would be used as a prosecution witness to contradict Myra's claim. After locking the maps and papers in the black briefcase the couple swept out of Bannock Street on the motorbike. Ian was in for a pleasant surprise.

When they arrived in Ashton they almost immediately chanced upon a market area, with its avenues of empty stalls. As they walked around it, Ian suddenly realised it was the same market he had visited with Peggy during his fortnight's holiday from Scotland: 'As soon as I recovered from this welcome recognition, I said to Myra; "We'll use the market for the pick-up area. Follow me." I led the way down a side street. A long dark backstreet ran alongside the market. There were no houses in the street or any threats of danger from over-looking windows. We could see only factory walls and the rears of commercial premises. The place fitted the bill. This would do fine.'

'We carefully planned the procedures for the pick-up, and selected the following Saturday, a busy day for markets everywhere. Back home in Bannock Street, we included the new information in selected guidelines from the master list.'

The working list they drew up included the usual range of abbreviations. For example, TOBAC = Tobacconist's Pick Me Up; OBV = Observation Points; TA = Target Area. The car would be parked in the dim backstreet they had inspected. Myra would walk to the target area by one side street, Ian to his first observation point by another, keeping a constant eye on her and looking for anyone paying her too much attention. After she had picked up the victim and was walking to the car, Brady would move to his second observation point, again watching for eyewitnesses.

If Brady saw any possible threatening complication from his observation points, he would go straight to the car and call off the operation with a prepared excuse to the pick-up. But if no worrying factors occurred, Ian would walk to a tobacconist's shop and wait for Myra to pick him up and drive to Saddleworth Moor. If there were a threatening eyewitness incident during the journey, again the operation would be aborted with a ready-made story to the pick-up. The preparations were backed-up by contingency plans for any unforeseen eventuality. If all else failed, there was lethal force.

It was nearly dawn by the time their plans were completed. Before catching a couple of hours' sleep and leaving for the office, they reached a decision about vehicles. They would replace them frequently and sell them in part exchange. For the operation they had planned, however, they would hire a car. Ian Brady later reflected upon that stage in his life: 'Miles across the darkened sprawl of Manchester, somewhere there slept a stranger whose life we were soon to enter. They were as yet unknown to us, and we to them. But our fates were drawing closer by the minute. The days of life left for that stranger were few, unless their benign god intervened to challenge my own deity – Death itself.'

Ian contacted his criminally minded friends for advice about stealing a car and holding on to it. He realised that numbers in the engine and on the chassis would have to be erased but was surprised to learn that the numbers could be detected by infrared. He wasn't going to take the risk to be arrested on what was, for Brady, a trivial charge. He was also in for a surprise when he arranged to meet his friend Alex.

As they sat drinking, Alex told him that not only was he still desperate to locate the elusive Gil, but that he had murderous intentions for another mutual acquaintance. Ian persuaded Alex, for the time being at least, to shelve his plans to kill the contact. Later, Ian reflected about the black comedy of this, considering the circumstances: 'Alex and I sat drinking in the pub. I couldn't help but ponder the irony of the situation; an irony he wasn't in on. I was cautioning him against murder. I reflected on what his response would be to the calculated carnage Myra and I had now been engaged in. I would have thought him raving mad if he had shared with me the plans he and his girlfriend had for murdering individuals on whim on purely philosophical, existential grounds. He would be a danger to me because of what he knew. He would be someone I would have to eliminate as soon as possible – after finding out the name and whereabouts of his girlfriend, so as to murder her too for what he might have told her about me.

'There it was in the clear light of clinical logic; yet, it was paradoxically insane. If he had my own convictions, and was behaving as Myra and I were, I would have thought him mad without hesitation. I asked myself, why did I not classify myself mad? The logical answer was simple. Because I was mad! I couldn't help laughing at the farcical implications of the situation. Alex put his beer down on the table, expecting me to let him in on the joke. His puzzled expression just made me chortle even more until beer came through my nose.'

This description prompted me to ask Ian Brady whether he and Myra ever considered the prospect of there being other individuals out there who showed the same contempt for law and human life as they did. 'But of course we took that not only as a possibility but also as an absolute certainty. Myra and I used a *Goon Show* apostrophe, which encapsulated the concept: "What! The gold I stole stolen! Is nothing sacred?"'

Ian and Myra hired a car from Warren's Autos on London Road in Manchester. It was booked a week in advance for use on Saturday, 23 November 1963.

Ian was emerging from another fugue and Myra was rubbing his neck to relieve a headache. She asked him if they were putting the suitcases into left-luggage: 'No, not this time. Hiring the car is just to put something in the records. The police would check with car hire firms as a matter of routine. It would show that we hired cars on days when no one disappeared. It diverts suspicion.' Myra couldn't remember discussing this particular tactic. Brady insisted they had.

After a minute's silence he suddenly changed his mind: 'Okay. We do it this Saturday. We'll deposit the suitcases to Central Station.' Myra expressed her delight with 'Zzzeee!'

On their way into the city, Ian bought two tubes of Pro-plus from a chemist's. It was a mild caffeine-based stimulant that could be bought over the counter. He used it before each murder. They needed to clock up a substantial mileage on the hired car to match the alibi. Where was it to be? They opted for Leek in Staffordshire.

When they arrived at Manchester Central, Myra waited in the car while Ian booked the two cases in left-luggage. He was walking back through the crowds in the station and overheard a man say, 'Kennedy's dead.' It was about seven o'clock in the evening on Friday, 22 November 1963.

Ian switched on the radio when he returned to the van. John F Kennedy had been shot dead in Dallas. It was an unforgettable night. As has already been noted, the novelist and philosopher Aldous Huxley had died during the day. The famous author C S Lewis would die in Oxford before midnight. At the time Ian Brady heard of the assassination, I was watching an episode of the long-running BBC soap series *Coronation Street*. The programme was interrupted with a news flash. In a moment of panic, I imagined that Russians had killed JFK and that World War III was about to break out.

The scheduled television programmes were abandoned for the evening as Myra and Brady discovered when they returned to Bannock Street. They watched, as I did, the blanket coverage of the assassination, the blurred pictures of the killing itself and the grainy footage of Jackie Kennedy at the hospital with her husband's blood on her clothes.

Ian Brady recalled that 'the theatricality of it all was mesmerising. It was live mayhem and madness by the hour.' After the initial shock and the news from Dallas sank in, Ian and Myra realised that the assassination had provided a massive diversion from what they were about to do the next day. Decades later, Brady reflected, 'It's an ill wind . . .' and quoted Horace: 'The changing year's progressive plan, proclaims mortality to man.'

Some books and articles on the Moors Murders have claimed that the assassination of President Kennedy triggered the murder committed by Brady and Hindley the following day. There was no question of this. After I raised the question with Brady, he wrote: 'All our arrangements and procedures for the target on 23rd November had already been finalised a week in advance.'

It's true that Ian Brady always linked the two deaths *afterwards*. When the video of the film *JFK* was released, he was fascinated by it and had watched it at least half a dozen times over a Christmas break.

In her confessions, Myra told Topping that Brady bought her a record to mark the second murder: Gene Pitney singing 'Twenty-four Hours From Tulsa'. Brady denied buying Myra records, as we have already seen. He did admit that the song evoked memories of the murder, though.

In the same confessions, Myra also told Topping that there was no research or reconnaissance for this or any of the murders. Anyone who has known Ian Brady would find this claim plainly false. Myra also assured Topping that no child had run away from them when they were approached; they had no failures. Brady strongly denied this to me. Some children had spurned Myra's overtures.

In December 2002, a woman claimed Brady and Hindley had approached her with a third person in August 1964. I asked Ian Brady about the alleged incident and he denied any knowledge of it. He assured me that Myra picked up all the known victims, apart from the final one, Edward Evans.

In number 7 Bannock Street, on the night before the murder of John Kilbride, Ian and Myra were replete with wine and the television coverage of the President's assassination. They went upstairs to bed to dream of committing their own private assassination. Like Lee Harvey Oswald, eventually they too would be news forever . . . but not yet.

In hindsight, Ian Brady thought of Anatole France's observation: 'It is human nature to think wisely and to act in an absurd fashion.' He couldn't have put it better himself: 'How true. But truth is the harlot of time, place and circumstance. Therefore, I ignored it.'

* * * * *

Sheila and Pat Kilbride were in their thirties and lived with their six children at number 262 Smallshaw Lane, Ashton-under Lyne. The house was two miles from Ashton market. John Kilbride was twelve and the eldest child. He shared one of the three bedrooms with his brother, Danny, who was a year younger. (As a man, Danny would campaign for years to keep Myra Hindley in prison.) The Kilbrides were a Catholic family. Just a few weeks before his death, John started at St Damian's Roman Catholic Secondary School.

Like Hindley and Brady, the Kilbrides watched the television coverage from Dallas on that Friday night. They felt some affinity with Kennedy, a Catholic with Irish ancestry. Pat Kilbride was Irish.

Saturday dawned. The date was 23 November 1963. Ian Brady and Myra Hindley rose from their beds with murder in mind. Breakfast for the Kilbrides was no different from normal, apart from talk about the cataclysmic event of the night before. Myra collected the hire car from Warren's Autos at 10 a.m. It was a two-door white Ford Anglia – registration number 9275 NB.

The foreman at the firm, Peter Cantwell, gave evidence at the Moors trial and said that Hindley was alone when she collected it. He recalled that she was wearing 'a pair of black trews, a leather jacket, a high-necked sweater and, I would say, black shoes.'

In the Topping interviews, Myra said that she drove from Warren's Autos to pick up Ian and his dog from Westmoreland Street. After their trip out to Leek they returned to Gorton at 4 p.m.

The clothes John Kilbride was wearing on the day of his death were crucial for the identification of his body when it was eventually found. Before going down to breakfast, he put on a white shirt, grey flannel trousers and his shoes – black chisel-toed Supa-Dukes, recently repaired at the local Co-op. Underneath, he was wearing his father's old vest, which his mother had taken in to fit John. After breakfast, John went round to Rowley Street to see his gran, Mrs Margaret Doran. He called on her every morning to put her stockings on and do odd jobs, sometimes weeding the garden.

The Kilbrides had fish and chips at lunchtime. In a television documentary, Sheila Kilbride said John was tormenting his brothers and sisters and that she had told him to go and see his film. John put on his sports jacket and went out of the front door. The buttons on his jacket were plastic, in the shape of footballs. His mother had kept a spare button that was also crucial in identifying John's body.

John met up with his pal, John Ryan, who was the same age. They went to the Pavilion cinema – the 'Pav' – to see Jack Palance in *The Mongols*. It was over by 4.30 p.m. and they walked to Ashton market to earn some pocket money by helping traders. A man with a carpet stall sent them to the nearby Charlestown railway station to collect a small truck. They were given six pence each and probably spent the money on ice cream from Roland Evans' stall, as usual. John's parents didn't know that he did odd jobs for market traders. One report claims that John's father had been in the market himself until 4.45 p.m., looking for a new pair of shoes.

A fog had descended on Ashton-under-Lyne by 5.45 p.m. John Ryan wanted to go home and left John Kilbride standing by a large salvage bin. The question is what happened next.

Hindley's story is at odds with Brady's. Brady said that everything went according to the plan described in previous pages. Myra spoke to the target, a boy, about a lost glove. Brady watched for signs of interest from the crowds of shoppers. Myra and the boy walked to the car and picked up Brady a few minutes later at the prearranged spot outside the tobacconist shop.

In Myra's version, she had put on a black wig – Brady denied this – and was waiting in a side street for Brady to return with a victim. Brady eventually arrived with John Kilbride, having enticed him with the offer of a bottle of sherry in return for helping them to search for a lost glove. John Kilbride sat alongside Myra in the front of the car after Brady had climbed into a back seat.

Myra told Topping that they drove to Saddleworth Moor and she parked in a lay-by on the opposite side of the road from where Pauline Reade was buried. From then on, she followed Brady's instructions. He took a torch from the boot of the car and she drove back down the hill to Greenfield as Brady and the boy walked on to the moor together. She parked next to the Clarence pub and waited there for half an hour after removing a rifle from the boot and putting it on the front passenger seat. Myra returned to the lay-by and flashed her headlights into the black landscape. She held her breath. Three tiny flashes answered in the darkness.

After a few minutes, Brady returned to the car carrying a spade and a shoe. He told her later that he had tried to cut the boy's throat with a knife that had a serrated blade. It was too blunt. He had strangled John Kilbride with a piece of string. The spade, shoe and string were put in the boot.

Years later, after the Topping investigations, Brady wrote to tell me that Myra's story about the role of the rifle in the murder could have been easily refuted. Brady claimed that Topping neglected to check the police records that would have shown that the rifle was purchased and registered in 1964 – a year after John Kilbride was murdered.

When I first raised the subject of John Kilbride's death with Ian Brady, he poured scorn on my brief summary of Myra's version, distilled as it was from *Topping*. Brady denied that the use of a knife – blunt or otherwise – played any part in the death of the boy. After all, he had almost decapitated Pauline Reade with a razor-sharp knife. Why would he try to use a knife with a short, blunt blade to kill John Kilbride?

Brady told me that all three of them walked on to the moor. John Kilbride, as young as he was, sensed danger and received no sensible answer to his questions. What were they doing there? John was afraid by now. It was too dark to look for a glove. He was miles from home with two total strangers. But one of them was a woman – there was nothing to be afraid of. With the agreed 'Groucho' movement of his eyes, Brady signalled to Myra to overtake him and guide the boy to do the same. Brady had to nod a 'Groucho' three times before Myra recognised his gesture in the mist and gloom of the moor.

Myra was a few feet away when Brady grabbed John Kilbride's throat from behind. He could locate the carotid artery easily – whether it was in the throat of a clerk at Millwards or a child on Saddleworth Moor. Myra joined in the struggle to restrain the boy, who was frantically defending himself. But John was no match for the combined efforts of Brady and Hindley and was forced to the ground. There was no protracted drama as there had been when Pauline Reade was killed. It was all over within a few minutes.

John was kicking wildly as Hindley held his wrists and Brady pulled the boy's trousers and underpants down. He tied a knot in John's underpants at the rear and sexually assaulted him. Brady strangled John to death with his hands as Hindley pinned the boy's legs together.

A spade was retrieved from a hiding place on the moor and Brady dug a shallow grave. Myra helped him to put John's body inside it, face down. Before Brady shovelled earth on top he slapped the boy's backside. Then he shook his fist at the night sky: 'I shouted, "Take that, you bastard!" This was my gesture in the face of whatever malignant force it is which underlies this universe, devoted only to chaos. I found a shoe nearby that I hadn't buried. I took it back to the car and we drove back to Myra's.'

John Kilbride had been buried at right angles to the A635 road, with his head facing south. The map showed that the grave was on a small area of the moor called Sail Bark Moss. It would be 23 months before his body was discovered.

In Bannock Street, Myra helped Brady to burn his clothes and shoes after making sure that John Kilbride's odd shoe was committed to the flames first. At the same time, in Smallshaw Lane, Ashton-under-Lyne, Sheila was wondering where her son had got to: 'I thought John had stayed in the cinema to watch the film round again, which you could in those days, as it carried right on.' She eventually phoned the police. She had no inkling that her son was dead and buried before she made the call. The police apparently arrived early on Sunday morning.

The same morning, Brady and Hindley cleaned the hire car and wiped fingerprints off all surfaces. At the trial, the foreman at Warren's Autos said that Myra was alone when she returned the car on Sunday: 'It was extremely dirty; it looked as if it had been through a ploughed field.'

As expected, the press coverage of John Kilbride's disappearance was sidelined by the news of another JK – President Kennedy. Nevertheless, hundreds of people joined in the search for John. Frogmen were used as well as cadets from the Preston Police Training School and soldiers from the Royal Army Pay Corps. When John's friend, John Ryan, told police that he had last seen him near a large salvage bin, the remains of burnt rubbish were filtered through for days, in case over-exuberant friends had thrown John into the bin.

John Kilbride's smiling face was reproduced on the thousands of posters that were distributed.

The police used the services of the psychic Annie Lansley, who lived in Ashton-under-Lyne, in an attempt to discover John's whereabouts. She saw John's resting place as '. . . someway down a slope, with the skyline completely barren and not a tree in sight . . . a main road on the right and quite near a stream.' This was a remarkably accurate description of the whereabouts of John's grave. Brady told me, 'There's no truth in the "psychic tosh", but if she had been accurate about the fate of the next target she would have been murdered.' He also referred to the use of a psychic in *The Gates of Janus*. He was discussing the accuracy of a psychic in the Hillside Strangler's case and made the following comments: 'The police used a psychic in my case. She, on two occasions, accurately described certain loci. Newspapers published her predictions and visions. After the first prediction, I, always overestimating the police on principle – far too generously, as I later discovered – put it down to inspired guesswork, or the police applying proactive methodology to force a wrong move. After the second prediction, I began to think in terms of having the psychic source neutralised by a third reliable party from another city. There was no known connection between myself and the third party, but I insisted that he should try to make the killing look like an accident.

'I still regarded the police predictions as guesswork, but was pragmatic enough to take into consideration the possible psychological and random consequences of such visions and predictions. As they were public knowledge, either the police might start searching for the loci described, or, possibly the greater threat, some member of the public might recognise the loci. Conversely, if none of these possible scenarios was valid and the psychic source was neutralised in a manner eventually discovered to be non-accidental, this might validate the visions and predictions in the eyes of the police, and possibly channel their activities in directions I was trying to deflect them from. There was also the possibility that, if the police were using proactive methods, they might be expecting an attempt on the psychic's life and be waiting in readiness. So it was Catch-22. I did, however, suspend a final decision on the proviso that no further accurate predictions surfaced. None did.'

Two weeks after the murder, Ian and Myra collected the cases from left-luggage in Manchester Central. Myra denied any previous knowledge of the suitcases to Topping, assuming that this was the first time Ian had taken this precaution. Myra claimed that she never knew what was in the cases. She was once tempted to open one and pulled it out from under the bed, but noticed that a human hair was trapped in the lock and feared that this was Ian's way of checking whether the case had been opened. She had second thoughts and pushed it back under the bed. Ian Brady laughed when I mentioned that Myra claimed to know nothing of the contents of the suitcases.

Brady drew my attention to a passage in Fred Harrison's *Brady and Hindley – Genesis of the Moors Murders*, in which Harrison wrote of the cruel morbidity of Brady and Hindley, claiming that they went to John Kilbride's home in Smallshaw Lane, posing as detectives. For half an hour, Brady and Hindley apparently questioned Sheila Kilbride and left the house with some of John's clothes, promising that, 'Johnny would be back home in a week's time'.

Brady denied that he and Myra ever went to the Kilbride home. Sheila Kilbride appears never to have mentioned it.

Myra told Topping that Ian used to take her on his bike to the top of Smallshaw Lane, where the Kilbrides lived. I mentioned this to Brady and he surprised me by agreeing with Myra for once. He said that she was simply using a principle he had taught her: 'Tell a small truth to hide a greater lie.' Brady said they sat on the bike at the top of the lane, eating fish and chips bought from a shop across the road.

One evening when they were there, Brady was scanning the horizon with his binoculars and realised that he was looking at the peaks of Saddleworth Moor. He could make out what he called the 'Needle', on the skyline of the moors: 'I was amazed by the criss-cross of Smallshaw Lane and the distant vista of the moors. Only Myra and I knew what linked these two places.'

In the weeks that followed the murder, Ian and Myra hired a car on two days, 27 November 27 and 21 December 1963. We saw earlier that this was part of their detailed ploy – the date 23 November wouldn't attract so much suspicion if a car were hired on other days. Ian Brady told me that Myra had kept the receipt for the car on 23 November without telling him: 'A big mistake.'

In the months that followed the murder, Brady himself breached his own criminal creed by committing two even greater mistakes. He had written John Kilbride's name in an exercise book in a list of several other names. He would have a lifetime to regret it and ponder the best-laid plans of mice and serial killers; he had fallen down on his own first principle and left a connecting thread.

Brady's second error would be even more damning for himself and Myra after their arrest. They checked the gravesites of Pauline Reade and John Kilbride on the third day of the New Year 1964, a day after Brady's 26th birthday. A few weeks later, Lassie gave birth to her puppies, crossbred tan-and-white collies. Myra kept one and called it 'Puppet'. The dog would have its day. It too would become a victim of the Moors Murders.

Brady and Myra took the puppy to the moors with them to check the graves again. He condemned himself for life when he found Myra and Puppet in his viewfinder and pressed the shutter. In the photograph the dog's head is peering out of Myra's coat as she stares down on John Kilbride's grave. After the arrest, police photographic experts put the negative of this picture under a microscope to reveal tiny scrape marks caused by the metal plate that supported the film in what was incontrovertibly Brady's camera.

The photograph would be impossible to explain away. But Myra tried: 'There could have been bodies all over the place.'

Janie Jones, in her book *The Devil and Miss Jones*, wrote that Myra was still denying, years later, that she knew she was looking down on the grave. Myra is quoted in Jones' book as saying, 'When the photograph was taken, John Kilbride had not even disappeared.'

Myra was still clinging to a semblance of innocence when she wrote to the journalist Duncan Staff. An extract of the letter appeared in the *Guardian* on 13 November 2001. She said that Brady, '. . . stopped me as I was walking and said to turn round, moved me a bit and told me to kneel down and look at Puppet. I now know, knew quite soon afterwards, that he's photographed me virtually kneeling on John Kilbride's grave.'

John Kilbride's disappearance, like all human tragedies, bred many other stories and brands of misery. Sheila Kilbride always set a place for John at meals. A few years after the death of his son, Pat Kilbride said, 'I just went haywire. I became an alcoholic.' Sheila and Pat divorced five years after John's murder.

Detective Chief Inspector Joe Mounsey joined Ashton police at the end of 1964 and read the files on John Kilbride's disappearance. He put a poster issued at the time of John's disappearance on his office wall. As a result of Joe Mounsey's interest in the case, John Kilbride became known as 'Mounsey's lad'. Mounsey would be on Saddleworth Moor when John Kilbride's body was found and took a major role in interrogating Brady and Hindley after their arrest.

*   *   *   *   *

Ian wanted to visit the Gorbals again. Early in February, Myra bought a car, a green Austin A40. They set out at midnight.

It was morning by the time they entered the Gorbals: 'Myra drove down to the close of number 56 Camden Street. It seemed as if the tenement had been waiting for us to come. Workmen had demolished and removed the stone and rubble of all the tenements but had unaccountably halted at my old close and were knocking down buildings from the other end of the street. I said nothing to Myra for a few minutes. I was absorbed by the question of what made the demolition crews stop at number 56. Was it some pagan deity, miraculously intervening on my behalf, granting a short stay of execution, allowing me to bid final farewell to the old stone that once was so familiar with my touch?

'The vanished tenements were still there in my mind's eye. As I led Myra through the dereliction, I felt the presence of the people and things that had gone forever.

'Myra and I had binoculars and cameras with us as we found our way into my old close and walked up the well-trodden stone stairs to the landing. I stood gazing down through the empty window frame at the dovecote, just about showing traces of the faded black-and-white paint that had once been so visible to me.

'I took a few photographs of the dovecote before going down to the backyards. They were once my total world, full of activity and noises of children at play. The wind blew litter across the backs. This was the only sign of movement. My camera didn't capture the bright sunlit days of long ago and the excitement of waking to fill the day with adventures. The camera caught nothing but uncomprehending, hollow-eyes, out of time, looking down on empty, squalid yards.

'I wondered what the few remaining inhabitants – squatters – made of Myra and me as we took photographs and scanned the scene with binoculars. We were the aliens from another time. Myra and I had loaded revolvers with us.'

In his prison years, Ian Brady's thoughts were ambiguous whenever he heard the final verse of the song, 'The Days of Pearly Spencer' and its reference to tenements, memories and origins.

Ian felt invigorated by their brief visit to Glasgow and Camden Street. After a few days he was disturbed again by flashbacks of Pauline Reade's eyes. He reacted, as he had done before, with contempt for the people who crossed his path from day to day. One of the first stories he recounted to me about himself belonged to this period. While he was with Myra, he went to the cinema alone if he was in a solitary mood: 'As I left a cinema during the final credits one night, to miss having to stand for the national anthem, a man in the aisle stood in my way as the anthem began. In a rage, I lifted him from the ground by his lapels and threw him between the seats amongst the litter. I stared at him, waiting for any justifiable excuse to murder him. I was furious at my crassness later, not for wanting to murder the patriotic cretin but for risking losing my own liberty for such a trivial reason. I mentioned the incident to Myra. She guffawed at the surreal spectacle I would have presented, strangling him to death in the ice-cream cartons to the tune of the national anthem!'

In these first weeks of 1964, he recalled how even trivial things caused him stress. He used his interest in the cinema to make the point: 'As a film-buff, I preferred the most expensive seats. Myra and I often queued, like many more; waiting for the commissionaire to shout what seats had become available. I hated taking up the offer when the dearest seats were called and no one in front took up the offer. I had to walk past the queue and into the cinema, unintentionally humiliating those who couldn't afford the seats.

'Again, when I was speaking to someone, I would stop myself using a word that may have been unfamiliar to my listener, and wasted time explaining my point in alternative ways. I wasn't being condescending. It was just good manners to me. Good taste may be poison to the mind, but we often learn something when we exercise it.'

On 6 May 1964, Myra exchanged her car for a white Morris mini-van, registration number VDB 893. It would be used to abduct two children. She re-registered it for four months on 16 January 1965 and sold it three months later.

I had asked Ian Brady, in a letter, how he and Myra felt about being confronted with individuals who were as ruthless as they were. I had also asked about their use of guns. He replied in November 1992: 'Whenever we were sitting in the car in darkness in isolated terrain, just sipping wine, smoking and enjoying the peacefulness, the car windows and doors were always shut, giving us the seconds to draw a revolver. In fact we wished for one of those lovers-lane prowlers you read about so much in the newspapers to turn up, just to see the surprise on his face, and provide us with some entertainment during his final span on earth. Even when walking in the wilds in daylight I carried the snub-nose .38 Smith and Wesson comfortably in a holster under my waistcoat, just in case we encountered some hillbilly-type with trouble in mind. Myra often carried the .45 Webley in a cosmetic case.

'You almost hit the target when you, intuitively, speculated that there would be acknowledged "admiration for someone else who was living without fear of the Unconditional." Apart from Myra, there were two people I really trusted. They were as ruthless as I was. So the operative word was not admiration but loyalty; mutual-loyalty. You might find that paradoxical – ruthlessness and loyalty. But not if you considered it's rather an exclusive club, in which you have to put your neck on the line to become a member. One of them got rid of a danger to me; in return, I got rid of a danger to him. I should add that the police know of this, but without names it means nothing. They also know locations, meaningless without the vital statistics – he favoured water, the River Ouse, I the North Sea Gas pipeline. Check the length of the Ouse and pipeline and you'll see what I mean.

'However, it wasn't a perfect circle. Although I trusted the two, they never did really trust (or like) each other. After my arrest and sentence, one of them was found dead – in water. So, you see, it was rather convoluted. The question of my giving the police the name of the survivor does not arise. Nor of giving the name of the danger or location, as this would also point the finger.

'You did well in intuition, considering it's rather an esoteric field in which, I assume, you remain a stranger.'

The two trusted friends referred to here can only be Alex and Gil Deare mentioned in earlier chapters. The comment 'I got rid of a danger to him' refers to the second 'happening'. I have already described the first 'happening', when Brady threw a woman into the canal at Rochdale.

This second 'happening' claimed by Brady, took place in May 1964, before the murder of Keith Bennett. The victim was an eighteen-year-old youth who was killed on the moors. A friend drove Brady and the youth to the moors. Brady didn't divulge the driver's name because it would implicate someone else who has since given up criminal activities and settled down.

Myra was not involved. Brady walked into the moor with the youth for about a quarter of a mile, before shooting him in the back of the head. He used the .38 revolver mentioned in the letter just quoted. Brady claims that he buried the body with a spade that lay hidden on the moor. A white handkerchief was tied to a road marker at the edge of the A635.

Topping investigated the alleged murder but could find no evidence of a youth – or a child – going missing at that time. Myra Hindley was questioned but claimed to know nothing about it. She said that she had never dropped off anyone on the moors except Brady and David Smith for shooting practice. Topping's team made a cursory search of an area of the moor but soon abandoned it. With only vague directions to guide them, they had an impossible task when faced with the vastness of the moors.

Ian Brady alluded to this particular 'happening' in *The Gates of Janus*: 'I regard personal disloyalty as the worst crime of all, and I have killed some guilty of it without a qualm.'

Early in June 1964, Brady and Hindley felt the urge to do another murder, but not before a trip to Glasgow. When they arrived, they found that the police were using white jeeps with cages at the back. Individual policemen there were as helpful as ever. The couple asked one of them for directions to Barlanark, and he kept them for ten minutes describing every possible route: 'I don't know if he was influenced by the fact that the pocket of the open car door was lined with bottles of rum, vodka, gin and whisky.'

The suitcases were put in left-luggage soon after their return to Manchester. If we are to believe her, Myra knew nothing about this or any of the detailed plans for the third murder she was about to be involved in. They were going to the moors again. She knew nothing more than this, she claims, until just before the event. The target area would be Longsight and a street near to the Stockport Road that linked the middle-class areas of Cheshire with central Manchester. Ian's own house in Westmoreland Street was in Longsight.

*   *   *   *   *

Keith Bennett was twelve years old, the oldest of four children and had his birthday four days before he was murdered. He lived at number 29 Eston Street, a cul-de-sac in Longsight. I walked down the street many years later and looked at the house he left on that fateful evening. Number 29 was the last house on the left, with an alley separating it from the brick wall at the end of the street. Keith used to kick a football against the wall with his friends. His mother Winnie was thirty when Keith disappeared, and seven months pregnant. The child, David, was born prematurely soon afterwards. She had been divorced and recently married her second husband Jimmy Johnson, a joiner. Winnie and Jimmy have had other children.

Keith and his sister Sylvia took turns to sleep on Tuesday nights at their grandmother's house. Mrs Gertrude Bennett was 65, and lived in Morton Street, Longsight, just a quarter of a mile from Eston Street. The day before the night in question Keith had taken part in his school's swimming gala. He swam the length of the baths for the first time and was given a certificate. During the evening he dropped and broke his glasses. He had been short-sighted since he was quite small.

On the night he went missing, 16 June 1964, Keith's mother had planned to go to a bingo session at 8 p.m. in St Aloysius School off Ardwick Green. Keith, without his glasses, left 29 Eston Street with his mother at about 7.45 p.m. They walked into Hathersage Road, across Plymouth Grove and along Plymouth Grove West. Keith was wearing a T-shirt, blue jeans, black shoes and a white leather zip-up jacket. He walked ahead of his mother. She was concerned about his safety until he crossed the busy Stockport Road at a zebra crossing.

In conversations about the murder of Keith Bennett, Ian Brady said that he was waiting in Ardwick, ironically in Bennett Street, while Myra was parked in Grey Street or Morton Street to pick up a victim. She saw Keith Bennett and offered him a reward if he would help her to carry boxes from an off-licence. The story about the lost glove was aired shortly afterwards as she drove to pick up Ian. In Myra's version, he was in the back of the vehicle already and had tapped the back window as a signal for her to stop and pick up Keith Bennett. She then drove to Saddleworth Moor and parked in a lay-by at Hoe Grain.

Brady said that all three of them walked into the moor to Shiny Brook, a stream that runs parallel to the road and three-quarters of a mile in. They then followed the stream bed. Keith was becoming anxious that his grandmother would wonder whether he was going to stay the night with her if he didn't arrive at her house in an hour.

Brady was mostly silent as they walked. His gaunt six-foot figure led the way. He knew where the three of them were going. So did Myra. She knew that just two people would return to the car. Myra offered Keith a few reassuring comments that he would be back in Longsight before long.

Brady told me that they had walked for three miles from the road before stopping. Myra had carried a spade and a rifle wrapped in a plastic mac.

Brady began to whistle 'When You Wish Upon A Star' for Myra to overtake the boy. As they entered a gully, Brady grabbed Keith's throat from behind. Keith sank to the ground and screamed in panic. His cry was lost in the wilderness and eerie silence of Saddleworth Moor. Myra held Keith's legs as he tried to kick Brady. Keith was fighting just as hard as John Kilbride had.

Myra pinioned the boy's legs as Brady pulled Keith's trousers down and sexually assaulted him. He then strangled him to death with his bare hands. It was all over in a few minutes, as John Kilbride's murder had been.

Brady photographed Keith as he lay on his back before Myra helped Brady to bury him. Brady put a large rock on the grave as a marker, 'like a headstone,' in Brady's words to me. Brady added that he was surprised that metal detectors hadn't located Keith's body from the metal zip on the jacket he was wearing. I informed Manchester police of Brady's statement. I do not know whether they took it further.

It was dark on their walk back to the road. Car lights guided them. Myra lost her shoe and they went back to find it. As they approached the car Brady unwrapped the rifle as a precaution against anyone waiting for them.

Myra's account of the evening is, as it was in the case of the previous two murders, at odds with Brady's. She said that she was some distance behind Ian and Keith as they walked into the moor, looking through binoculars for any threatening signs of human activity. Ian signalled Myra to stop at one point, as he walked on with Keith into a dip some thirty yards ahead.

She stayed there on lookout until Ian returned alone after half an hour, carrying a spade. She had heard no sounds while she was on watch. Myra asked Ian whether there had been any sexual activity. He said, 'Why, does it matter?' Myra denies that she saw Keith's dead body. Brady dismissed Myra's account. When I asked him where Myra was at the moment of Keith's death, I received a very brief reply: 'She was a yard from me. I couldn't keep her away – she enjoyed it!'

After returning home to Myra's, Ian burned his trousers and counted the buttons on the rest of his clothing. He ticked off items on a disposal list Myra claimed never to have seen before. Their shoes showed the remains of shale from the Moor and were also burned. The vehicle was cleaned the same night and more thoroughly again the next day in daylight. Ian developed the photograph two days after the murder at his house in Westmoreland Street. Myra's house didn't have a bathroom. She saw the print of Keith with his trousers down and blood on his body. Ian destroyed the photograph. It was blurred. Ian and Myra agree on that point.

Myra told Topping that she had put on a black wig in a side street before they picked up Keith Bennett. Brady denied this. There was no black wig that night.

There was a report that Keith Bennett had been seen with a blonde woman on the day he disappeared. Brady told me that this was the only actual sighting in the whole Moors case. Myra did wear a wear a black wig for their criminal activities afterwards. He rejected Myra's claim again that he gave her a record on the day of the murder but agreed that the song they always associated with it was Roy Orbison's number one hit, 'It's Over'.

Early in the morning after the murder, Keith's grandmother walked to Eston Street to ask Winnie why he hadn't spent the night at her home in Morton Street. She usually brought Keith back to Eston Street on her way to her cleaner's job at the TocH centre in Victoria Park. Both women became anxious. Winnie went to Keith's Victoria Park secondary school and the local clinic, in case he had been there about his broken glasses. Keith hadn't been seen at either place. She went to the police but was told that her son would have to be missing for 48 hours before they could do anything.

Keith's stepfather, Jimmy Johnson, had the misfortune to be the first suspect. He was to suffer the same ordeal three more times in the two years after Keith's disappearance. The police took up the floorboards at the house in Eston Street and discovered that all the houses in the row shared a common underfloor space. They searched the whole length of it and the grounds of an old people's home that backed on to Winnie's garden. There were rumours that Keith's body had been found in a river or that he had run away to London.

Keith's grandmother blamed herself for his disappearance and spent two years searching for him on derelict sites around Manchester. In the Topping interrogations, Myra said that during a picnic with Ian in the Shiny Brook area of Saddleworth Moor, the dog they had with them wandered off and sniffed around a dead lamb. Ian grabbed the carcass and threw it away. She assumed that it must have been where Keith Bennett was buried.

I put this to Brady and he replied in a letter: 'If she did say that "lamb" rubbish to Topping, why then didn't she take him to the spot when she was up there? Irrelevant questions. She knew anyway, without the cock and bull lamb story.' Brady added in conversation that the only dead lamb they had seen in their travels together was one that had obviously been killed by a car. They dragged it to the side of the road and cursed the guilty motorist.

The police showed Winnie photographs of Brady and Hindley after they were arrested. She had never seen them before. She was later shown the clothes of a boy found on the moor. The clothes were those of John Kilbride, not Keith. Winnie's mother wouldn't allow her to go to the Moors trial, as it would be too distressing. Ian Brady mentioned Keith's name once during the trial when he referred to questions put to him by detectives asking about the disappearance of Keith and Pauline Reade. This was the only allusion to Keith in the whole trial.

Thirty-seven years after Keith's death, Myra Hindley drew a map marking the place where she stopped to be on lookout as Keith walked out of sight with Brady to his death. The map was published in newspapers in November 2001. I referred to the press coverage in a letter to Ian Brady and he dismissed Myra's claims of innocence and distance from the scene of the murder. He had always said the same in my conversations with him.

Brady and Hindley had now murdered three children. All three walked to their deaths, were killed in the open air and buried on the spot. Their fourth murder was committed indoors, in the tiny bedroom of a council house. This killing was unique in British criminal history: the victim's pleas were recorded on tape.

In her later prison years, Myra Hindley said that the children walked quietly and willingly on to the silent moors, 'like lambs to the slaughter'.

Brady and Hindley didn't expect to be caught. They felt omnipotent. Ian Brady said to me: 'We were nineties people living in the sixties.' I asked him if they had thought about the prospect of living into middle age, or even beyond. He said they had discussed a long-term plan to convert a farmhouse in the Manchester area: 'We looked at two of them. One had an artesian well in the cellar.'

CHAPTER FIFTEEN

CHRISTMAS PAST – THE SHADOWS OF THINGS THAT HAVE BEEN

Ian Brady was asleep in bed with Myra at her home in Bannock Street. He aroused suddenly, lashing out blindly and hitting her. She made a sleepy and reproachful sound: 'It touched me and I drew her warm body close for comfort.' He had woken up from a recurring nightmare: 'The sun baked and cracked the earth and on the hilltop I sat with two other men outside a ramshackle hut. The hot tropical sun was insufferable and there was an overwhelming air of unkempt lethargy. The two men in tattered, threadbare clothes were dirty and unshaven. I couldn't trust them but I knew that I would never be free of them. I was gazing at a beautiful white beach far below me at the bottom of the hill.

'A small group of sailors had rowed to the shore from a ship in anchor. They were spotless in gleaming white uniforms. I wanted to go down to meet them but knew that I would be arrested as soon as I was recognised. I was in Haiti. The very air was fetid with corruption. It was stifling and oppressive. I knew I was marooned and would never leave that place. I felt wretched with ennui. I was slowly dying.'

Brady said that the symbolism of the nightmare was obvious without explaining why. Was it a premonition of a lifetime in prison? Whatever the case, the nightmare had a Pavlovian effect upon him: 'Whenever I saw a tropical scene, I experienced the same nausea, loathing and rage. Nevertheless, it had its uses – in a situation when violence was required. I simply imagined the scene in my mind to evoke insane fury.' I arrived at Ashworth on one occasion and Brady told me that he had woken from a dream a few hours before, conscious of the fact that he had been speaking in a language he had never learned.

Ian told Myra about his trip to the fifty caves of Arrochar in his childhood and wanted to pay a return visit. They made their usual midnight departure from Gorton: 'When we arrived there, I felt full of pagan power. I felt invulnerable. We left the car to view the wooden bridge. It hadn't changed at all. I had. I had returned to the scene with a Smith and Wesson strapped to my chest. I lit a cigarette and stared down at the water, thinking of all the water that had passed under the bridge since I first visited the place with my pals all those years ago. As we neared the hut, I imagined the little gang that had been there. The door was padlocked. There was no trace where our fire had been, nor any trace that we had lived in that place for a short time. The meadow, the mountains and the forest were as I remembered them.

'We strolled along the western shore of the loch to the mountain torrent running under the road and filled a large container. The sun was hot and I mixed the wine with the icy water to make us cold negus.

'Feeling refreshed we drove along the western shore road towards the hills and the forests, unconscious of the short time left to us.'

Ian Brady claims to have killed a man during this trip to Scotland. I found fragmentary notes about this incident in Brady's property. This was the third 'happening'. Myra had driven through the village of Arrochar in the mini traveller and parked at the roadside near the banks of Loch Long.

There was bright sunshine. Brady was looking through his binoculars when he spotted a hiker. He was in his twenties with a heavily packed rucksack. He was approached by Brady, who said later that he just wanted to hear a Scottish accent. 'I said something and he turned around.' The hiker spoke with a southern English accent. Brady watched the shadows of the clouds drift across the landscape and felt a sudden sense of heat and rage: 'I nodded to Myra and patted my gun holster. She nodded a "Groucho" in return and I shot the man through the back of the head with a single bullet.'

It was the gun found by police when Brady was eventually arrested. Brady opened the victim's rucksack and found a trench tool to bury him: 'I propped the body up to look as though he was sitting and relaxing. I used the binoculars to scan all around till dark'. He didn't bury the rucksack but threw it into a pine forest, 'a strange place full of brambles on the way to

222 IAN BRADY — THE UNTOLD STORY OF THE MOORS MURDERS

Stirling.' Years later, Brady said he could still remember exactly where he buried the body. It was near a pinnacle, a natural rock about thirty feet high.

Myra was asked about this 'happening' during the Topping sessions but said she knew nothing about it. She remembered camping with Ian several times at Loch Long. They slept in the car. She said that Ian often went for walks alone while she was preparing meals. After the arrest, the Scottish police suspected that Brady had committed a crime in the area and searched along Loch Lomond and not Loch Long. Four miles of land separate the two lochs. Strathclyde Police had no undetected murders in the area at the time in question. A German tourist disappeared in the Loch Lomond area in the summer of 1961, before Ian Brady and Myra were together. The missing man wasn't dressed as a hiker and had no rucksack.

A few weeks later, Myra's sister Maureen married David Smith at All Saints register office on Saturday, 15 August 1964. Smith was still only sixteen. It was a few days before Maureen's eighteenth birthday and she was seven months pregnant. None of her relatives attended. Her mother Hettie was ashamed and Myra didn't believe in marriage. Maureen and David went to live with his father Jack in Wiles Street, Gorton, two doors from where Pauline Reade's parents lived. The newlyweds would divorce nine years later. (Ian Brady's mother Peggy had married Pat Brady at All Saints register office fourteen years before.)

It was Ian's idea to take David and Maureen for a day out, as a honeymoon present. The following day, Sunday, Myra drove them with Ian to the Lake District. It was Act I, Scene I – a drama that would banish normality from the lives of the four of them forever.

Ian bought six bottles of Australian wine for the outing. Maureen sat with Myra in the front and left the men to talk and drink wine in the back of the mini traveller. They arrived at Lake Windermere and found it crowded with tourists. They moved on to Bowness and went for a steamboat trip on the lake. Ian bought an 'Ambleside'-inscribed brass horseshoe from a small gift shop and I found this in his property. On the journey back, Ian raised the subject of making money with David – the opening lines in a story that would end in Ian and Myra's nemesis. Before the four of them went back to Myra's house in Bannock Street, Ian bought a bottle of whisky from an off-licence. Ian and David stayed downstairs talking for three hours after the two sisters had gone to bed. This was the first of a series of late-night drinking sessions.

As far as murder went, Brady and Hindley were members of an exclusive club with only two members. Brady hardly knew the sixteen-year-old David Smith at this stage and some aspects of Brady's criminal schemes were gradually revealed to Smith only later into their friendship.

In September 1964 Myra and her grandmother were re-housed to a new Manchester overspill estate of four thousand homes on the green meadows of Hattersley, near to the Domesday Book village of Mottram-in-Longdendale. Ian Brady had been sleeping most nights at Myra's and it meant a move for him too. He went with Myra to see the site foreman in Hattersley and asked to be given a house at the edge of the estate closest to the moors. They were allocated number 16 Wardle Brook Avenue, the end of a terrace of four houses overlooking the road between Hyde and Mottram, ten miles from the summit of the moors. The house faced the rear of the New Inn pub on the main road.

Myra's mother refused a house offered to her on the new estate. At the time she was having an affair with Bill Moulton, a driver, and it wasn't convenient for her to move miles away to Hattersley.

In number 16 there was a living room with a window at each end, a serving hatch to the kitchen and a fireplace. There were two bedrooms and a bathroom. Three pets moved in with the three human beings: Mrs Maybury's Lassie, Myra's Puppet and a budgie, Joey, in a cage on a stand in the living room. All three pets would be present at the scene of two murders.

By the time Myra, Ian and Mrs Maybury were settled in, the living room was painted pink with wallpaper around the fireplace in the style of imitation brickwork. There was a red carpet square on the floor, a red moquette settee that converted into a bed and a green armchair. A cigarette machine was installed in the house, refilled every Sunday morning and emptied of half-crown coins. Myra was smoking forty cigarettes a day and walked over to the New Inn when she ran out. After the trial, the locals recalled her asking at the bar for 'Twenty Embassy, please', in her Mancunian accent. In these early days, there were no shops on the estate and everything was sold from vans – except cigarettes.

Ian Brady added his own touch to the living room décor: 'I put an SS dagger on the wall. I bought it from an antique shop. It had a metal scabbard decorated with Rune stone signs and an eagle holding a swastika. My mother sold it after the arrest. If its origin had been known, it would have been snapped up by dealers in crime memorabilia.' Upstairs, Brady fitted a deadlock to the door of the small bedroom. Ian and Myra paid rent on a lock-up garage in the vicinity. They never used it and the police never knew about it. The couple would have used it as a hiding place in an emergency.

In the terrace of four houses, number 10 was at the level of the road but number 16 was ten feet above it. Access was along the path from number 10. Ian and Myra scrambled up the grass to save walking from the end of the row.

A Jamaican family, Phoenix Braithwaite, his wife Tess, and their three children, lived next door to Myra at number 14. Their house soon became known as 'Jamaica Inn'. Mrs Elsie Masterson lived at number 12 with her six children. She had been married three times. Her eleven-year-old daughter, Pat Hodges, became friends with Ian and Myra after calling at number 16 to ask if her mother was there. Myra used to take Pat in the car to pick up Ian from his mother's house in Westmoreland Street, Longsight, whenever he had called there after work at Millwards. Myra gave her a puppy called Duke.

Myra and Ian often took Pat to Saddleworth Moor to spend the evening sharing their wine and, occasionally, to bring back soil for the garden. She sometimes went with them on longer journeys – Leek, Whaley Bridge, Crowden and Glossop. After the arrest, Pat Hodges guided police to their favourite parking places on the moor where bodies were found. Two other children who lived nearby, Carol and David Waterhouse, sometimes went out on trips with Myra and Ian.

Brady and Myra liked to visit Whaley Bridge in particular. I asked Brady why. 'Because there's a moor there. There are moors all around the Manchester area. People just think of Saddleworth Moor. I discovered a gun shop in Whaley Bridge town. In that dump! It was a great gun with an extension handle. I would have smashed the window and taken it, given the opportunity.'

It was October 1964 and the three occupants of number 16 had settled in. Maureen and David Smith visited for a drinking session and Ian brought up again the subject of making money. As Brady admitted at the trial, October was the month when he and Smith got down to 'brass tacks'.

Ian Brady remarked to me once that people who read about the Moors Murders assume that he and Myra spent their days stalking the moors with their hands dripping with blood: 'Just the opposite! Most of the time we were laughing. Criminals are not criminals *all* the time.' He mentioned the occasion when the two of them were sitting in the car observing the comings and goings of an electricity board office as they spat grape pips at each other.

Between them they invented a game called 'Who for many years . . .', based on the 'ludicrous obituaries written for the aristocracy, politicians and other notable parasites; so dead, at least they were good for a laugh.' Either Ian or Myra would start the game by mentioning someone's name and adding, '. . . the boring old ham – who for many years was known as Erasmus Croakstutter of no fixed abode . . .' The other would take over, '. . . and who for many years was a close friend of Cardinal Ima Liar, world-famous chicken-wrestler . . .'

There's sparse evidence to show that anyone appreciated Brady and Hindley's company or their sense of humour. After the arrest, Millwards' manager, Tom Craig, was asked about Brady and Hindley as employees. He spoke about the morose Ian Brady: 'He was so bad tempered about anything that upset him. If you ticked him off about something he would fly into a rage. He had a shocking temper and his language was dreadful, but I used to pass it over just to keep the peace. He was reasonable at his job but he would have been sacked long before if it hadn't been that it was difficult to get staff. In the six years he worked here, I can't say I ever got to know him at all.

'In an office, the lads usually chat a bit about football or something like that, but Brady wasn't interested in anything like that. Sometimes in the morning he might join in a conversation about what was on the TV the night before, but I noticed he only talked about the crime films or the *Alfred Hitchcock Hour*, things with a bit of horror or brutality in them.

'He often had a book with him – I don't remember any of them, but they were always those paperbacks with a bit of filth in them. I think it was his first clerical job and he was just adequate and no more. He wasn't the sort of fellow I liked to have around.'

What of Myra Hindley? Tom Craig continued: 'She was a good shorthand typist, I'll say that for her, and she was always smartly dressed. She wore these short skirts and boots and fancy stockings. But she would have been fired, too, if it wasn't that it would have been difficult to get a replacement. With most of the girls in the office you have a bit of a lark around, you pull their legs and everyone tries to get a bit of fun out of their work. But Myra was heavy going. You got no response out of her at all. She was surly at the best of times and aggressive if you spoke to her the wrong way. She didn't come in contact much with the other girls, but still she managed to have a bad effect on everybody. The pair of them were just plain surly and unsociable.'

* * * * *

It was a few weeks before Christmas 1964. Ian had been with Myra for almost two years. They had acted together in the murders of three children. Their surveillance of the movements of money had yet to lead to robbery, an action they both knew could easily lead to their capture. Murder was another matter. Killing a stranger, particularly a child, had far fewer risks. The inspiration came out of the blue.

According to Myra, she and Ian saw an advertisement for cut-price wine on sale at a branch of Tesco in the Miles Platting area of Ancoats, and left in their lunch break to stock up for Christmas and New Year's Eve. Posters for 'Silcocks Wonder Fair' were pasted on walls and lamp-posts near the supermarket. The fair came to Hulme Hall Lane every Christmas and took over waste ground that went to the edge of the main road. It was the 'Red Rec' to the locals. The posters were everywhere. Ian and Myra hardly had to say a word. Funfairs mean one thing – children. (Brady denied that they saw posters about the fair.)

Myra drove Ian to Manchester Central after they had stripped number 16 of anything that would arouse suspicion if the police came. It was Thursday, late on Christmas Eve, when Myra asked Pat Hodges at number 12 if she would like a trip out to Saddleworth Moor. It would be Christmas Day within an hour or so and her mother let her go as a treat. The three of them sat in the car on the moor, looking down on the city lights and drinking wine. It was 1 a.m. when they decided to drive home, shivering with the bitter cold on Saddleworth. Pat was dropped off at number 12, but Ian wanted to go back. Myra put blankets and more cut-price wine into the vehicle and drove back to the moors.

Pat Hodges escaped with her life that night, according to several writers on the case. They claim that Myra and Ian had second thoughts about killing her. I have described the detailed preparations for their first three murders, particularly the care taken to eliminate any connecting thread linking them to the victim, despite Myra Hindley's claim that no research went into any of the murders. We have only to imagine entries on their working list: 'Pick up Pat Hodges from her home for an evening's ride out to the moors. Rape, kill, bury her and return home without her.' The very idea is as implausible as anything could be. I cannot believe that Brady and Hindley ever, for one moment, entertained the thought of murdering Pat Hodges.

Christmas Day in number 16 Wardle Brook Avenue was much like any other day. Myra's gran dozed in the armchair, being 'selectively deaf' as usual, as Ian Brady would tell me years later. The cheap wine was flowing, thanks to Tesco in Miles Platting. In Miles Platting itself, a family was enjoying Christmas for the last time. Ann Downey (36), lived with Alan West in a maisonette flat in Charnley Walk, with four children from her marriage to Terry Downey: Terry (14), Lesley Ann (10), Tommy (8) and Brett (4). Miles Platting was part of the inner-city district of Ancoats, whose inhabitants were immortalised as matchstalk figures in the paintings of L S Lowry.

Lesley Ann unwrapped her presents, leaving a mysterious box till last. It was a toy sewing machine. She could hardly put it down all day. Her mother promised to help her make some proper dolls' clothes with it as soon as there was peace and quiet to follow the instructions. Lesley's brother Terry gave her a string of white beads he had won at the fair. She would be going there herself tomorrow. But Lesley didn't live to use her sewing machine. The white beads would be buried with her. The police described Lesley as frail-looking, of slim build, four feet ten inches tall, with blue eyes, brown curly hair and of fair complexion. She wanted to be a hairdresser when she left St Mark's School in Ancoats.

It was Saturday, Boxing Day in Wardle Brook Avenue. At 2 p.m., Myra drove her gran over to the only surviving son from her first marriage, James Burns. He lived in Combermere Street, Dukinfield. Myra knew him as uncle Jim. She transported her grandmother there every fortnight, but Boxing Day happened to be uncle Jim's birthday. Myra said that she would collect her gran at 9.30 p.m.

It was 4 p.m. in Miles Platting and Lesley was just leaving to go to the fair. Her older brother Terry wanted to go with her but he had flu. This didn't cause any problems, however. Mrs Clark from downstairs would take Lesley with her own daughter, Linda, as well as Tommy and two other friends, Roy and Ann. Fatally, Mrs Clark then decided not to go after all and the five children walked down Iron Street and Hulme Lane to the fairground without an adult.

Lesley was wearing a red tartan dress with lace trimmings, a pink cardigan, red shoes, a blue coat edged with white and Terry's string of white beads. She had sixpence to spend.

The money had gone in an hour and the five children drifted back home to tea. The exotic sights and sounds that interrupted the routine of life in Miles Platting – the movement, the lights and the music – enthralled Lesley. She told her friends to start back without her. She wanted one last look and would follow in a few minutes.

After the investigation, Bernard King (11) said that he saw Lesley by the dodgems at 5.30 p.m. Had he watched Lesley for a few minutes more, he would have seen a woman with dark, unnatural hair, talking to her. A minute more, and he would have seen the woman leave the fair with Lesley as the two of them walked together out of the coloured lights and into the darkness. He wouldn't have seen a tall man in a long dark coat watching the scene in the shadow of a fairground generator. But he was there.

Myra Hindley's story to Inspector Topping is – predictably – at odds with the version related to me by Ian Brady. The accounts diverge from the beginning. Myra said that Ian Brady was with her when they dropped boxes near the girl, to entice her and be part of their calculations. If she helped them with the boxes they would give her some money.

Myra remembered the music blasting out from the tiny cubicle of the man operating the dodgems – 'Little Red Rooster' by The Rolling Stones – and stated that the boxes were stacked to hide Lesley from public view as she drove her two passengers nine miles to Wardle Brook Avenue. Ian Brady denies all of this and claims that Lesley was already in the vehicle when Myra stopped to pick him up a few streets away from the funfair.

What isn't in doubt is that Lesley wasn't kicking and screaming when she went with Hindley and Brady. Like the three victims before her, she stepped calmly into a vehicle that would take her to her doom. But all of the victims would scream, struggle and fight before they died. For all of them, the tragic nightmare began innocently as an interesting, brief adventure that would take up no more than an hour of their time. The small reward at the end of it may well have remained a secret and belonged to the secret world that all children inhabit.

Myra was driving on the Mottram Road, turned right just before the New Inn pub, and left into Wardle Brook Avenue, stopping at the grass slope beneath number 16. In Charnley Walk, Ancoats, Lesley's mother and Alan West made snowballs to throw down on Tommy and Lesley when they arrived home from the fair. Ann Downey, later to become Ann West, takes up the story in *For The Love Of Lesley*. After making the snowballs, Ann said that she would go back indoors to prepare for tea: 'So we went in and tidied the sitting room and enjoyed the last hour of unspoiled happiness in our lives.' (Tommy and his own daughter were to die 38 years later in tragic circumstances at the same time of year.)

Myra, Ian and Lesley walked into the small hallway of number 16. The door on the right led into the living room: the kitchen door was directly in front of them and the stairs were to their left. Whatever else happened, we know for certain that Brady, Hindley and Lesley were in the small bedroom together for at least sixteen minutes. The sounds and voices were recorded on the notorious tape discovered shortly after the arrest. The transcript has been included in *The Moors Murders: The Trial of Myra Hindley and Ian Brady* by Jonathan Goodman (see bibliography), which is an edited transcript of the whole trial. It has been reprinted several times over the years. In fact, before she died, Ann West wanted parts of the tape of the death of her daughter played in a Moors Murders documentary.

A small minority of writers has argued that the tape recording was made after the photographs that recorded some of the events of that night had been taken. Emlyn Williams does so in *Beyond Belief*. He finds it hard to believe that it took two adults almost seventeen minutes to gag a child. Williams claims that Lesley Ann was struggling on the tape because she had dressed after the photographs were taken and was being made to undress again for even more sinister purposes.

At the trial, both prosecution and defence lawyers assumed that the photographs had been taken after the recording was made. Williams comments that this assumption favoured Brady and Hindley. If Lesley Ann was alive at the end of the tape, there could be some credibility to the view that she was taken away from number 16 alive and well by the two men who allegedly brought her to the house for a photographic session.

After entering the house, Myra said that Ian and Lesley began to climb the stairs as she walked into the kitchen to attend to the dogs. She knew that Ian had set up his photographic equipment and floodlights in preparation. She heard Lesley shout and assumed that Ian was taking the child's coat off. Brady denies Myra's account of these first few minutes in number 16. The tape dating from that night is a record of Brady and Hindley forcing Lesley to pose before the photographs were taken.

Lesley Ann's words on the tape show that she is doing all in her meagre power to fight off Brady and Hindley's attempts to put a gag into her mouth. The tape begins with the child screaming. She starts to cry and Myra Hindley can be heard to say, 'In your mouth. Hush, hush! Shut up or I'll forget myself and hit you one!'

Lesley Ann appeals to the non-existent parental instincts of her killers: 'Can I tell you summat . . . Please take your hands off me a minute. Please, Mummy, Daddy, please.' In her desperation she appeals to a higher power:

'Please, God. I will swear on the Bible.' She couldn't have known that that was the most futile appeal of all to the ears of Brady and Hindley. One of her final, desperate appeals is perhaps the most poignant statement in the whole saga of the Moors Murders: 'I have to go home for eight o'clock . . . or I'll get killed if I don't, honest to God.' It was, ironically, a simple statement of fact.

The tape closes with two pieces of music – 'Jolly Old St Nicholas' and 'The Little Drummer Boy'. As the music fades, there is the sound of three loud cracks. The tape ends with sounds of footsteps.

The three loud cracks were the sounds of the tripod being opened. The music came from Myra's small brown transistor radio; a present from her uncle Bert. It was tuned to Radio Luxembourg and Myra had simply turned up the volume. When the tape was found after the arrest, sound engineers explored all the possible ways in which the music came to be there, the most favoured of which was that it was added later by taping from a record player. A witness at the trial gave a brief summary of the possible theories. In conversation with me, Brady commented that the truth was much simpler. Ray Coniff and his singers sang the two songs on the radio, which was playing in the room at the time.

Myra claimed that she did not know the tape recorder was on. It was under the bed out of sight. I asked Brady about Myra's story: 'She knew. In any case, whatever Myra says about the tape recording, it puts her into a Catch-22 situation. If she did know that the tape recorder was on, she was on her best behaviour. If she didn't, then her actions and words reveal how she normally behaved. The tears she shed when she was forced to listen to the tape by the police, were tears of self-pity because she could not lie with the evidence on tape.'

We know for certain that at least nine photographs were taken of Lesley naked, apart from her shoes and socks. A scarf was wrapped around the bottom part of her face to hide her identity. The photographs were found in one of the suitcases recovered from left-luggage by the police. They show Lesley in various poses – kneeling, praying and arms outstretched.

The photographs would become exhibit number 144 at the trial. Ann West allegedly gave permission for one of the photographs to be shown publicly for the first time in a three-part series on the Moors Murders, made by Chameleon Television, broadcast in 1999. She wanted the sheer evil of her daughter's killers to be revealed in all its starkness. She also allegedly agreed to the playing of extracts of the notorious tape, but it was thought to be too harrowing for the listening public.

The police matched markings on the bed head in the photographs with the bed found in Myra's bedroom. The same Channel 5 television programme showed a photograph of the bed head with the markings identified and numbered.

In her various later accounts, Myra distances herself from what actually happened in that bedroom. She said that she was looking away, anxious that Lesley's screams would be heard through the open window and front door open downstairs. The naïve response to this is to ask why she didn't simply shut the door and the window to relieve her anxiety. The very idea that Brady and Hindley would calculate in detail to commit murder, and leave windows and doors open, beggars belief. We know too much about the meticulous planning that went into the murders to accept this patent nonsense.

During the Chester trial, the Attorney General questioned Myra's claims to have been innocent of the events in the bedroom on Boxing Day. He said, 'It's not the Albert Hall. It is a small room and you were there.' On the tape she had actually threatened to hit Lesley. 'I wouldn't have hit her much,' Myra said in the witness box.

The tape recorder was disconnected so that the floodlight could be connected for the photographs. In response to Topping's questions, Myra said that Ian told her to run warm water in the bath after he had taken the last photograph. She said she waited in the bathroom long enough for the water to become cold, then pulled out the plug and filled the bath again. After a few minutes, she went back to the bedroom. She saw Lesley lying face down on the bed. She was dead. There was blood on her legs and Myra assumed that she had been raped.

Hindley's version is simply not credible. One minute she is threatening to hit Lesley Ann. A few minutes later, she is completely removed from the scene of the action, meekly waiting in the bathroom, patiently running water to wash the child's corpse. The water was not warm for Lesley Ann's comfort. She was dead and growing colder by the minute.

Brady's version is very different. In Brady's copy of Topping he has written 'lie' against Myra's claim to be in the bathroom when Lesley Ann was murdered. Myra had taken part with him in the sexual acts committed against Lesley. Brady and Hindley were themselves partially clothed by now. They had both struggled to hold Lesley down as she fought for her life. Myra straddled Lesley Ann just as she had straddled Pauline Reade.

The child begged for mercy as she fought with something so totally beyond her experience. She pleaded with Brady and Hindley with the only words she knew that meant love and complete safety – 'Mum' and 'Dad'. Lesley Ann couldn't have known that Brady and Hindley were well used to ignoring the hopeless cries of doomed children. They were past masters.

Myra insisted on strangling Lesley Ann herself with a length of silk cord while Brady held the child down.

Brady said that Myra openly played with the cord in pubs for a few weeks, revelling in the deadly secret it represented. I asked Brady whether the bath was used, as Myra claimed. He said that it was. They washed fibres and dog hairs from Lesley's dead body in it. Brady commented to me, 'Hindley can kill in cold blood or in a rage.' He used these words in a letter to the BBC in 1997, adding, 'In that respect we were an inexorable force.'

We can imagine a little of what happened in the bedroom from a slip Brady made when he was being questioned about the photographic session during the trial: 'After completion, we all got dressed and went downstairs.'

When Dr David Gee gave evidence about his post-mortem examination of Lesley Ann he ruled out strangulation by ligature as the cause of death. When I pressed him on the question, Brady insisted that Myra's silk cord strangled the life out of the child.

Myra checked that Wardle Brook Avenue was deserted. Brady carried Lesley's body down the narrow stairs and put it in the back of the mini traveller. They had already selected a spot for the burial, not far from Pauline's Reade's grave on the same side of the road. They had travelled only a short distance of the ten-mile journey to Saddleworth Moor when snow reduced their speed to a crawl. They telephoned for a road and weather report and realised it was pointless to travel in conditions that would be much worse on the bleak moors. They drove back to Wardle Brook Avenue and put Lesley's body back in the bedroom.

What were they to do about Myra's grandmother? Myra drove over to Dukinfield and parked the vehicle some distance from her uncle Jim's house. It was about 11.15 p.m. when she knocked on his door. She said that the roads were too treacherous for driving her grandmother back to number 16. There was only a sprinkling of snow on the roads in Dukinfield, however, and an argument followed that lasted several minutes. Mrs Maybury would have to sleep on the floor. Myra's uncle was puzzled. Myra would have to drive back herself anyway, so why couldn't she take her grandmother?

Jim eventually realised the real reason and was questioned about the evening during the trial. Myra had left his house saying flatly that she couldn't take her grandmother back to number 16. Of course she couldn't; but it had little to do with the weather.

In Charnley Walk, Ann Downey and Alan West were frantic. Tommy had returned home from the fair without Lesley. They knocked on doors and searched the streets for their daughter. They contacted the police at 10 p.m. Lesley was long dead by then, lying on a strange bed belonging to two total strangers who were waiting for the snow to clear. Her killers were downstairs on the divan bed, sleeping fitfully, replete as they were on the numbing consolations of Tesco's cut-price Christmas wine.

Sunday, 27 December 1964. Myra and Ian were up with the dawn. Myra led the way as Brady followed her upstairs. She unlocked the small bedroom. Lesley Ann's cold, naked body lay face down on the bed with her clothes on top of her, where they had been thrown the night before. In Miles Platting, Lesley's mother and Alan were out of their minds with worry. Meanwhile, in Hattersley, Myra and Ian were merely anxious. Would the roads to the Saddleworth Moor be clear of snow?

The roads were passable by now. Myra stopped the vehicle near where Pauline Reade was buried. When the coast was clear, Brady ran with a spade up the incline and out of sight. He began to dig a shallow grave through the layer of snow, about 90 yards from the road.

Myra watched and waited. To her horror, a police car pulled up beside her. The policeman asked if there was something wrong – one of the classic understatements of the Moors case. Myra said that she was drying out her spark plugs. Brady assured me that Lesley Ann's body was in the back of the vehicle. Myra was silently praying that Ian Brady would not appear over the rise of the hill.

The policeman accepted the explanation and drove away. Brady returned and ran with Lesley's body up the incline. He put Lesley into the grave with her legs doubled up to her abdomen and lying on her right side. Her clothes, including the string of white beads, were buried at her feet.

In the *Sunday Times* of December 1994, Myra spoke about her thoughts as she waited for Lesley to be buried: 'I looked up and said, now I know there is no God, now I am sure.'

In her confession to Topping, Myra admitted that a policeman had once stopped to ask her if she was in difficulty while she was parked on Saddleworth Moor, but added that there was nothing sinister about the occasion. Ian Brady and David Smith were simply engaged in some shooting practice out of sight on the moor.

Myra drove back to Hattersley and Ian said he would go and spend the rest of the day with his mother in Westmoreland Street, Longsight. He slept there that night.

Myra picked up her grandmother from Dukinfield at 10.30 a.m. By that time, the police were taking Lesley's disappearance seriously. The fairground was dismantled and house-to-house enquiries were made. They dragged the Ashton canal and used frogmen in the futile search. Ironically, the song Hindley and Brady always associated with Lesley's murder was 'Girl Don't Come', by Sandie Shaw. (Alan West was taken in for questioning after Lesley Ann's disappearance. When I met Alan many years later, he told me that if he had been interrogated much longer, he would have signed a confession.)

Life returned to what was curiously thought of as normal in Wardle Brook Avenue. At some point Brady developed the photographs of Lesley. Myra looked at them and unthinkingly left her fingerprints on them for police to find after the arrest. Two copies were made of the tape. Police found them in one of the suitcases together with the original tape. Pat Hodges' voice was also found on one of the tracks. It was recorded in the living room of number 16 during the first day or so of the New Year.

Brady was using the tape recorder with the microphone turned on as Myra chatted to Pat about a headline they were looking at in the *Gorton and Openshaw Reporter*, dated 1 January 1965 – 'HAVE YOU SEEN TEN YEAR OLD LESLEY? BIG SEARCH FOR LOST GIRL'.

'You see that girl at Ancoats?' asked Pat.

'Yes . . . just now,' said Myra.

'She lives near my friend,' commented Pat.

'And she lives near her house?' said Myra.

'Yes.'

'Did you know her?'

'I don't know.'

After the taped conversation came to light, the police treated it as an item in the collection of perverse memorabilia found in two suitcases after the arrest. Myra's brief conversation with Pat was used as evidence to support the view that Ian and Myra got a kick out of a child reading innocently about a gruesome secret they alone shared. Myra rejected this interpretation. She said that she wanted nothing to remind her of the murder and couldn't bring herself to sleep again in a bedroom that haunted her dreams and daytime memories. I mentioned this to Ian Brady and he said they never slept in the bedroom anyway. They slept on a divan downstairs so that they could watch television in bed.

Like many others, Pat Hodges was innocently drawn into the saga of the Moors Murders and played a significant part in helping to locate the graves of two of the victims.

Making tape recordings was an obsession with Brady and he carried it well into his prison years. When I eventually received his property, it contained many cassette recordings from the radio and master tapes of collections for duplication.

Pat Hodges stopped calling in at number 16 some time during February 1965. It is not clear why she stayed away. It may be that she had found new friends, or because she had been told off by Ian for taking a short cut through his garden, as one report claims.

*   *   *   *   *

There was nothing but misery in Charnley Walk. Ann Downey would keep Lesley's Christmas presents forever. On a Sunday school outing, Lesley had bought her mother a little plastic dog filled with perfume of freesias: 'It's one of my dearest treasures.' In May 1965, five months after the murder, Ann Downey lost the baby she was expecting by Alan West, who was now her husband.

Ann couldn't bear the memories associated with Charnley Walk and asked to be re-housed. Her family moved to Bowden Close in Hattersley, just half a mile from Wardle Brook Avenue. Brady denied that there was any truth in the story that he and Myra went to Ann and Alan's local pub to gloat.

When I met Alan and Ann West in the early 1990s, Ann signed my copy of *For The Love Of Lesley* with the words 'God bless you, keep you safe.'

A few weeks after burying Lesley Ann, Brady and Hindley took photographs of each other, smiling at the camera, standing near the child's grave. They were unmistakably sixties pictures. There was a transistor radio at their feet where they stood on the rock.

Decades later in captivity, Myra Hindley – still claiming that Ian Brady had killed Lesley Ann – wrote to a journalist: 'I just find it hard to believe that I could have been such a cruel, cruel bastard.'

To the journalist Yvonne Roberts, who visited her in Cookham Wood before she made her confession (*Observer*, 17 November 2002), Myra said: 'The girl shouldn't have been out at that time of night.'

CHAPTER SIXTEEN

CIGARETTES & WINE AFTER MIDNIGHT – THE RAG DOLL MURDER

When Myra Hindley looked back during her prison years, she reflected upon the ten-month period that followed the death of Lesley Ann Downey and which ended with her arrest after the murder of Edward Evans. It was the longest gap between any of the murders that Hindley and Brady committed together. In one of the sessions with Inspector Topping, she said this ten-month interval was, '. . . the most peaceful time in my life'.

Myra contradicted this in various remarks she made after she broke with Brady after corresponding with him for six and a half years in captivity, in which she said she had been afraid she would eventually become one of Brady's murder victims herself. I mentioned this to Brady and he said, 'She was never in danger. I was about to leave her on two occasions, having thrown clothes and guns into a bag ready to walk out the front door. She begged me to stay. She wanted to go down with me at the trial and wrote to me for years before the break.'

When Myra lodged her appeal for parole to the then Home Secretary, Jack Straw, in 1997, Brady wrote a letter to the BBC and commented on Myra's perception of the murders: 'She regarded periodic homicides as rituals of reciprocal innervation, marriage ceremonies theoretically binding us ever closer. As the records show, before we met my criminal activities had been primarily mercenary. Afterwards, a duality of motivation developed. Existential philosophy melded with the spirituality of death became predominant. We experimented with the concept of total possibility. Instead of the requisite Lady Macbeth, I got Messalina.'

Whatever Myra meant by calling that ten-month period a peaceful time, she could only have been speaking in relative terms. Violence was never far from the surface with Ian Brady, even though he contained his rage for most of the time. In a letter to me of June 1992, Brady wrote about an occasion when the *black light* gleamed and he came near to losing control completely: 'Myra and I were in a Manchester pub one night when I shouted threats at a group of men. I wasn't drunk, though it was a silly move to make. They were staring at Myra. First, I outstared them, but that wasn't enough. I wanted blood. Unobtrusively, I slipped one hand into my overcoat pocket and, with finger and thumb, prised open the lock-back knife I always carried – the entire knife made of stainless steel and without ornamentation of any sort, like a scalpel. I had also chosen what bottles I would use as weapons on our table. But the men were ignorant of these calculations. Actually, I felt marvellous once committed to physical confrontation. The men apologised. It was only later that I scolded myself for being sucked into such stupid heroics. Myra remained silent throughout the whole scenario. I didn't even bother to explain anything to her afterwards. However, knowing that audience potential had pushed me into confrontation, I, especially when going for one of my much-loved strolls in the Gorbals of Glasgow, always went alone. Though I risked us going into the Gorbals by car in daylight, showing her my tenement, old primary school, etc., and carrying a revolver under my waistcoat.'

On 5 April 1965, Myra sold her Morris Mini-van to a firm in Stretford. She bought her third vehicle on 27 April, on hire purchase: a surf blue Austin Mini Countryman with the registration CNC 153C.

Ian and Myra were becoming bored with their crimes: 'Most power, once attained, becomes a curiously empty experience.' They looked for a diversion. In a letter of January 1993, Brady mentioned two options they considered: 'Myra and I extensively discussed and researched the psychological and logistical mechanics of creating a small race war. We toured the Moss Side area of Manchester (known as "Little Africa"). However, we had no political or racial motive. To us it was simply an existential challenge, an end in itself. In tandem, we also discussed and researched the existential challenge of derailing an express train.'

On 24 April 1965, four months after the death of Lesley Ann Downey, David Smith and Maureen lost their six-month-old daughter, Angela Dawn. She died of bronchitis a few hundred yards from Charnley Walk in

Ancoats hospital. David and Maureen were devastated. Some reports claim that David tried to vandalise the hospital ward and later threw his baby's clothes down a railway embankment. He couldn't face living in the same house again and asked the council to re-house them.

Maureen, her mother and David went round to Wardle Brook Avenue to break the news of the baby's death to Myra. Ian was watching a television version of *Richard III* and resented the interruption. Myra drove round to the Smiths' house. Ian stayed in the car while she took in flowers for Angela Dawn. With heavy irony, her card read 'Another flower for God's garden'.

Maureen and David became more involved with Myra and Ian as a result of Angela Dawn's death. Two days after the child died, on Saturday, 26 April, the four of them drove to Saddleworth Moor. It was about 11.30 p.m. and Ian wanted David to walk with him on to the moor to look down on the lake below them in Greenfield. David wondered about the attraction of trying to see the moon's reflection on water on such a cold and dark night. He didn't know he was standing on John Kilbride's grave.

In the weeks and months that followed, Myra drove Ian and the Smiths on trips that included picnics in the pine forests of Derbyshire. At other times, the girls sat in the car as Ian and David practised shooting at an old oil drum on the moors. Wherever they had been, they usually ended the day with long drinking sessions at Wardle Brook Avenue or David's house in Gorton. Myra and Mo retired to bed eventually and left the men to drink more wine and talk. Ian continued his efforts to seduce Dave into the ways of making easy money. Dave didn't like work and admitted it during the trial when he said he was liable to 'regular tonsillitis'.

Ian spoke about armed robbery and, after all, Dave was usually free enough during the day to observe the activities of banks and building societies. But David wasn't keen on using real bullets. Ian was thinking several steps ahead, and knew that David wouldn't be keen on the idea . . . yet.

In the small hours, the wine served its purpose by putting Brady and Smith to sleep in their chairs. At some point Brady introduced a new dimension to their conversations – murder. He gave Smith an orange-covered paperback to read, *The Life and Ideas of Marquis de Sade*. Brady drew his attention to one particular passage: 'Should murder be punished by murder? Undoubtedly not.' This idea ultimately proved too much for David Smith. Along with many teenagers, he would have found another of de Sade's ideas more realistic: 'Happiness lies in the senses and virtues gratify none of them.'

I mentioned to Brady that David Smith said it was like metal-to-metal when the two of them talked together. Brady said, 'No, it was metal to mush!'

* * * * *

Ian woke up one morning on the divan in the living room of number 16: 'I looked at the side table. On it there was a glass of red wine from the night before. The sun is shining on it, right into the wine glass and seems to be illuminating a diamond in the middle of it. The gun on the table is glinting in the sunlight. I reach for the transistor radio and turn it on – "Mr Tambourine Man" by The Byrds. It had just entered the charts. It was mid-June 1965 and time Myra and I visited Scotland again.'

Myra eased the Austin Mini out of Wardle Brook Avenue for their midnight run. They were on their way. It was a pilgrimage to places Ian had visited as a child. In his first letter to Myra after they had both been imprisoned, he reminisced about their visit to St Monans. Brady described the day to me: 'As we approached the village via a route unfamiliar to me, I saw a dark tower in the distance. I was delighted. It was the castle! It was sixteen years since I had last seen it.

'We drove into a field in St Monans to have our usual snack of wine and cheese. We smoked cigarettes for a while, left the car and went for a walk, taking the loaded .38 Smith and Wesson revolver in a petite zip case. We wanted to be prepared for any development in England while we were away from Manchester. We were ready for the police if they tried to catch us off guard to make a surprise arrest.

'As we walked around I lived the old times with Ma and Da and the family. I found myself smiling at the pleasant recollections.

'Early the following day we headed north in search of Dunning, a small village in Perthshire. I had spent a fortnight's holiday there with Peggy and May. We lodged in a tiny whitewashed cottage. Oil lamps were the only means of lighting. They lent enchantment as we drank cups of Oxo in the semi-darkness.

'Dunning was as I remembered it, except that Myra and I could see no trace of the whitewashed cottage. We quartered the village in search of the whitewashed cottage, but without success. I received a letter some years later in prison, telling me that the cottage had been demolished. There remained only a single stone – the remains of the front doorstep.'

Myra and Ian visited Glasgow before they returned home. If Brady's recollections are accurate, it was here that the fourth 'happening' took place. The fragments I found in Ian Brady's property contradict Topping's record of Brady's version of the incident. Brady's notes deny that the attack took place near a canal and railway arches. Brady was in the Salt Market area of the city when he saw a man ill-treating a woman who was obviously a tramp: 'She was a wino in a man's cap with bedraggled hair. I said, "All right?" to her. She said, "Bugger off!" '

Her matted hair aroused Ian's memories of the fetlocks of the dying Clydesdale horse he saw in his childhood. Brady's notes of that incident read, '. . . pathetic, heaving, massive, the large eyes.' He was filled with rage and ran after the attacker through several streets, into the Carlton district of Glasgow: 'I had my .38 revolver but preferred to use the sheath knife attached to my wrist.'

In Argyll Street, he attacked the man from behind and stabbed him several times with the knife. He wrapped the knife in a handkerchief to prevent the blood staining his coat pocket. He returned to Myra and said nothing about it. In Manchester, the following day, he submerged the blade in nitric acid.

Brady claimed that he still had the knife when he was arrested and it was returned to Peggy after the trial. The man may have survived the attack. Strathclyde Police had no record of an undetected murder that could be linked with the description and the time.

On 1 July 1965, Brian Simpson, manager of a photographic shop in Ashton-under-Lyne, sold Myra a Fujica camera after she had placed a Ross Ensign as a deposit. The police were handed the Fujica shortly after investigations began into the Moors Murders.

David Smith and Maureen moved into Underwood Court, a block of flats a few minutes' walk away from Wardle Brook Avenue. They were allocated flat number 18 on the third floor. It was 23 July 1965, Myra's 23rd birthday. Pets were not allowed in Underwood Court but the new arrivals ignored the rule and took their dog Bobbie with them. They would be threatened with eviction because of it.

Maureen was now only minutes away from her sister and this was the cause of some irritation to Ian. He had got to know Maureen and David well in the period since their wedding and had grown bored with their rows. Myra was now on the doorstep to give solace to her sister in the domestic strife that had simply moved ground from Gorton to Hattersley.

I was with Ian Brady one afternoon when David Smith's name came into the conversation. Ian said that he regretted not killing David Smith when he had the chance. I asked what he meant. Brady told me that on one occasion Maureen arrived on the doorstep of number 16 asking to be driven to her mother's house in Gorton after a bust-up with David. Myra obliged. An hour or so later, David Smith came round to Wardle Brook Avenue to ask about Maureen. Ian nodded a 'Groucho' to tell Myra that this was a golden chance to get rid of his nuisance once and for all. They could offer to take him to Gorton to see his wife and make an excuse to drive up to Saddleworth Moor en route. Once there, they could dispose of him. There would be no connecting threads. They had taken Maureen to her mother's and could claim to know nothing else about the matter.

Myra talked Ian out of it for her sister's sake. Ian spent a lifetime regretting listening to Myra. He could so easily have eliminated the single cause of their eventual ruin.

* * * * *

Ian Brady told me of the time he hit Myra while she exceeded the speed limit through the streets of Manchester. He had asked Myra to wait for him in a road that runs off London Road, directly under Piccadilly railway complex. Ian told me that he was late meeting Myra because he had been washing blood from his hands in the toilets of Piccadilly Station.

Myra's story to Topping was that she had driven Brady to Manchester city centre after work and dropped him off at the Queen's Hotel. He told her that he was going to the cinema alone, which angered her. She was told to pick him up at Store Street near Piccadilly Station at 11 p.m.

Myra killed time by going round to Underwood Court for her sister to put her hair in rollers. She put a headscarf over her rollers and drove to the city centre for the time arranged.

Brady wasn't there when she arrived and eventually turned up drunk two hours later. She had no idea what he had been up to. For the first time in their relationship she dared to ask him where he had been. Brady said that it was none of her business.

At one point on the journey home, she drove at high speed to give vent to her feelings then suddenly slammed the brakes on, causing Ian's head to hit the windscreen. Ian imbedded a roller into Myra's head as he hit out at her. She had taken the needless risk of being stopped by police for speeding. After a minute or two Ian burst out laughing and talked to Myra as though nothing had happened.

I listened to this and asked why he had blood on his hands. Brady said that he had been drinking heavily and became involved in an argument with someone who looked like a workman in baggy trousers. Brady grabbed a brick or a piece of concrete and battered the man to a pulp, to use his own words. This would have been the fifth 'happening'. Brady told me that Myra was angry when she heard, because she had been left out of the murder.

Police records show that 55-year-old William Cullen was found dead on waste ground near Piccadilly Station in St Andrews Street, probably killed by a piece of concrete found near his body. Topping commented that this would be an obvious killing for Brady to claim, since he was questioned about it two months later when he was under arrest.

Brady noted in the margin of Topping's book: 'One minute he says my memory is unreliable, next he claims I remembered obscure murders and suicides in paper.' Topping adds that Brady couldn't have known that the murder of William Cullen was solved 22 years later in 1984.

On Saturday, 25 September 1965, Myra and Ian visited David and Maureen in Underwood Court for a late-night drinking session. After the girls had gone to bed, Ian and David talked about robbing the Gas and Electricity Board shop in Hyde Road on Saturday, 9 October 1965. David Smith was asked about this after the arrest and replied that the robbery was only to take place if Brady 'felt it was right' on the day. If not, another date would be planned for. It would be another Saturday. Brady and Smith had discovered that there were only two men in the shop on that day, and at one stage, only one.

When the wine had taken effect, Ian introduced a topic he had raised before – murder. 'Are you capable of murder?' he asked Smith. 'I've done it. I've killed three or four . . . You don't really believe me, do you? Their bodies are buried on the moors . . . You and Maureen were sitting near one of them.'

After his arrest, when he was questioned by detectives about David Smith's report of these conversations, Ian Brady answered that his claims to have committed murder were 'part of the fiction to impress him'.

Some of the books and articles on the case state that Brady told Smith that he waited in Myra's car until someone walked past and climbed out to kill them on the spot. This is nonsense. Brady and Hindley committed murder, but not by such simple, literal methods.

A few days later, on 2 October 1965, Ian talked about killing people, and under the influence of wine again, told Smith that he had photographs to prove his murders: 'I'll do another one. You don't believe me . . . it will be done. I'm not due for another one for three or four months, but this one won't count.'

In the Topping interviews, Myra wondered whether Ian Brady had committed a murder after Lesley Ann Downey was killed and before the murder of Edward Evans. The second murder had been committed four months after the first. The third and fourth were separated by a sixth-month interval. If the two 'happenings' had in fact taken place, it would make sense of Brady's comment that another killing was not yet due.

As arranged, David Smith bought a parcel of books to number 16 on the evening of Tuesday, 5 October. It contained the books Brady had lent to him: *Justine*, *Kiss of the Whip*, *Tropic of Cancer*, *The Perfumed Garden*, *Orgies of Torture and Brutality*, *Mein Kampf* and an exercise book in which Smith had copied out various quotations. Myra took the parcel from Smith and put it on the living room table. Brady took it upstairs and packed it with other items he had ready. There were two reels of tape containing the Lesley Ann Downey recordings and two radio programmes: *The Goon Show* and a commentary by Freddie Grisewood on the rise and fall of Adolf Hitler.

The other articles were two coshes, a black wig, books on sexual perversions, gun cartridges and a few letters. Brady appeared a few minutes later with two suitcases: one black and the other blue. This was part of the regular steps to 'clean' the house before the robbery on Saturday. Brady told me that 'the house was so clean, a nun couldn't object.'

Brady was still worried that Smith's nerve would 'crack' during the robbery. If this happened, he would have to shoot Smith. This would lead police directly to Myra and himself. Brady had thought of testing Smith's nerve by taking him up to the moors with a victim and making an excuse to stop the car. Brady would hand the gun to Smith and ask him to kill the stranger. If he didn't have the nerve to do it, Brady would ask for the gun back and shoot them both.

Myra and Ian drove to Manchester Central Station later on Tuesday evening and deposited the cases in left-luggage as usual. When they awoke on Wednesday morning, 6 October 1965, they had no idea that the events of the day would mock their meticulous plans and rob them of their freedom forever. Myra and Ian coasted through the day's routine at Millwards. It was a day like any other. They returned to Wardle Brook Avenue after work and Myra began to prepare the tea. Ian Brady described to me what happened next: 'Myra was busy in the kitchen and I took the two dogs, Lassie and Puppet, out for their daily run. The weather was glorious. I wanted to use up the half-dozen pictures left in the film and took five photographs of the dogs chasing a stick. I was near Underwood Court, or "The Towers" as Myra and I called it, and heard Smith calling to me from their third-floor balcony. He shouted down to tell me to wait there for him.

'He told me that he had a letter threatening eviction if the rent arrears weren't paid and their dog Bobby removed from the flat. Smith and Mo owed £14 and 8 shillings. He asked me to lend him the money and I said I was broke. I told him that there was nothing he could do about the dog. It would have to go. I felt even more concerned about Smith's nerve. We had a robbery planned for three days' time, and here he was worrying about a few quid, when the takings from the raid on the gas and electricity shop would pay his rent arrears many times over. Why couldn't he take a broader view? During our conversation, I suddenly realised that here was a chance to put Smith's nerve to a real test.

'I told Smith I would try to get some money for him by "rolling a queer". This was sixties parlance for enticing a homosexual with the promise of sex and then robbing him of his cash. He would be unlikely to report the incident to the police because homosexual acts were illegal then.

'I went home for tea and told Myra we would be going out in the evening. The girl from next door was in number 16 when I arrived back, so I finished the film by taking one of her with Myra and the dogs in the living room. It was the last photograph I ever took. I still have an enlargement of the picture.

'The murder was conceived and executed within the space of five hours. There were none of the preliminaries of Tarot cards, Pro-plus, and so on. The suitcases were in left-luggage by chance in preparation for the robbery on Saturday.'

*   *   *   *   *

At the time Myra and Ian were eating their tea, Edward Evans in the Ardwick area of Manchester was preparing to go out for the evening. He was seventeen and lived at number 55 Addison Street with his mother Edith and his father John, a lift attendant. Edward's brother and sister also lived there. Edward was an apprentice – a machinist at the AEI electrical works on Trafford Park Estate. He had arranged to go with his friend Michael Mahone to see Manchester United play Helsinki at Old Trafford soccer stadium.

Eddie put on a white shirt, blue jeans, dark brown Italian shoes and his best suede jacket. He left home at 6.30 p.m. to meet his friend in Auntie's Bar on Oxford Road. The licensee, George Smith, remembers seeing Eddie at 7 p.m. He had known him by sight for three or four months. Michael Mahone didn't appear. Eddie left the bar to go to the city centre alone. He was six days older than David Smith.

In Hattersley, Myra was wearing her leopard-skin print dress as she drove out of Wardle Brook Avenue with Ian for their rendezvous with a stranger. Ian Brady would later re-decorate the homely pink living room with the victim's red blood. It was 7.30 p.m. They were bound for the city centre but went first to Longsight to buy wine in Grey Street.

Myra told Peter Topping she remembered that at some point in the evening a car in front of them hit a dog. She stopped the car and offered to take the dog to a vet. The owner said that his dog's injury wasn't serious enough for that. Myra attached great importance to this incident as she tried to convince Topping that they would hardly be prepared to be diverted by a triviality if she and Ian had more sinister plans in mind. I asked Brady if there was any truth in Myra's story about the dog. He said that it was true.

At 10.30 p.m. Myra parked the car close to Manchester Central Station while Ian went to the station buffet to buy more bottles of wine. She had parked on double yellow lines and a passing policeman told her that if she was still there when he returned, he would book her for a parking offence. Myra used this incident as further evidence to Topping that there was no plan to pick up someone and murder him or her. Why should she take the risk of having her number taken by a policeman so close to the spot where Edward Evans was last seen alive?

Ian arrived at the buffet to find the doors locked. The buffet had closed two minutes before at 10.30 p.m. Ian recognised a young man standing at a vending machine nearby. He had seen him in a Manchester gay pub a couple of times but the two had never spoken. He walked over to Eddie and asked him if he wanted to come back for a drink. Eddie was only too happy to salvage what was left of a wasted evening by accepting what – according to Brady – was a covert invitation to sex. As they settled into the vehicle, Ian told Eddie that Myra was his 'sister' to deepen the deception.

Myra stopped the mini-traveller at the grass slope below number 16 in Wardle Brook Avenue. Ian said to Myra, 'Fetch Smith,' and whispered to tell her to stay in Smith's flat for a while. It's not possible to say, with confidence, exactly what happened next. At some point in the late evening, Myra changed out of her leopard-skin print dress into what were later called her 'killing clothes', which included a shabby skirt with the hem hanging down. She may have changed clothes before she went to fetch Smith or after she returned with him. David Smith said that she had changed her clothes by the time she made her late night call at Underwood Court.

Myra walked to Underwood Court and pressed the button for flat number 18 – there was an entry-phone system at the time. There are different versions about who answered the entry-phone and what happened in flat number 18. At the trial David Smith said that he was in bed when Myra called. Myra insisted that Smith was dressed and waiting for her to call. This would support the claim she made years later, that Brady and Smith had planned the murder of Edward Evans without her knowledge.

There was some agreement about what was said in the flat. Maureen asked Myra why she had called so late. Myra said she had a message for her mother, who was working with Maureen at the time. She would call in on Friday to do her mother's hair and borrow a pair of her shoes. She had forgotten to call round earlier.

Myra asked David Smith to walk back home with her as the lights on the estate were out and she was afraid of the dark streets. Hyde Corporation would, in fact, give evidence at the trial to confirm that the street lights were out at that time of night. David put on his moccasins and told Mo he would be back soon. Before he left, he picked up his dog-walking stick. It was nearly two inches thick and between two and three feet long. It had a long length of string wrapped round the end and would play a part in the drama that was about to unfold.

Would Smith's nerve crack? It was a question answered before the population of Hattersley rose from their beds on Thursday morning.

Another one of the mysteries of the Moors Murder case is what happened in number 16 while Myra was with David and Maureen in Underwood Court. When police found Edward Evans' body, he was not wearing his shoes and the flies on his jeans were undone. Forensic evidence proved that dog hairs from the house were found on the anus and legs after the jeans were removed from the corpse. Under interrogation, Brady denied any sexual involvement with Evans. During a discussion of the murder, Ann and Alan West told me that David Smith had described to them how Myra Hindley cavorted naked in front of Edward Evans before he was axed to death.

According to Brady's answers to questions from the police, in the time Myra was away, Evans had gone upstairs to the toilet – which explained the dog hairs. The truth is that Brady did take part in sexual acts with Edward Evans. These included oral sex.

Myra and David left Underwood Court and took the short cut to Wardle Brook Avenue, across Pudding Lane and down Sundial Close. They arrived at the front of number 16 and Brady answered the door. In an unusually loud voice, 'for Edward Evans to hear', he asked David, 'Do you want those miniature wine bottles? They are in the kitchen.' Myra and David walked into the short hallway as Brady fetched the bottles and said that there were some whisky and brandy miniatures in the next room. Brady entered the living room and walked behind the settee that Eddie was sitting on. He told me what happened next: 'I picked up an axe that had been placed out of sight and I brought it down with great force on to Evans' head. I was aiming for the back of his head to kill him instantly but he turned round at the last split second and the blade of the axe bounced off the crown of his head. It should have taken only one hit.

'Evans screamed out as I rained down blows to his head. He was writhing on the floor to protect himself. Myra was in the room watching. The two dogs were excited and barking in the kitchen.

'Myra's grandmother had been woken up by the noise and shouted down to ask what was happening. Myra shouted something in reply but I was too occupied to know what it was.

'Evans was still alive after I had hit him about a dozen times. I went into the kitchen to fetch a length of electrical flex. I put a cushion cover over his head and strangled him by wrapping the wire round his neck. Evans stopped gurgling. It was suddenly quiet. The walls, floor and carpets were spattered with blood. I handed the axe to Smith so that his fingerprints were on the handle.

'I lit a cigarette and muttered something about it being the messiest murder I had committed. Myra made a comment about the terror in Evans' eyes as he was being flayed.

'I opened Evans' wallet and found a green National Insurance card giving his personal particulars. His occupation was given as "engineer". There was also a pay packet and an old letter from a girl named Wendy in North Wales. I put the wallet, the axe and Evans' shoes in a carrier bag with other rubbish. I had sprained my left ankle and realised that this would delay the disposal of Evans' body. We would have to put the corpse in the empty bedroom upstairs until tomorrow. I unwound the string wrapped round the end of Smith's stick and used it to tie up Evans into a foetal position. Myra claimed that she knew nothing of string from David Smith's stick. She was lying.'

'Myra spread a white cotton blanket on the floor and we lifted the body on to it. The blanket was knotted around the torso. We wrapped a large sheet of polythene around the bundle. A grey blanket was used to carry Evans cradle-fashion. Myra held her grandmother's bedroom door closed as Smith and I struggled upstairs.

'I was wearing a shoulder holster and a gun that was hindering my movements. I took them off and put them into Myra's empty bedroom. This was a fatal mistake. I should have asked Smith to carry Evans single-handedly. I would then have no reason to put the gun upstairs. It would have been under the divan bed downstairs and I could have used it at the arrest. I have since remembered that I was at my strongest when I was Smith's age. He should have carried Evans.

'It took the three of us almost three hours to clean up the blood in the living room, using buckets of soapy water and rags. The carpets were the most troublesome.

'I found it incomprehensible that the police couldn't find traces of blood on the carpets. This incompetence led them to assume that I had taken up the carpets before Evans arrived in preparation for the slaughter. Even Smith said that the carpets were down all the time.'

The room was as clean as it could be until daylight would dawn to reveal the overlooked marks of the mayhem. At that stage, Brady felt that Smith had passed the initiation test. He seemed calm as he left number 16 to return to Underwood Court and the waiting Mo. Ian Brady later reflected on those hours after midnight: 'We drank wine till 3.30 a.m., during which I tended my sprained ankle – the minor injury which led to delay, loss of impetus, the cracking of Smith's nerve and our capture.'

Myra had put a cold compress on his ankle. Brady denied David Smith's claim that Myra put her feet up on the mantelpiece when the action was over. As the three of them drank the wine, they had what Brady called an 'ad lib discussion' about what was to be done. He wrote out a hasty disposal plan using abbreviations in five columns. (I mentioned in a previous chapter Brady's explanation of the abbreviations on the list that were never deciphered by the police.)

Brady already had Penistone in mind as a burial site for their next victim. Now he was having second thoughts. There were no connecting links to number 16 and so there was no need for immediate disposal.

Bonfire night was less than a month away. Why not burn Evans? Brady had suddenly remembered a film in which the central character disposed of the leading lady on a fire. He dismissed this idea and another suggestion that they bury the body in the garden. Why not use a pram for moving the body into the back of the car? Maureen and David had held on to Angela Dawn's pram after her death. The pram was kept at David's grandfather's house. Brady said that a large bundle in a pram wouldn't attract attention: 'People put washing in prams in the north.'

The three of them agreed that David would be waiting outside Millwards at 5 p.m. the next day, Thursday, and Myra and Ian would take him to collect the pram.

Brady lied about the evening's events at the trial to save Myra from conviction. He said that Myra wasn't in the room when Evans was killed. According to him, she was in the kitchen, 'overwrought' and 'hysterical'. Myra embroidered the lie several times during her imprisonment. She told fellow prisoner Janie Jones that she was in the kitchen when the screams were heard, with her hands over her ears: 'I never entered that room except to go and mop up the blood.'

The marks of blood on Myra's shoes were not smears. If they had been, it would be plausible to say that the marks were made as she helped to clean up. The blood on Myra's shoes was arterial. The shoes must have been very near Evans' body as a blow was struck. Her explanation for this was that she wasn't wearing the shoes at the time. They just happened to be in the room when the bloodbath was taking place. However, there was no blood inside the shoes, which means that someone must have been wearing them at the time.

David Smith, according to Ian Brady, also played down his contribution to the evening. Smith said he was in the doorway of the living room when he became aware of the violence and heard the screams. There was just a small television light on and it was difficult to see what was happening. Brady was swearing violently as he brought an axe down again and again on what appeared to be a man-size marionette in the dimly lit room. Smith used the graphic image of a 'rag doll' during his evidence at the trial, prompting Ian Brady's lawyer to suggest that the newspaper paying Smith for his story had supplied the colourful phrase.

At some point between 3 a.m. and 4 a.m., David Smith said that it was time he went back to Maureen. He was afraid he would not be allowed to leave number 16 alive. He ran in the darkness up Sundial Close and across Pudding Lane, his mind full of terrors as he ran. Had Brady and Myra jumped in the car to intercept him before he could reach the safety of Underwood Court? The lift had never taken so long to open and ascend so slowly.

After Myra's death, 37 years later, David Smith reflected on the events that night in number 16: 'I just stood there, froze. You think you would jump out of a window or run into the street shouting blue murder, but I knew if I did that, I wouldn't even make it to the front door, and that Evans's murder wouldn't be the only murder that night.

'It was an almost animal self-preservation that clicked in. I knew I had to show no emotion, no bad reaction to what he had done or I wouldn't be going home. It frightens me to think I was capable of that.'

Myra and Brady were alone in the living room. Brady said that she would have to go into work. A break in routine might arouse suspicion. He would send in a sick note and invent a story about his ankle injury.

There was silence for a few minutes. Myra Hindley and Ian Brady drank what was left in the wine bottles as they chain-smoked without speaking. The spectre of his beloved Dostoevsky hung over the exhausted Brady. The fictional anti-hero of *Crime and Punishment*, Raskolnikov, had triggered the Moors Murders when he sank an axe into the skull of the moneylender. The character of Raskolnikov took factual form in the murdering consciousness of Ian Brady as he sank an axe into the skull of Edward Evans. Edward was as defenceless as the moneylender. The moneylender's death started it and Edward's death brought it to a close.

Myra broke the silence and told Brady that the chain needed to be locked on to the steering wheel of the car. She said she couldn't face the darkness of Wardle Brook Avenue. Brady nodded and left the room.

Brady limped down the grass slope to secure the car for the night. His wallet dropped on to the car seat as he stooped to put the chain on the steering wheel. He put the wallet on the dashboard for a moment and forgot to pick it up before he locked the car. The disposal plan was in the wallet waiting for someone to find. Ian slipped into bed on the divan to get a couple of hours' sleep. Myra said that she sat in the darkness wondering what the morning would bring. Brady said she then climbed into the bed – for the last time.

Ian Brady wrote to me in September 1992, commenting on the final murder and the dark thoughts that he believed everyone has: 'There is a Mr Hyde in everyone (chained down) but subconsciously straining for release;

meanwhile, he must make-do with vicarious thrills through the actions of others. It is rather ironic that the final victim's name was Edward and that it took place in Hyde: Edward Hyde.'

Ten years later, Brady wrote that, 'The serial killer is in effect your alter-ego, that facet of character you strive so hard to conceal and repress.'

The song that Myra and Ian associated with the murder of Edward Evans had entered the charts early in September. It was Joan Baez's version of Bob Dylan's 'It's All Over Now Baby Blue'.

It was far from over for Ian Brady and Myra Hindley. Their misery would begin with the dawn. It was all over for Edward Evans. He began the day breathing in a glorious October Indian summer morning and ended it trussed up in a bundle in a stranger's house. The police would find three paperbacks on top of the lifeless parcel: *Tales of Horror*, *The Road Ahead – A Children's Poetry Book* and *Among Women Only*.

Edward Evans' body grew cold in the black hours. It was in the same small bedroom where Lesley Ann Downey had been murdered. She too lay cold in the night, waiting for burial. Yet Edward Evans would be given a proper burial a short time before Lesley Ann. His death led to the discovery of Lesley Ann's body on Saddleworth Moor. They were brought close in death. Lesley Ann's grave is a few feet from Edward's grave.

CHAPTER SEVENTEEN

THE ONLY DATE I REMEMBER

David Smith was covered in blood as he opened the door to flat No. 18. Maureen was in bed. Between retching and vomiting in the bathroom, David stammered out what he had witnessed in No. 16. There was no alternative: they had to call the police.

Maureen reflected in the early hours: 'These things don't happen in Hattersley. And not to our Myra.'

But what if Brady was waiting near Underwood Court, watching to see if David could be trusted? It would be daylight in an hour. Better wait till then.

The two of them slipped out of Underwood Court at the first signs of dawn, armed with a knife and a screwdriver. They hurried through the paths of Underwood Walk and Paynton Walk on to Hattersley Road West. The nearest telephone kiosk was on the corner of Hare Hill Road: Hyde 3538.

Constable Keith Edwards answered the telephone at 6.07 a.m. in Hyde police station: 'My name is David Smith . . .' said a voice, 'I'm speaking from Hattersley . . . There's been a murder.' PC Antrobus drove off to investigate. In the meantime, the panic-stricken Smith telephoned again. When the police car arrived, he jumped in the back with Maureen before it had come to a halt.

PC Antrobus contacted Detective Inspector Wills at 7.20 a.m. In turn, Detective Inspector Wills telephoned his own superior, Superintendent Bob Talbot. Talbot had been appointed just five weeks before and he was about to become a central figure in the investigations into one of the most notorious crimes in British criminal history. He was due to begin a fortnight's leave that very day. It would be a long time before

THE ONLY DATE I REMEMBER

he could take it. He left for Hyde police station to meet up with his detective Sergeant Carr.

First of all, the detectives needed to be sure that a crime had actually taken place. David Smith told the story of the night before and spoke of other murders and bodies on the moors. He warned the police that Ian Brady had guns in the house. As fanciful as Smith's account seemed, the police had no alternative but to take it seriously. Superintendent Talbot ordered 24 uniformed and six plain-clothed policemen.

The police cars turned off Mottram Road and parked in the vicinity of Wardle Brook Avenue, blocking all surrounding roads. Smith had said that Brady left for work at 8.20 a.m. every morning. No one had surfaced from number 16 by 8.35 a.m.

Craig's Pantry van was in Sundial Close with its driver delivering fresh bread. Talbot commissioned the deliveryman's white coat and a basket of loaves. He walked up the front path of number 16, went to the side of the house and knocked on the back door.

Myra Hindley answered and was surprised to see a bread man. She was ready to leave for work in her tweed jacket and skirt and white stiletto shoes. One of the dogs came to inspect the visitor. Talbot looked at the woman's backcombed honey platinum hair, thick black eye make-up and lipstick. The superintendent thought she must be about 35. She was 23. Who was she? Never in a thousand years could he have known that her face would haunt the front pages of the tabloid press for a generation and go down in the annals of murder as Britain's first female serial killer.

'Is your husband in?'

'I haven't got a husband.'

'I am a police superintendent and I have reason to believe there is a man in the house.'

'There's no man here.'

'I have received a report that an act of violence took place here last night and we are investigating it.'

'There's nothing wrong here.'

Talbot swept past Myra, taking off his white coat on his way. Myra said, 'He's in the other room in bed.' The policeman entered the living room and almost bumped into the budgerigar's cage near the door. Ian Brady, dressed only in a string-vest, was sitting on a divan bed. Myra described the moment: 'I'll never forget his face when I took the police into the living room the morning after the murder of Edward Evans. It was expression-less, as it often was, but I saw him almost shrink before my eyes, helpless and powerless, just as the victims had been, but now, thank God, there would be no more victims, it was all over, and I felt free.' Freedom was the last thing she should have expected; she showed no signs of 'feeling free' in the interrogations that followed.

Superintendent Talbot looked around the room and heard Sergeant Carr enter the kitchen behind him. The young man on the bed was writing with a green ballpoint pen. Ian Brady didn't stop writing. Talbot wanted to go upstairs. Myra led the way. He opened the door of one bedroom and saw Mrs Maybury sitting up in bed sipping tea. Myra explained who she was. Talbot asked for a key when he found that the second bedroom was locked. Myra said the room was locked because she kept her firearms in there. She said that the key was at the office and it wasn't convenient to fetch it.

Talbot walked downstairs followed by Myra. He said he wasn't leaving the house until he had checked the bedroom. One of his men would go to Millwards for the key.

Ian Brady had finished writing. It was a letter to his boss, Tom Craig:

Tom,

Sorry I could not phone yesterday, my family are at Glasgow this week. I was crossing the road in town last night when someone on a bike came around the corner and knocked me down, except for a few bruises. I was alright until I got up this morning, my ankle would not take my weight. I must have weak ankles or something, if its no better tomorrow; I'll have to see a doctor.

Ian

No one was speaking in the living room. Myra looked at Ian for help. Ian broke the silence: 'You had better give him the key. A fight got out of hand last night. It's upstairs.' This was for Myra's ears. He gave her the story to tell.

Upstairs, the superintendent looked around the small, sparsely furnished bedroom. The floorboards were bare, so were the walls. There was a narrow bed, a small table, an armchair and a jumble of cardboard boxes and suitcases.

Under the window there was a large parcel covered with a grey blanket. A few paperbacks rested on top. There was a carrier bag on the floor with a hatchet inside. Alongside it was a stick covered in blood and a cardboard box containing two loaded revolvers. Talbot felt the grey bundle and soon discovered he was touching a human foot. David Smith hadn't lied. The policeman wondered whether there was any truth in the other things he had said.

Talbot walked back down the narrow stairs into the living room. He told Ian Brady to get dressed. Brady put on his shirt and trousers and slipped into his shoes, watched by the two policemen.

Brady intended to kill both of them where they stood and had decided which one to shoot first. He bent down to tie his shoe laces and covertly felt underneath the divan bed with his right hand for the loaded revolver. There was nothing there. The superintendent had already found the guns in the bedroom, where Brady had absent-mindedly thrown them a few hours before. Ian Brady realised he was finished.

Brady once stopped in mid-sentence, stared blankly at me and said, 'October 7th 1965 – it's the only date I remember.'

The policemen – Talbot and Carr – never knew how close to death they came. Brady and Hindley had agreed to shoot and kill anyone if they were cornered. If the situation was hopeless, Brady would shoot Hindley in the back of the head, put the gun into his own mouth and blow his brains out. Commenting to me more than thirty years later, he mused, 'If only the gun was where it always was. But here I am.'

Brady told me that they could have driven across the grass – on the other side of the road from number 16 – on to the Mottram Road and turned left immediately into what he called the Rain Lane, opposite the New Inn pub. It was just wide enough to take a car. Brady and Hindley called it the Rain Lane after being caught in a torrential downpour there once while walking the dogs. Brady reflected on the arrest: 'In the final confrontation, with the house surrounded by the police and all exit roads blocked, I still believe that if we had been given the ten-second warning to reach the revolvers and rifle, we could have reached the car and escaped by the Rain Lane they hadn't thought of blocking. And then? Well, that would be mere speculation. But probably death in hours or days. The media would have been furious at us for depriving them and thirty-odd authors and playwrights of the lucrative profits they have made from the case over the years. Our departing message to the media would have been the same as Nixon's when he withdrew from politics: "You guys will have to find someone else to kick around now."'

Neighbours stood and watched as Ian Brady was escorted to a police car. Myra's grandmother was bewildered by all the activity and Myra went with her to a neighbour's house in Wardle Brook Walk, at the rear of number 16. The two dogs, Lassie and Puppet, went with them. Mrs Maybury was told there had been a road accident. She never spoke about what happened on the fatal night.

Shortly after Ian Brady was led out through the front door to the waiting police car, a young man visited the house where Myra and her grandmother were temporarily taking shelter. He was Clive Entwistle, a freelance reporter, who was at Hyde courts when he heard there had been a murder at Hattersley. Had he but known it, the next twenty minutes were to be the most memorable in his professional life.

Clive saw a young blonde woman sitting in the living room. He was about to be the first person to interview Myra Hindley: 'I sat down and basically had a 20-minute chat with Myra Hindley, not realising in any shape or form the enormity of what was about to be revealed. As far as the police were concerned it was an open and shut case, a straightforward murder.

'They had got the bad guy who had admitted it and he was in custody. I got her name out of her and asked what she knew about the killing. She just stared away. I introduced myself and handed her a cup and saucer, which she held but never drank from.

'I asked whether she knew the dead man and all I got was silence. After a while I changed tack and asked her boyfriend's name. She said, "Ian Brady". I asked what happened and I was just stonewalled. It was a one-way conversation and after 20 minutes I got up and left.

'All that appeared in the papers was that a man had been charged with murder after police discovered the body of a young man trussed up in the back bedroom of a house on a housing estate near Hyde. That was all there was.'

A few hours later, Detective Chief Superintendent Arthur Benfield, in charge of the CID, walked into number 16 with Dr C St Hill, a Home Office pathologist. Dr St Hill discovered that Edward Evans had a fractured skull and deduced that the ligature used to strangle him accelerated his death. There were fourteen lacerations to the scalp.

Arthur Benfield – Brady and Hindley referred to him as 'Big Ben' – examined the two revolvers found in the bedroom. He realised he was not dealing with an ordinary killer when he found that the guns had five loaded chambers and the empty sixth was opposite the firing pin. Brady knew that one pull of the trigger lined up a bullet. It was quicker than having to release the safety catch before shooting. This was Benfield's first step into the labyrinthine, cunning mind of Ian Brady.

As Superintendent Benfield and his colleagues were looking over the empty shell of number 16, Ian Brady was being interrogated in Hyde police station. I asked Brady about his relations with the detectives in the Moors Murders case. He said that Mounsey, Mattin, Leach and Tyrrell were shouting a foot away from each ear from both sides: 'I answered their questions as though they were dog shit!'

Brady had to give a statement, whatever he thought of the detectives. He implicated David Smith and removed Myra from the scene of the murder: 'Last night I met Eddie in Manchester. We were drinking and then we went home to Hattersley. We had an argument and we came to blows. After the first few blows the situation got out of control. When the argument started, Dave Smith was at the front door and Myra called him in. Eddie kicked me at the beginning on the ankle. There was a hatchet on the floor and I hit Eddie with it. After that the only noise Eddie made was gurgling. When Dave and I began cleaning up the floor the gurgling stopped. Then we tied up the body, Dave and I. Nobody else helped. Dave and I carried it upstairs. Then we sat in the house until three or four in the morning. Then we decided to get rid of the body in the morning, early next day or next night.'

Myra was kept apart from Ian and was questioned by a detective policewoman, Margaret Campion, in the station canteen. She wanted food for Puppet but the detective insisted that she answered some questions first about the death of Edward Evans. After a few minutes, Campion realised Myra was going to be a tough nut to crack. Myra just stonewalled: 'I didn't do it, Ian didn't do it. I am saying nothing. Ask Ian. Whatever Ian has done, I have done.'

Myra was willing to say a few things about her movements with Brady before Evans was killed in number 16. She said that her story was the same as Brady's. They left the house at 8 p.m. and went to Longsight to buy some wine. Then they drove to Glossop near the moors and drank the wine as they talked. They had done the same on many evenings before. Myra didn't know that Brady, in another room, had said that they drove into Manchester – the opposite direction from Glossop.

Margaret Campion walked across the road to buy a tin of dog food for Puppet.

At Millwards, Tom Craig and a few of the staff were wondering why Ian and Myra were hours late for work without phoning in. Irene ran to Tom when she heard on the one o'clock news that a man had been murdered at Myra's house. Everyone in the office jumped to the conclusion that the victim must be Ian Brady. Had he lost his temper once too often in a fight?

Tom Craig could never have guessed that Ian Brady had written a letter to explain his absence from work. He would never receive it. It would be an exhibit at the Moors trial and Tom Craig would have to testify that the letter was in Brady's handwriting. (Millwards Merchandise Ltd never recovered from its innocent association with the Moors Murders and eventually closed down.

Myra was medically examined and gave saliva and blood samples. Her uncle, Bert Maybury, arrived with his sister Hettie, Myra's mother, to find out why Myra was in trouble. Myra's clothes were retained for forensic tests and she changed into clothes her mother had brought.

The police had taken over number 16 and Myra was refused entry. They dug to a depth of three feet in the garden. The police search of the house uncovered, among other things, a tartan-covered album with many moorland scenes featuring either Myra or Ian in the picture. An exercise book containing Ian's doodles and drawings was found in a wardrobe.

When he found time, after the immediate drama of the arrest was over, Superintendent Talbot looked through the book. He noticed that Brady had written the name 'John Kilbride' in it. Detective Chief Inspector Joe Mounsey was then drawn into the enquiry. As I mentioned earlier, he had taken a particular interest in John Kilbride's disappearance. When questioned, Brady said that the name in the book was that of someone he knew in Hull Borstal. A check revealed that no one by that name had ever been there.

Brady was photographed in a cell corridor against a white sheet with a box camera. This security photograph, together with the one of Myra taken a few days later, would haunt the popular press for decades. Myra said that her security photograph was taken after four sleepless nights. She was told to sit on a chair in the middle of a bare room. She tried to contain her fear by glaring at the policeman. There was a flash. For years, the *Sun* would call her 'the most evil woman in Britain' and they had the gift of a Medusa-like picture to prove it. Brady's security picture was exhibited 34 years later in the 'Faces of the Century' exhibition at the National Portrait Gallery, London. (These first security photographs of Brady and Hindley would sometimes be 'doctored' by the use of shadows to make the pair appear in their most demonical form in newspaper articles and on book covers.)

Brady was charged with the murder of Edward Evans and made a three-minute appearance in Hyde court on Friday, 8 October, the day after his arrest. He gave his solicitor strict instructions not to involve the Sloans in any way. If they wrote to Brady, he would not reply.

Myra wasn't charged after she had been questioned on the day of Brady's arrest. She went to live with her mother and made the best of her four days of freedom. Myra used the days to destroy what she could of any incriminating material. She went to Millwards on Saturday morning, 9 October, and asked that she and Ian be sacked. On the same visit she went into the old invoice storeroom in the warehouse. Brady said to me that she 'destroyed the master list, addresses, photographs and negatives. Thank Christ the police didn't discover those!'

Twenty years after the arrest, Myra told Peter Topping that she had burned the envelope in an ashtray without looking at the contents. She assumed they were plans for bank robberies. Naturally, Topping was sceptical. Brady told me she burned its contents in a fireplace, knowing full well what they were. The photographs and notes she destroyed, according to Brady, could have helped to locate Keith Bennett's grave. He made notes to this effect in the margins of Topping's book.

The left-luggage ticket was in the spine of the prayer book in the living room of number 16. Brady commented: 'A policeman was on guard outside the front door of number 16. The prayer book was deliberately left on open display on the chest of drawers near the back window. Myra was deterred by the police presence. If I had been free, nothing would have stopped me from retrieving that ticket and destroying the contents of the two suitcases.'

Myra was charged with the murder of Edward Evans at 3 p.m. on Monday, 11 October, at Hyde police station. In the morning of the same day, men had been at work on Saddleworth Moor looking for signs of disturbed ground and circling the spot with yellow dye. From the air, the circles looked like giant marigolds.

Edward Evans was blood group 'O'. Traces of his blood were found on the clothing of Brady, Hindley and Smith.

In Hyde police station Ian Brady was coming to terms with his fate and the inevitable guilty verdict at the trial. I mentioned the crime magazine *Ellery Queen* to him in the course of one visit. Brady remembered that he had read copies of the magazine to combat boredom in the cell at Hyde. It prompted him to tell me how he could have escaped from there. He was shaving when he noticed in the mirror that the constable had been distracted by a telephone call. A window was open and it would have been so easy.

Brady mentioned another chance to escape that presented itself while he was held on remand at Risley. There was a dense fog one night when he was being escorted across a car park: 'It would have been easy to slip out of sight and climb over the low fencing.' I asked him why he hadn't taken his chances: 'I didn't want to leave the girl,' a word he often used whenever Myra cropped up in our conversations.

David Smith told the police about the two suitcases a few days after Myra had been charged. He claimed that he had forgotten about them. Brady said that Smith had hesitated to tell the police about the cases because he knew that some of the material inside incriminated him. Smith became less worried when he discovered he would be immune from prosecution for helping the police.

The police were credited with the discovery of the left-luggage ticket in the spine of Myra's prayer book. Brady said that after Smith's tip-off, the police opened suitcases at Manchester Central until they found what they were looking for. Brady wrote: 'Presented with the cases I was asked where the ticket was. I told them. Tyrrell actually ran from the room!'

Brady was referring to the detective John Tyrrell, who found the ticket number 74843 in the spine of Myra's prayer book after Brady had told him where it was hidden. It was the last piece of evidence to link Brady with the suitcases. Brady told me that he couldn't help but smile when Tyrrell accepted the praise of the trial judge for his thoroughness in finding the ticket in such an obscure hiding place.

There was intense police activity on several fronts in the days following the arrest. It was some weeks before the police could relate each separate discovery into an overall picture. The police were naturally asking questions about Brady and Hindley's possible links with unsolved crimes, including murder. The names of Pauline Reade and Keith Bennett, among others, were mentioned during the interrogations.

Brady and Hindley were confronted with the tapes and photographs found in the suitcases and described in an earlier chapter. Brady said that he had only taken the photographs of Lesley Ann Downey. He stated that she had left number 16 alive in the company of David Smith and another man, who had been waiting outside in a car. Myra Hindley was presented with the same material and showed brief signs of remorse. As she listened to the tape she began to cry. She bowed her head and said, 'I'm ashamed.' But she quickly recovered and stayed tight-lipped. Myra didn't want to say much more until she knew the story Brady was telling. (As we have seen, Brady said much later that Myra's tears were those of 'self-pity because she could not lie with the evidence of the tape'.)

Meanwhile, the police were trying to make sense of Brady's disposal plan found in the car. At this early stage in the investigation, they believed that WH referred to 'Woodhead' on the A628 Manchester to Sheffield road. We have seen that it referred to 'Warehouse'. REC referred to 'records', not to 'reconnaissance' as the police assumed.

In their door-to-door enquiries, the police discovered that Pat Hodges had been on trips to the moors with Brady and Hindley. Pat was a passenger in Detective Constable Peter Clegg's car as she guided him and police-woman Slater through Greenfield and up the slow climb to the places where Myra and Ian used to stop the car for a picnic or simply to drink wine. Brady and Hindley knew that although the police were looking for Lesley Ann Downey, they were walking over the grave of Pauline Reade.

Lesley Ann Downey's body was found soon after Pat's visit, 70 yards into Saddleworth Moor from one of the spots she had pointed out. On Saturday, 16 October, at 2.50 p.m., the policemen searching Saddleworth Moor decided to call it a day. PC Robert Spiers told his colleagues to wait while he walked over a rise to answer the call of nature. He was about to return to the police coach when he saw a bone sticking through the mud and peat. He called his sergeant, who scraped mud away to reveal the remains of the arm of a young person. Joe Mounsey of the Lancashire police was called to the scene in case it was John Kilbride.

Speaking after Myra Hindley's death 37 years later, retired journalist Derek Rigby recalled the scene: 'It was a horrible, misty night and bitterly cold. The lamps shining through the mist on the moors was haunting. There were just these yellow blobs in the mist.'

Lesley Ann's body was found as it was buried, in the state and con-ditions described in chapter fifteen. Her cherished white beads dropped out of her scraps of clothing when they were cleaned of the clinging peat. Lesley's mother identified the body the following day; Alan West wasn't a blood relative and wasn't allowed to spare his wife the sight that would take natural sleep from her for the rest of her life. She was only allowed to see the part of Lesley's body that had not been ravaged by animals. She was also required to look at two of Brady's photographs of her daughter and listen to a minute or so of the tape as part of the formal identification.

Detectives covering the John Kilbride enquiry had contacted every car-hire firm in Manchester and had found what they were looking for. Myra Hindley had hired a Ford Anglia, number 9275 ND, for a period of 24 hours from 10 a.m. 23 November 1963 – the day John Kilbride disappeared.

Four days later at Hyde, on Thursday, 21 October 1965, Brady and Hindley were charged with the murder of Lesley Ann Downey.

After Lesley Ann's body had been unearthed on the moor, police realised that one of Brady's photographs had been taken a few feet from her grave. Had he photographed other graves? One picture in particular made them wonder. It was the photograph, described in chapter fourteen, of Myra holding her dog and staring down to the ground.

The Scene of Crimes officer Mike Mascheder had been responsible for producing John Kilbride's photograph for mass distribution when the boy went missing in November 1963. He developed the negative of the picture of Myra and her dog, producing a photograph that showed a skyline of a stone outcrop not visible on Brady's print. Mike Mascheder's colleague, Ray Gelder, was taking photographs on Saddleworth Moor and recognised the stone formation on the picture that Mike had fully developed.

Photo in hand, Joe Mounsey walked around the area of Hollin Brown Knoll on the north side of the A635, the side where Lesley Ann had been found. Just before abandoning his search for the day, Mounsey crossed the road to the south side.

He could scarcely believe his eyes. By looking at the photograph and the actual skyline of Saddleworth Moor, to the north, he located what must have been the exact spot Myra was staring at, by matching the stones in the foreground of the picture with the stones still there on the moor. Light was fading in the late afternoon and Joe Mounsey called it a day.

He was back on the moors the following morning with Inspector Chaddock. Mike Mascheder had his camera ready and pushed its three legs into the soil. By looking through the viewfinder and readjusting the legs several times, the settings of the camera, and that of the photo held by Joe Mounsey, were matched.

All three men held their breath as Inspector Chaddock pushed his long stick into the ground. He pulled it out and sniffed the end of it. He recoiled from the smell of putrefaction. They had located the remains of John Kilbride. Joe Mounsey was moved to be there to witness the discovery of the body of the gap-toothed boy, whose picture had haunted him since he took on his job in the Lancashire force.

As with Lesley Ann, John Kilbride was found in the state in which he had been murdered. The body was in a stream bed and badly decomposed. It was placed on the same slab in Uppermill Mortuary that had borne the remains of Lesley Ann Downey. Only John's teeth were discernible. His mother, Mrs Sheila Kilbride, identified her son by the clothes he was wearing on the day he disappeared.

The police also looked at another photograph that was probably also taken on the day that Myra was pictured looking down at John Kilbride's grave. In the photograph Myra was dressed in the same clothes and holding Puppet. Police photographers and detectives calculated that Myra, in the photograph, was obscuring a sign for the trans-Pennine methane gas pipeline and possibly looking down on another grave. The cost of digging up the site would run into millions of pounds.

While police and the accused were arguing, funerals were taking place. Father William Kelly said a special Mass for John Kilbride at St Christopher's Roman Catholic Church, Ashton. Later in the day there was a Mass attended by the Kilbride family. Sheila Kilbride would die in 2002, three months before Myra Hindley. Mrs Kilbride's ashes were placed in John's grave in Hurst cemetery.

Mike Mascheder worked on enlarged photographs of the marks on the bed head in Myra's bedroom to show that it was the same bed head that appears on Brady's photographs of Lesley Ann Downey. Lesley Ann was buried two days before John Kilbride, on Tuesday, 26 October. There was a service at Lesley Ann's church, Trinity Methodist in Butler Street, Ancoats. The minister looked down on the small white coffin and quoted Christ's words: 'those who cause these little ones to stumble . . . it were better that a millstone were put around their neck and cast into the sea.' Lesley Ann was buried in Southern Cemetery, Fallowfield. Ann West graphically describes the day in *For the Love of Lesley*. I mentioned this book once to Ian Brady and he said, 'Don't send that book to me!' I said that I had visited Southern Cemetery and had seen Edward Evans' grave no more than a yard or so from Lesley Ann Downey's. 'I never knew that,' Brady told me.

On the day that Lesley Ann was buried, an RAF Canberra jet bomber used its photo-reconnaissance equipment to look for unusual ground formations as it flew over Saddleworth Moor. Two days later, Hindley and Brady appeared for a two-minute hearing in Hyde Magistrates' court. Lesley Ann's natural father, Terry Downey, and her uncle, Patrick Downey, were present to see the couple accused of killing her.

Two days after Lesley Ann's funeral, Myra was questioned by detective John Tyrrell at Ashton-under-Lyne police station about her relationship with Ian Brady. Tyrrell asked: 'Since you and Brady have been associating together, has he, so far as you know, ever been out on his own?' Myra was emphatic: 'Never. Wherever he has gone, I have gone.' At the trial, sixth months later, she gave a very different answer to the same question: 'He often preferred to go out by himself.'

The police had to determine the age of Puppet, who was being held by Myra in the photograph of John Kilbride's grave. An X-ray of the dog's teeth would reveal its age and determine whether it had been photographed before or after John Kilbride's death. An X-ray was only possible if the dog was anaesthetised. Puppet died under anaesthetic at Ashton Kennels. Superintendent Benfield broke the news to Myra, who shouted 'Murderers!' in response. During an interview with the police, immediately after Brady's arrest, Myra had casually mentioned that Puppet had been born in January 1964. She did not realise how significant this remark would turn out to be. No one was surprised when the dog's X-ray confirmed the timing of events. The photograph was taken after the murder of John Kilbride, as Myra had unguardedly admitted.

Capital punishment was abolished in the UK with effect from 9 November 1965. Sidney Silverman's Murder (abolition of Death Penalty) Act had been passed the day before; some policemen called it 'Silverman's Folly'. The Moors Murders were the first case of mass murder under the new act. Ian Brady never tired of telling me that it had only been passed in the House of Commons. It had still to go through the House of Lords at the time he and Myra were under arrest. Lesley Ann's uncle, Patrick Downey, stood as a pro-hanging candidate against Sidney Silverman in the General Election in the Nelson and Colne constituency in north-east Lancashire. Although he failed to win the seat, Patrick Downey attracted a few thousand votes.

Ian Brady's mother Peggy stood by him after the arrest. Reporters looking for a story hounded her night and day. Ian described to me the circus his mother had to endure. He told her to tie a knife on the end of a broomstick and poke it through the letterbox when journalists shouted through it.

Ian and Myra were held on remand at Risley, thirty miles from Hyde. While they were there they had the same solicitor, Mr C L Fitzpatrick, and were in touch with each other every day. Writing in the *Guardian* thirty years later, Myra recalls this time:

Arrest and Risley prison symbolized freedom to me. But to Ian it symbolized a living death; something he told me he couldn't endure.

He had a jar of jam brought in with other things on a visit from his mother and he intended killing himself with the glass. I begged him not to, not to leave me, he was all I had lived for. He said I couldn't be found guilty if I went on trial without him; that his influence would pall and I'd be able to rebuild my life. But he said he would wait and see what happened at the trial.

I felt that he needed me even more than I'd ever needed him and for the first time in the whole of our relationship I knew that he loved me. He deplored what he thought of as sentimentality and had never said he loved me, and afraid of annoying him I'd never told him I loved him.

In his first letter to me on remand he wrote at the end, in German, that he loved me, and I poured all my love for him into my letters to him. I knew he would never be able to come to terms with our arrest, particularly because it was the result of David Smith going to the police, which to Ian was a betrayal of the worst kind.

In a letter of January 1995, Brady wrote about his feelings while on remand, and the question of his suicide: 'I had planned my death as a final spit in their faces, but I was set on attending the trial in an attempt to keep Myra free, and spat at them from the witness box instead. Then, after sentence, I just drifted into acceptance of the situation, and the weekly correspondence between Myra and I, from our respective prisons for six-and-a-half years before we broke up.'

Myra and Ian used a private code in the letters they were allowed to send to each other. Faced with separation for years into the future, they abandoned their rejection of convention and filled in forms to the Home Office for permission to be married. Married prisoners were allowed contact with each other. Their application was turned down.

Ian and Myra had worked out their own secret code for letters between them before they were arrested. It was called the '6-7-8' code. If the date was underlined at the heading of a letter, there was a hidden message in the sentences that followed. To anyone who didn't know the code, what was written would still make complete sense as a normal letter.

The secret text in the letter would start on the sixth line. The seventh and eighth words would be the first two words of the message. The seventh and eighth words of each alternate line would be the remainder of the message. Thirty-five years after their time on remand, Brady threatened to reveal the secret letters that passed between them. Myra tried to anticipate and limit any possible damage to her by the revelations by saying that Brady had asked her to write 'stimulating' letters to him on a variety of topics. She added that by 'stimulating', Brady meant sexually arousing subjects such as causing pain to children.

Myra claims to have kept a copy of one such letter she sent to Brady while they were on remand. The first line of the following extract was the sixth line of the original letter. The secret message, therefore, begins with the seventh and eighth words. The hidden words are printed in capitals below but, of course, were not in capitals in the letter Myra claims to have sent to Brady:

> 'I've been thinking for a while, WHY DON'T you ask if you can go to church on Sundays so we can at least see each other there? YOU GET someone to help with this.
> See the Governor if necessary. There are places in the chapel for people in your situation Ian, so ask SOMEONE TO look into it for you. There's someone here who goes with two officers. She is in here for killing her own children and also for attempting to THROW ACID in her boyfriend's face. No one likes her; she's on Rule 43, of course. Re: your mention of facial expressions in your last letter . . .
> I could have seen the one ON BRETT. His face was a picture when you stared him out!'

The hidden message is about Brett, the four-year-old brother of Lesley Ann Downey: 'Why don't you get someone to throw acid on Brett?'

I raised the subject of the letter's authenticity with Brady. He said tersely, 'It's a fake.'

At no point in the legal processes leading up to and during the committal and trial was it suggested that either Brady or Hindley were mentally ill and had acted out of diminished responsibility. The resident psychiatrist at the Risley remand centre interviewed them and they were seen for the defence case by a forensic psychiatrist, Dr Neustatter. The doctor later said that he learned very little from them but that they were perfectly sane.

In March 2000, when Ian Brady was fighting his case to be allowed to starve himself to death in Ashworth high security hospital, Angela Neustatter (*Guardian*, 10 March 2000) spoke out about the spectre of Ian Brady that had hung over their family since her father had pronounced Brady sane. She recalled that visitors to their house were forever asking her father about 'what made Brady tick'. She was opposed to capital punishment, but she felt that his crimes push him some 'way beyond the usual concerns of compassion and protection. I would not sanction the active killing of him but I would happily see him do it himself. Apart from moral justice it would be a relief to know his spectre could be ushered out of my life.'

On 2 December 1965, Ian Brady was charged with the murder of John Kilbride and Myra with being an accessory after the fact. Like it or not, Myra and Ian were involved in the due processes of law. English law is based on the presumption of innocence until proven guilty. There had to be a case for the defence if they pleaded not guilty. Myra wrote an article in the *Guardian* in December 1995, describing the stark choice she faced:

> When I first met my barrister he told me the only way he could defend me was by prosecuting Ian Brady. I told him I couldn't allow that, and if necessary would have to find another barrister. I couldn't allow it not only because I believed in my heart that of the two of us I was the more culpable, but also because I had never given Ian Brady any inkling of what my real feelings were.

Myra Hindley might have been spared what became her irrevocable fate if she had joined David Smith as a prosecution witness against Ian Brady. She was deeply compromised by the tape of Lesley Ann Downey's final minutes on this earth and would clearly have been jailed for her undeniable complicity in the events that led to the child's murder. It's difficult to say now how she would have been treated if she had admitted her involvement in the photographic session and her helplessness in the face of Ian Brady's unstoppable reign of terror.

The committal proceedings for the murders began on 6 December 1965 at Hyde's fifty-year-old magistrates' court. The town of Hyde has some-times been called an S-bend with fish and chip shops. It was, however, about to become the centre of the nation's attention. It would be so again, 33 years later, when a GP in the town, Dr Harold Shipman, was found to be a multiple murderer.

A committal decides whether there is a prima facie case to answer before the accused is sent to a higher court. Two years after the Moors case, The Criminal Justice Act reduced the amount of time spent on a committal and restricted press coverage. Before that, all the evidence presented at the committal stage had to be repeated in a criminal court if there was a case to answer. Nevertheless, the Hyde magistrates could have ordered no publicity in 1965. The jury's neutrality is obviously compromised if the case has received wide exposure beforehand.

There were three magistrates listening to the evidence at Hyde. Mrs Dorothy Adamson was in the chair assisted by Harry Taylor and Sam Redfern. David Lloyd-Jones was counsel for Brady, Philip Curtis for Hindley and the prosecutor was William Mars-Jones. On the first day of the committal there were forty-five women and nine men in the public gallery. More than fifty reporters represented the world's press, radio and television.

Shortly after 10 a.m., Ian Brady appeared in the dock wearing a grey suit, waistcoat and white shirt. He was chewing gum. Myra Hindley followed him wearing a black-and-white flecked suit and a yellow nylon blouse. Her hair was bleached blonde. Brady and Hindley were both holding a notebook and pen.

The hearing opened with a surprise. David Lloyd-Jones asked the magistrates to hear the case in camera, arguing that the government was considering legislation ruling out the reporting of committal proceedings. Referring to the case of Dr Bodkin Adams, in which the committal had been heard in private, Lloyd-Jones pointed out the high profile nature of the Moors Murders case and the difficulty of obtaining an unbiased jury uninfluenced by pre-trial publicity. Myra Hindley's counsel and the prosecutor both supported the application.

The magistrates deliberated for just thirteen minutes and ruled that the whole case would be heard in open court. It would last 15 days. There would be 86 witnesses and 179 exhibits. On the second day of the hearing, the fog was too heavy for the journey back to the remand centre at Risley. Ian and Myra spent the night in the cells at Hyde. After the second day, BBC television and radio issued no bulletins on the proceedings, judging the details to be too shocking for its viewers and listeners. ITV continued to release brief daily bulletins.

David Smith, the prosecution's major witness, was questioned for a total of six and three-quarter hours. Myra's sister Mo, sporting a fashionable bouffant hairstyle, gave evidence briefly to explain how much Myra had changed since going with Ian Brady. Senior police officers were questioned on their evidence.

A moment of high drama came when Lesley Ann's mother entered the dock. Ann Downey was soon in tears and screamed across the courtroom at Myra Hindley, 'I'll kill you! . . . I'll kill you! . . . An innocent baby . . .

She can sit staring at me and she took a little baby's life . . . the beast!' In the well of the court, Detective Constable Frank Fitchett grabbed the water carafe in the dock before Ann Downey could reach for it.

Ian Brady told me that he had no recollection of Ann Downey's outburst. When I met her 27 years later, her rage was less strident but the hatred hadn't diminished. The court was cleared on 15 December, when the tape of Lesley Ann was played in private to the three magistrates.

Patrick Downey, Lesley's uncle, and Terry Downey, Lesley's father, were arrested outside the magistrates' court for attacking a police car that they had thought contained Brady and Hindley; the two figures under the blankets were decoys. The two men were released but the police warned that they would be charged if they attempted it again. Patrick Downey bought a gun and was determined to kill Brady. His wife persuaded him to hand the gun to the police; he realised he might kill a decoy by mistake.

The hearing concluded on 20 December 1965. Ian and Myra pleaded not guilty to the charges. To no one's surprise, they were committed for trial. Brady spoke to me about the circumstances that led to the committal. He mentioned the day of the arrest: 'I was deceased on October 7th 1965.'

Two of my friends lived in Hyde for many years. I was walking with them in the town's main street one day when they pointed to a huge faded sign painted on the side of a building. It read 'PSA' and had always mystified them. By chance, I knew it stood for 'Pleasant Sunday Afternoons', an organisation that had existed in England many years previously and had held meetings at which elevating religious talks were given on Sunday afternoons. Mystery solved.

The day after the committal, there was a mass exodus of the journalists who had taken over the town for two weeks. Hyde was at peace. That is, until Dr Harold Shipman arrived in 1977 and later set up his surgery in Market Street, routinely consigning the town's older residents to eternity with caring injections in their homes. My friends were Dr Shipman's patients but too young for the gentle doctor's compassionate needle. They would have been too old for the tastes of Ian Brady and Myra Hindley. If only they had known it, my friends were in the safest place in England; particularly on pleasant Sunday afternoons.

Journalists descended on Hyde once more on 13 January 2004 when Dr Shipman was found that morning, hanging in his cell at Wakefield Prison. Many of the relatives of his victims were in despair at now having little prospect of knowing why he murdered their loved ones.

In the long months between the close of the committal and the opening of the trial, Ian Brady had many hours in which to reflect on his fate. Sometimes he thought about the father of his pal Ginger, who 'shopped' the gang and his own son to the police. Brady had been 'shopped' by the husband of Myra's sister. Brady commented, 'It should have been carved into my mind that, remembering Ginger's father, blood is not thicker than water.'

As I write, I have Ian Brady's copy of *The Rubaiyat of Omar Khayyam* in front of me. He has written his name inside and the date, December 1965. It was a Christmas present from his solicitor. Ian Brady was, of course, on remand with Myra at Risley at this time. Brady was fond of quoting from the book. He had marked one passage in particular:

> The Moving Finger writes:
>   And, having writ,
> Moves on: nor all thy Piety
>   Nor Wit
> Shall lure it back to cancel
>   Half a Line,
> Nor all thy Tears wash out
>   A Word of it.

CHAPTER EIGHTEEN

IT'S NOT THE ALBERT HALL

The trial date was fixed for Tuesday, 19 April 1966, at the assizes in Chester Castle. Ian Brady told me that Myra and he had their say about the location: 'We wanted to deprive the Old Bailey of the pleasure. While we were on remand, Myra was still saying she wanted to share my certain fate of life imprisonment. I told her that if she was really serious about that, why not do her best to get off the charges, buy a shotgun, kill Mo and Smith and then get a life-sentence? All my evidence at the trial was to get the girl off. But Myra had instructed her lawyer Heilpern that she wanted no cross-examination that damaged me.

'There were months of media coverage – an international circus – before our trial. And when our barristers argued that we could not have a fair trial because of publicity, the judge stated that, as there wasn't a person in the country who didn't know all about the case, the point was irrelevant!'

Ian Brady's comments were prompted by the trial of three police chiefs involved in the Birmingham Six case who, in November 1993, were released by the judge, who ruled that they couldn't have a fair trial because of the publicity.

Brady reminded me that, 'the queen was in Chester for the races in the first week of the trial. Several members of the "Ascot set", in Chester for the same reason, attended the trial for an entertaining diversion, making full use of their lorgnettes. We looked up at them in contempt. I picked the winner of the Gold Cup race but couldn't back it. A policeman near the dock told me the horse had won.'

The police warned Patrick and Terry Downey not to attend the trial. If they did, detectives would be assigned to be with them full time. Myra and

271

Ian were driven to Chester every day from Risley, 25 miles away. The route changed each day. On the first day of the trial, there were sixty seats available to the public in No 1 court. There were 23 people in the distinguished visitors' gallery. One hundred and fifty journalists were there to report the case to the four corners of the globe. Someone attending the trial took illicit photographs of Brady and Hindley in the dock. The pictures were published immediately after Myra Hindley's death in November 2002. The photographs were first published in Anthony Syme's – now very rare – *Murders on the Moors*, released in Australia soon after the trial. It could not appear in the United Kingdom since the two photographs were taken illegally.

The judge was Fenton Atkinson. The prosecutor was the Attorney General, Sir Frederick Elwyn Jones, who was assisted by William Mars-Jones. It was the first time an Attorney General had acted as prosecutor since the trial of Dr Bodkin Adams in 1957. Elwyn Jones had been a prosecutor at the Nuremberg war crimes trial and would now be cross-examining Ian Brady, who allegedly had sympathies for Nazism. Brady commented to me about this alleged coincidence: 'At the trial, much was made of the fact that I had tapes and books on Nazi figures. I also had tapes of Stalin and Churchill, but these were of no interest to the prosecutor, Sir Elwyn Jones. His discrimination can, perhaps, be explained by the fact that he was a British prosecuting counsel at the Nuremberg trials of Hess, Göring and other Nazis.

'No one could identify with Hitler; he was unique. My interest in the Third Reich was based on aesthetic, not political grounds. I admired the will, boldness and the courage with which Hitler put his beliefs into effect. But, in fact, I held left-wing views. So ends another plagiarised myth about the Moors Murders.'

Godfrey Heilpern and Philip Curtis defended Myra Hindley. Godfrey Heilpern was absent from the court on the first day. He had been informed that his sister-in-law had been murdered. The three remaining top lawyers in court on the first day were all Welsh. Ian Brady's counsel was the Welsh-speaking Liberal MP Emlyn Hooson, assisted by David Lloyd-Jones. The only hope for Hindley and Brady was for their defence teams to discredit David Smith as an accomplice or a participant.

In the opening minutes of the trial, Emlyn Hooson and Godfrey Heilpern made joint submissions to the judge. They argued that Brady and Hindley should be given separate trials and that the first indictment – the murder of Edward Evans – should not be linked with the remaining two indictments – the murders of John Kilbride and Lesley Ann Downey. They were not founded on the same facts. The judge rejected the submissions.

The murders committed by Brady and Hindley have been described in earlier chapters and there is no need to repeat the material that was examined during the trial. For anyone unfamiliar with the case, it's necessary simply to know that Brady and Hindley were charged with only three of the murders – those of John Kilbride, Lesley Ann Downey and Edward Evans. The admissions of guilt for the murders of Pauline Reade and Keith Bennett were made twenty years after the trial. Hindley was not charged with the murder of John Kilbride at the committal, but only with harbouring Brady, knowing that he had killed the boy. This charge was changed to murder at the trial.

When they entered the D-shaped dock at Chester, Ian Brady was 28 and Myra Hindley 23. The front row of seats behind the dock was kept empty. There was a four-inch-thick glass screen around the back and sides of the dock. When asked, the police said it was a draft excluder! The clandestine photographs already mentioned clearly show the glass screen.

Ian Brady was wearing a grey suit with a white handkerchief in the pocket, a white shirt and a blue tie. Myra Hindley wore a black-and-white speckled suit, a blue blouse and white shoes. Her hair was lilac-blue; it had become bright yellow by the time she was sentenced.

The defence counsels challenged the four women in the jury. Four men replaced them.

Brady and Hindley pleaded not guilty to the three charges of murder. Myra's sister Maureen was the first witness to be questioned. She was taken out of sequence because she was in an advanced state of pregnancy and could give birth at any time. She testified against Myra's claim that she was unfamiliar with Ashton-under-Lyne, stating that Myra shopped in the market there, particularly for diamond-patterned nylon stockings. She also recalled a conversation with Myra about a report in a newspaper that Ann Downey was offering a reward of £100 for anyone who could find Lesley Ann. Maureen said that the girl's mother must think a lot of her, at which – according to Maureen – Myra simply laughed. Myra was to say this was 'a wicked lie'. (The two sisters were worlds apart at the trial but were reconciled before Maureen suffered a sudden, early death.)

Under cross-examination, Maureen admitted that a newspaper had given money to her husband David for his story. If Brady and Hindley were convicted they would receive a large sum when the story was syndicated to other newspapers. The judge commented later that the defence had been given 'a stick with which to beat Smith', who now had a vested financial interest in a guilty verdict.

On the fourth day of the trial, Myra Hindley's lawyer asked David Smith whether he would be in touch with the newspaper over the luncheon adjournment. The judge interjected, 'They are probably standing him lunch!' It transpired that the newspaper involved was the *News of the World*. After the trial, the Attorney General announced to the House of Commons that there would be no prosecution against the newspaper.

The Smiths' involvement in 'cheque book journalism' was responsible for a change in the code of practice governing newspapers and their involvement with witnesses in criminal cases. Ian Brady told me that the *News of the World* tore up the contract with Smith. The Moors Murders case was cited as a precedent in 1979, when a newspaper attempted to make a similar arrangement with a witness in the trial of former Liberal Party leader Jeremy Thorpe.

The Smiths' admission of being in the pay of a newspaper was not ultimately damaging for the prosecution's case. The police had David Smith's original statement describing the murder of Edward Evans, made before any arrangement with the newspaper. In that statement Smith had said that Myra had been in the room when Evans was murdered and that the hatchet grazed the top of Myra's head as Brady swung it in the air. Under questioning at the trial itself, however, Smith said that he couldn't remember whether Myra was in the room.

David Smith spent some hours in the witness box and was at first very ill at ease. He kept touching the microphone. He was eighteen and was dressed, like many of his contemporaries of the time, in tight trousers and a velvet coat. After one lunch break he returned to the dock wearing a tie in deference to the solemn proceedings.

He was questioned about his non-existent religious beliefs and the passages he had copied out from a book by the Marquis de Sade on the subject of murder. One particular passage states that the only punishment a murderer should fear is retribution from the victim's family. The Marquis de Sade had written: 'In a word, murder is a horror, but a horror often necessary, never criminal, and essential to tolerate in a republic. Above all it should never be punished by murder.'

Ian Brady's lawyer said that David Smith was 'a crumbling rock on which to found anything.' However damaging the cross-examination was meant to be, though, it was never likely to persuade a jury that Smith was involved in the murders on the word of Brady and Hindley. For one thing,

Smith would have been very young at the time of John Kilbride's murder.

The claim that Smith had taken Lesley Ann away from Wardle Brook Avenue alive after being paid for the photographic session was staggeringly implausible. Smith would hardly have reported Brady to the police for the murder of Edward Evans if he had, himself, led Lesley Ann away from number 16. The body of Lesley Ann was found, as she appeared in Brady's photographs – naked. Furthermore, why would the little girl ask Brady and Hindley what they were going to do to her if she was being paid ten shillings to be photographed?

David Smith told the police that Brady had boasted to him about the photographic proof of his murders. It turned out to be the case in the minds of the jury – how could David Smith have known that there was photographic proof if Brady had not told him so? In a conversation with me, thirty years later, Ian Brady commented: 'I hope Smith lives a long life – worried in case there is a knock on his door late one night.'

There were 67 witnesses for the prosecution. Myra Hindley gave evidence for six hours and Ian Brady for eight and a half hours. Before being questioned, both of them pushed the Bible aside and affirmed. It was ironic that the court should hear, as part of Lesley Ann's pleas to be released, the words, 'I'll swear on the Bible.' It is touching that she felt the appeal to the Bible would influence the two strangers in their treatment of her. The Bible meant nothing to her killers, whether in the small bedroom or in a court of law.

There was only one defence witness – Myra's mother, Mrs Hettie Hindley. She testified that David Smith could be responsible for putting Myra in the dock. However, although Mrs Hindley said that she looked after Maureen's baby on Christmas Eve and Christmas night of 1964, she admitted that she did not have the baby on Boxing Day that year. If Lesley Ann Downey was in the hands of David Smith on Boxing Day 1964, it couldn't be said that Mrs Hindley was looking after the Smith's baby, Angela Dawn.

The tape was played on the sixth day. The tape recorder, with leads attached to the amplifier in the courtroom, stood on a table in front of the jury box. There were three minutes of virtual silence on the tape before Lesley Ann's first scream. Brady commented: 'No one left the courtroom when they were warned that it was about to be played.'

Many people who listened to the tape, and even more who have read the transcript of it since, believe that what Lesley Ann was having forced into her mouth was not a gag, but Brady's penis. The prosecuting lawyers, in fact, claimed that it was a scarf or some kind of gag. They argued that

Lesley Ann died of suffocation and that the photographs confirmed it. Brady was, of course, glad to agree that it was a scarf but deny that she died because of it. For what it is worth, when I asked Ian Brady what Lesley Ann was forced to put in her mouth, he said that it was a handkerchief held in by a scarf. He denied that she suffocated because of it: 'Myra strangled the Downey girl with cord.'

Myra Hindley was as defiant as Ian Brady in the witness box. In the time they had together as they were driven to and from Chester, Brady warned Myra that she would have to show some remorse in the dock. Brady said, 'I told her to put some small flakes of tobacco in her eyes to at least give the appearance of crying. She ignored my advice.' As for himself, Brady added: 'I felt detachment and contempt during the trial. I was finished and all the huffing and puffing around me meant nothing. I stared at the judge at one point and smiled. He nearly had a heart attack!

'I cast my mind out into deep space, looked back at the speck of dust called Earth, and imagined all its pomposities and little wars and laughed. It put everything in the right perspective.

'What could I do that could possibly matter on that speck of dust? What could anyone do? It would be as dead as the moon one day. All mankind's dead will be forgotten.'

In *Moving Targets*, Helen Birch reflects on the persona of Myra Hindley as seen by an incredulous world as the trial proceeded. Hindley may have been the worst of her kind, but she belonged to a female type in the public imagination, whether they were conscious of it or not. Helen Birch observes:

> The spectacle of the treacherous, sexually active blonde has become a popular cliché since the Second World War. The sirens of film noir – Barbara Stanwyck in *Double Indemnity*, Rita Hayworth in *Gilda* – set the tone for a period in which the most potent cinematic representations of women linked the blonde with perverse sexuality and social aberration. And from there, these films implied, it was just one more metaphoric step to murder . . .
>
> It is into this tradition of the unknowable blonde with a heart of steel that the image of Myra Hindley has been co-opted, and from which it has acquired some of its force.

After Myra broke with Brady in the prison years, she frequently claimed that she was the unwilling tool in Brady's evil plans. In the trial, however, she showed no such subservience to Brady. Under interrogation after the arrest, she had said to Inspector John Tyrrell: 'I made my own decisions . . . Ian never made me do anything I did not want to do.' She was stony-faced throughout the court hearing and once put her tongue out to one of the reporters who was staring at her. When questioned about her feelings for Ian Brady, Myra replied, 'I became very fond of him. I loved him . . . I still . . . I love him.'

No defence counsel could have extracted Myra Hindley from her involvement in the murders. She had been photographed staring down at the grave of John Kilbride. Her voice was on the tape threatening to strike Lesley Ann Downey – 'Shut up or I'll forget myself and hit you one!' She was in the house where Edward Evans' body was found. There was a particularly poignant moment when she said she was in the kitchen with her hands over her ears as Edward Evans was screaming. The Attorney General said to Myra: 'This court has heard more than one scream in the room where you were?'

Myra said, 'Yes.'

'The screams of a little girl of ten – of your sex, madam. Did you put your hands over your ears when you heard the screams of Lesley Ann Downey?'

Myra said, 'No.'

Ian Brady, in his evidence, would try to exonerate Myra by saying that she was in the bedroom in order to placate the child and act as a witness in case someone claimed later that Lesley Ann had been interfered with during the photographic session.

Myra had admitted to the Attorney General that she was not merely clay in the hands of the potter. Yet Brady seemed more concerned for Myra's acquittal of the charges than she was herself. When he was asked whose views would prevail when the two of them differed, Brady replied, 'Mine. She was my typist in the office. I dictated to her in the office and this tended to wrap over.'

Brady was asked if he hated David Smith. He replied, 'I don't think he is worth hating.' Throughout his evidence, Brady was resigned to a guilty verdict. He said at one point, 'I'll be convicted anyway.' Brady looked back on his own court performance in a letter to me in January 1993: 'During my cross-examination at the trial, I deliberately let loose my contempt for the Attorney General, judge, jury and public, in order to convince the jury that I would not bother to lie for anyone and thus persuade them to accept the innocent role I created for Myra. Emlyn Williams' book says I "struck terror" into the courtroom; another author described me as "demonic". All quite flattering, but I was not reaching for metaphysical heights, only exemplifying the Great Contempt, the Great Down-Going.

'I felt total indifference for everyone except Myra. I deliberately treated questions about Myra with throwaway gestures of indifference. Her Counsel, whom I had briefed as well as my own Counsel, commented that I should've shown more feeling in response to such questions; I was astonished that he hadn't grasped my aim. The freedom that lack of hope creates is tremendous; the power of total possibility surges up with delight, and contempt for all barriers had me almost laughing at the expressions on the faces of the courtroom. That height of contempt is a delight, like it or not. It is, simultaneously, to experience self-abnegation along with total self-expression. Even in those who rebel there is a subconscious wish to be accepted in the context of universality. A paradox. But add total lack of hope and you will see the face of the Unconditional, and the fear it creates in others. Call it " insanity" or whatever else you like.'

It took five hours for Judge Fenton Atkinson to sum up. He said that there was no question that Brady and Hindley were mentally subnormal. Writing in the *Guardian* in December 1995, Myra commented: 'I've so often wished that I had suffered from some affective disorder and been diagnosed accordingly. This would have provided some kind of explanation for my actions. As it is, what I was involved in is indefensible.'

The jury retired at 2.40 p.m. to consider their verdict and took with them three of the trial exhibits: Brady's notebook with John Kilbride's name written inside, the disposal plan for Edward Evans and Myra's shoes spotted with blood.

The jury returned at 4.20 p.m. to ask for the judge's clarification of dates: the dates when the guns were purchased and the date of Brady's letter about the investment establishment found in one of the suitcases.

Finally, the jury returned to give their verdict at one minute past 5 p.m. on Friday, 6 May, the fourteenth day of the trial. They found Ian Brady guilty of all three murders. They found Myra Hindley guilty of the murders of Lesley Ann Downey and Edward Evans and guilty of harbouring Ian Brady, knowing that he had killed John Kilbride. The judge asked the accused if they had anything to say before the sentences were passed. Myra Hindley had nothing to say. Ian Brady said, 'No – except the revolvers were bought in July 1964.' He buttoned his coat with a brief glance at Myra to his left and listened to the inevitable: 'Ian Brady, these were three calculated, cruel, cold-blooded murders. In your case I pass the only sentences which the law now allows, which is three concurrent sentences of life imprisonment.

'Put him down.

'In your case, Hindley, you have been found guilty of two equally horrible murders, and in the third as an accessory after the fact. On the two murders, the sentence is two concurrent sentences of life imprisonment, and on the charge of being an accessory after the fact to the death of Kilbride, a concurrent sentence of seven years' imprisonment.

'Put her down.'

The judge's comment, 'the only sentence which the law now allows' is an allusion to the fact that capital punishment had been abolished. The last two men to hang were Peter Anthony Allen and Glynne Owen Evans, who killed a laundry van driver. They were hanged four months before Lesley Ann Downey's death. Pamela Hansford Johnson, who attended the trial and was the author of the book *On Iniquity*, observed that after the final verdict, 'we did feel a lack of catharsis: something violent should have happened to put an end to violence. Throughout, we were missing the shadow of the rope.'

Many authors have commented on the pedantry of Ian Brady in making an apparently trivial point about the dates the guns were purchased. I asked Brady why he made the remark before sentence was passed. This is what he said in a letter of April 1993: 'All through the trial the police, the Attorney General and the judge were determined to back-date the purchase of the .38 and .45 revolvers as far as possible. Myra and I were equally determined to forward-date their purchase. The jury saw the significance – an hour after they retired to reach a verdict, they returned for information and direction from the judge. "On what date were the revolvers purchased?" The judge gave them the *police* date. A further hour later, the jury returned with their verdict. The judge asked if I had anything to say before being sentenced, and I got the last word on the trial transcript by repeating *my* date re purchase of the revolvers.

'So, it was not mere pedantry, as the half-witted press and authors suggested. I was sure that the police had inside information that the guns had been used, hence their back-dating the date of purchase. And I was determined to forward-date just in case they, the Attorney General and the judge knew.'

I asked Ian Brady about his and Myra's immediate reaction to the sentence. He said that in view of the overwhelming evidence, it was a minor miracle that Myra got away with the harbouring charge on the John

Kilbride indictment. I asked him what was said in the police van on the way back to Risley for the last time. Brady said, 'Nothing. We would never show weakness in public. I chain-smoked cigars all the way back. The air was blue.'

Two days after the trial, the judge wrote a letter to the Home Secretary: 'Though I believe Brady is wicked beyond belief without hope of redemption (short of a miracle) I cannot feel that the same is necessarily true of Hindley once she is removed from his influence. At present she is as deeply corrupted as Brady but it is not so long ago that she was taking instruction in the Roman Catholic Church and was a communicant and a normal sort of girl.'

Speaking in 1994, Arthur Benfield, the retired police superintendent said, 'She should have hanged. She was pure evil. It might be fairer for her to rot in prison.' Almost thirty years after the trial, Ian Brady wrote to tell me the fate he would have preferred: 'I'd choose lethal injection. In fact, when a person is sentenced to life or 30 years, they should then go from court to a special unit where on the table in the cell there is a capsule of potassium cyanide. They should be told that the capsule kills in 10 seconds. If, by morning, they have not chosen to take the capsule, they should know that they will serve thirty or forty years in the garbage cans that pass as prisons in Britain. The Home Office would be embarrassed by the flow of bodies, indicating the nature of their prisons. It would be popular with the public as it saves money.'

Jonathan Goodman edited the book on the official transcript of the trial and presents a faithful record of what was said by all the participants. The book, *The Moors Murders: The Trial of Myra Hindley and Ian Brady*, was first published in 1973 and reprinted a few times. I mentioned casually to Ian Brady that Jonathan Goodman's record of the trial had just been re-issued. Brady said, 'I hope he dies of cancer!' I should have said that Jonathan Goodman was a friend of mine. But it would have made no difference. I could see that Brady needed the afternoon medication to mollify his rage.

After being sentenced, Ian Brady and Myra Hindley spent their last night at Risley remand centre. They were allowed to speak briefly in a corridor before they parted. I asked Ian what they said to each other. He couldn't remember. Myra recalled that she asked Ian not to carry out his threat to kill himself.

They were never to see each other again. In the morning Ian Brady would be driven north to Durham prison; Myra Hindley would be taken south to Holloway prison in London. Night descended on Hattersley council estate. The morning would reveal that someone had smashed every window of number 16 Wardle Brook Avenue.

*   *   *   *   *

Tabloid newspapers would make millions of pounds out of the case in the following years. In the immediate aftermath of the trial, T-shirts were sold bearing the security photographs of Brady and Hindley. A pop group named The Smiths released a song that featured names and images taken from the Moors case, with a Myra Hindley lookalike (actually Viv 'Spend, Spend, Spend' Nicholson) on the sleeve. Brady called the song, 'Suffer Little Children', a 'dirge'.

Four words Ian Brady once said to me put the trial at Chester Assizes in its true perspective:

'We were all lying.'

CHAPTER NINETEEN

NEW WORLD IN THE MORNING

As soon as dawn broke, Myra Hindley was driven south to Holloway prison in London. Ian Brady travelled north-east to Durham. Within hours, they were in prisons 250 miles apart. He would be in Durham for five years, she in Holloway for eleven.

Brady was contemptuous throughout the reception procedures, which all new prisoners had to undergo. Myra was humiliated in Holloway when she was inspected for lice and venereal disease.

Within a couple of days of the verdict in the Moors trial, Leo Abse, the Labour Member of Parliament for Pontypool, told a meeting of Cambridge University Labour and Liberal groups that the whole community was ultimately responsible for the evil deeds of Brady and Hindley. The *Daily Telegraph* reported, ironically, that Abse had beaten all the other progressive public figures to this age-old pronouncement against the doctrine of Original Sin.

Ian Brady wrote his first prison letter to Myra on his sixth day in Durham. It was timed at 8.30 a.m. on 12 May 1966: 'Dear Myra: It's a beautiful morning, clear blue sky, a sharp early tang in the air and the sun's radiance hot on the skin.

'There's an old clock tower near here, the chimes ring out every quarter of an hour; that sound combined with the warbling of the birds helps to produce a pleasant backdrop, and reduce the stark realities of the present cheerful country sounds.

'I work in my cell during the day sewing mailbags which may not be an ideal mode of work but it's surprising how quickly the time goes while doing it.'

'Well, Myra, I hope you've now gotten over the initial shock of your sentence. I at least got what I expected but you should never have been on any charge except harbouring.

'Keep your chin up. The day you are released will be the happiest day of my life. I expect none happier.

'So clear your mind of well-justified hate and bitterness and approach each day in hope and each person as an individual; never express despair, you have a future and I will see you begin life anew, and so, I'll dwell once more in freedom as seen through your eyes.

'But for now, keep your eyes looking towards the sky; ignore the grimy ground till you again tread grass underfoot. I'm counting on you, by gaining your freedom, to bring me back to life. So don't let me down, Kiddo.'

Ian Brady then reminds Myra of their visit to St Monans, described in an earlier chapter: 'Firstly we reached the round, stone structure on top of the cliff, the daisy-strewn valley diving down and up to the castle.

'We progressed at a leisurely rate, your photo and mine taken on a resting place of my childhood 17 years in the past.

'Off towards our fated night's resting spot, the Y-sign street, the meal, the manoeuvering about till situated in an ideal spot, the couple with their children.

'The final setting down, the warmth as we lay together, the radio playing and wine sipped lazily as the summer dusk darkened around our glade, the solitary bird calls dwindling to peaceful silence, the soft beat of our hearts leading us to blissful slumber.'

Brady interrupts his reminiscences to refer to the trial that had ended less than a week before: 'I heard the news on TV last night; the Att General is taking no action against the *News of the World*, but he's introducing some new laws to stop recurrence. I hope you were correct about Smith losing the £1,000. I wonder if Big Ben has started digging yet, (joke). Working has given me an appetite . . . '

(As I noted earlier, 'Big Ben' was Ian and Myra's way of referring to Superintendent Arthur Benfield.) Ian reverts back to his first few days in Durham: 'I heard *Round The Horn* [sic] the other night; it's just as good as ever. Here's a part I remember: "He stood straddling the fireplace, his pipe clenched firmly between his teeth and his teeth firmly clenched in his hand."

'There are some musical birdcalls around this area that I've never heard before, one bird in particular has an extensive range of melodies.'

'I hear it first thing in the morning and last at night.

'I wish I knew where you are and how you are feeling. Only a week since I saw you but it seems an age. Absence makes the heart grow fonder – or breaks it!

'Let's make sure the latter does not apply to us. I know that I will love you more as time passes. I know I can never love you less.

'Where my love is, there I will be. That and little else is certain. So much has been lost; our love for each other is all that remains and will always remain. Everything else was only an accessory to our love.

'So, when one looks at life from that angle, we have really lost little. However, cynical logic does not wipe the realities from our minds, but it makes them easier to accept.

'Funny, but when I write of our love my letter tends to read rather sombre; whereas I am in excellent spirits.

'I'll keep this letter back till I know your address. Keep cheery!'

Brady signs off with '*Ich werde sie nicht vergessen*' – German for 'I will not forget you' – and 'I love you' in English. He ends the letter with seven kisses.

Myra replied from Holloway prison nine days later on 21 May 1966. She devotes one brief sentence to the birth of her sister's first child, Paul, born shortly after Maureen gave evidence at the trial. The Smiths would have two more sons, David and John. Myra comments on her appeal: 'I don't for a minute, think they'll grant it, but I've got nothing to lose by trying, and what's a year, with sentences like ours? Anyway, I've been convicted and branded a murderess, so I'm not just sitting back and accepting it. We know each other, and one day, in the fullness of time, the truth will out. It must be so! I dreamed last night that Smith had died, or left Maureen, and she came forward and said she'd lied about . . . Ashton Market, etc. She had her baby last week, a boy. I think her conscience will start bothering her pretty soon.

'Here I am, Sunday, 7.30 p.m. There's a strong wind blowing, rattling the leaves on the many trees in the gardens outside my cell. It sounds just like home. There's a weeping willow in the centre of the lawn. I feel rather like one myself tonight. I feel desolately . . . Not because I'm on my own of course, but because you aren't here. I miss you all the time, but sometimes more than others. I hate Sundays anyway – You've read, of course, about all the publicity concerning the girl at school whose mother kept her off because she wasn't allowed to wipe her cutlery on a napkin? I read yesterday that the *People* have bought her "story" for £800 and the BBC have paid her £130. What a waste of money!'

'I'll sign off again until tomorrow. I wear wax earplugs some nights. The girl in the next room (these are strip cells for difficult women and punishment. Mine is lined with plastic, rendering it completely sound-proof to the outside, but I can hear anyone in the next cell) sometimes spends her nights crying for "sister" so I put the plugs in, and cut that noise off. This cell is perfect for peace and quiet. I wish I could remain here indefinitely. However, if I move to the star wing, I hope to remain under Rule 43, and cherish any solitude, it suits me fine.'

Ian and Myra were both on Rule 43 – isolation from fellow prisoners. Brady was always at pains to tell me that in his case it was not Own Request Rule 43 but Good Order and Discipline Rule 43 (GOD) imposed by the prison authorities to avoid the trouble that a 'nonce' – a sex offender – usually attracts. Mainstream prisoners regard a 'nonce' as worse than an informer or 'grass'. Even 'screws' are more highly esteemed than 'nonces' or 'grasses'. Brady told me that he stayed on Rule 43 until television was introduced on to the open landing: 'I realised what garbage most television programmes were after being exposed to great literature in the solitary confinement of my cell.'

In the 1990s, I mentioned to Ian Brady that I had given a talk at Durham University the day before, but saw nothing of the prison. Brady said, 'How could you miss it! It's a blackened pile on a hilltop facing the Cathedral.' This prompted me to ask him about his early weeks in Durham prison: 'The first thing I felt was a drastic drop in income. I stopped smoking right away to avoid showing a weakness and to provide a lever. The only money I spent of my pittance was on a 2lb bag of sugar every two weeks.

'Madame Tussaud's in London wrote to me asking for personal details – eye colour, etc. – and a set of clothes for a wax model they wanted to make of me for the Chamber of Horrors. I tore up the letter.

'I wrote to Myra every Friday morning so that she would receive the letter in Holloway on Saturday morning. Myra wrote to me every week. The prison authorities copied all our letters, of course. We wrote the criminal bits in code. I kept all of Myra's letters received from her over a six-and-a-half-year period. The *Sun* has written to me over the years saying that they would be willing to publish Myra's letters. I bet they would!'

Peggy's husband, Pat Brady, dropped dead in the street in June 1966, a month after the trial. He was 48. I mentioned this to Ian but he just shrugged, 'I never really knew him.'

The police gave Ian Brady typed sheets of the property found in number 16 Wardle Brook Avenue that were still in their possession and not exhibited at the Moors trial. I have these lists, heavily annotated in Brady's writing. They include everything from ammunition to books and documents. There are two letters addressed to Brady and dated 5 and 8 October 1965. They were sent from Glasgow and arrived a day or so after Brady's arrest. They were frozen in time – like flies in amber – from a family whose innocent world would be shaken to the foundations before the letters were opened. Brady's written comment on the police sheets is, 'I have not read these and want them sent to me.'

The lists also include items found at Millwards. Brady told me that he asked police to send him all photographs in their possession that were not used as exhibits at the trial: 'I received the photographs in Durham a year after I had asked for them. I destroyed all the incriminating pictures that the police had failed to connect with my crimes and kept the rest.'

In Durham, Ian Brady was in the maximum security E wing. Three special security wings had been set up in 1964 after the Great Train Robbers' trial in 1963 – at Parkhurst, Leicester and Durham.

The E wing at Durham was eventually closed in 1971, four years after the Mountbatten Report, commissioned by the Home Secretary following the escape of the spy, George Blake, from Wormwood Scrubs in October 1966. The report condemned conditions in all E wings 'as such no country with a record for civilized behaviour ought to tolerate any longer than is absolutely necessary as a stop-gap measure'. Mountbatten recommended that prisoners should be divided into four main categories – A, B, C and D – according to their security risk. Category A prisoners were those 'whose escape would be highly dangerous to the public or the police or to the security of the State.'

Durham's E wing was an L-shaped block of cells, four storeys high, with three landings. Ian Brady was isolated with another sex killer, David Burgess, on the second landing. Burgess had killed two children. The wing was rarely out of the news with its stories of escape bids, disturbances and hunger strikes. The journalists who reported the trials and tribulations of E wing saw themselves as members of an exclusive club and had their own club tie.

In its seven years, the wing held some of the most notorious criminals in Britain: the train robbers – Goody, Reynolds, Wisbey – Eddie and Charles Richardson, Ronnie Kray and other members of his 'Firm', Dennis Stafford, the Shepherds Bush police killers, Walter Probyn, David Burgess, the escapee John McVicar, the Cannock Chase child killer Raymond Morris and, of course, Ian Brady.

Meanwhile, Myra Hindley was adjusting to the traumatic new world of prison in Holloway. Myra displayed a white card on her door to indicate that she wanted no chaplains to visit. She had a photograph of Ian Brady on her cell wall. On the maximum security wing Myra found herself with the two spies, Ethel Gee and Helen Kroger.

Myra Hindley had appealed against her sentence on the grounds that she should have been tried separately from Ian Brady. On 17 October 1966, at the Criminal Division of the Court of Appeal, Lord Chief Justice Parker turned down her appeal on the grounds that Brady had, at all times, sought to exonerate her during the trial. To that degree, it was an advantage for her to be tried with Brady.

It was just before Christmas 1966, their first in prison, when Myra looked at the photograph on the cell wall and put pen to paper: 'Dearest Ian, hello my little hairy *Girklechin* . . . I had a beautifully tender dream about you last night and awoke feeling safe and secure, thinking I was in the harbour of your arms. Even when I realised I wasn't, the thought of your presence remained with me, leaving me tranquilly calm and strong. Each day that passes I miss you more and more. You are the only thing that keeps my heart beating, my only reason for living. Without you what does life mean? Nothing, absolutely nothing. Freedom without you means nothing too. I've got one interest in life and that's you. We had six short but precious years together, six years of memories to sustain us until we're together again, to make dreams realities.'

Anyone reading words like these could be forgiven for thinking that Myra Hindley was Ian Brady's devoted lover – then. Many, perhaps most, passionate love affairs die the death of a thousand familiarities before the break and the realisation that it was, after all, 'just another Winter's Tale'. Love grows old and waxes cold, something those most practised in the art accept as inevitable as the rain.

The great question facing anyone who claimed to be a friend of Myra Hindley is why she continued to offer undying love to a man she later claimed to be in dread of, at a time when she was absolutely safe from any conceivable harm he could possibly wish on her. They were 250 miles apart, both in maximum-security cells and yet she wanted to have meetings with him as his common-law wife. In August 2001, the *Independent* published a statement from Myra to a reporter in which she explained – for the umpteenth time – her version of her involvement in the murders:

288 IAN BRADY - THE UNTOLD STORY OF THE MOORS MURDERS

I was under duress and abuse before the offences, after and during them, and all the time I was with him. He used to threaten me and rape me and whip me and cane me. I would always be covered in bruises and bite marks. He threatened to kill my family. He dominated me completely. He raped me anally, urinated inside me and, whilst doing so, bit me on the cheekbone, just below my right eye, until my face began to bleed. I tried to fight him off strangling me and biting me, but the more I did, the more the pressure increased.

As we have seen, years after her incarceration, Myra said that immediately after the arrest she had felt free at last from the nightmare. Yet at the time she wanted to be reunited, however briefly, with the author of all her miseries. When she was eventually given a job in the kitchens at Holloway, she learned that a worker there was married to a prisoner in Durham and was allowed visits to see her husband. Myra pleaded that she could be allowed to travel north to Durham with this woman – it would cost nothing to have another inmate from Holloway in the van. She was turned down.

Ian Brady was as obsessed as Myra. In a letter to me, he wrote about the only weapon left to him to press his case for a meeting with her: 'In the sixties and seventies I carried on a series of hunger-strikes – 28 days, 52 days, 72 days and 21 weeks. I was force-fed by having a block of wood put between my teeth, and – through a hole in the centre of the block – a rubber tube was forced down my throat and into my stomach. Fear evaporates in the absence of hope. Although a prisoner, I was an individual, not simply my prison number – 605217. The strikes gave me a powerful "high". I was more contented slowly dying than living under the conditions I was forced to endure. Fasting feeds the mind. Religious orders throughout history have realized the truth of this. I frequently experienced the *black light* when I was starving myself but have no idea whether any monks were familiar with such an altered state. I have never read any account of the phenomenon occurring in a monastic setting.

'In spite of being locked in my own form of monastic cell for 24 hours a day, my mind was both deepening and expanding. I experienced an inner serenity and freedom which mocked my surroundings. Spiritually, I was transcending my confinement and – paradoxically – feeling genuine sympathy for the screws' own captivity, with their addled minds, entombed in their overweight bodies running to fat; all of them squabbling among themselves in pursuit of egregious ambitions.

'Some nights, in the total darkness of my cell, I would see the aura of the *black light* outlining my physical frame, which was becoming more skeletal by the day. To the outward observer, I was losing and dying. In reality, I was winning and pulsating with life.'

When speaking about spiritual release, Brady sometimes said that you must first probe the character of the locks and the doors you wish to be opened.

The religious fasting that Brady refers to has certainly been part of the Christian mystical tradition, among others used to produce what today would be called altered states of consciousness. In the accounts left by Christian mystics it is called 'fasting to a vision'. All of Brady's hunger strikes were given coverage in the press. One tabloid newspaper counted out each day of Brady's hunger protest by printing the latest number of days on the front page of every issue.

I pressed Brady about force-feeding in his Durham days: 'Ronnie Kray looked like a corpse if he went without food for three days. I could go for a fortnight without it and no discomfort. That length of time would just be a toning up period for me. It all depends on your metabolism.

'They fed you with "complan" that solidifies in the stomach after a few minutes. The screws hadn't got the sense to keep you talking while this happened. I used to throw it up as soon as they had left the cell. The mouth tastes of pear drops after a period on hunger strike. It's obvious to anyone who walks into the cell.' (Brady told me that during his incarceration in another prison, Parkhurst, he had witnessed the death of a fellow prisoner being incompetently force-fed by a doctor.)

There were three riots on E wing while Ian Brady was held there. One of the riots made the headlines early in 1967 as the 'Football mutiny'. On Thursday, 9 February, a dozen men from the security wing were in the exercise yard playing football. The ball was kicked into the barbed wire and a prison officer refused to let them retrieve it. In the early evening about thirty-five inmates began to throw everything they could find on to the guards in the yard below – dishes, cups and burning pieces of clothing. About a dozen men barricaded themselves in their cells and held out for three days. The men were eventually punished by loss of privileges and forfeiture of remission. Public allegations of brutality were made against prison officers. Another serious disturbance would occur a year later.

Ian Brady always put his name and prison number – 605217 – in his books and sometimes wrote a date on the inside cover. It's clear that he was doing some serious reading in the isolation of his cell. The three books I am at present looking at are all dated April 1967. The first one is the complete *Poetical Works of Wordsworth* and is inscribed 'To Ian, with love from Myra', with kisses. It has pressed purple heather for bookmarks, as do several of Brady's books. Brady has marked the Wordsworth book throughout. The second book is the complete *Poetry and Prose of William Blake*. The marks show that it too has been read from cover to cover. The third is a Penguin edition of Machiavelli's *The Prince*. Brady's name and 'E wing' are written boldly on the cover.

Traditionally, *The Prince* was thought to be inspired by the Devil: a book on the evils underlying statecraft. Brady would say that we are all somewhere on the sliding scale of evil; whatever mask of good will we wear to face the world. He was making this point during a visit when he suggested I try an experiment when I returned home: 'Dial any number and just say, "I know" before hanging up. Everyone has something to hide.' Brady said to me once that if 'evil' individuals had no good qualities, it would be a simple task to identify them and clear the streets of criminals.

I had seen a television documentary about Aleister Crowley, the self-styled 'most evil man in the world' and asked Brady what he thought about the programme. He said that he hadn't watched it but commented that anyone who claimed to be the most evil man in the world just couldn't be so: 'Evil is spontaneous and unselfconscious, merely complementing good. Real evil is only found in governments and authorities.' Ian Brady claimed that not only were the masses unaware of their tainted innocence, but 'lack even the intellectual capacity to argue their spurious case. To them, Machiavelli is a brand of spaghetti.'

Brady's copy of *The Prince*, as is the case with his other books, has his German annotations in the margin. Ian and Myra had decided to study German in prison as a pact of togetherness. They already had a smattering of the language as lunchtime students in the office at Millwards. Ian sat an examination after six months of study and acquired his German 'O' level.

Ian Brady mentioned the sociologist Laurie Taylor to me from time to time. On the first occasion, I said that I had never read any of his books but remembered seeing him hosting a group chat show of the kind that has become the staple diet of daytime television. The subject was the male menopause – or the non-existence of it. The studio had a range of men who had their mid-life story to tell: bank clerks who had become teachers, teachers who became bank clerks, men who had ditched their wives for much younger women, and so on. Towards the end of the programme Laurie Taylor said something like, 'For heaven's sake! Why don't you all become a bit more philosophical and spiritual about your lives? Can you imagine St Paul, after his Damascus road experience, saying "Right! I'll take up jogging."' I forgave Laurie Taylor for being a television sociologist.

I'd forgotten about it until Ian Brady raised the subject. Ian gave me his copy of a Penguin book by Stanley Cohen and Laurie Taylor, *Psychological Survival: The Experience of Long-Term Imprisonment.*

In November 1967, Laurie Taylor and Stanley Cohen began a series of weekly classes in social science for long-term prisoners on Durham's E wing. The book is an account of their time there. It has some engagingly honest passages about the nonsense and conceit of the academic dogma that they were presenting an objective view: 'Rather like the tourists who went by coach to visit the hippies in Haight-Ashbury, we have felt ourselves to be doing no more than gazing at our own images in mirrors held up by our intended subjects.'

Inevitably, there were tensions between the lecturers and prison staff, who thought the lecturers were in league with the inmates. The prisoners on E wing made it clear that they thought the screws were insensitive and 'thick'. As Taylor and Cohen acknowledged, 'We are university teachers, they are Category A prisoners. Outside on the landing sit the plebs.' I have lost count of the times Ian Brady said to me that 'the real indignity of captivity is having to endure anthropoid screws, and Pavlovian psychology that – in their hands – wouldn't fool a dog! Capital punishment would be blissful release.'

The book was published in 1972, a few months after Durham's E wing had been closed down completely and Ian Brady transferred to Albany prison on the Isle of Wight. Brady appears in the book briefly under the pseudonym 'Frank', and a short account is given of his hunger strikes on the 'Fours', the upper landing in which the isolated sex criminals were segregated.

Two years after Brady's longest ever hunger strike, which began at the end of September 1999 – and which was still in progress when we met – Brady told me that he had not heard from Laurie Taylor for a long time. He remembered the Durham days and said that Taylor was once a firebrand: 'He's just another establishment hack now. They all get bought off in the end and become sausage-machine pundits for the middle-class – windbags

292   IAN BRADY − THE UNTOLD STORY OF THE MOORS MURDERS

who bore everyone but love their own voices and end up giving fatuous advice on talk shows to people with trivial problems not worth listening to – diet, sex, pimples, etc.'

After a year in Durham, Ian Brady was quietly involved in the pursuit of learning. The great and the good appeared occasionally. He saw John Profumo of Christine Keeler fame. The Labour Home Secretary James Callaghan walked into Brady's cell and commented that he too had read the Russian classics he saw on Brady's shelf.

Ian Brady wouldn't have known it, but Edward Evans' father, John Evans, died on 17 August 1967, almost two years after his son was murdered. He had never recovered from Edward's death. His name was added to Edward's gravestone, a few feet behind Lesley Ann Downey's.

The reported attacks on Myra Hindley in Holloway were featured in the tabloids at regular intervals. There is no need to add to the account of these described in Jean Ritchie's book *Myra Hindley – Inside the Mind of a Murderess*. Maureen Smith read the newspapers, but Myra ignored her sister's requests to see her.

In February 1968, however, Myra heard news about her family that she couldn't ignore. Her grandmother, who had given Myra a home from the age of four, was seriously ill. Myra was allowed to spend a week away from Holloway in Risley Remand Centre and visited her grandmother twice. Mrs Maybury died a few weeks later in March 1968.

It was at this time that Myra showed she had a sense of humour. She worked with others in the tapestry workroom on an elaborate carpet for the Polish Embassy. She wrote 'Myra Hindley made this carpet' on a cigarette paper and put it into the hem.

At about the same time, there was another serious disturbance on E wing in Durham. John McVicar described the riot in his book *McVicar By Himself*. Prisoners were protesting against the governor's new clothing rule on the wing. The inmates stormed the administration office and barricaded themselves in. McVicar and a few others wanted to take advantage of the chaotic situation and lock Brady and Burgess in the office with them. It was not possible. McVicar comments, 'they would both have died that night, probably as painfully as their victims.'

E wing was reorganised after the riot. The top landing was for the sex cases. Brady shared it with three others.

After the history of disturbances following the creation of E wing at Durham, most of the less dangerous inmates were removed elsewhere. Brady said, 'We were supplied with all food uncooked. I cooked for my landing, Ronnie Kray for his. Steak every day; doors open fourteen hours a day. Conditions like those will never again occur in an English prison.'

One of the inmates on Brady's landing was John Straffen. He had killed a child and was sent to Broadmoor, but he escaped and killed again. I asked Ian Brady about him: 'Straffen was a simpleton. He was bald and we called him "Mekon" after the bald-headed character in the Dan Dare weekly feature strip in *The Eagle* comic. He was tolerated because he ran errands for us. He was the only person I have ever met who watched the adverts and got up to make a cup of tea when the programme started. He was sentenced to life while I was still at school.'

Straffen had been in jail for fifty years on 10 August 2001 and was Britain's longest-serving prisoner. The *Mirror* did a small feature on the day and reported that lawyers had medical evidence to show that he had a mental age of nine-and-a-half and had not been fit to stand trial in the first place.

I asked Ian Brady about Ronnie Kray. He said that Kray was quiet and no trouble: 'Remember that these individuals are only famous for their crimes, not for their personalities. Criminals never measure up to their image, as you know. After the first five minutes of meeting someone notorious, they are all pretty mundane; a fact which becomes depressingly obvious, day after day, year after year.'

Lord Longford entered the saga of the Moors Murders towards the end of 1968. Longford – Frank Pakenham – was a Christian aristocrat who championed prison reform in the tradition of William Wilberforce and Lord Shaftesbury in their reforms of the slave trade and factories, respectively, in the nineteenth century. He had a double first at Oxford but was described as having a mental age of twelve by his Labour prime minister, Harold Wilson. Peter Stanford, Lord Longford's biographer, believed that Longford dreamed of being a reforming Home Secretary. This prompted Longford's friend Evelyn Waugh to quip 'and then we would all be murdered in our beds'.

Myra Hindley had heard of Lord Longford's work for prison reform and his years of prison visiting. She thought that he could be instrumental in helping her fight for conjugal visits with Ian Brady. In one of his autobiographies, *Avowed Intent*, Longford recalls the opening gambit in a protracted game that turned sour on him, although he would never have accepted that judgement:

> I was astonished to find that the peroxided gorgon of the tabloids was in fact a nice-looking, dark, well-behaved young person. She was

desperately anxious to be allowed to meet Ian Brady with whom she was still infatuated or, to use kinder words, deeply in love. In my arguments with the Home Office I seldom believe them to be in the right, but they were absolutely right to refuse to permit a meeting.

Lord Longford goes on to record his impressions of Ian Brady: 'Having visited him subsequently over a period of many years, I have no doubt that he was powerfully, almost hypnotically attractive . . . Ian Brady is a man of natural intellectuality. It is almost incredible that someone brought up in a very poor area, not knowing who his father was, packed off at one point to Borstal, should, by the time he went to prison, have developed such an impressive knowledge of writers like Dostoevsky, Tolstoy and Blake. When I look back at his earlier letters, I am still astounded at the contrast between this young man of genuine culture and idealism and the author of such dreadful crimes.'

Both Myra and Ian were to have a love-hate relationship with Lord Longford. In the end, they both refused to receive his visits. At the beginning, even Longford's wife Elizabeth was opposed to him visiting the two of them. She had always supported her husband's prison visits in the past but drew the line at the Moors Murders: 'I didn't want Frank to have anything to do with these people. I wanted him to keep his hands clean of these monsters.' Lord Longford visited Myra four times a year, with the governor present on each occasion. He denies that it was he who converted her to Catholicism.

Longford was often described as being naïve, but there was at least one occasion when he performed a favour for Brady and Hindley in both their eyes. A film director in the United States wanted to convert Emlyn Williams' book *Beyond Belief* into a film. Both Myra and Ian were given contracts to sign and were told they could name their price. Topping claims that Brady urged Myra to accept the money because the film would be made anyway. Brady disputed Topping's version. He explained to me that Longford had just resigned from the cabinet but still had access to James Callaghan, who was Home Secretary. Callaghan announced that if the producer tried to make the film of the Moors Murders, his work permit would be refused.

A number of unsuccessful proposals to screen feature films of Brady and Hindley have surfaced over the years. Gary Oldman and Meryl Streep were to play the title roles in one of these. Writing in the *Guardian*, 16 November 2002, Jonathan Glancey reflected on the inevitable:

Bonnie Parker, the young American gangster, seems glamorous today, but this is because the person we see in our mind's eye is not the real-life scrawny, 4ft 11in, 23-year old freckled blonde, but the gorgeous Faye Dunaway in the 60s movie *Bonnie and Clyde*. A film, *Myra: the Manchester Medusa*, will surely flicker across the silver screen soon enough; the Lancashire blonde will be played by a beautiful woman, lovingly lit, carefully shot. The old photograph will lose its power to shock.

I sent Ian Brady a newspaper cutting of a plan for Gary Oldman to play him in a film of the Moors case. Brady told me that if he ever had a say in the matter he would choose the Scottish actor Brian Cox to perform his part on screen. Brady said that Brian Cox looked like him and was the appropriate age. Cox had played Dr Lecter in *Manhunter*, the film to which *The Silence of the Lambs* was the sequel. Brady couldn't resist pointing out the obvious coincidence that 'the killer is held in a top security mental hospital.'

In May 1991, the *Sunday Telegraph* printed a conversation between the author Brian Masters and Lord Longford. Brian Masters asked Longford whether Myra Hindley was wicked. Longford replied:

Not now. I cannot think of two people more unlike than Brady and Myra. He's a mental case. He's much more to blame than she is. For good or ill, you can blame a person more if they're well balanced, I know, but there's no question that Myra's not mad. People who have never set eyes on her say all sorts of things about her. But those who have met her share my view that she is an honest woman. She's really very delightful.

Masters pressed Longford further on Ian Brady:

Well, I didn't know him until two or three years after the crimes. Here was a boy from the slums, with no schoolmaster or anybody who took an interest in him, yet, do you know, by the time I knew him he had a thorough knowledge of Tolstoy and Dostoevsky, he really was interested in the moral elements; that appealed to him. When judgement comes, in view of Ian Brady's background, and taking into account all my advantages, will St Peter say to me,

you've got to occupy a lower place than Brady? I don't know. I
don't know what the calculation will be.

I showed Brady a copy of the interview and asked him what he thought. He
said, 'Typical! But the St Peter comment redeems him. Longford was a
relativist after all!' In 1974, Longford published *The Grain of Wheat* and
devoted a chapter to his correspondence with Brady, having first obtained
the latter's permission. Ian Brady commented: 'Longford asked me if he
could write a book devoted exclusively to me. I refused. It would all be
about theology and get me a bad name!'

Ian Brady was in prison on the Isle of Wight when *The Grain of Wheat*
was released. Brady hated his time in the two prisons on the island. The
letters show that he much preferred the conditions on E wing in Durham
and regarded that period as a 'golden age'. In a letter to Longford dated
22 January 1973, Brady writes with his usual candour: 'Our correspondence has been pretty stilted and foreign these past few months. I
think back to our letters at Durham. The early years of our correspondence
were both the best and the most constructive. I suppose you recall the
Dietrich Bonhoeffer books which acted as a spring-board for our lengthy
dialectics on religion.

'I have all your letters, of course, and draft copies of my early replies. I
recently re-read our early correspondence and was struck by the closely
reasoned objectivity and balance of my replies, and was left with the
impression that a better person wrote them, not I.' It is a mystery to me
how Ian Brady could read Lord Longford's writing!

I asked Brady how he felt about Longford's visits in retrospect:
'Longford was a visiting junkie who couldn't live without journalists. He
did some good. He had a good brain. His contributions to debates in the
House of Lords were very much to the point although he had to take some
stick because of his appearance.

'The visits were sometimes acrimonious. I told him that he would be
remembered as the friend of Myra Hindley even more than "Lord Porn" in
his campaign for censorship against sexual obscenity. The fact that he was
in charge of the Berlin zone after the war, and later leader of the House of
Lords in Harold Wilson's cabinet, would be forgotten. I asked him whether,
if he had gained access to Hitler, he would have assassinated him to save
the lives of millions. He said "No". I was contemptuous of his reply.'

Lord Longford often took prisoners he had visited to lunch at the House
of Lords on their release. He believed that Myra Hindley would eat with

him there one day. Myra eventually realised that Longford was a curse rather than a blessing in her cause for freedom, however, and allegedly called him 'a stupid old moron' behind his back. His visits ceased.

I asked Ian Brady why he refused Longford's visits: 'He travelled up to Liverpool by train and took a taxi from Maghull station to Ashworth, paid for by the hospital. A newspaper paid for the taxi on one visit and two journalists were waiting in the car park for comments from Longford when he returned. He told me he had to give them a quote since they had paid for the taxi. I told him to tell them to fuck off. He said he couldn't possibly use such language to them. I told him that was too bad. I banned his visits after that.'

I asked Lord Longford if he would care to visit the college where I taught and talk to the students about penal reform and Myra Hindley. He called me one Sunday morning to say that he was happy to come, provided his train fare was paid for because he was a pensioner. I said there would be no problem about that. Furthermore, he added that he wanted a drink at lunchtime: 'I mean a real drink.' I realised after a minute or so that he wanted a glass of wine. I assured him that wine was offered as a matter of course to speakers, if they wanted it.

As it turned out, he never did come to speak. No doubt the old campaigner was thirsting after righteousness somewhere else.

Trouble walked into Durham's E wing in February 1969. The Cannock Chase child killer Raymond Morris had been sentenced to life for the murder of seven-year-old Christine Darby from Walsall in the West Midlands. Christine's body was found three days after her disappearance on Cannock Chase, a vast wooded area fourteen miles from her home. The police suspected that Morris had also killed two other young girls.

Ian Brady despised Morris within seconds of meeting him. The killings had taken place not far from where I live and so I was very familiar with the Cannock Chase Murders, as they were called. Brady may have belonged to the metaphysical realms of evil beyond belief; Raymond Morris was just a plain, repulsive, nasty piece of work.

Brady told me that he attacked Morris three times in Durham: 'Punching him in the TV room; punching him down a flight of stairs; scalding him with a jug of tea. When I ended a 28-day hunger strike, a prisoner tipped me off that Morris intended to retaliate while I was still weak; he tried and missed, and I chased him along the landing until he banged his cell door shut. Still, even an attempt has to be avenged in the shark-pool of the prison culture; I waited patiently for eleven months

298   IAN BRADY – THE UNTOLD STORY OF THE MOORS MURDERS

and, at Albany, stuck a pair of scissors in him. All these attacks were published in newspapers.'

The second attack, described above, was at least partly prompted by external factors. On 12 December 1969 the Home Secretary had informed Ian Brady that his petition to see Myra Hindley had been turned down. Something inside Brady snapped and he threw scalding hot water over Morris. Prison officers intervened. Brady told me that the impression of a screw's buttons was imbedded into the right side of his face for hours afterwards. Raymond Morris took revenge a few weeks later. The *Daily Telegraph* reported the incident on 21 January 1970, under the heading, 'Ian Brady in Hot Water':

> Raymond Morris, at whom Ian Brady, the Moors Murderer, threw hot water five weeks ago, has thrown a jugful of hot water at Brady, who was sitting reading a newspaper in the recreation room in the top-security wing of Durham Prison.
>
> As a result, Morris has been confined to his cell for twenty-eight days, which is the same punishment as that given to the tea-throwing Brady, who, during his confinement, went on hunger strike and was fed by tube.
>
> Morris is one of five prisoners who are allowed to associate with Brady because of the nature of their crimes. Other prisoners are kept away from him for his own safety.

Brady told me that he attacked men, 'who had committed two or more murders like me – Copeland (the Carbon Copy killer), Burgess (Beenham gravel pit), Gypsy Smith and McGreavey (the triple killer). After studying psychology I realised I was attacking myself by proxy. I stopped doing it. I was sure that Morris had used my disposal plan that Emlyn Williams published in *Beyond Belief*. I didn't attack Morris again but I still despised him.'

Brady described one attack on a fellow murderer he didn't name: 'I went for him with a sharpened spoon. You could cut steak with it. I jammed it into his stomach and he ran into his cell. I chased after him and was about to ram it into him again when I looked down and saw that the spoon was completely bent backwards! It looked comic. I just collapsed in laughter.'

In conversation, I mentioned to Brady that there was a book on the Cannock Chase Murders by Pat Molloy, one of the detectives in the case.

Many of the people who met him assumed that he was the detective involved in the Moors Murders and he grew weary of having to explain that he wasn't. Molloy gave his book the title – *Not the Moors Murders*. Brady said, 'It proves my point.'

* * * * *

Manchester police still had two missing children on their files: Pauline Reade and Keith Bennett. Detective Douglas Nimmo visited Ian Brady in Durham. In his book on the reopening of the Moors case, Topping wrote that Brady would say nothing to Nimmo. Ian Brady told me that, in fact, the interview lasted an hour. Nimmo drew a blank when he approached Myra Hindley shortly afterwards: 'Ask Ian.'

Beyond Belief was published in 1967. In September 1969, I was in London on a week's course connected with my degree at Bristol University. A few of us went out for the evening to the Apollo Theatre in Shaftesbury Avenue to see Alan Bennett's play *Forty Years On*. Alan Bennett played a part himself but Emlyn Williams topped the bill. I was interested in seeing Williams in the flesh. I had read a copy of his book but found it hard going at the time because of the peculiar dialogues in Manchester dialect. Years later several of my own students found it difficult for the same reason. And yet it was a best-seller, going through several editions.

Beyond Belief is still selling, although it is very dated, containing nothing of the developments in succeeding years. Myra Hindley detested the book and dismissed it as 'faction'. Ian Brady gave me his own early paperback copy of Williams' book, covered in brown paper, on which he had written his own opinion of the book in large capitals on the cover – BELIEF.

After years of contact with Ian Brady, I realised that Emlyn Williams' book was more of a novel than a record of what actually happened. Perhaps that is what Williams had intended anyway.

David Smith was tainted by the Moors trial despite the fact that he was a witness for the prosecution. He was sacked from jobs as soon as his employers heard of his background. Smith was goaded by total strangers and eventually snapped. He repeatedly stabbed a neighbour, William Lees, and was sentenced to three years on 18 July 1969, in the same court at Chester where Brady and Hindley were sentenced. Ian Brady watched the television news and enjoyed the rest of the evening.

David and Maureen separated while he was in prison. Maureen couldn't cope alone with the children and had them put into care. David gained custody of his three sons – Paul, David and John – on his release and went to live with his partner, Mary. David and Maureen were divorced in 1973. She subsequently met Bill Scott, a man 22 years older than herself. They had a child, Sharon, and married eighteen months after she was born.

The secure wing in Durham prison was still having its moments. John McVicar escaped. He was in prison for armed robbery, and was Britain's most wanted man while he was on the run. Ian Brady told me that he watched the escape from his cell as McVicar climbed across rooftops in the prison: 'It was pure farce. It reminded me of a Laurel and Hardy escapade.' McVicar eventually acquired an education and became a journalist on *Punch* magazine. He published a book in 2002, *Dead On Time*, about the high-profile murder of the television personality Jill Dando, for which Barry George was sentenced to life.

*   *   *   *   *

I asked Ian Brady about his last days in Durham: 'E wing was becoming emptier by the week as prisoners were transferred. In the end there were just two of us – Straffen and me. Straffen was moved to Parkhurst on the Isle of Wight. Then there was one.

'One morning, in August 1971, prison officers arrived at my cell door to tell me I was being moved. They didn't say where. Even the officers driving me south didn't know. They had sealed instructions to be opened en route after calling for refreshments at Gartree prison in Leicestershire. The buff envelope was opened. It was Albany prison on the Isle of Wight.'

CHAPTER TWENTY

SHE TOOK HER WAY – I TOOK MINE

Ian Brady loathed being in Albany prison on the Isle of Wight. He would be transferred within a few years to Parkhurst on the same island and loathe that prison even more. He hated the isolation from the mainland: 'We felt so cut off – the screws did what they liked.'

Brady had been on a long hunger strike at Durham at the time he was transferred. He carried it over into Albany for a short time. He wrote to Lord Longford: 'I want to prove myself, not by doing useless jobs such as mailbags year in, year out, but by giving something tangible and worthwhile. I mean, not so long ago, after a previous hunger-strike, at the risk of making a fool of myself, I seriously considered the possibility of inquiring about donating a kidney to some hospital, for the satisfaction of knowing I'd done something real to balance the past. But I eventually decided that such a gesture would be perhaps too ostentatious and that my motives would be misinterpreted or construed as the passing fad of a mental defective.'

Lord Longford visited Brady in Albany and gave him George Steiner's *In Bluebeard's Castle – Some Notes Towards the Re-definition of Culture.* Longford's dedication is dated 22 November 1971. One of the four chapters is entitled 'A Season in Hell' and is heavily marked by Ian Brady's pen. It spoke of his condition. Steiner was arguing that hell is above ground and Brady felt that he was living proof. He often quoted to me a verse from the *Rubaiyat of Omar Khayyam*:

301

I sent my Soul through the Invisible,
Some letter of that After-life to spell:
And after many days my Soul returned
And said, 'Behold, Myself and Heaven
          And Hell.'

Ian Brady was growing more conscious by the year of the magnitude of his crimes. He recalled a scene in *A Christmas Carol*. The Spirit of Christmas Past shows Scrooge a scene in which his young lover tells him that they made their promises when they were poor and content to be so. A new idol – money – had replaced her in his affections. Scrooge begs to be shown no more. As I mentioned earlier, Brady had set up mental blocks to protect himself from the memory of the terror in the eyes of the children who had gazed upwards in despair at the tall black figure towering over them and the blonde woman with a hook nose a few feet away, looking down without pity.

I talked with Brady years later about George Steiner's books, the work of a gifted polymath. I wondered sometimes what Steiner would make of his ideas being discussed by such strange bedfellows. Then I realised that if Steiner meant what he said, it was proof that hell was, indeed, above ground. Brady would add that we shouldn't confine our description of this visible hell to the acts of individual murderers: 'How many centuries of "criminal" murders would it take to, for instance, equal the 50 million death-toll of World War II?! The sub-culture violence in prisons is, again, mere child's play compared to the violence of the forces of "law and order" – people with permission to beat-up or kill. With permission, there is no remorse or guilt, only rewards and honours. You see why I've always despised the hypocrisy of the Establishment. And see how I copied them. Created my own microcosm, with its own rules and laws. Armed my "government" with revolvers, rifles and blades. We emulated our "betters"; were morally superior to them, for we ran the risk of penalty. Even dignified our victims with identity and remembrance – as individuals, not mere scraps of dead meat in a hill of 50 million corpses created by our "betters". As Balzac said – "Behind every great fortune there lies a crime". And "They want us to repent; but refuse us pardon. They too have the instincts of wild beasts." Do such sentiments and views justify my being described as "evil" and (at the trial) "demonic"?'

Myra's friend Carole left Holloway prison and she no longer had anyone to draft her letters to Ian Brady. In February 1972 Myra broke with him for good. She wrote to him to say that the love affair was over and she would return his letters unopened. Myra wrote to Lord Longford about the break with Brady on 13 March 1972: 'The decision was an agonizing one which cost me dearly. It shattered me because previously I had deemed it impossible that my feelings for him could ever change and this, coupled with my long religious struggle which took place before my complete reconciliation with God, convinces me for, at the moment, some inexplicable reason, that I am doing the right thing, however much it may cost. I know he fears that I am growing away from him which, to a certain extent is true, since we are no longer on the same wave-length and feel no affinity at all with him in a religious sense.'

Two months later, in May 1972, she wrote: 'Although my feelings for him are only a mere shadow of what they used to be the fact remains that at one time, and for a long time, I literally idolized him. Flaubert once said we should never touch our idols because some of the gilt rubbed off on our fingers and this is all too true. For a long time I had him on a pedestal and he was always just out of reach and there was always an air of mystery surrounding him, which I could never solve, never quite touch.

'But in the past few years I have been able to look at him and the past, through eyes of reason rather than the heart and so much of the gilt rubbed off that I find it virtually impossible to recapture even a shred of my previous feelings for him. I wish to put him out of my life as totally as I do all the unhappy, destructive and Godless aspects of my past life with him, and I must admit that I rarely think of him now. At times I tend to blame him entirely for my involvement in things, which is unfair, since I was not a mindless idiot without the ability to say no to the things I acquiesced to.

'Although, of course, had it not been for him, I would never have been involved in any of the things that brought me to prison. However, I made my own bed and so I lie in it, even though I often complain of its unpleasantness.'

Myra claimed that Ian Brady threatened to kill himself if she renounced him, nine months before the final break. I asked him about this and was given a terse reply: 'She flatters herself.' Whatever the truth of the matter, Myra saw the break from Brady as a break from her own past. She changed her name to Myra Spencer. The rest of the world took no notice. Brady commented to me: 'She took her way and I took mine. She tried to please the mob. I spat in their faces and always will.'

Sometime after his transfer to Albany, Ian Brady asked permission to transcribe books into Braille for blind children at St Vincent's school just ten miles from Ashworth Hospital near Liverpool. He eventually began the work when he was transferred to Parkhurst. I asked him about the circumstances: 'A blind person had done a favour for a friend of mine and I wanted to repay it in some way. The prison authorities agreed on the condition that a few of us made an economical unit. I persuaded four other prisoners to join me and we were in business. The first book I transcribed was a volume of Blake's poetry for a blind woman in her eighties.

'Dickens points to the penalty of withdrawing from humanity. When Marley's ghost orders Scrooge to survey the dark sky, he sees the air, "filled with phantoms, wandering hither and thither in restless haste, and moaning as they went. Every one of them wore chains like Marley's ghost; some few (they might be guilty governments) were linked together; none were free. Many had been personally known to Scrooge in their lives. One old ghost . . . cried piteously at being unable to assist a wretched woman with an infant, whom it saw below, upon a doorstep. The misery with them all was, clearly, that they sought to interfere, for good, in human matters, and had lost the power forever."

'Even after decades in prison, I hadn't "lost the power". In spite of resistance from the prison authorities, I was occupied for some years transcribing books into Braille for schools for blind and partially sighted children. One of the schools was in Liverpool, just a few miles from where I ended up. I did not do this for plaudits or personal gain from any section of society (I shall die a prisoner), and I regarded praise of any sort as intolerably patronizing, causing me to lose my temper whenever it was given. The intense satisfaction I gained from transcribing was more than enough.

'Through my grasp of Braille I did, in fact, read in the dark. Sighted people read in a linear way, using both eyes. Blind people have, in effect, another eye at the fingertips of both hands. They read a line with one hand while the other is reading the next. The so-called "visually handicapped" children can read at twice the speed as those who can see. This supports the often-made point that there are vast resources of untapped intelligence of which we are unaware.'

Myra Hindley had been petitioning for her Category A status to be reduced to Category B. She succeeded and could now walk around the prison without an escort. She could also be taken outside Holloway at the governor's discretion. The governor could take out prisoners without seeking permission from the Home Office, although this was normally sought as an extra precaution to avoid controversy. In September 1972,

Holloway's governor Dorothy Wing took Myra out for a walk on Hampstead Heath, an outing which lasted about two hours. Myra walked in large open spaces for the first time in six years and particularly enjoyed the company of Mrs Wing's pet Cairn terrier Piper.

A prisoner had seen Myra leave Holloway and newspapers were told of it within hours. All hell broke loose. The tabloids, the police and victims' families raged against the apparent stupidity of the act. Mrs Wing hadn't informed the Home Office of the intended outing but no official rules had been broken. However, everything to do with Myra Hindley was potentially explosive.

Questions were asked in the House of Commons and the Home Secretary, Robert Carr, publicly criticised Mrs Wing for an 'error of judgement'. The Home Office issued a statement denying that the trip out was part of preparations to release Hindley in the near future and announcing that they were reviewing the procedures for allowing Category B prisoners such privileges.

Myra wrote to Lord Longford to tell him that the two hours on Hampstead Heath were the 'happiest and quickest hours of my life'. She added that she felt wretched about the treatment of Mrs Wing. Myra knew that there would be no outings for her in the future. She resolved to experience the open spaces that knowledge gave, to explore her own mind and enjoy some kind of inner freedom, the only kind she could probably hope for. She enrolled as a student for the Open University to take a Humanities degree.

Two months after Myra's notorious outing, David Smith was in the news again – for a mercy killing. His father had cancer and he died shortly after David Smith gave him a milk drink containing 20 crushed sodium amytal tablets. Smith was given a nominal two-day prison sentence on 8 November 1972 for administering the overdose. Under questioning from Peter Topping fifteen years later, Myra Hindley said that she would one day like to write to David Smith to ask for forgiveness for the damage she had done to him. Ian Brady wrote 'crap' against the appropriate passage in *Topping*.

Ian Brady was on hunger strike again, even though Myra no longer wished to have any sort of contact with him. Lord Longford questioned the sense of a hunger strike when even Myra had no intention of seeing him. Brady wrote: 'In regard to the present demonstration, you say you cannot understand my intellectual reasons. It is essentially a spiritual choice. It is between two futilities. That of doing nothing. That of doing something. To do something naturally infers a degree of hope, no matter how infinitely small or subconscious. To do nothing acknowledges complete hopelessness. It is like either being dead or alive.'

Early in January 1973 Myra became involved in a plot to escape from Holloway. Ironically, at the same time, Lord Longford was becoming more vociferous in his campaign to have her released. In the *Guardian* of 6 January 1973, he said: 'The more one looks into the case, the more one comes to accept her [Hindley's] insistence that she was never directly involved in any act of murder. The tapes, horrible though they are, prove nothing in that respect.'

I asked Ian Brady if he had known about any plans to spring Myra from prison before they split. He said that he had encouraged Myra to get involved in the plot after she raised the possibility of it in a coded letter to him. Jean Ritchie has given a detailed account of the escape attempt in her book as previously mentioned. It is only necessary to give a summary of it here.

Myra and her lover, Tricia Cairns, hatched the plot. Myra and Tricia had the impossible dream of working as missionaries in Brazil. The two of them persuaded another prisoner, Maxine Croft, to be involved in the plan. Maxine was 22 and serving three years for passing counterfeit money. She was a 'trustie' in Holloway and given access to parts of the prison out of bounds for other prisoners. She cleaned the officers' sitting room and used an empty clock in a cupboard there as a pick-up point for written messages and other forbidden items. After a few attempts, Maxine managed to make impressions of Tricia's keys from modelling plaster.

In November 1973, eleven months after the escape plan had been devised, Maxine was allowed a day's parole out in London since she was just twelve days away from her release date. Maxine met up with Tricia to put the key impressions in left-luggage at Paddington station. They arrived to find that no luggage could be deposited because of the IRA's bombing campaign in London at the time and so they left the impressions with Maxine's friend at a car workshop in Ilford.

By chance, a detective inspector called as a customer to the workshop later in the afternoon. Maxine's friend mentioned the package to him and wondered whether it was a bomb. The detective examined it and realised something criminal was afoot when he was told that Maxine was a prisoner in Holloway.

As it turned out, Maxine told prison officials about the escape plan when she returned to Holloway in a distressed state after her few hours of freedom in London. She realised the gravity of what she had done. When Myra saw that an investigation was in process, she concocted a farcical story about a former assistant governor who had made the key impressions to sell when they left Holloway. Myra warned Maxine that if she didn't give the same alibi, she would have no protection while she was in prison. Maxine told the truth.

Myra, Tricia and Maxine came to trial at the Old Bailey in April 1974. People were shocked to see the change in Myra's appearance since the Moors trial – the defiant, tarty look of Myra in the notorious first police photograph had given way to a plainer looking, dark, short-haired woman in her mid-thirties. All three were charged with conspiring to effect the escape of Myra Hindley from Holloway. All three pleaded guilty. As usual, Lord Longford could be expected to put in a good word for Myra and he did so at the trial: 'Only the Almighty can tell us whether to try to escape when there is no hope of being let out is a sin, although it is illegal and wrong. This woman has suffered and she is anxious to do what she can to atone.'

Tricia Cairns was given a six-year prison sentence and Maxine Croft eighteen months. Myra was sentenced to an extra twelve months to be served consecutively to her other sentences. Maxine appealed and was released immediately when the court heard how another prisoner had been treated after attempting to inform on Myra and Tricia. In her book *The Devil and Miss Jones*, Janie Jones wrote of her time with Myra in Holloway and quoted her as saying that Tricia Cairns was 'the instrument of God's grace' for her. God clearly has a sense of humour. Ian Brady told me that Janie Jones had sent him a copy of her book in which she described Myra as 'ruthless'. Brady had used the same word to describe Myra to me on another occasion.

Having mentioned her several times, one should explain that Janie Jones was a singer in the exclusive nightclubs of London in the sixties and friends with several big names in the world of pop music. She was arrested in May 1973 and sentenced to seven years' imprisonment for controlling prostitutes and attempting to pervert the course of justice. Janie writes about Myra's attempts to have an affair with her when glamour had walked into the corridors of Holloway. She recalls the occasion when Myra told her that she had dreams and premonitions of being a silver-haired old crone of ninety being pushed out of the front gate of the prison in a wheelchair. This was an ironic comment by Myra. She didn't live to be ninety, but she was in a wheelchair just before she died – still in custody.

Myra was emphatic in her claims to Janie Jones that she had never heard of any of the murders other than that of Edward Evans: 'I am perhaps one of the only people concerned who still does not know where the alleged graves were.' Myra told Janie how much she detested Ian Brady although she admitted that he had 'fantastic good looks' when she first met him.

After her release from prison, Janie Jones championed Myra's cause for freedom. She sat alongside Lord Longford on television programmes and advocated Myra's innocence in the light of the years of friendship with her in prison. I watched a programme on which Janie Jones appeared some time after Myra's eventual confession — she revealed that she had screamed with anger when she heard the news about Myra. Brady gave me his copy of Janie's book and I asked him what it felt like to be called the scum of the earth in it. I realised how thick-skinned he had become when he replied, 'I enjoyed the book very much. It shows great insight into Myra.'

After a relatively short stay in Albany, Ian Brady was transferred to another prison on the Isle of Wight: Parkhurst. As far as Brady was concerned, this was the 'scum hole to end all scum holes'. Again, it was the isolation from the mainland that depressed him more than anything. This was no doubt one of the reasons Albany and Parkhurst were built in such a location. Brady was doing his Braille work but was becoming aware of psychotic changes in himself, changes which had shown themselves years before in his memory blanks. I asked him what led him to think this: 'I woke up one morning in Parkhurst convinced that there was a revolver in my cell; one I had managed to secrete since my first imprisonment in Durham. I searched my cell for six hours until I realised the futility of it. How could I possibly have a gun?

'Some weeks later I emerged from a daydream thinking I had been released from prison for a few days. I remembered the streets I had walked down. I kept asking myself where I had been and why I had been given the freedom. After a few hours of intense self-examination it dawned on me. It was an absurd idea.'

There was another notorious killer in Parkhurst, Graham Young, the so-called St Albans poisoner. I had read books about him and asked Ian Brady if Young was the pure psychopath he seemed to be: 'Graham Young was a psychotic manic-depressive. He was very sharp, highly intelligent and conversed on a wide range of subjects although his favourite topics were poisons and Nazi Germany. Young cultivated a Hitler moustache until his upper lip was red raw with the razor's attentions. The screws had to stop him doing it. He wanted to be known as the greatest poisoner of all time. Young saw his destiny in Wagnerian terms. He used to sit in his cell imagining that he was in Hitler's Berlin bunker and listened with a fixed gaze to *Twilight of the Gods (Gotterdammerung)*.

'Graham Young was the nearest thing to a natural born killer that I have ever met. His first and only ardent love was murder. Not the garish public variety, rather more of a secret intimate relationship or fleeting liaison of which only he knew the details and fatal result. Those he embraced with his art died without knowing how or why, perhaps suspecting bad food, bad karma or simply awfully bad luck, before giving up the ghost. He also had the good manners, but hardly good taste, to attend the funeral of those he had lovingly relieved of all the world's travails. A truly professional mourner – unique, in that he could, with absolute certainty, rehearse his condolences with some exactitude far in advance of the actual expiration.

'I played chess with Graham Young virtually every day. He beat me in some individual games, but never in a series. He chose the black pieces, likening their power to the Nazi SS. He was psychotic rather than psychopathic. We used to laugh until the tears rolled down our cheeks. Graham dropped dead in his cell one morning. I suspected that he had given himself an undetectable poison. Nothing was found at the post-mortem.'

(One of the questions in the game of Trivial Pursuits is: 'Who beat John Stonehouse, the former Labour MP, in the chess final at Wormwood Scrubs?' Answer – 'Ian Brady'. Stonehouse had faked his own death because of money problems. He wrote his own account of the events in *My Trial*.)

Brady gave me the chess set he used in prison through the years. He devoted a chapter to Graham Young in *The Gates of Janus*. I pressed Ian Brady about his time at Parkhurst. He told me that Donald Neilson, the Black Panther, was there but that their paths never crossed.

While at Parkhurst, Brady witnessed an escape attempt by two men. They nearly made it. A prisoner who was serving eighteen months pressed the alarm button in his cell: 'If the buzzer goes off on the landing a metal flag goes clunk outside the cell with the cell number on it, so everyone knew who had pressed the button. Brooms on torn strips being swung out of the cells above broke the windows of the informer's cell. He was transferred within hours.' Shortly after this incident, Ian Brady was himself transferred suddenly – to Wormwood Scrubs in London.

Meanwhile, in Holloway, Myra Hindley was becoming more depressed by the month. Some of her letters to John Trevelyan from this period were printed in the *Sunday Times*. Late in August 1974, she wrote:

> Something is slowly dying inside me, and it's the will to live. I don't know whether it's because of the acute depression which makes me feel, deep in my heart, that I'll never be released, or if so, not until I'm quite old. I feel tortured with grief and remorse about the disaster I have caused others and I can hardly live with myself. I feel I just want to drag myself into a corner in the dark, as does an animal when it knows it is dying, and if I had no moral responsibilities and didn't owe so much to so many people I think I could quite easily do so now . . .
>
> Some of the sunrises I see when going to collect the breakfasts are extraordinarily beautiful. I found myself thinking how fervently I wished that there was no one whom I loved or loved me so that I could tell life to go to hell and simply lie down and wait to die . . .
>
> I would like a child, perhaps even two. I would like to have a child before I reach forty but I'd like to have a couple of years free in order to cram in as much living as possible to make up for the years of merely existing. I'll be thirty-three soon, which leaves seven years for me to realize my ambitions. I fear I am living in dreams.

In a later letter to John Trevelyan, on 8 May 1975, she revealed her black moods: 'What is life for? To die? Then why not kill myself at once? No. I'm afraid. Wait for death until it comes? I fear that even more. Then I must live. But what for? In order to die. I can't escape from that circle.'

At this time, Myra was still seeking the consolations of religion. In Christmas 1974 she took part in the nativity play at Holloway. She played the part of Mary and an entire wing walked out of the prison chapel.

Ian Brady would spend eight years in Wormwood Scrubs. If Parkhurst was the worst, Wormwood Scrubs was the best. He worked on the hospital wing and had regular contact with between seventy or eighty inmates. The rapid turnover in young, short-term prisoners, gave the place an energy he had not experienced in prison before. Many of the new prisoners, on first meeting, didn't know who he was and knew nothing of his crimes. They found out later, but, 'I'd met them simply as another individual and that was marvellous. We talked to each other, however briefly, as ordinary human beings. I cherished anonymity more than anything else. People who deliberately seek fame or notoriety are fools.'

Apart from his Braille work, Brady worked mainly as a cleaner and barber in Wormwood Scrubs. I asked him who cut his hair. He said, 'I do. In the Scrubs I had some tuition from a short-termer who had worked for Vidal Sassoon. I used to cut the screws' hair. Imagine that! Ian Brady behind you with a pair of scissors!'

Ian Brady said that he felt part of the prison community in Wormwood Scrubs, as he did in no other prison. He helped prisoners with their parole applications, stressing the importance of family connections and educational opportunities they had used during their sentence: 'I always advised them to state that they were pursuing private theological studies. If they were in for burglary, I used to give them a sheet of cellophane paper with my fingerprints on it to be left behind at the scene of the first job they did after they were released. I loved the prospect of detectives scratching their heads about how Ian Brady could have been there when he had been locked up for years.'

Ian Brady began a correspondence course on psychology with Aldermaston College: 'Psychology was on the proscribed list until I challenged it. I was trying to expand my mind. I was going nowhere so the mind was the only place I could expand.'

Brady continued to study the classics and actually read Plato's *Republic* in the punishment block – 'chokey' – following some misdemeanour. This particular occasion revealed a vulnerable side of Ian Brady. He was on punishment, but during association a prisoner offered him a cigarette. Brady ignored him, thinking that the man was trying to send him up. Later, Brady was in the 'chokey' cell with just a mattress and a chair. A tiny rolled package dropped through the spy or Judas hole that happened to have no glass in it: 'It was rolled tobacco, a match and a piece of sandpaper to strike it on. I felt very bad about snubbing him before.'

Years later, Ian Brady wrote, 'Kindness has no place in a penal institution. It is also a sensible practice not to read any books which might induce human or altruistic sentiment.' Why, then, did he read *A Christmas Carol* every year?

Brady felt re-energised after his transfer to Wormwood Scrubs. He ran a book on title fights: 'Not for the profit but for the fun. I organised games with marbles after two of them had been thrown over the prison walls. The screws confiscated the marbles eventually. I started a trend by using plastic medical syringes as cigarette holders. Some of the prisoners didn't cut them short enough and they looked like Noel Coward! There was a relaxed atmosphere in the Scrubs in those days. They were the days of pirate radio stations and I tuned in to Radio Caroline.'

Brady entered the Koestler Awards painting competition and came second with two abstract pictures: 'I didn't try again. Why bother if you can only come second?' The two paintings still exist. Brady told me that they would form the covers of his autobiography.

In Holloway, Myra Hindley entered a prison song competition and won it with the three songs she submitted, 'Don't Make Promises', 'Prison Trilogy' and 'Love Song to a Stranger'. The prize was £10. Janie Jones, a professional singer, came second in a competition that had hundreds of entries.

I asked Brady about his experience of drugs in prison. He said that he avoided them so that he could be alert at all times: 'I was offered marijuana in the Scrubs. I listened to what they said was the amount to smoke and then reduced it in case it dulled my senses. That was my one brief encounter with drugs. I have never seen hard drugs like heroin in prison. Neither have I seen any evidence of LSD. Without the prison authorities' toleration of drugs, prisons would be destroyed.'

Brady told me about the draft of a novel he wrote in Wormwood Scrubs. The central character was a Labour supporter pretending to be a Tory sympathiser, who killed right-wing Labour MPs and trade union leaders. The killer escaped to Scotland from London by using the canal system after assassinating the Labour politician Michael Foot: 'When I was told I was being transferred back to Parkhurst, I tore up the manuscript. It's still in my head, though. I could write it out again.'

Ian Brady spent some time on the psychiatric ward G2 on west wing in Wormwood Scrubs. It was there that he met Peter Sutcliffe, the Yorkshire Ripper. It's hard to resist asking one of the most intriguing questions concerning the subject of twentieth-century murder: 'What did the Moors Murderer say to the Yorkshire Ripper?' I couldn't resist the temptation: 'Sutcliffe was reserved and deferential with a pleasant mien. The general impression was that he was ordinary without any charisma.

'He had no sense of humour, although he did have a sense of irony. He showed casual indifference to his crimes. He was not purely psychopathic; he had a psychotic side. He read the Bible obsessively everyday. He was convinced that he heard the voice of God in his head. I asked Sutcliffe whether God spoke to him in Hebrew or English. Sutcliffe seemed not to hear the question. He spoke of the murders in a very matter of fact way, perfectly convinced that he had done the right thing in carrying out a God-given mission. He felt no need to justify his actions further than that. This mundane attitude reduced the conception and enactment of his crimes to the mere commonplace. A paradox, as he claimed his accomplice to be no less than God. At a later date, he said it was the devil's voice he heard.'

'When I first met him, Sutcliffe recognised me right away. He had seen a model of me with Myra Hindley in Blackpool waxworks but felt that it was a poor likeness. I told him, "There's a model of you alongside me there now."

'Sutcliffe's physical appearance had changed from being slim to positively podgy, mesomorphic physically but not psychologically, a side effect of the daily medication he was forced to take to artificially maintain mental equilibrium. There was no intellectual capacity in his conversation, no philosophical or even theological structure. Instead, there was simply a calm, almost prim self-righteousness. Yet there had been sexual assaults upon the victims. He sometimes used a screwdriver as a penis substitute to violate his victims. The use to which he put the screwdriver clearly indicated sexual inadequacy, leading to self-contempt, which, perhaps, comprised at least part of the root of the cause of his psychosis, and the eventual schizophrenic descent into homicidal religious mania. By periodically destroying the object of his mania, he was simultaneously attempting to eradicate his guilt, the homicidal urge and unclean desires.'

The question put to Sutcliffe about which language God used to address him is vintage Brady. When *The Gates of Janus* appeared, there was a chapter devoted to Sutcliffe. Brady includes the sentence, 'I had the opportunity to interview Sutcliffe at length when I was passing through the south of England.' No prisoner before has described their time in Wormwood Scrubs in this way.

* * * * *

The mid-seventies were a period of mixed fortunes for Myra Hindley. She had seen nothing of her sister for ten years. Out of the blue Myra told her mother that she wanted to see Maureen. A month later, Maureen went with her husband Bill Scott and new baby Sharon, to see Myra in Holloway. Hugs and tears.

Lord Longford was still campaigning on Myra's behalf and persuaded the editor of the *Sunday Times* to print her letters to publicise the acceptable face of Myra Hindley.

Myra was now encountering younger prisoners who had not even lived through the publicity of the Moors Murders ten years before. They only learned of it when newspapers and magazines did features on the case. Myra's friends were particularly protective of her on the days these stories went into print. The *News of the World* published an article with pictures on the tenth anniversary of the Moors trial. A young prisoner in Holloway, nineteen-year-old Josie O'Dwyer, read the feature and launched a vicious physical attack on Myra Hindley that broke her nose. I remember reading a magazine article about the attack: 'She beat Myra Hindley to a pulp', by Alix Kirsta, author of *Deadlier Than The Male*. Myra had surgery to her nose in an outside hospital where she was treated as a patient under the name of Susan Gibb.

Prison officers opened Myra's cell door at 5 a.m. on Saturday, 25 January 1977. Without warning she was transferred to Durham's H wing. Myra had been in Holloway for eleven years. She was in a distraught state when the door was locked behind her for the first night in her new cell.

Myra Hindley despised Durham as much as Ian Brady loathed Parkhurst. She was only allowed to have books in her cell that were essential for the immediate needs of her Open University course. She had to disperse the books she had collected over ten years to her friends. Myra suspected that her food had been urinated in and spat upon and chose a diet comprising foods that were safe from contamination, such as boiled eggs and fruit. She was allowed far fewer visits than she enjoyed at Holloway.

At that time, Myra and Brady were two of only three prisoners serving more than ten years who had never been considered for parole. Apart from her studies, Myra set herself the task of writing a detailed plea for parole that would take her eighteen months to complete. She received spiritual guidance from the Catholic chaplain, Father Algy Shearwater, who introduced her to a method of praying and reading the Bible through a Jesuit book, *The Spiritual Exercises*.

The sexual freedom she had enjoyed was now much more restricted, although she had a serious affair with another prisoner, Dorothy, a Scottish woman who was married with children. When they were discovered together, Dorothy was transferred to Styal. After the incident, no prisoner was allowed to close the door while another prisoner was in the cell. Myra eventually recovered from the loss of Dorothy and had other relationships.

In Wormwood Scrubs, Ian Brady had completed his course of study with Aldermaston College and was awarded a certificate for his success in Practical and Applied Psychology. The certificate is dated 27 April 1977.

Myra finished her long parole submission in 1979 and sent it to the Labour Home Secretary, Merlyn Rees. Four years later, the *Sun* acquired a copy and proposed to publish extracts before it was stopped in its tracks. The contents are an open secret now. There is little point in describing the contents in detail here, since Myra herself admitted to Inspector Topping years later that her submission to Merlyn Rees was 'a pack of lies'.

Some idea of the self-delusion in Myra's statement is evident in her comment that the moors 'represented nothing more and nothing less than a beautiful and peaceful solitude that I cherish. Of the bodies and graves I know nothing.' Her only crime, she wrote, was her blind love for Ian Brady. She went further, after describing the miseries of prison life, and claimed that 'Society owes me a living'. She wrote that she *now* believed that Ian Brady was guilty of the Moors Murders. This is another one of the greatest understatements of criminal history.

The Open University awarded Myra her degree early in 1980, but she was refused a graduation ceremony. Her disappointment was dwarfed by the sudden death of her sister. Maureen and her husband had gone out for the evening to a pub near their home in Manchester. Maureen complained of a headache and they returned home. The following morning, she was violently sick and was admitted to Crumpsall, the hospital where Myra was born. Mo had suffered a brain haemorrhage and was operated upon. Myra was rushed from Durham to her bedside to find that her sister had died an hour before.

Knowing that her presence at her sister's funeral would probably cause pandemonium, Myra did not ask for permission to attend. She sent flowers instead. John Kilbride's father, Pat, and Ann West were there to attack Myra if she appeared. Bill Scott's daughter, Ann Wallace, was mistaken for Myra Hindley and there was a scuffle. In *For the Love of Lesley*, Ann West claimed, in error, that she looked Myra Hindley in the eyes at the funeral.

In the early months of 1980, the press had sensed the imminent release of Mary Bell. Mary Bell, at the age of eleven, had killed two small boys in Newcastle in 1968. Myra began to hope that the tide had turned. Perhaps the powers that be would extend their clemency to her, imprisoned as she was for the murder of children. Mary Bell was released on 14 May 1980. There was nothing in the air to suggest that Myra stood any hope of release in the near future.

Myra's plight was not completely without hope. It was the day of small things. In 1981 the Home Office brought the United Kingdom in line with the European Community and allowed ex-prisoners to have contact with prisoners still in jail. John Trevelyn's daughter, Sarah, who was visiting Myra regularly in Durham, put her in touch with the man who became her new lawyer. Michael Fisher was in his early thirties, keen for the fray and relished impossible cases.

While Myra was at Durham, Ian Brady was transferred back to Parkhurst. He wondered whether the prison authorities had assumed he had forgotten about the death of a fellow prisoner at the hands of a doctor while he was in Parkhurst eight years before. Brady asked to speak to the police. Nothing came of it. Detective Chief Superintendent Geoff Rimmer spent seven hours with Ian Brady, but to no avail. The visit was reported in the press. Brady may have staged the meeting with the police to worry Myra Hindley into thinking that he had been talking about the murders of Pauline Reade and Keith Bennett. Brady stayed in Parkhurst for thirteen months before being transferred to Gartree.

In Durham, Myra had heard that a new section was being opened in Holloway. She submitted a request to be sent there in February 1982. She preferred anything to Durham. The new unit was still not open in November 1982, but Myra renewed her request and said that she was happy to go to Holloway and wait. During 1982, the Tory Home Secretary William Whitelaw announced that Myra Hindley would not be considered for parole for another three years. Brady released a statement in which he said that he would never seek parole and that the nature of the Moors Murders justified permanent life imprisonment for himself and Myra. Referring to his own contribution he said: 'They were the acts of a madman. I don't deserve any sympathy and I would never seek it. I want to spend the rest of my life inside. I want to die in jail.'

CHAPTER TWENTY-ONE

THE SECOND COMING – TWO GHOSTS ON SADDLEWORTH MOOR

On 30 March 1983, after a three-week hunger strike, Myra Hindley was transferred from Durham to Cookham Wood prison in Rochester, Kent. It had been open just five years and had been built in the grounds of the original Borstal. Myra optimistically thought that the move could be connected with her eventual release on parole.

A new man entered Myra's life in 1983. He was David Astor, former editor of the *Observer*. I met David Astor some years later and asked him how he became involved in supporting her. He commented: 'I had been a friend of Frank, Lord Longford, for many years and felt that he had become the object of ridicule. He had lost his way in his high-profile defence of Myra. He told me that he couldn't face St Peter at the end if he had missed an opportunity to do her good. His critics even suggested that he was in love with Myra. Auberon Waugh referred to Frank's "crucifixion complex".' David Astor went on: 'Frank just couldn't resist speaking to journalists and insisted that anyone who claimed to be a Christian must agree with him. I first visited Myra in September 1983 and Peter Timms came with me. It went on from there. My support for Myra was low-key compared with Frank's. I took over from him. Frank found it difficult to accept that his tactics to champion her cause were self-defeating and doing her more harm than good.'

317

Ten years after David Astor's first visit to Myra, it came to light that he had been giving her money through two Methodist ministers. There was nothing illegal about this arrangement. Anticipating Myra's release, Lord Longford commented that, 'It won't be easy for her to get a job. But she is a good friend of David Astor and he is not a poor man. It will be all right, I'm sure of that.'

Myra's father had disowned her after the arrest because of her failure to tell him that her mother was having an affair with Bill Moulton, a lorry driver. He disowned Myra's sister for the same reason. Out of the blue, in June 1985, Myra's mother spoke publicly about Myra for the first time. Over the years she had turned down a fortune from newspapers for her story. She was now married to Bill Moulton and was living in a two-bedroom council flat in Gorton when she made her comments to the *Sun*. 'Myra should die in prison,' her mother stated: 'It's better she dies there than comes out of prison and gets killed out here. Myra's been in prison all these years now, so what difference does it make if she stays there forever? If Myra came out she couldn't come here. I don't know where she would go. People wouldn't let her alone. She might as well die in prison.

'Poor Myra. Life means life or Myra. For others it means just a few years. When they call her a beast or a devil, they don't know what they are talking about. They don't know her. She is still my daughter. I love her just like I always have done. Something like that does not change.'

Brady commented to me once that if the victims' relatives were serious about wanting to kill Myra, they should shut up, abandon their campaign against her, wait for her to be released and then kill her. This was pure Brady-logic.

Ian Brady was at Gartree prison at Market Harborough in Leicestershire, having been transferred from Parkhurst. Many years later, I invited a tutor from a police college to talk to my students. In conversation I discovered that he had been a governor at Gartree prison while Ian Brady was there. Without prompting, the former governor told me that he had seen Brady in a hopeless condition: 'He was clutching a radiator and talking to it as though he was speaking to God or the Home Office.'

On 28 December 2002, the novelist Patrick McGrath spoke to *The Times* about his childhood in the surroundings of Broadmoor, the maximum-security psychiatric hospital, where his father was medical superintendent. His father had told him that in thirty years of practice he had encountered only two patients who were untreatable. One of these was Ian Brady:

'There's nothing I can do with this guy,' he reported, 'he's cold, there's no humanity there. I can't create any kind of empathy with this man.'

This has led some writers on the Moors Murders to assume that Brady was in Broadmoor for some time. This is not so. When I mentioned *The Times* article, Brady said that, 'The true version is I sent McGrath packing in prison, describing Broadmoor as a political dustbin in the Russian psychiatric tradition.'

I asked Ian Brady about his time in Gartree prison: 'After the transfer from Parkhurst, I gave up the exercise periods out of doors. To move out of a match box into a shoebox is no choice. I kept fit doing press-ups on my knuckles. I developed hard skin doing this and it used to catch my trouser pockets. I used sandpaper on the hard skin to stop this. I still did my Braille work but I was in a bad way at Gartree. I went from thirteen to under eight stone. My only visitor was Lord Longford. I refused to see my mother. I could never get warm. I didn't go to bed for three years.

'I spent the nights sitting in a chair, clutching a big plastic bottle full of hot water. The low flying planes were noisy anyway. When it was illuminated at night, the prison was like a wedding cake; a convenient marker for the RAF's training flights.

'There was one spell in Gartree when I attacked anything that moved. I used to deliver karate chops to the cell wall. I broke my hand doing it.'

On 29 November 1984, a journalist for the *Sunday People*, Fred Harrison, visited Ian Brady at Gartree. He was the first person to have visited him – apart from Lord Longford – for nine years. Harrison was shocked by Brady's physical and mental state. He looked seventy.

During Harrison's second visit, on 21 January 1985, Ian Brady vaguely suggested, for the first time in almost twenty years, that he was responsible for the murders of Pauline Reade and Keith Bennett. Brady didn't disclose to Harrison how these two children died. In the course of later visits, without giving details, Brady disclosed that he had committed other murders – the 'happenings' that have been described in early chapters of this book.

Harrison's first article on the disclosures was published on 23 June 1985 under the headline 'MY SECRET MURDERS'. On 27 June 1985, Harrison was informed that he could no longer visit Ian Brady. A year later, Harrison published a book describing his involvement in the Moors case – *Brady and Hindley: Genesis of the Moors Murders*. The book has been overtaken by later events and its theory about the abduction of Pauline Reade now appears particularly fanciful. In the book, Harrison wondered whether he was part of a private vendetta against Myra Hindley.

Harrison has appeared from time to time in television documentaries claiming to have 'solved' the murders of Pauline Reade and Keith Bennett. In a programme broadcast in February 2002, Harrison complains that Brady had 'used' him. Ian Brady saw the programme and told me that Harrison's comments were 'satirical in view of his book and serialisation profits'.

The then Home Secretary, Leon Brittan, released a statement on 23 May 1985 that Myra Hindley wouldn't be considered for parole until 1990. Myra collapsed with nervous strain on hearing the news and went on hunger strike for ten days. She later dismissed Brady's admissions about the deaths of Pauline Reade and Keith Bennett as 'fabrication'.

It was at this stage that Peter Topping became involved in the Moors case. The Home Office and the Director of Public Prosecutions had asked him what he was doing about Ian Brady's fragmentary admissions to Fred Harrison. As a result, Topping visited Ian Brady in Gartree. The detective was as shocked as Harrison had been by Brady's condition. In the event, Brady told Topping: 'Go away.'

Ian Brady had been fighting the authorities for years for his right to be committed to a mental hospital for treatment. He had been 'certified' five times in prison for attacking fellow prisoners. Doctors at Gartree examined Brady and concluded that he was suffering from acute paranoia and a type of schizophrenia. He had been suffering from hallucinations and delusions for a long time. On the recommendation of his doctors, the authorities decided to transfer Brady to a secure mental hospital under Section 47 of the Mental Health Act.

I asked Brady why he had succumbed to such a physical and mental state while Myra Hindley seemed to have survived for twenty years comparatively unscathed. He replied with one word: 'Hope.' He then quoted the Monty Python legend, John Cleese: 'The despair, I can stand the despair . . . it's the hope I can't stand. Myra had hope; I had no hope. I had done everything I could during the trial to secure her release. I told her to stick to the alibi I gave her and build upon what I called the three pillars: maintain family ties, study and get religion. And shut up! If she had kept quiet she would be out in 25 years. But she didn't. She said that it gave her a chill down the spine to think she might be in the same cell as me.'

Ian Brady described his transfer from Gartree on 29 November 1985: 'Screws came to my cell and told me I was being moved. They didn't say where. They put me in handcuffs and I climbed into the van. There were police cars in front of the van as we drove off and after a few minutes I could see that there were police cars following.'

'We had been on the road some time and I moved my body as far as I could to catch sight of road signs. I saw a sign for Kirby and I knew we must be somewhere on Merseyside. Eventually, the van swept into Park Lane secure mental hospital at Maghull in Liverpool. I saw the convoy of police cars sweep away once the van was safely inside.

'The police opened the Black Maria to let me out. A doctor was there waiting for my arrival and was angry when he saw I was handcuffed. He told the police to remove them immediately.'

Just a week after Brady's transfer to Liverpool Myra wrote to Janie Jones: 'So he's got what he's been after for the past sixteen years at least. This is why I'm reserving judgement about these things. I don't think he's as mad as he's made the doctors believe he is, and although he's obviously got problems, he's as shrewd and intelligent as he always was.'

Park Lane, later known as Ashworth, is ten miles north of Liverpool city centre and is one of three secure hospitals in England. There had been hospitals on the same site since 1878. Park Lane was opened in 1979 to reduce overcrowding at Broadmoor secure hospital at Crowthorne in Berkshire. Park Lane is distinct from the nearby Moss Side hospital, which became Ashworth South. The third high-security hospital is at Retford in Nottinghamshire.

Ian Brady told me that he had no memory for five months after arriving at Park Lane. He was in a prolonged fugue. It was the medication that eventually helped him to recover. He was given various strong drugs from morning till night, but principally chloral hydrate – known as 'Mickey Finn' to old-time American gangsters.

Brady was put in Newman Ward with older inmates to avoid the trouble that might have arisen with younger patients. Brady eventually realised that his Braille machine was not around. It was thought to be a possible danger with its metal parts that he could have used to harm himself. Lord Longford visited him eventually and noticed a change: 'He looked like a scarecrow in prison, but now he has put on a lot of weight and is looking better.' Ian Brady's mother visited him on 2 January 1986, his 48th birthday.

Ann West wrote to Brady in March 1986 about the other two Moors victims, Pauline Reade and Keith Bennett. Brady sent a letter to the BBC, an address he would use more and more for his pronouncements, to say that he was prepared to meet Ann West. The substance of his letter was broadcast during the *Nine O'Clock News* on Friday, 14 March 1986. In *For the Love of Lesley*, Ann West claims that Ian Brady wrote to her three times between May and August 1986, admitting that for some time he couldn't bring himself to read her first letter. She added that David Smith had been writing to Brady at Park Lane hospital but had received no reply.

I asked Ian Brady about this exchange of letters. He had written to say that his remorse was axiomatic and painfully deep: 'I despise useless, empty words and prefer positive action to balance part of the past; i.e. the Braille I have done for schools this past 18 years and which the authorities here are making it difficult for me to do.'

I spoke to Brady about this a few days after a television programme on Charles Manson. Manson had made the point that the question was not whether he, Charles Manson, was 'remorseful', but whether he was 'sincere'. Brady had seen the programme and approved of Manson's comment. Brady said that nobody knows where the dividing line is between remorse and self-pity or where self-interest lies: 'Can you think of a thought or action not attributable to vanity?'

Brady told me that Charles Manson had read up on the Moors Murders and felt some affinity with Brady. When Brady's book *The Gates of Janus* was published, an American critic commented that, 'Charles Manson, though iconic, doesn't get nearly the amount of spilled ink in America that Brady gets in England.'

Sometimes authors have linked Brady with an observation by the Marquis de Sade: 'Remorse is just an illusion. Merely the whining of a cowardly soul – too cowardly to stifle and kill it.' In *The Gates of Janus* Brady asks: 'To whom should I apologize and what difference would it make?'

*   *   *   *   *

Peter Topping realised that he had to do something about Pauline Reade and Keith Bennett. They had been on the police's missing persons list for twenty years until Ian Brady's admissions turned the fate of the two children into murder cases. The police had to investigate murder. When he was later criticised for the protracted search of Saddleworth Moor, Topping said, 'God help us when we come to the day in this country when we don't investigate murder.'

Topping was already familiar with many of the basic facts about the Moors Murders. He had lived with his family above his father's barber's shop in Gorton Lane, a stone's throw from Myra Hindley's house. Topping began to study the papers in the case in depth. Because Edward Evans' body had been found in Hattersley, the Cheshire police held the case files.

Eventually, four other forces were involved: Derbyshire, Lancashire, Yorkshire and Manchester City.

The relatives of Pauline Reade and Keith Bennett had read about Brady's admissions to Fred Harrison and were impatient for action by the police. Paul Reade, Pauline's older brother, pleaded with the police: 'Please take those two monsters back to the moors to find my sister's grave and end our agony.' Police activity was already taking place, albeit in a very low-key way. Topping had asked Yorkshire force's dog handler Neville Sharpe to spend the summer of 1986 with his collie dog searching Hollin Brown Knoll on Saddleworth Moor and the nearby Shiny Brook. Neville Sharpe found nothing of significance.

In the autumn and winter months of 1986, two things happened to Myra Hindley that speeded up the police's investigations into the two missing children. She received a letter from Mrs Winnie Johnson, Keith Bennett's mother, and a visit from Peter Topping.

In her letter, Mrs Johnson explained that she was a simple woman who worked in the kitchens of Christie's Hospital. She added that it had taken her five weeks to compose the letter. She begged Hindley to tell her what had happened to her son. She hoped that Christianity had softened her heart. Could a Christian condemn a pleading mother to the purgatory of grief for the years left to her?

Peter Topping was three years older than Myra Hindley and two years younger than Ian Brady. I asked Brady about Topping. Brady said that he was 'unctuous': 'He used the Moors case to become a "personality" like John Stalker. It never happened for him.'

Topping's first visit to Myra Hindley in Cookham Wood took place on 17 November 1986, just a fortnight after she had received Mrs Johnson's letter. Topping intended to search the moor whatever she said. He would warn Myra and her solicitor that he was not cautioning her and that nothing said during the interview would be used as admissible evidence. Topping was warned by those who knew Myra to expect nothing from her. She would be polite and respectful, but nothing more.

Topping was in for a surprise. He assumed that Myra's appearance would be different from the notorious first security photograph, but couldn't have anticipated what she was about to say. Myra calmly said that she would help him in his search for the bodies of Pauline Reade and Keith Bennett.

Peter Topping had many questions on his mind. In the original investigation it had been assumed that the victims were murdered elsewhere and transported to the moors. The bodies would, therefore, have been buried a short way from the road. Another question concerned photographs that seemed to be innocent pictures of views on the moors. Could they have been taken before Lesley Ann's death and be photographs of Pauline Reade's grave? Myra issued a statement through her solicitor, Michael Fisher, in which she denied any involvement in the disappearance of Pauline and Keith – and put in a plug for her own future release: 'I received a letter, the first ever, from the mother of one of the missing children and this has caused me enormous distress. I have agreed to help the police in any way possible and have today identified, from photographs and maps, places that I know were of particular interest to Ian Brady, some of which I visited with him. In spite of a 22-year passage of time, I have searched my heart and memory and given whatever help I can give to the police. I'm glad at long last to have been given this opportunity and I will continue to do all that I can.

'I hope that one day people will be able to forgive the wrong I have done and know the truth of what I have and have not done. But for now I want the police to be able to conclude their inquiries, so ending public speculation and the private anguish of those directly involved.'

Brady reacted by issuing a statement through his own solicitor, Benedict Birnberg: 'He is very concerned about things that have been said by Myra Hindley implicating him. That has stung him. He wants Myra Hindley and her advisors to know that letters she wrote to him over a period of years when they were first in prison and before their relationship broke up are still in existence.'

In the margins of *Topping*, Brady wrote a terse comment on Myra's statement that she wished Winnie Johnson had written to her fifteen years earlier: 'She only ever regrets when caught out.'

Lord Longford's reaction to the news of Myra's willingness to help the police was predictable. He said that if Myra were a character in a Dostoevsky novel she would be a heroine. He expected her release from prison and commented that anyone who said she was the most evil woman in the country should be certified and receive psychiatric treatment.

The search of the moors began in earnest on 20 November 1986, with thirty men and dogs. Six days later, the *Daily Telegraph* reported that detectives had interviewed Ian Brady, with his solicitor present, for two hours in Park Lane secure hospital.

Topping and his trusted band of detectives conducted the daily routine search for the bodies from then on. They marked out areas of the moors with a grid system and removed the top layer of peat that had covered the ground over the previous twenty years, looking for signs of disturbance in the ground beneath it. Some critics wondered why lay workers – experienced in the careful uncovering of land sites – were not used. Should detectives have been employed to spend months full time on their knees with a trowel when there must have been equally pressing matters elsewhere and for which they were trained? Brady commented: 'Topping wanted the search group to be as small as possible to give him an exclusive story.'

People involved in the Moors case at all levels were expecting a significant breakthrough. Mrs Johnson travelled down to Kent at the *Sun*'s expense and stood outside Cookham Wood prison. Ann West turned up on the front doorstep of the house of Ian Brady's mother. The Tory MP for Saddleworth, Geoffrey Dickens, wanted the search called off. Ian Brady was to be merciless – as only he can be – towards Dickens in his letters to me.

Myra Hindley and Ian Brady both eventually made two visits to the moors with Topping and his men. Myra's first visit was made before her confession to her involvement in the murders of Pauline and Keith. Her second visit was made after her confession but before it was made public. Ian Brady's two visits took place after Pauline Reade's body had been found.

The police operation to bring Hindley and Brady back on to the moors was called 'Little Chef' after the numerous meals Peter Topping and his colleagues had at roadside restaurants when they were engaged on the case. In the course of researching this book, I drove up to Manchester to walk the streets the Moors victims walked on their appointment with death. One of my visits was just before Christmas and I called in to have a meal at a Little Chef restaurant during which piped music played 'The Little Drummer Boy', the song recorded on the Lesley Ann tape.

Myra's first visit to the moors was nine days before Christmas 1986. She was taken by car in the early hours to West Malling airfield for the flight in a Metropolitan Police helicopter to the A635 road on Saddleworth Moor. David Mellor, a junior Tory minister in the Home Office, told Radio 4's *Today* programme that Myra was on her way to the moors. Topping commented later that this 'drove a bus through my plans'. As a result of the announcement, the press were given the time to hire helicopters in the hope of being able to take photographs of Myra on the moors.

Roadblocks were set up at either end of the A635 road that cut its way across the moors. Patrick Kilbride had come prepared with a knife to attack

Myra Hindley, if given the chance. The police stopped him in his tracks. Two photographers from the *Daily Mirror* had trudged five miles across Saddleworth Moor for a picture but were stopped by police. Decoy parties had been put on to the moors by police to distract the media. The *Today* newspaper printed an aerial photograph of 'Myra Hindley' the following day. It was, in fact, a policewoman in one of the decoy parties.

The Home Secretary announced that there was no promise of parole to Myra Hindley for her cooperation; 'Time will tell if she knows something.' Topping reports that Myra was emphatic to him during the day's search that she was not seeking parole. She did, however, plead to stay one more day on Saddleworth Moor. Topping explained that it was impossible.

Some suggested that Myra's visit to Saddleworth Moor was a pantomime staged to divert attention from the controversy surrounding John Stalker, the Deputy Chief Constable of Greater Manchester (and who headed the so-called Stalker Inquiry into an alleged 'shoot to kill' policy in Northern Ireland). Stalker had been accused of associating with known criminals in Manchester. One of the reasons he gave for his eventual resignation from the force was that he had not been informed of Myra Hindley's visit to the moors, despite the fact that he had actually been directly in charge of police operations in Manchester during the period in question.

A few days after Christmas 1986, Myra's solicitor, Michael Fisher, Topping and his assistant, Geoff Knupfer, had lunch at the house of the Revd. Peter Timms, a Methodist minister very experienced in counselling long-term prisoners and who had been governor of Maidstone prison. Years later, Peter Timms became a friend of mine and told me about the post-Christmas meeting at his house. After lunch, they went to see Myra in Cookham Wood and it was agreed that Peter Timms would counsel her. Myra said that she couldn't talk to the Catholic priest in the prison and the approval of the Home Office was sought for Peter Timms to become her spiritual counsellor.

Pauline Reade would have been forty years old on 18 February 1987. By this time, Mrs Johnson had sent Myra a second letter saying that her hopes hung on a thin thread and she couldn't accept that Myra's visit to the moors was just a day out for her, as many had said.

Myra claimed that she hadn't written a reply to Mrs Johnson's first letter because of the publicity. When she did write back in answer to the two letters, Myra said that if only Mrs Johnson had written to her fourteen years before, after she had broken with Ian Brady, she would have helped the police with the search for Keith. In the light of later events, this is a strange claim. For years after her break with Brady, Myra had consistently declared her innocence.

In the first few weeks of the New Year 1987, Myra's 'confession' was in the wind. She had been seeing Peter Timms and I knew from conversations with him, years later, that it was during those sessions that Myra had confessed to her involvement in the murders. David Astor arranged for Myra's various advisors to meet the lawyer to the rich, Lord Goodman, to ask his advice. Should she confess? Lord Goodman said she should. And so it was that Myra Hindley admitted to her role in the abduction and murder of Pauline Reade and Keith Bennett.

On Thursday, 19 February, the first day of interviews with Peter Timms present, Myra spoke informally to Peter Topping, having been told that she was not under caution. Nothing that she said would be recorded in notes or on tape. On three subsequent days, 20, 23 and 24 February, Myra's confessions were taped. She compared the sessions to 'watching a malignant tumour being removed without anaesthetic, feeling the pain as you are watching it being done.' She commented to Topping that, 'I just hope that some day, in some way, I can be forgiven for making those families wait 22 years.'

Brady responded by saying, 'Liar! Hypocrisy. They would have had to wait forever, had I not confessed and re-opened the case.'

On later reflection, Topping was quite cynical about Myra's motivation. She was looking to be released one day. She said how much Mrs Johnson's letter had moved her, but Topping commented that she had had plenty of opportunities to put the parents out of their misery. Topping believed Myra's account of the abductions, but was sceptical of her role in the murders themselves. She always put herself somewhere else when the killings took place.

Myra visited the moors for the second time on 24 March 1987, having already given her version of her role in the murders of Pauline and Keith. She spent most of the time walking in the Shiny Brook area. Her confession was made public in April 1987, after her second visit to the moors. This visit escaped the media's attention. Journalists learned of it two days after the event. Even Myra's solicitor, who had been with her during the first visit, knew nothing of it.

The day before the visit, Myra had been smuggled into a flat at the Greater Manchester Police Training School in Prestwick.

Ann West said that she would try to raise the money to brief a barrister to prosecute Myra Hindley for murder in a new trial. Myra said that she felt

that she had been on trial for twenty years anyway. Lord Longford
described the release of Myra's new revelations of her guilt as 'a very
brave and fine statement that I would expect from Myra.'

Maureen's husband, Bill Scott, stopped his visits with his daughter
Sharon to Cookham Wood after Myra's admission of guilt. The Home
Office withdrew Peter Timms' right to visit Myra freely and counsel her.
Speaking about Myra's confession, Peter Timms said, 'I can't say I admire
her . . . but I respect her courage.' He was convinced of the truth of her
version of events. Ian Brady said to me that, 'documentary proof in my
autobiography will crucify Timms. Myra found her "confession" about
Lesley Ann Downey's death the most distressing because it was harder to
explain away.'

Peter Topping spent more time in interviews with Ian Brady than he
did with Myra. One session on 1 May 1987 lasted five hours. Yet
Brady told him hardly anything of significance. Topping admitted as
much. Brady offered to confess, provided he was given one final
human week – 'a last week of pleasure' – during which he could watch
videos, eat meals, drink alcohol, all of his own choosing and then be
given the means to kill himself at the end of it. Naturally, these
conditions were impossible to meet. Years after he retired, Peter Topping
reflected on his relations with Ian Brady at this time: 'He was always
asking the impossible. He knew he could not have it, but he's a control
freak.'

Topping reflected that Brady was reluctant to confess because it could
result in another trial and his possible return to prison. By contrast, Myra
Hindley probably welcomed the prospect of a new trial to show that she was
not an evil monster. Ian Brady told me that Myra only gave Topping a
'confession' – false as it was – because 'she thought I had told the police
everything.'

Brady was in the depths of a fugue for the whole period Topping had
contact with him: 'I couldn't remember much during the fugue. Topping
never suspected this. I fed him with fragments of information – song and
film titles and so on – that would find their way back to Myra and give her
the impression that I had divulged more than I had.'

Throughout the years I knew him, Ian Brady often spoke about suicide:
'Ideally, I'd prefer what I call the double entry bookkeeping method – a
bullet through the head seconds after swallowing potassium cyanide. I
wouldn't want to bungle the suicide and survive it to be an invalid, at the
mercy of these bastard screws.'

Brady had, of course, witnessed many suicides in prison. Several attempted suicides were 'just scratching their wrists – "wrist ticklers". There was a fearless South African doctor I liked who told me that you had to cut your wrists just below the pulse if you really wanted to die. If I decide to commit suicide I shall send my solicitors a letter a few days before, instructing them to stop an autopsy.' Brady went on: 'The screws and the doctors here think they have all the cards. But I have the ace – my instinctive relativism that nothing matters and that I don't have a life. The screws have their little lives – a mortgage, family, etc. They don't realise that when I decide it is time to go, I could simply go up to them and kill and take away their precious, cosy world.'

Ian Brady sometimes made veiled requests for me to smuggle potassium cyanide into him at Ashworth. In one letter after a visit when he had spoken to me about the subject, he wrote, 'Here's a "Thought for the day" – photographers use cyanide.' I raised the subject with Brady on my next visit. I commented to him that, quite apart from any other considerations, wouldn't I be an automatic suspect as likely accomplice? Brady's response was: 'I've worked out all implications, and dealt with them. I'm surprised you asked.'

Brady often quoted the opening sentence of Albert Camus' *The Myth of Sisyphus*: 'There is but one truly serious philosophical problem, and that is suicide.'

* * * * *

On 16 June 1987, the 23rd anniversary of Keith Bennett's death, Myra wrote an open letter to Ian, made public through the media: 'If you are withholding vital information, for God's sake help these poor families . . . for your own selfish and morbid gratification you don't ever want this whole ghastly nightmare to end. What difference can it make now to acknowledge those two crimes? We both know we will never be free.'

Ian Brady issued a statement through his solicitor, Benedict Birnberg: 'He has not received this letter and he does not wish to receive it. If the letter arrives he will instruct the hospital authorities to send it back unopened. He regards the whole thing as a publicity stunt.'

Peter Topping was interviewing Ian Brady in Newman Ward at Park Lane hospital on Wednesday, 1 July 1987, when he was called away to answer a telephone call. Pauline Reade's body had just been found. Topping returned to Brady and told him only that there had been a significant 'development'.

Pauline's body had been well preserved in the peat but was stiff and hard. It had to be immersed in a solution of polyethylene glycol before Dr Geoffrey Garrett could carry out a post-mortem. He later described all the circumstances and findings in detail in his book *Cause of Death*. Dr Garrett's examination confirms Ian Brady's account of the moments immediately before and after Pauline's death. She had died from a deep cut across the front of her throat. There were two cuts. The smaller one was Brady's first attempt.

After the discovery of the body, Brady issued a statement through Benedict Birnberg to say that he was willing to go to Saddleworth Moor with no conditions attached. As a result, Brady visited the moors with Topping and his men two days after the discovery of Pauline on 3 July 1987. Brady said that he would pinpoint Keith Bennett's gravesite but didn't want to witness the exhumation.

On the day, Brady seemed disorientated in the open spaces of the moors and couldn't locate Keith Bennett's grave. Topping was convinced that Ian Brady was devious enough to take a chief super-intendent on a fool's errand across Saddleworth Moor to check that the police hadn't got close to the grave. I asked Ian Brady whether Topping was justified in his suspicions. His reply was evasive: 'It was weird seeing the place again, all that space and vastness. Keith Bennett is buried three miles into the Moor from the A635. I put a boulder on his grave as a marker after we buried him. Myra knows this. She was a few feet away. I didn't indulge myself on the day, thinking about the luxury of walking on the moors I had loved so much when I was free. I knew I would be back in my matchbox within hours.'

Ian Brady wrote to the BBC on 4 August 1987 claiming that Topping wasn't interested in the five 'happenings' he had confessed to. The detective was furious. Brady told me, 'Topping was angry to lose the exclusive.'

Amos Reade, Pauline's father, identified her from clothing he was shown. An inquest was opened on 3 August 1987 at the Magistrates' Court, Oldham. The full inquest eventually took place eight months later, on April 12th 1988. Three days after the inquest, Pauline's brother Paul took out a private prosecution against Brady and Hindley. The Director of Public Prosecutions stopped it within hours.

Joan Reade was escorted from Springfield Mental Hospital in Manchester to attend Pauline's funeral on 7 August 1987 at Gorton cemetery. Among the many mourners were Winnie Johnson, Ann West,

Pat Kilbride and two of John Kilbride's brothers. I visited the cemetery and found Pauline's grave on my third visit. The inscription on her gravestone is: 'In Loving memory of PAULINE READE died 12th July 1963 Aged 16 years'. Myra Hindley suffered attacks by prisoners in the week leading up to the funeral.

Peter Topping called off the search for Keith Bennett on 24 August 1987 and broke the news to a heartbroken Winnie Johnson. In fact, it was not the end to Keith Bennett's story by any means; Ian Brady was taken for his second visit to the moors a few months later, just before Christmas 1987.

The discovery of Pauline's body, and her Christian burial, was a turning point in Joan Reade's recovery from the depths of depression. Mrs Reade later spoke about this period in her life: 'I was in hospital and I remember my husband saying that Pauline had been found. I had her shoes brought to me. A terrible feeling. Out of my mind I was, really. It was a dark world.

'Two nurses brought me home to the funeral. I remember everything about the funeral, everything. I remember following the coffin and the people putting flowers on, throwing flowers down. I remember putting the dust on Pauline and putting my flowers on.

'Well, as years went on, I was saying my prayers about it and it seemed to lift me like a cloud lifting off my shoulders. I began to feel more pleasant about it, although I never forgot her any day. Even now I think about her every day and the way she had to go. That's never to be forgotten.

'She's not suffering now. Nobody can hurt her now. I feel her that close now, you see. That seems to buck me up a lot. I feel her so close to me. But I miss her very much. I still do. She's my little girl.'

Peter Topping's answer to those who criticised him for reopening the case and the protracted search of the moors was, 'Look at Mrs Reade!'

Ann West wrote her first letter to Myra Hindley the day after Pauline's funeral. Winnie Johnson had written to Ian Brady but received no reply. He couldn't bring himself to read her letters knowing that her son's body was still undiscovered. Ann West had been writing to him since March 1987 about the possibility of a face-to-face meeting with her. Brady had replied to her letters, although he told me later that Mrs West wouldn't be allowed within a mile of Park Lane hospital.

Ann West's letter to Myra began, 'Many years ago my daughter begged you for her life.' Myra replied two months later. The letter was a detailed expression of remorse for the suffering she had inflicted on Ann West and the other relatives of her victims.

Ann West's reaction to Myra's reply was withering – 'Liar!' Peter Timms always made the point to my students that Myra's reply was hawked around newspaper offices in Fleet Street, to be sold to the highest bidder. The *Daily Mirror* published it on Monday, 12 October 1987. Ann West was quoted as saying that she had set a trap for Hindley and the murderess had fallen into it.

I mentioned to Brady the charge that the Moors victims were 'tortured'. He wrote in a letter of May 1994 saying that reporters simply dream up such tales to sell newspapers: 'They and authors all say the victims were "tortured", without heeding the fact that no such allegation was mentioned by the police or the Attorney General at the trial, and not a scrap of medical testimony even suggested such. Press and authors have invented "tortures" for thirty years to make their boring repetition more salacious – without thinking of the relatives who, again curiously, seem to wish it to be true; I suppose they wish it in order to make the authorities and public hate us all the more, but whether they, the relatives, actually believe it I've no idea. The media add insult to fiction by piously implying that, out of consideration for the relatives, they've held from publishing some of the more horrific details. A nice way of stimulating the prurient imagination of the public without having evidence to produce. That's show business.'

The Housing Department responsible for Hattersley eventually admitted defeat in its efforts to persuade tenants to live in 16 Wardle Brook Avenue for more than very brief periods. They took a decision to demolish the house on the day of Myra's first visit to the moors. In the autumn of 1987, number 16 was pulled down. Ian Brady had written to a correspondent: 'I expect you saw of the grotesque scenes on the news when No 16 was demolished because tenants wouldn't live in it. Previous occupants claimed to have heard ghosts screaming. Crowds descended on Wardle Brook Avenue. It was a last opportunity to pick up sinister souvenirs as crime memorabilia. Some people visited the site during the night.

'It was a bitterly cold day but my body became strangely very clammy. I felt tightness in my neck as though I was being strangled. It was frightening. I never want to see the place again. The demonic lives on. I'm convinced of it. Demons were in my head that day.'

On 12 November 1987, Topping visited the Home Office in London to seek permission for Ian Brady to revisit the moors for a second time and for Myra Hindley to be hypnotised and possibly recall important clues about the location of Keith Bennett's grave. The Home Office ruled out hypnosis for Myra, but agreed to Brady's second visit to Saddleworth Moor.

The question of hypnosis surfaced again in January 1995 and Brady issued a statement to the news agencies: 'Eight years ago, during the renewed Moor searches, I offered to take sodium pentothal – the truth drug. Hindley immediately copied by offering to be hypnotised, and has been using the gambit as a public relations exercise ever since. People of strong will cannot be hypnotised. Therefore she will control and exploit the whole theatrical event. However, drug-induced hypnotic trance is another matter, undermining the will and probing the sub-conscious. Therefore, if Myra Hindley genuinely wishes to confirm the truth already given by me, she will submit herself to a drug-induced hypnotic trance.'

Peter Topping arrived at Park Lane at 5 a.m. on 8 December 1987 to take Ian Brady to the moors for a second time. Brady refused to get out of bed initially but eventually left Park Lane at 7 a.m. with police officers. There were just a handful of officers with Brady and Topping on the moors. They spent nine hours in Shiny Brook but found nothing.

On his return to Park Lane, Ian Brady sat down to write a letter to Alan West explaining that he had been able to rectify a big mistake he made on the first visit. Brady knew 'without doubt' that the gully and the area they were searching were there. Brady told Alan West that he was deflated when Topping said that the weather was too 'inclement' and that no further search was planned.

Early in the New Year, on 14 January 1988, the Director of Public Prosecutions, Allan Green, announced that it was not in the public interest to put Ian Brady and Myra Hindley on trial for the murders of Pauline Reade and Keith Bennett. However, the Greater Manchester police were considering charging Myra for the murders fifteen years later, just before her death in November 2002.

In a television documentary about Myra Hindley, broadcast in 2003, Keith's mother Winnie Johnson is shown movingly fighting back tears as she spoke about her visits to Saddleworth Moor to be closer to her son's undiscovered body. She said that she took flowers up to Saddleworth every Christmas and Easter, as well as on Keith's birthday and the anniversary of his death. She added that she felt on top of the world when she was there, while still longing to have him back home.

* * * * *

In January 1988, Myra's council, Mr Edward Fitzgerald QC, echoed the sentiments of Lord Longford and David Astor that Myra's was the only case in which a 'secondary party' to murder was given natural life.

Journalist Jean Ritchie's book *Myra Hindley – Inside the Mind of a Murderess* was serialised in the February 1988 editions of the *Sun*. Ritchie acted as the ghostwriter for Topping's book on the Moors Murders a year later.

Topping's book was published in 1989 as *Topping – The Autobiography Of The Police Chief In The Moors Murder Case*. Jean Ritchie, in her own book, *Myra Hindley*, comments that, 'The documents in Peter Topping's possession are undoubtedly the truth . . . The confessions will reveal . . . that she did not take part in killing any of the victims.'

In 1990 I asked Peter Timms to join in seminars with my sixth-form students on the subjects of evil and crime. As a Methodist minister, the issue of forgiveness was never far away from Peter. He became a regular visitor just before Christmas in the years that followed. The sessions with the students were often heated and Peter absorbed a great deal of flak for being a spiritual guide to Myra Hindley. In the sessions, Peter never said that Myra should be released – only that she should be considered for parole under the same terms that were applied to all life-sentence prisoners. Myra was a different woman now, he would say. If nothing else, she looked different from the notorious photograph familiar to the students.

In 1991 Gordon Burn's novel *Alma Cogan* appeared, featuring Myra Hindley's familiar security photograph on the cover. Ian Brady commented that the photograph bore no relation to the contents of the book: 'It was a purely cynical device to sell copies of the novel. The use of the picture on the cover was totally irrelevant and gratuitous.'

In the same year that *Alma Cogan* was published, David Astor and Peter Timms released a set of photographs of Myra Hindley as she was at the time, in 1991 and therefore 25 years after the trial. Peter gave me a set of the slides. She was pictured in her Open University graduation gown and also receiving her degree certificate in the chapel at Cookham Wood prison. Another photograph showed her playing with dogs in the prison grounds.

When the photographs were released, Peter Timms was questioned about the asking price for them. The tabloid newspapers were willing to pay thousands for a current photograph of Myra in prison. Peter said that there was no charge. He was happy enough for the newspapers to see what Myra Hindley looked like 25 years on.

When Ann West saw Myra Hindley's graduation picture, she said that 'Hindley is wearing the cloak of Satan', while Paul Reade simply stated, 'Satan in satin is still Satan.' Myra's former solicitor Michael Fisher commented: 'She shouldn't have smiled for the camera ever.' He added that people would think that she felt the murders were 'fun' for her.

A few days after Hindley's graduation photographs were released, ITV's *Weekend Live* programme staged a studio confrontation between Peter Timms and a tabloid journalist to a backdrop of two large photographs of Myra as she was in 1965 and as she appeared in the newly released pictures. Afterwards, Peter needed police protection back to his hotel because of death threats.

Some time later, Ian Brady told me that Park Lane hospital wanted to take a photograph of him after Myra's new pictures were released. In prison, inmates are photographed at regular intervals to ensure that there is a recent likeness available in the event of a prisoner escaping. Brady told the authorities that he was in a hospital and not a prison. In any case, some patients had been in Park Lane for decades without being photographed: 'I told them that if they wanted a current photograph of me, ask the *Sun*.'

*   *   *   *   *

Colin Wilson entered Ian Brady's life in 1991. Wilson became famous overnight when his first book *The Outsider* received wide acclaim. That was in 1956, when Wilson was just 24. I mentioned earlier that Ian Brady introduced the book to Myra Hindley. Colin Wilson has written many books since *The Outsider* on a very wide range of subjects. I shall have more to say about him later. It's enough for now to say that an attractive, young blonde woman turned up on the doorstep of Wilson's home in Cornwall just after Easter 1990.

Christine Hart was writing an autobiography and wanted advice about using letters she had received from Brady. The Moors Murders fascinated her and she believed, in fact, that she might be Ian Brady's daughter. Ian Brady had heard on the grapevine that someone was writing a book about him and that Colin Wilson was in some way connected with it. Brady wrote to Wilson in November 1991, asking if there was any truth in the rumour. After the initial contact they wrote regularly to each other for ten years.

Colin Wilson, Christine Hart and Ian Brady were an unlikely threesome from the beginning, as time would tell.

CHAPTER TWENTY-TWO

THE CHARISMA OF CERTAINTY – FACE TO FACE WITH IAN BRADY

I read Ann West's book *For the Love of Lesley* when it appeared in 1989. I knew from other books that Mrs West's body and mind had been ravaged by her daughter's murder. Peter Timms always said a few words about Ann West when he debated with my students. He told them that he prayed for her, but knew that she probably wouldn't thank him for it. Ann and Alan West interrupted a Sunday service he was leading to protest about his support for Myra Hindley. Peter gave me a copy of the *Sunday Post*'s report about the demonstration that included a photograph taken by a press photographer who was on the spot to record the event.

I wrote to Ann West after seeing her in a studio debate broadcast to the Midlands region. She responded within a very short time and we arranged a date for her to come and take part in a few sessions with the students. I had a long-standing engagement to give a talk to the Manchester University Students' Buddhist Society on the subject of Zen. It was a fortnight before Mrs West's visit and I arranged to call at the Wests' home in Fallowfield on the same evening to give Alan West directions for finding the college in the labyrinth known as the Black Country.

A few students travelled with me north to Manchester and we were given a warm welcome as we walked into the living room to see Ann West sitting up in bed. A friend of the Wests had painted the large portrait of Lesley Ann on the wall above her mother. It was a house in the shadow of pain and loss. Ann West told us that she couldn't face visiting Lesley's grave because it had been desecrated by Hindley's supporters, who had sprayed 'Release Myra' on the gravestone. She also told us that Hindley had support from some students at the university. We chatted for a time with Mr and Mrs West before we left to attend the students' society and theorise about the Buddha's central teaching that all life is suffering and wonder how we can wake up from the dream.

Ann and Alan West travelled south on 13 February 1992 to talk with the students about Lesley Ann, Myra Hindley, suffering, forgiveness, loss and crime. It was a new experience for the students, to meet people directly affected by the misery and despair that the murder of a child brings. Half an hour after one session, three students came up to my room to tell me that they had walked out of their Sociology class. For the rest of the day at least, they couldn't take academic theories seriously.

I mentioned earlier that Ann West treasured a small bottle of freesia perfume that Lesley had bought for her on a holiday with the local church Sunday school to North Wales. Freesias meant the *presence* of Lesley Ann for Ann West. A student presented Mrs West with a bunch of freesias just before the end of the final session. Several of the students were visibly moved by Ann West's reaction.

The day after, some of them said that they appreciated Mrs West's frankness about her own weaknesses. For example, when she confronted Myra's mother outside number 16 Wardle Brook Avenue, as it was being emptied, she shouted, 'You brought a monster into the world!' She also admitted pulling clumps of hair from the head of Myra's sister Maureen, after barging into the Smiths' flat in Underwood Court.

When she was asked about the way her health had declined since the death of Lesley Ann, she said, 'Hindley doesn't know it, but she's keeping me alive. I've no intention of dying until I'm sure she's locked up forever. I want her to die before me and then I will die in peace. The tape of Lesley should be played every night to Hindley – let her live it over and over again.'

In fact, Ann West died before Myra Hindley. Aged 69, she died of liver cancer on 9 February 1999. In a television documentary after his wife's death, Alan West said, 'Ann's nightmare was that she could never close her eyes.' In her book, Ann West had confessed that she had resorted to hysterical attempts to keep her sons safe. Her son Tommy had turned 21 when she confronted him in a pub with his mates and asked why he hadn't called to tell her where he was.

Ann West died at home in Fallowfield, Manchester. She asked to be buried alongside her daughter. Before her death she said, 'I believe that I am going to be with my little girl – that after all this pain and torment we

IAN BRADY – THE UNTOLD STORY OF THE MOORS MURDERS

will finally be together again.' The location of their grave was not disclosed. Lesley Ann's body was exhumed because of the vandalism to her gravestone and buried in an undisclosed place. Alan West reflected: 'When you think of it, my Lesley's been buried three times.'

Tragically, after his mother's death, Lesley Ann's brother Tommy died on New Year's Eve 2001, in a fire at Alan West's home in Princess Road, Manchester. Tommy and his seven-year-old daughter Kimberley died, trying to escape from a fire that had been started by a 41-year-old female friend of the family. She had set fire to curtains in the early hours of New Year's Eve hoping to attract attention to herself by starting the fire and then 'heroically' saving the people sleeping in the house. Alan West himself was not in the house at the time. Tommy carried a nine-year-old boy to safety but became trapped inside the burning building when he went back for Kimberley. Caz Telfer was found guilty in September 2002 of two charges of manslaughter and two of arson. She was sentenced to eighteen years' imprisonment. I mentioned the incident to Ian Brady. He knew of it, but had no thoughts to offer.

*   *   *   *   *

In one of my conversations with Ann and Alan West, as I have already mentioned, they suggested that Ian Brady would probably respond if I wrote to him and put some of the students' questions about the case. At that stage, the idea had never entered my head. I accepted the received wisdom – that Ian Brady was a crazed and evil psychopath, lost in the depths of madness beyond the reach of the contained sanity that allows questions to be asked and sometimes answered. In any case, at students' requests, I had already made a couple of attempts to contact the super-sinners they were discussing.

I wrote to Peter Sutcliffe, the Yorkshire Ripper, and – having seen television programmes about his correspondents and visitors – I was relieved when his doctor replied to thank me for my letter and to regret that Sutcliffe didn't wish to enter into correspondence. I had no appetite for the tedious, gushing platitudes of Mr Sutcliffe.

I wrote to Myra Hindley herself after Peter Timms had taken part in seminars at our college. I explained that – with the experience and wisdom Peter brought to the case – we were trying to give a fair and sympathetic hearing to her predicament. After all, such an approach was virtually non-existent everywhere else. Despite the empathy for her cause, and the stamped addressed envelope, she never replied.

As trivial as it may seem, this points to one of the major differences between Myra Hindley and Ian Brady. Brady claimed that he replied to every letter, however briefly, unless they were blatantly exploitative or 'from journalists who were clearly on the make'. Myra's time in prison is peppered with allegations of how she stopped writing to and receiving visits from good friends. If this is true, as strange as it may seem, this would be completely alien to Ian Brady's character – he would not drop or ignore people he had contact with if he had no good reason to do so.

I'm sure that the book you are reading would have been a very different one if Myra Hindley had replied. In fact, it's unlikely that the book would have been written at all. But so it was, that on a February evening in 1992, I picked up a pen and wrote to ask Ian Brady why an intelligent and well-read man would commit such hideous crimes.

I gave my own ill-informed suspicions about his motives to students if they asked, but wasn't expecting the sheer scale of Brady's explanations that would emerge through my contact with him. From the beginning of his imprisonment, Ian Brady had become well aware of the mixed motives of those who wrote to him. As Brady observed, correspondents 'invariably rationalise their prurient intrusion in the name of science and the furtherance of human illumination.'

Brian Masters had been intrigued to learn from a newspaper article that the multiple killer Dennis Nilsen possessed the collected works of Shakespeare. How could the world of high culture have breathing space among the suffocating depravities of a serial murderer?

My first approach to Brady was, as I have said, at the suggestion of Ann and Alan West. Perhaps the students could become a little more informed about the story that had appeared by the week for decades in the newspapers read by their parents. Who knows? Maybe I could discover a few clues about the reasons for his murders, or even what actually happened. Nevertheless, I was aware of R. D. Hare's warning: 'A good psychopath can play a concerto on *anyone's* heartstrings'.

I learned later that, like Nilsen, Brady too possessed the single-volume complete works of Shakespeare. He eventually gave me the book. It was a present from Lord Longford – 'Frank' in the inscription written at Christmas 1973, when Ian Brady was in prison on the Isle of Wight. It is dedicated 'To a . . . lover of the Bard'. Brady would quote long obscure passages from it during my visits and had obviously read the book from cover to cover. We have already seen that, as a schoolboy Brady was bored to death by Sir Walter Scott's books but electrified by Shakespeare. Perhaps it was premonition.

The mature Ian Brady recognised, from first-hand experience, that Shakespeare had a profound understanding of what it was to commit murder. Brady admired even more Shakespeare's genius for mercilessly exposing, in sublime language, the mercenary motives and self-delusions human beings excrete through every pore of their bodies, often under the guise of benevolence and love.

Brady's reply to my first letter to him was dated 2 March 1992. He made a few responses to my questions and told me that the ball was in my court.

I expected him to be defensive. For a long time, he wrote in red ink and block capitals across the pages of his letters: 'Personal and Confidential' – 'Not For Publication'. This was standard practice until he felt he could trust the person receiving his letter. He had, of course, decades of experience in separating the wheat and the chaff. The most crass attempts to hoodwink him were from journalists using the headed notepaper of the hotel where they happened to be staying. Commenting on my own involvement with him, Brady once said; 'If you were a journalist you would be in a very favourable position.'

Brady had blanket contempt for journalists apart from a small number he wrote to from time to time. Brady usually wrote to the BBC to obtain publicity for particular issues he was concerned with. For several years, the BBC's crime correspondent, Peter Gould, had special responsibility for news connected with all aspects of the Moors Murders. Ian Brady had nothing but good things to say about Peter Gould: 'A rarity. A journalist with integrity.'

Ten years after his first letter to me, Ian Brady reflected on the people who write to high-profile murderers: 'Many of them simply want contact with imaginary danger or notoriety, from a distance and safely caged, of course. Lends romantic license, and the advantage of a captive recipient. They then actually become possessive, believing they should have a monopoly and resenting it when they discover the prisoner actually has contact with other people. They're suffering from the Schweitzer syndrome, dispensing charity and becoming disturbed when people of similar bent invade their territory, regarding such accepted intrusion as personal betrayal. Makes them bitter and vengeful. That type is best avoided. You have to be selective, choosing the balanced and intelligent. Only takes a couple of letters to distinguish which is which, usually. Most are harmless and disappear with the novelty eventually.'

Brady told me that he sometimes received requests for his signature that were transparently for good causes – however bizarre that may sound. He always obliged. He gave me an example of a letter from a man who was to be best man at his friend's wedding, and who wanted to give the bride and groom a book of signatures written by the famous and the infamous, and to raise money for charity in the process.

Looking through the letters we exchanged in the first two years, it's clear that Brady preferred to write about philosophical, religious, literary and psychological issues – four areas in which he was at ease. He had no interest in economic and financial concerns, but would occasionally make barbed comments about the passing and transient political scene. He was not interested in crime and rarely watched documentaries about murder cases: 'I've had enough of anything to do with crime. The programmes are a busman's holiday to me.'

My first letters to Ian Brady were written in the year of the serial killer as superstar – 1992. I sent him a copy of *The Silence of the Lambs* when it was released on video. Brady sent me his reflections: 'Lecter? He has largely been portrayed as an insane, cold, calculating monster. Most of the public will have missed, or misinterpreted, the less dramatic psychological factors – his small, silent wince of empathy as Clarice relates the story of the lambs; the lingering touch of fingers through bars; "people will say we're in love" quip, cynical banter hiding affection; the caring phone call at the end, simply to assure her that she is in no personal danger from him and that the world is a better place with her in it. These psychological triggers worked at a subconscious level in most of the public, hence the popularity of the film. But perhaps I'm being generous in not concluding they simply thirsted for other people's blood. What's your opinion?'

Ian Brady was 55 on 2 January 1993 and, in a letter to me that day, he commented on Anthony Hopkins' performance as Dr Lecter: 'I see Hopkins has received a knighthood. I wonder when my turn will come – for my contribution to the entertainment industry over the past thirty years?! Not to mention my services as national folk-devil and scapegoat.'

Brady asked me to try and obtain a video of *Reservoir Dogs* despite the fact that it hadn't been released at the time. One of my students presented me with a pirate copy within days. I found the scene where a policeman's ear is cut off difficult to watch, and told Brady so in a covering letter. He gave me his impressions of the film and once again commented on the serial killer phenomenon that was obsessing the media at the time. His reply conveys the style and atmosphere typical of his letters to me in the early years: 'Many thanks for your letter and *Reservoir Dogs*, which I enjoyed. The dialogue had a Dostoevskian air, that odd mixture of realism/violence/comedy/absurdity. Did you notice old-timer Lawrence Tierney (the bald leader) who, in the 1940s played *Dillinger* – only movie buffs would appreciate this line in RD, "Dead as Dillinger" . . .

'The torture scene in *Reservoir Dogs*? The American troops in Vietnam used to collect ears of the VC they killed. No horror was expressed at that, nor over the burning alive with napalm. You see how I am an instinctive moral/amoral relativist. Galley's massacre of the rape and killing of a whole village (over a hundred) with his troops in Vietnam only got him 4 years of house arrest. You see, you can't beat "respectable" people for wholesale slaughter and torture – with no remorse, as they had official permission – Dresden, Hiroshima, genocide of 2 million Biafrans with British arms and official backing to recapture British oil interests there . . . You see, it is all absurd! Serial killers? Mere amateurs who didn't ask permission; mix them with the socially-acceptable psychopaths of the SAS and you won't be able to tell the difference! . . . The subculture of violence in prisons is, again, mere child's play compared to the violence of the forces of "law and order" – people with permission to beat up or kill. With permission, there is no remorse or guilt, only rewards and honours.'

I knew that Brady had taken steps to check that I was what I said I was; a teacher in a sixth-form college. He told me that he would love the chance to teach students in that age group. In one letter, he asked me if I had any promising students who were, perhaps, lacking in motivation and incentive. He referred to the strictures that naturally govern a teacher and wrote; 'You are circumscribed by entrenched conservatism, but I am not . . . Who can tell how my address might accidentally fall into the hands of a questing student, one *dissatisfied with the extant structure of society*? A much more stimulating and inspired alternative to rotting on the dole.'

I made a point of *not* leaving his address lying around. Apart from any other considerations, I knew that he would probably relish letters from someone who knew me, which would give him the edge in the correspondence we exchanged. I don't think that this concerned him in later years, after some form of mutual trust had been well established. He told me once that people assumed that his world was hermetically sealed: 'They would have a heart attack if they knew the information I have about them. They think I'm safely contained and they're beyond my reach. The advantage of having had the exclusive company of criminals and madmen for decades – many now free – means I have a very unorthodox circle of friends.'

Whatever his suspicions in the early days, Brady always sent me a Christmas present and a card. His Christmas cards were those sold for the protection of wild birds. The wrapping paper was secondhand – scavenged over the years. Everything is precious in captivity.

*   *   *   *   *

Meanwhile, Myra Hindley remained in Cookham Wood prison, still hoping for release on parole some day. In the decade, 1990–2000, her life was lived on a roller coaster of ups and downs. The 'ups' were appeals for release on her behalf by herself, her friends and her solicitor; the downs were the decisions of a succession of home secretaries. Just before Myra was about to appeal to the European Court of Human Rights, Ian Brady issued a statement; 'If I revealed what really happened Myra would not get out in a hundred years.' In time, I realised that this was true. As far as the victims' relatives were concerned, Pauline Reade's mother, Joan, put the issue simply and clearly: 'She should never be set free. Our children are not free. They deserved to have lived in this world.'

Judges who issue mandatory life sentences usually advise the Home Secretary about the tariff period – the minimum time to be served in the light of all the evidence at the trial. The tariff is the term that must be served for retribution and deterrence. If the tariff is less than twenty years, the date for the first review is three years before the end of the tariff. If it is more than twenty years, the first review is seventeen years after the sentence.

Justice Fenton Atkinson, the judge at the Moors trial, sentenced Ian Brady and Myra Hindley to life imprisonment. He didn't give a tariff date for Myra, but wrote that she should be imprisoned 'for a very long time'. In March 1978, Lord Chief Justice Lord Widgery said that he couldn't decide on the precise number of years Hindley should serve. Brady issued a public statement: 'I accepted the weight of the crimes both Myra and I were convicted of justifies permanent imprisonment, regardless of expressed personal remorse and verifiable change.'

Four years later, in January 1982, the succeeding Lord Chief Justice, Lord Lane, recommended that Myra should serve a minimum of 25 years. In 1985, the then Home Secretary, Leon Brittan, increased this to 30 years.

A new Home Secretary, David Waddington, increased Myra's sentence in July 1990 to the rest of her natural life. She wasn't informed about this.

In 1992, four prisoners serving life sentences for murder challenged the Home Secretary's right to silence. The Court of Appeal ruled that the secretive system of assessing release dates was unlawful. The Home Secretary was legally bound to give a tariff date. Myra's solicitor, Andrew McCooey, submitted a ten-page letter to Home Secretary Michael Howard on 5 December 1994 asking for compassion and Myra's freedom after almost thirty years in prison.

Two days after the letter was sent, Michael Howard announced that life sentence prisoners with whole life tariffs would have their cases reviewed by ministers and not by the Parole Board. Before this new development, Myra Hindley had been told that a Parole Board review for her case would take place in August 1995. Michael Howard announced that this would still take place whatever decision he reached about her future under the new ruling.

On 16 December 1994, Myra Hindley was handed a letter by the prison governor, Mrs Chris Ellis, to say that she would never be released. Ian Brady was given a letter with the same tidings. On 24 January 1995, he sent a letter to Reuter's, the news agency, reacting to reports that Myra was 'upset' by the news that she would be locked up till she died, and ridiculing her hopes of release.

The Parole Board met in August 1995 to consider Myra's case as planned. They concluded that she was no longer a danger to society and should be released. Michael Howard didn't agree.

Around this time, a visiting prison counsellor at Cookham Wood, Joe Chapman, appeared in a documentary about Myra's campaign for freedom and had nothing but good things to say about her – 'You would like her if you met her' – he told viewers. Joe Chapman changed his tune in a later programme after Myra had dumped him following her move to Durham: 'I was hurt and disappointed. It was as though I didn't exist.'

Early in 1996, the student editors of the Oxford University Law Society's journal, *Verdict*, asked Myra Hindley to write an article for them. The students were looking for ways to increase their circulation and Myra was grateful for the chance to put her case for release. Peter Timms had spoken to Myra Hindley the night before he joined my lessons for the day in March 1996. He gave me a photocopy of Myra's *Verdict* contribution in her own handwriting. Myra Hindley and Nina Wilde had signed their names as joint authors. By this time I had started visiting Ian Brady. He had read a feature on the *Verdict* piece in the *Daily Mail* and mentioned it when he phoned me a few days after Peter Timms' visit to the college. I handed Brady a copy.

Ian Brady drafted a rejoinder to the *Verdict* article and Myra's long statement to the *Guardian*, published on 18 December 1995. He sent his letter to the news agencies the day before the mass murder of a number of children in their school in Dunblane, Scotland. After that event, the newspapers naturally had greater priorities than reporting Brady's statement. The *Daily Mail* eventually gave it a two-page coverage on 6 April 1996. Brady's letter concluded: 'The self-serving Stations of the Cross in Myra's confessions over the . . . years, took the following expedient shapes:

'(1) "I vaguely knew something, so I'll take the police to places which interested Ian."

'(2) "I confess I knew everything. But I saw nothing, heard nothing and did nothing."

'(3) "I confess I was evil, wicked and corrupt . . . but it was Ian, uncle Tom Cobbley and all, who were really to blame."

'In thirty years of imprisonment, I have never applied for parole and never shall. I will die in captivity. Myra is enmeshed in an unenviable "Catch 22" net, the warp of which progressively tightens each time she makes a public statement: (a) Until she tells the truth, she will never be released; (b) But if she tells the truth, she will never be released anyway.'

Two years before this was published, I asked Brady about his feelings for Myra twenty years after the split: 'I'm not even out to get her. I can still think affectionately about the old days. I still love her for the innocent good times we had together. As for what she has become – that is another person, one I feel nothing for and can demolish with objectivity and equanimity; a caricature of no importance.'

Ian Brady would take a harder line two years after his reply to Myra's *Verdict* article. In a letter to Home Secretary Jack Straw in 1997, Brady removed any ambiguity about his current feelings for Myra Hindley. She had stepped out of the compartment in Brady's life where he would have protected her: 'For twenty years I continued to ratify the cover I had given her at the trial whilst, in contrast, she systematically began to fabricate upon it to my detriment. Therefore, when I learned from the *Panorama* programme this week that she was now claiming I had threatened to kill her if she did not participate in the Moors Murders, I considered that the lowest lie of all. The fact that she continued to write several lengthy letters a week to me for seven years after we were imprisoned contradicts this cynical allegation. Perhaps her expedient demonomania now implies that I exercised an evil influence over her for seven years from my prison cell three hundred miles distant? In character she is essentially a chameleon, adopting whatever camouflage will suit and voicing whatever she believes the individual wishes to hear. The subliminal soft sell lured the innocent and naïve.'

I knew that Brady had a Smith Corona typewriter/word processor and in July 1993 he asked me to find him a script or italics printwheel, 'for literary purposes'. I would realise the significance of his request only later, but had my half-suspicions anyway.

*   *   *   *   *

In one of his earlier letters to me, Brady had said, 'Personally, I only open up to full throttle when face to face in privacy.' I took the hint and offered to visit him. My name was put through the Home Office computer to find out whether I was an undesirable. Brady said, 'Your name is already in their files as one who corresponds with me. I ran a check on you myself with the help of a retired member of the SAS.'

I have already described my first meeting with Ian Brady on a Sunday in March 1994. At the end of the visit, he made some parting comments before he left for his room: 'I don't feel mad – I just say what I think from my objective relative point of view. I would rather be "mad" if it means being different to the morons out there.

'People who live conventional, dull, boring lives are mad.'

From then on, I visited him every month in Newman Ward. Each ward on the site at Ashworth was named after a famous writer – Lawrence, Tennyson and Forster – and is effectively a separate island inside the perimeter high walls of Ashworth Hospital. I had studied Cardinal Newman's books at university and saw his picture on the entrance wall each time I was admitted into Newman Ward. It amused me to wonder what Cardinal Newman would have said about his picture finding its way into a ward named after him in a high-security hospital.

As I walked towards the interview room I often thought of the words of Newman's famous hymn, 'Lead, kindly light, amid the encircling gloom . . . The night is dark, and I am far from home'. Talking to Ian Brady about all the developments that had taken place since he and Myra were young lovers, I thought of Newman's words, 'To live is to change. To live long is to have changed much.'

For anyone unfamiliar with the practices of high-security hospitals, a few comments may help to set the scene and describe the procedures used to control the arrival of a visitor, such as myself, in the corridor of a secure ward. I parked the car and walked into the main entrance. After the routine procedure of booking in at the reception desk, I joined the other visitors waiting to be called. I was usually called first. Mr Brady didn't like to be kept waiting. All gifts for patients had to be transferred from plastic bags to brown paper hospital bags. Once called, a sliding door admitted me, alone, into a short sealed corridor fitted with cameras. I could see the outline of a figure, my escort, waiting for me behind the glass door at the other end. After a minute or so, the glass sliding door at the far end of the corridor opened and my escort walked with me to a very high steel fence. He unlocked the door and we walked into a large open area free of buildings.

It was a few minutes' walk from there to Ian Brady's ward across this surprisingly broad grassy expanse. I saw rabbits and families of ducks and tiny ducklings in that no-man's-land. Brady told me that he fed the ducks with rice crispies through his window in the early hours. Once the first heavy security door to the ward was unlocked, there was a yard or two before the final door.

Brady took care not to book a visit for me when what he called the 'shit shift' was on duty. He preferred to see me when there were nurses working on the ward with whom he could relate. He never referred to any of the staff as 'nurses', because he said they were all members of the POA – the Prison Officers Association. When talking to me about them, he called them 'screws' or 'warders' and regarded his own room as a 'cell'.

I was alone with Brady in the interview room unless an inmate called in to offer us cigarettes. Brady pointed out the psychopaths, paranoid schizoids and psychotics to me. Close daily contact with them made it relatively easy for him to differentiate between them. His life depended upon it: 'You have to watch your back with psychopaths. They may kill you to have something momentarily exciting to do, merely to break the boredom. The psychotics are the most interesting to me. Psychopaths are completely lacking in emotional depth and concern in all but self-interest. They lack any trace of humour, but can nevertheless simulate laughter and all the social graces. They are part of their simulated persona. An observer with experience can quickly discern the unsmiling eye, the hollow tone. They are usually beyond psychiatric treatment.'

Visiting hours were from 2 till 4 p.m., but they invariably went on much longer, sometimes till 8 p.m. if Brady's preferred shift was on duty. One winter, I left Brady's ward so late during the darkness that the hospital's public address system boomed, 'Who the hell's that!' as I walked with a large package in the open area towards the entrance.

I always gave Brady several packets of Gauloises, strong untipped French cigarettes, and a box of Carousel iced sweets: 'I like to feel the tar hit the back of my throat. Cigarettes made in Britain are all the same, whatever the brand. I want all the nicotine and tar there is! One of the advantages of knowing I'll die in captivity is that I don't fear cancer. Tipped cigarettes are for cowards. The French still care about cigarettes, wine and food. In other words, "life".'

I am looking at a letter from Ian Brady dated August 1994: 'Thank you for today's visit. Towards the end, after four hours of stimulating conversation, I was beginning to run down, having been working on the computer till 3 a.m. and not having eaten – I can go days without food.' During a normal visit he would show no signs of 'running down'. Quite the opposite. Since he had hardly spoken to anyone during the day, he let fly when he had the chance to speak openly. Everything came out. It was like standing at point-blank range in front of the barrel of a Centurion tank and being blasted non-stop for four or five hours. Another letter dated February 1995 begins, 'As usual, thank you for the visit, cigs, chocs. We talked non-stop for five hours, I realized later.'

Looking back on my years of contact with Brady, I never for one moment thought I was speaking with someone who was insane. I felt that he was incandescently evil sometimes, as his grey eyes penetrated the fog of French cigarette smoke. But not that he was mad. This is probably a reflection of my own ignorance of the forms insanity takes. The scales of insanity and evil are blood relations. They are both sliding scales. A few psychologists have suggested that many people are at some point on both scales.

While reading Antonio Melechi's book *Fugitive Minds*, in which he describes the 'frenetic highs of psychotic illness', I came across a passage that spoke directly to my experience of Ian Brady face to face and through his letters. Melechi was referring to the psychotic's absolute conviction, the ability to explain everything in terms of one overriding, unshakeable belief. The psychiatrist Anthony Storr calls this the 'charisma of certainty':

the state in which the psychotic finds confirmation of his beliefs in whatever he encounters. Earlier, I mentioned that Malcolm MacCulloch, Brady's psychiatrist for some years, described him as 'charismatic'. I do not think that MacCulloch had in mind the so-called 'creative illnesses' that charismatic spiritual leaders experienced.

After a visit I felt completely drained as I eased my car out of Ashworth's car park to face a journey home of 111 miles. Sometimes Brady's parting words were, 'You had better go back down on the motorway, or you'll miss Cilla Black on *Blind Date*.'

Once home I would usually walk to a pub and down a few lagers. On some occasions, when the Moors case was in the newspapers for some reason, people sitting next to me in the pub would be talking about Ian Brady. I smiled to myself and thought, 'It's okay to talk about him. I've just been battered by him for five hours.' I never gave into the temptation to point this out to the people chatting next to me, but did have to restrain myself from saying, 'You think he is bad. Look at the state I'm in!'

Brady was so well read and had such a lively, astute mind that you could never relax in discussions with him. He would put you on the spot and expect an immediate response. The question could be just about anything. Once he asked me if I had seen Gary Cooper's film *High Noon*. I said that I had seen it two or three times. Then came the question: 'Who sang the theme tune "Do Not Forsake Me, Oh My Darling" for the film?' I knew it was Tex Ritter and said so. 'Funny,' Brady said, 'people usually say Frankie Lane.'

Brady used my car keys to pry the stubs from his small cigarette holder. During a normal day he rolled his own cigarettes by mixing strong pipe tobacco with the moist tobacco from the French cigarettes. If there is a smell associated with the Moors Murderers, it is that of strong tobacco. Whenever I opened a letter or a book from Ian Brady – or even unpacked video machines and typewriters he gave me – they reeked of tobacco. I was always reminded of this whenever I saw the long-running television advert for strong pipe tobacco – 'It's that Condor moment'. The *Guardian* journalist Duncan Staff wrote that as he opened a bag containing Myra Hindley's broken typewriter, he was met with a blast of Golden Virginia.

Brady always gave me a gift on each visit – a book, a video or other items. He brought a large flask of black coffee into the interview room and we drank it slowly for the duration of the visit. He had scratched his name on the side of the flask and I came to know that he personalised all of his property in some way as a guard against theft in that small world he occupied. I saw the enduring traits of his meticulous planning even in the smallest of things. At the beginning of each visit he would bring in the usual nine items and check them against the nine-point list he had written out – 'cigs, book, spoon,' etc.

If he was already waiting in the room, it meant that he wanted me to do something for him. Sometimes Brady would try to dismantle the receiver on the wall phone in the interview room to check for bugging devices.

Ian Brady's mother visited him from time to time. She had become frail after a fall and Brady would only allow her to visit if she was transported by car from her home in Manchester to Ashworth Hospital. Brady found his mother's visits a strain. There were long silences. In Peggy's world, emptying the bin was an event.

I asked Brady if he would attend his mother's funeral. He said that Ashworth had considered the prospect some time before. He wouldn't attend. It would be a media circus. I could tell from the greetings cards Peggy sent to Brady that she still had strong affection for him. She usually sent him shirts and sweaters at Christmas time. Speaking to me of his mother on one occasion Brady said, 'Munificence in everything was part of her nature.'

Ian Brady told me that he woke up every morning with the thought that he was the Moors Murderer, enclosed and trapped by four walls: the walls of fellow inmates and screws; the hospital's boundary wall and the wall of the world at large. He was alone in his room for most of the day and avoided any significant or 'eclectic' conversations with staff or inmates. Apart from other reasons he said, each ward had a 'Conversations' book in which the nurses could enter details of things said to them or which they overheard. Brady suggested a new police caution: 'Anything you say will be taken down and sold to the *Mirror*, unless we receive a better offer from the *Sun*.'

Very few of the large staff at Ashworth saw Brady. If he suspected someone was visiting the ward to catch a glimpse of him, he made sure to stay in his room. Over the years, only one or two of the chief executives of the hospital caught even a passing glance of him.

Patients were taken in groups on trips to a seaside town occasionally. Naturally, Ian Brady was never given the pleasure. If he had to move within the grounds of the hospital – to the dentist, for example – he was always given a police escort. Brady would do almost anything to avoid appearing in need of the hospital's services. Periodically he sat on his glasses and gave them to me to have them repaired. I had to make excuses to opticians who wanted to know why the anonymous owner couldn't call in himself for a proper fitting.

I asked Ian Brady about many issues and incidents in the Moors case that puzzled me. Brady had obviously set up mental blocks to keep the realities of his crimes at bay, as I suggested before. He would often hand me detailed notes to answer questions in a letter or an earlier visit. These couldn't be read by someone in Ashworth as his outgoing letters could be. Even if these notes were read, the reader probably wouldn't be able to understand the abbreviations. I have made full use of these notes for this book. Some of the notes gave lists of his friends in his gang in the Gorbals, for example.

As I noted earlier, Brady was given doses of chloral hydrate at set times during the day: 'The medication would put a normal person to sleep in a very short time. It just makes me tolerant. I go without food to enhance its effects. It's like drinking alcohol on an empty stomach.' I grew to know when the calming effects of the chloral hydrate were wearing off and when he needed another dose. It was usually about two hours into a visit, at 4 p.m. Sometimes I would tell him that I had heard the bell for 'Meds' even though I hadn't. Within five minutes after taking it he was relaxed, in control of himself again after being in a rage about something – usually the Home Office, Myra Hindley or the prison system – and calm enough to indulge himself in his own particular brand of irony: 'I am fully rehabilitated. I'm a hundred times more dangerous. I would commit mass murder now.'

* * * * *

I visited Ashworth on Sunday afternoon 17 July 1994 and looked down the ward corridor to see Ian Brady already sitting waiting for me, flask at the ready. I knew something was in the offing. I walked into the room and noticed there was no brown paper hospital bag with his usual gift in it.

Halfway through the visit, Brady asked me if I had a safe at home. I said no. He stood up and looked up and down the corridor. He left the room for a few minutes and returned with a parcel inside a hospital bag. He wanted me to put the parcel in a bank vault as soon as possible. He told me to carry the bag through the hospital as though there was something light in it. The only comment he made about the parcel was that he didn't want it to be in his room if he was transferred elsewhere without warning. No one asked me what I was carrying as I left Ashworth.

The double-sealed parcel was addressed to Brady's solicitors in

London. I would take it to Brady's solicitors in Liverpool when he asked me to do so. From there, it would be sent to London by the secure internal legal delivery system. Brady had signed his name nine times under Sellotape, where he had secured the folds. I put the sealed package into the vault of my own bank in Stourbridge in the West Midlands on 21 July 1994. The receipt read: 'One sealed envelope – contents unknown to the bank.' Ian Brady rang me a day or so after the visit to ask if the parcel was secure in a bank vault.

I knew that the sealed parcel contained Ian Brady's autobiography, to be published on his instructions – probably after his death. The script printwheel he had asked me to send was used to type his soliloquies on the 'green vision' and the 'voice of death'. I was already familiar with the material that may have been in the parcel, through letters, telephone conversations and visits. As I mentioned earlier, passages in his letters to me may have been distillations of sections of his autobiography.

Selections from these letters and conversations have been used liberally in the first three-quarters of this book. Brady's incoming mail had always been censored. But in October 1996, patients in Ashworth were informed that all their outgoing letters would be opened and read before being sent. It was impossible from that time for Ian Brady to write anything of a confidential nature to me. However, he had been phoning me for some time and continued to do so after the new ruling about outgoing mail.

New wards had been built nearby on another of Ashworth's sites and Brady was transferred to one of them. The new wards were named after semi-precious stones and he was assigned to Jade, adjacent to Amber ward. He told me that 'Jade' was short for 'jaded'! I visited him for the first time in Jade in June 1995. A few of the tabloids, particularly the *Sunday Express*, had a field day over the change of location, with headlines screaming that Ian Brady was now to have a life of luxury. Some members of Ashworth's staff were quoted as saying that it would be much easier for Brady to escape from the new ward. Having been there many times, I found it difficult to imagine how anyone could get out without the help of a group of people armed and equipped with the means of overcoming the barriers of high walls, interior fenced areas and a series of locked doors.

I gave Ian Brady three large film posters for his new room – *Pulp Fiction*, *Reservoir Dogs* and the closing airport scene with Humphrey Bogart in *Casablanca*, as I mentioned in an earlier chapter. He had a small statue of the Buddha with its enigmatic smile; a surreal image of enlightenment in that room of all places. There was also a carved wooden figure of Don Quixote standing beside it – an ironic touch. In the eyes of many people, Ian Brady had been tilting at windmills for much of his time in captivity.

In Brady's new surroundings, a born-again Christian member of staff, who may have seen the Buddha statue, pushed his luck and asked Brady if he would like to join a Bible study group. Knowing Brady's thoughts on born-again Christians and the expletives that would follow, I said, 'Please don't tell me!' He replied, 'I'm going to tell you anyway. I asked the Bible study screw if he was familiar with the writings of Bonhoeffer, Teilhard de Chardin, Tolstoy, etc. He had never heard of them. I knew more about the subject than he did. I told him where to go.' I should add here that I have Ian Brady's own copy of the Bible and he had obviously read it – although he hasn't marked it with his pen in the way he did so with his other books.

Unprompted, Brady wrote out of the blue, in November 2001, to give me written permission to use his letters and notes if I wrote more books. In the following chapter I have allowed space for a little light relief by considering the tale of an aspiring author who did want to use Brady's letters. I have ignored, so far, virtually all of the many newspaper and magazine stories concerning Brady and Hindley since the trial. If I had mentioned them, this book would have been documented to death. For anyone unfamiliar with the genre, the next few pages describe one of the many side-shows that have helped to sell tabloid newspapers by the million.

CHAPTER TWENTY-THREE

THE DAUGHTER IAN BRADY
NEVER HAD

Colin Wilson received a visit late one evening from a young woman who was writing a book about her own life and her fascination with Ian Brady. She particularly wanted Wilson's advice about the copyright laws governing her use of letters from Brady. She could have found this information easily without travelling all the way to Cornwall. This was a bad omen of things to come.

Christine Hart had been brought up in children's homes and at one stage was told that her father was a notorious criminal. With no real grounds for thinking so, she became carried away by the fantasy that her father was Ian Brady. Apparently, after trying for years, she eventually received a reply from him. Was it possible that Ian Brady knew her mother nine months before Christine was born? Colin Wilson encouraged Christine Hart to write her story.

In the autumn of 1993 Brady mentioned to me that Christine Hart's book was about to be published. He said that it was being backed by £50,000 worth of promotion and would be the subject of a television documentary and serialisation. I was surprised that someone so astute as Brady should have believed so readily such an unlikely story.

He told me that despite what she said in published interviews and on television programmes, Christine Hart only visited him twice. One visit lasted just ten minutes.

Christine Hart had asked Ian Brady for a second visit to attract some publicity for her book and its flagging sales. The visit took place in January

1994. At 5 a.m. on the morning of Sunday, 12 June 1994, nurses woke Brady in his room on Jade Ward to tell him that the *Sunday Express* had run a front-page story accusing him of sexually assaulting Christine Hart in his room. The headlines were:

BRADY ABUSED ME IN JAIL SAYS HIS 'DAUGHTER'
My sex ordeal with Ian Brady
'We will be alone. Are you afraid I may bite you?'

I had read many sensational articles connected with the Moors case, but this was breaking new ground.

In response to an apparent attempt to sell the Hart story to the *Sunday Express*, through his solicitors, Brady submitted a writ for Malicious Falsehood against the newspaper.

In his statement to the press about Hart, Brady included the following points: 'In today's three-page allegations printed by the *Sunday Express* she now alleges that I "abused" her during the single visit I allowed her last January. A visit which took place in an interview room with a glass door and staff supervising outside, as the hospital staff will confirm. Next day Hart gave an interview to Manchester Radio; after that, she appeared on TV's Ann Diamond show. On both these occasions she expressed how much she had enjoyed the visit to me.'

In the months that followed, Christine Hart allegedly showered Ian Brady with letters and audiotapes asking to be forgiven for lying about him. Brady commented: 'She told me that she hadn't really profited from her lies because she had spent all of the money on therapy,' and he went on to be abusively critical about her motives and state of mind.

A hearing was set for 12 December 1994 in order to determine whether Ian Brady's writ should proceed to trial. Brady expected to be taken to appear in a court in Liverpool. Instead, a makeshift court was arranged within Ashworth Hospital itself to avoid the public disturbances that were still likely to happen thirty years after the Moors trial.

The court was presided over by Justice Michael Morland, the judge who had sentenced the young killers of the child, James Bulger, in Liverpool. Lawyers for the *Sunday Express* accepted that their story of the allegations by Christine Hart was false and maliciously published. Despite this admission, Justice Morland ruled that there was no remedy available to Ian Brady in English law. The case could not proceed to trial. Brady was given leave to take his case to the Court of Appeal.

One of the ironies in the Christine Hart pantomime resulted from an article by Professor David Canter accompanying the *Sunday Express*'s original story. In the article he speaks about the 'cold logic' of Ian Brady's criminal mind and that of other murderers: 'The only objective these men have is to use and exploit people for whatever ends they can.'

The newspaper admitted that the story of the allegations was maliciously published. Brady had no remedy in English law.

*   *   *   *   *

Ian Brady decided to write his own analysis of serial killing. Colin Wilson claims to have suggested the idea in his introduction to *The Gates of Janus*. At this early stage, Brady was insisting that the book would have to be published under a pseudonym. Wilson put him in touch with a publisher he knew and allowed events to take their course.

The publisher contacted Wilson to say that he had read a typescript by Brady on serial killers but didn't want to publish it. Wilson asked his friend to send him the typescript. Ian Brady flew into a rage – as only he can – when he discovered that Wilson had been sent the typescript without his permission.

Whatever else happened between Wilson and Brady, Wilson sat down in November 1995 to type a letter of several pages to Ian Brady, pointing out what was wrong with the typescript and how it could be improved.

In February 1996 Ian Brady asked me what he called an 'academic' question: 'If you were asked to do a foreword for a book by an anonymous criminal, what would be your reaction?' I said that I would be happy to read a manuscript and make a judgement. I suspected immediately that the manuscript was his own. I was becoming familiar with his convoluted ways and knew that he was a past master at hiding his little plans and true intentions from the Ashworth authorities.

In March 1996 Brady raised the question again and admitted that he was the author of the manuscript in question. He had a title: *The Gates of Janus*. Janus was the two-faced Roman god of doorways – beginnings and endings – from which, of course, we derive the word 'January'. Knowing Brady, I realised that the title was redolent with meanings. Brady's book would look in two opposite directions. He was a convicted murderer looking into the minds of serial killers and the minds of those tracking them down. The title could also be an allusion to the two sides of Brady's own personality.

The gates to the temple of Janus in the Roman Forum were closed in peacetime and open when Rome was at war. Perhaps Brady used the image to suggest that his gates were metaphorically open: he was doing battle with the 'sane and civilized' world. I asked Brady why he chose the title. He simply said, 'Partly the definition, partly the symbolic allusion.'

Brady wanted to use the pseudonym 'Nemo', Latin for 'nobody'. I commented that 'Nemo' was the pseudonym used by Mark Chapman – John Lennon's killer. I added that although I had written books on the philosophy of religion and Zen, in the publishing world of true crime I was myself a 'nobody'. Why not, I suggested, ask a 'somebody' – like Colin Wilson – to write the foreword or an introduction in some form? Brady's answer was an emphatic 'No!'

In the conversation that followed, I realised that his relationship with Colin Wilson was one that had never run smoothly. Brady said that Wilson was too well known: 'I keep him at a distance and have never allowed him to visit. He wanted to write a full scale book about me and the Moors Murders but I turned him down.' Brady suspected that Wilson had a book on the Moors Murders three-quarters written in the word processor.

Wilson sent copies of his books to Ian Brady and he passed many of them on to me. Consequently, I possess a shelf full of Colin Wilson's books all signed and dedicated: 'For Ian, warm regards, Colin'.

I visited Brady in April 1996. He told me that a draft of his book was secreted in a case containing a portable typewriter he wanted me to take out of the hospital that night. Brady stressed that my foreword should give no clues as to the real identity of the author. He had decided to use the pseudonym 'Francois Villon', a fifteenth-century criminal poet, instead of 'Nemo'.

For reasons that will become clear later, I also carried out his video recorder the same evening. On top of the pile was his usual monthly gift – on this occasion a commercial video of the controversial film *Natural Born Killers*. No one checked me as I staggered out of the hospital, burdened as I was with this world's goods. When they eventually realised that Brady had published a book, the Ashworth Hospital authorities sought an injunction to stop sales of the book in the United Kingdom.

Ian Brady wanted me to give him a couple of new books on the psychology of crime so that he could compare some of the received wisdom current in academic circles with what he had written from his own experience in prison. Secretively, he handed me the revised manuscript in late August 1997 to send on to his solicitor, Benedict Birnberg.

Even after suggesting a few potential publishers to Mr Birnberg, I realised that it would probably be a long time – if at all – before the book was published, and gave it little thought after that.

CHAPTER TWENTY-FOUR

THE DAYS GROW SHORT WHEN YOU REACH SEPTEMBER

Peter Timms sent a note asking if I would meet with him and David Astor for an informal conversation. As I mentioned earlier, David Astor had taken over Myra's cause from Lord Longford. Astor's mother was the famous Nancy Astor. He had inherited his family's newspaper, the *Observer*, in 1942 and edited it himself from 1948 to 1975. He once said that the *Observer* was 'trying to do the opposite of what Hitler would have done'. David Astor gained wide respect for the way he held on to his high, humane ideals throughout his time as editor.

Myra Hindley was still receiving 'pocket money' from David Astor on a regular basis. Some estimates put the amount as high as £250 every month. Ironically, when Astor's newspaper reported the Moors trial in 1966, it stated that the *Observer* found it easier to empathise with Jack the Ripper than with the Moors Murderers.

Peter Timms met me at London Euston and drove me, with his friendly female assistant, to David Astor's house in St John's Wood. My train was late and David Astor phoned Peter's mobile to say he had sandwiches ready and what was the delay? We arrived in St John's Wood eventually. Peter and David wanted to know if they could make a new case for the secondary role Myra played in the murders. Had Ian Brady said more about this than the remarks he made during the trial, remarks that were designed to exonerate her? I told them the good news and the bad news as far as I could see it.

In that context, my good news was that Ian Brady would completely dominate anyone in a relationship if they showed an atom of weakness. He would eat them for breakfast.

The bad news was that, if Brady is to be believed, the confessions Myra made to Peter Timms and then to Peter Topping bore little relation to the truth. Myra was just not the kind to be eaten for breakfast.

I added that Ian Brady had kept all of Myra's letters in which he claims 'she waxed lyrically and nostalgically' about the murders for years after the trial and before she broke off the relationship. Furthermore, Brady had written a long and detailed autobiography and, from time to time, threatened to publish it before his death. I knew that the contents of his autobiography would sink Myra without trace. Her single, major mistake was deviating over the years from the alibi he gave her at the trial.

David Astor appeared a little downcast when he heard about the autobiography. I told the two of them that I was not unsympathetic to their cause but I was sure they had bigger fish to fry. They admitted that the new evidence of the kind they were looking for would probably only be accepted in court if it was given by a qualified psychiatrist and not by a lay visitor to Ian Brady.

Before we left for Euston, Peter's assistant wanted us to call in on the local Oxfam shop to see what clothes the wealthy residents of St John's Wood gave to charity. Peter chose a book and his assistant bought something off the rail. In the car, on the way to the station, she said that David Astor was the salt of the earth. I was inclined to agree.

* * * * *

I can't remember the exact circumstances, but during May 1996 Ian Brady asked me to put a bet on a few horses for him. Brady was gambling on horses as a diversion from the daily tedium of life in Jade Ward, and as the weeks went by he asked me to do this more frequently. I knew nothing about gambling, but I had to learn the mysteries of horse racing quickly not to look a fool in the inner sanctum of the betting shop.

Brady would give me the name of the horse, but not the venue or the time of the race – details that are now required before the bet can be accepted. He couldn't accept that times had changed since his old betting days more than thirty years before. Consequently, I had to have a newspaper ready to make sense of the list of horses he was giving me over the telephone.

To compound the problem, Brady had no real sense of time and often gave me the horses a few minutes before the 'off'. When he wanted to bet on continental races, I had to try and find the names of the trainers, jockeys and 'the going' – the state of the course. I established telephone contacts all over the place.

Brady had a phenomenal memory for the horses he backed before prison. He remembered the jockeys, the trainers and the odds. Brady commented to me once that he was betting with the same income, in Ashworth, as he had thirty years before: £12 a week. He recalled the days when he used the betting shop near Millwards, a time when punters had to use a betting name. His was 'Gorgon'. I assumed that this was to give his bets a subtle connection with the Greek monster with serpents for hair. 'No,' he said, 'it was short for "Gorgonzola" – my favourite cheese.'

When Ian Brady hit a losing streak, he gave me some of his possessions to sell and offset his losses. These included typewriters and video recorders. He gave me his signet ring when one losing spell lasted for two weeks: 'Take it to a jeweller and sell it off for its scrap gold value.' I did not, in fact, sell any of these items. I thought that he might have given them to me in a temper and regret disposing of them when his luck improved.

By July 1996, I had realised that I could save myself a great deal of trouble by recording every call he made. I then had time to work out the names of the horses by listening more than once to his Scottish pronunciation. I did this daily for well over a year – and still have the tapes. In time, he spoke about things other than horses and would speak in code if he thought someone could be monitoring the call.

During one visit, Brady drew my attention to the white plastic Ashworth telephone cards he had bent and discarded in a small pile below the wall telephone. Sometimes he would ask me to phone a bet through in the interview room while he sat puffing away in a thick cloud of French cigarette smoke, shouting out the horses' names. The smoke in the room was usually as dense as fog on the Tyne and set the fire alarm off frequently. Brady said (expletives deleted), 'I'll wait till it's quiet in the early hours and smash that alarm in the ceiling with a broomstick.'

*　*　*　*　*

Ian Brady was feeling his mortality. He welcomed the final meeting with his oldest friend – Death. In July 1996, he reflected on the prospect: 'I think of death on a daily basis. Whether I die tomorrow or the next day means nothing to me. All my affairs are arranged; wills signed and witnessed, instructions re publication projects, public statements, etc., all in the hands of my solicitors. What remains of so-called life bores me, as you know. I'm 59 next January and don't give a shit about 60. The years are passing like months.'

Brady wrote this shortly after a visit during which he suddenly felt pain in his chest and heart. He thought he was having a heart attack. So did I. Was he about to die on me? The pains passed after a few minutes and he proceeded to chain-smoke his way through a blue packet of Gauloises as though nothing had happened. As far as he was concerned, nothing had. It wasn't fatal.

Ian Brady asked me to withdraw his autobiography from the bank vault in Stourbridge and send it to his solicitor, Benedict Birnberg, in London. I went to collect it from the bank and was kept waiting for some time while the assistant was away locating it. She eventually returned and told me that it must have been mislaid. It couldn't be found.

The possible consequences almost paralysed my brain. How could a major bank 'lose' a large parcel in a vault? How could I explain it to its owner, sitting in a small room in Liverpool, brooding that very minute over whether the precious manuscript had arrived safely with Mr Birnberg? I couldn't divulge the contents to the bank employee. I pleaded with her to keep searching. She called on the help of a senior manager and they both returned to the vault.

After an eternity, they returned with the manuscript, full of apologies. They would never know that, for a short time, they had a walk-on part as extras in the never-ending drama of the Moors Murders. I crossed the road from the bank to the post office and sent the sealed package by special delivery to Mr Birnberg right away. Two years later, in March 1998, for 'logistical reasons' Brady asked me to collect the autobiography from Mr Birnberg and deposit it in the vault of a London bank. He gave me a letter of authorisation, but changed his mind at the last minute.

In April 1992 Ian Brady gave me a brief description of the structure of his autobiography: 'It was conceived as two books; the first dealing with up to the age of sixteen, the second from there to the present. The whole comprises of at least six hundred pages, including maps, diagrams and unpublished photographs. I use a stream-of-consciousness style to capture ethos, psychology and philosophy most of the time. I had a lengthy struggle with the publishers, who wanted the two books in one volume. Eventually, I agreed, on condition that the two books be clearly defined within the one volume. I obtained written permission from the relatives of all the families involved, as only they had/have the right to decide whether the true story be told. None of the myriad of authors and playwrights which dealt with the case over the decades – using speculation and inventive sensationalism – bothered to do so. Some even published the working "disposal plan" – a single blueprint to avoid detection and capture. Yet I had to keep debating with myself whether to reveal the voluminous detail of the "master list", illustrating multi-methods for various crimes from robbery to murder, which, if emulated by other criminals, would practically guarantee they'd never be caught. As you know, it was only because of Smith that we were arrested.'

Brady's almost ceaseless private attack on the establishment ceased for a week or so after the death of Princess Diana in August 1997. Brady wrote to me a few days later: 'When the first reports of the Princess Di accident interrupted films in the early hours, stating she had only received injuries, I thought it cynically typical that such people get all the luck. Then, when I heard eventually that she had died, I felt sadness. She had, I recalled, always set herself apart from the English establishment and evinced none of its collective hypocrisy, and had at least tried to help the victimized and dispossessed very unfashionably. An unlikelier mourner of Royals could not be imagined.' Princess Diana visited Ashworth Hospital four years before her death, but saw nothing of the likes of Ian Brady. There are places where even princesses cannot go.

Brady cut his losses and gave up betting in November 1997. A few months before, to simplify life, I opened an account with William Hill, the bookmakers, and told Ian Brady to telephone Hill's directly, using my name and account number. He was a little surprised that I trusted him to do this: 'Don't you realise I could wipe you out financially?' I said, 'There's nothing to wipe out.' It never entered my head that he would take advantage.

As I observed earlier, and as paradoxical as it may sound, loyalty was a religion with Ian Brady. I never used the account, so no one at William Hill's was familiar with my voice. Brady told me once that when he phoned a bet through using my name, a young woman asked for the details and invariably addressed 'me' as 'mister'. Brady added, 'I always correct her and say, "It's 'doctor'."' I laughed to myself later. He regularly sent me lists of bets he had made and accounted for every penny.

Brady had read somewhere in a newspaper that anyone with an account with William Hill could send for a free pair of binoculars. I knew that he used binoculars all the time when he was out on trips with Myra. I claimed the free pair and handed them to him on my next visit. I never thought there was any sinister motive involved. I assumed that he wanted the binoculars to remind him of old times. I received them back when his property was delivered to me.

I once asked Brady why he stopped gambling. He replied very ironically: 'There's a dwarf on my shoulder giving me lousy tips. I have the Midas touch – everything I touch turns to lead – especially betting on horses.' His comment was an allusion to Nietzsche's famous book in which Zarathustra has a malign dwarf on his shoulder.

Over a very long period during which I was visiting Ian Brady, I was suffering from depression. No medication had any effect. Brady noticed my hand shaking on one occasion while I tried to drink a cup of his black coffee and I explained the trouble. At first, Brady said, 'It's "world sadness". We all get it at some time. That whirlpool going round and round, down and down, sinking lower and lower with no way out.' He went on to speak for a long time about his own long periods of depression, with the 'shakes' in prison. Brady made much more sense than all the doctors I had been referred to. He said that when he was in this state he used to give himself simple tasks to do and use self-contempt by saying to himself, 'Surely you can manage that!'

Brady had often spoken about the 'auto-hypnosis' techniques he had learned in order to cope. Sometimes he would ask me to stare intently at a spot on the interview room wall: to put all my attention into the spot. He suggested I put a small spot on my classroom wall and tell no one about it, explaining that if I stared at it when I felt in the depths, it would help.

I took up the suggestion. Brady said that if I carried out the exercise often enough, everything would fall away in my mind except the spot. After long explanations about the method, he said, 'I've just one more thing to say: whisky is quicker! Go down to the pub tonight and have a few Drambuies.'

The spot is probably still on the classroom wall. I realised much later that Brady's method resembled the Hindu practice of *tratak*: staring at a fixed object. This too is related to the method of meditation that focuses intensely at the spot – the *bindhu* – in the centre of a mandala. When the person's whole being is centred in the spot, the spot itself disappears – indicating liberation.

*   *   *   *   *

Ian Brady often found himself taking issue with the authorities in Ashworth. From October 1996, as I mentioned earlier, all patients' outgoing mail was opened before it left the hospital. Brady took up the matter with his solicitors, claiming that Ashworth's new censorship was in breach of the Mental Health Act. He sent me copies of letters that he had sent out to various groups known for their advocacy of prisoners' and mental patients' rights. On 30 November 1996, Brady sent me a copy of his application to the European Commission for Human Rights with the request to send it to the Commission if he died and the solicitors gave up.

On a lighter note, for some time, inmates at Ashworth had been allowed two cans of beer at Christmas. For Christmas 1996, the chief executive of the hospital, Mrs Miles, reduced it to one can. Brady sent her a greetings card with a skull on the front, inscribed 'Happy New Year for cutting the beer!' The title of the skull picture on the card was, 'I've got a bone to pick with you'.

Ian Brady's computer was seized on 17 April 1998. He had used it to write to MPs, solicitors, the House of Lords, the European Commission and the Home Secretary, Jack Straw, to complain about the conditions at Ashworth. An Ashworth employee said: 'Brady's devastated. It was the only thing that kept him going.' Ashworth Hospital later issued a statement that computers were taken away from all patients and not just Ian Brady.

Brady was eventually told that a nurse would sit in the interview room with him when he had visitors. He refused to accept visitors under these new conditions and asked me to write to Lord Longford, who was expecting to visit him for the first time in ten years.

Brady also asked me to visit him once more, a few weeks later in June, to discover just what the Ashworth authorities meant by a supervised visit. When I arrived at the hospital I was told that I wasn't on Brady's visitors' list. I left the usual bag of cigarettes at the reception desk and returned home.

A few days later I had a letter from Brady, commenting on the irony of the incident: 'I'm not surprised you're puzzled after being told you are not on my visiting list after visiting me for the past ten years . . . Thanks for the Gauloises left when you were turned away by the scum here after travelling so far.' Two years later he commented in a letter: 'I miss the long interesting talks we used to have. I speak to none of the staff here . . . Keep well.'

I wrote earlier about the authorisation letter I was to give to Benedict Birnberg for the collection of Ian Brady's autobiography. The letter was dated 20 March 1998, and apart from Brady's instructions about his autobiography, there were instructions to his solicitor to hand me a sealed brown envelope addressed to a woman whom I assumed to be one of Brady's visitors. I was to hand it secretly to Brady on the next visit.

From the wording in Brady's authorisation, I realised he had ceased to have contact with the woman in question. It was none of my business, so I didn't question Brady about it. On 28 June 1998, the mystery was solved. The *Sunday Express* published a three-page story about Ian Brady's plot to escape from Ashworth, based on the claims of a former visitor, Una Forsyth, a psychiatric nurse from Halifax, West Yorkshire.

The *Express* listed the many items Brady had allegedly asked Una Forsyth to obtain. These ranged from a hacksaw to a 25-foot rope and documents to conceal his true identity, if challenged. Forsyth was reported as saying that Brady may have seen her as his last chance. Brady told me that he was taking legal action about the allegations.

Ian Brady had occasionally fantasised about what he would do if he found himself alive and free after a nuclear attack on Britain. He went into great detail about the items he would need to survive, before heading north to the remote areas of Scotland. Never once did Brady mention any intentions to escape from Ashworth. On the contrary, he said time and again that he wanted to be carried out of Ashworth in a box. He had released several statements to that effect to the press over the years. Brady had no wish to be released or to escape.

During one of my visits, a 'warder' was sitting outside the interview room looking in. Brady commented that 'the hospital authorities obviously expected me to stroll to freedom through the outer brick wall of the visiting room, and over three security fences and a fifteen feet-deep dry moat.'

Ian Brady's legal action, pressing for a judicial review against the Ashworth authorities, alleging their breach of patients' rights, was still proceeding. In August 1998, Brady instructed his solicitor in Liverpool, Robin Makin, to appoint me as 'next friend' in the proceedings, to satisfy the rules of the court.

In November 1998, Ian Brady wrote to me about his computer, which had been confiscated six months earlier: 'I won't be getting it back. It has CD-ROM and Word Perfect. Over £1,400 value.

'If you are interested you will have to collect it. In return, after you have checked all is working properly, I would wish you to get me a 22ct

Gold Full Sovereign Coin pendant from Argos, catalogue No 234/3648, value £179.99, plus some Condor (strong tobacco), which you yourself can decide.'

I told Ian Brady that I was willing to help but didn't have the cash to buy the pendant and the tobacco.

Brady eventually asked me to collect his computer from the main store at Ashworth Hospital and – with a hammer – destroy the hard drive on the car park before leaving for home. I said I was happy to do this. In the event, my journey north to Liverpool was not necessary. Brady had disposed of his computer by other means. I didn't pursue the point.

Judge Peter Fallon delivered his report on Ashworth in 1999. Seven years earlier the Blom-Cooper inquiry described Ashworth as 'a brutalizing, stagnant, closed institution'. Judge Fallon recommended that the hospital should be closed down. His report described 'years of abuse, corruption and failure' and referred specifically to the availability of alcohol, drugs and child pornography on the wards. A girl of eight, the daughter of an ex-patient, allegedly visited the ward housing paedophiles. In July 2000 a House of Commons health select committee would recommend that the three high security hospitals – Ashworth, Broadmoor and Rampton – should be replaced by eight smaller regional centres.

After the Ashworth hospital ruled that all patients' outgoing mail would be opened and read, Brady invariably included a mercilessly worded paragraph on Ashworth in the knowledge that a hospital employee would have to read it. The following is typical: 'This is an admin which believes that "morals" are pictures painted on a wall, and "ethics" some form of foreign currency. "Scruples", they scratch when no one's looking.'

Meanwhile, events at Ashworth were to put Brady's complaints on a new footing. It was morning in Jade Ward on 30 September 1999. Brady gave me his account of what happened: 'I was sitting on my bed, door wide open, writing legal notes on the Channel 5 television programmes of 28th, 29th, 30th on my case.

'A crowd of warders dressed in riot gear – visored crash helmets, padded suits and plastic shields – rushed in, wrenched my arms up my back violently and held my head down to the floor. For over an hour I was dragged and bundled around in this position, stripped and searched, and wrenched to Lawrence Ward – made notorious in the Fallon Inquiry because half-a-dozen patients committed some trivial misdemeanours.

'My wrist was too severely bruised and swollen for X-rays to penetrate clearly for bone damage. A splint on it for 12 days, my hand was X-rayed another three times. A consultant said the bone is cracked and said it needed a plaster cast.

'On 30th September I ceased eating up to the present, taking only milkless, sugarless tea, over my treatment by the riot squad.'

Brady told me that he repeatedly told the riot warders, who were dragging him that he could walk – and was ignored.

At the judicial hearing held in the High Court Liverpool, on 10 March 2000, Justice Kay in his public summing up referred to 'an undisplaced crack fracture of Ian Brady's right arm'. The primary reason for the attack on Brady stemmed from the discovery of a bucket handle taped under a sink in the ward's laundry room. Later, the hospital provided more reasons. Ashworth's senior officials were concerned that Brady might be planning to commit suicide. In addition, security staff were worried that he was vulnerable to attack from outside the hospital grounds. Brady was in Jade Ward on the edge of the Ashworth complex, visible through a wire perimeter fence. A sniper on a nearby motorway bridge could take aim at Brady using a rifle with telescopic sights. Jade itself was thought to offer the potential for escape – or a break-in by an assailant.

As Brady states in his letter, he protested against the attack by beginning a hunger strike on the same day. From 29 October 1999, he was force-fed through a naso-gastric tube, an action that is apparently allowed under the Mental Health Act 1983. Brady described the process: 'Permanent tube up nose and down throat and chained to a slow motion machine that takes up to 11 hours 40 min. to force-feed – prisons do it in 15 minutes. Being kept under "observation" by two warders 24-hours a day (including sitting outside my open cell door at night to ensure I get next to no sleep and they get plenty of overtime).'

Brady added that it took three attempts and three X-rays to insert the tube. The first attempt went into his duodenal. Staff syringed freezing fluids straight from the fridge into his stomach. He has been wearing an overcoat ever since.

Ian Brady described his transfer to a new unit, created 'to store political embarrassments like myself': 'A mortuary. Therefore, my having spent my 15 years on mental illness wards here, as you know, the shallow mediocrities and penal rejects who now run this place, sycophantically decided that, to assist the Home Office protozoans in their plans, I would be attacked and dragged to the Personality Disorder Unit and thus re-classify me. It is more publicly acceptable to dump "personality disorder" patients, usually referred to as "violent psychopaths". (The fact that in

35 years I have never touched a prison official or prison warders, being ignored).'

Ian Brady's fear was not Death, his faithful friend. His real horror was growing old, feeble and sick, he said, and at the mercy of the 'screws'.

Brady told me that the riot squad warders had 'trashed' his room in Jade Ward for four hours after he was dragged to another ward. I eventually received what they had cleaned out of Brady's room when his property was delivered to my door some time later. I found newspapers and magazines in his property that, from their dates, had obviously been lying around in his room on Jade Ward on the day of his removal. They were frozen in time.

Each day, Brady marked the programmes that interested him. He had highlighted programmes to watch on Wednesday, 29 September 1999 in the *Daily Mail*'s magazine, *Weekend*. Brady had also marked the second part of Channel 5's television series on the Moors Murders. He had watched the first part the night before and was, in his words, 'attacked' the following morning. Newspapers and magazines had been scooped into a hospital bag shortly after Brady's transfer to the Personality Disorder unit in Lawrence Ward. The ward housed the most seriously disturbed psychopaths and was located in the most secure part of Ashworth's grounds, behind high walls.

Brady told me that his arms were black and blue and he couldn't write legibly for ten days after the attack. His clothes and toiletries were given to him some days later, but he found he no longer had his catalogue for ordering Christmas cards from the Royal Society for the Protection of Birds. In view of his uncertain future, he asked me to send him a supply of cards so that he could send them right away. For the first three of the eight months Brady spent on Lawrence Ward, he claimed, the only furniture he had was a bed. He was then given a chair but no table. He used a Samsonite briefcase on his knees as a desk. He commented to me: 'I would've been content, had they dumped me on an empty ward, with peace and quiet to think and contemplate.' The hospital eventually moved him to Forster Ward.

Three months into his hunger strike, on Boxing Day 1999, Brady collapsed and was taken to a hospital unit at Fazakerley amidst intense security. He was taken there again early in 2000 and gave me some idea of the security that still surrounded him: 'My 11th January trip to Fazakerley hospital for tests was even more zoological and absurd than the first. They trussed my hands together with one pair of handcuffs and attached me to the five-warder escort with a second pair. The van was then escorted by police cars and armed response vehicles, for the 20-minute trip. At Fazakerley another unbelievable army of armed police filled the courtyard and empty corridors. I've never seen such a farcical show of overkill in 35 years; a total waste of public funds designed exclusively to demonise Ashworth patients (the most cowed subnormals I've ever seen), fan public fears, dramatise Ashworth warders, all as wage lever devices, overtime and overmanning. This dump is a preventative detention political prison. All this for a 62-year-old weakened by a 4-month death-strike. They wouldn't even take the cuffs off during the medical tests. Back in the van, in disgust I slumped in my seat, eyes closed – and that's when they got the illegal photo (*Liverpool Echo* sold it to the *Daily Mirror* front-page), touched up to fit the Ashworth propaganda slant making me look fat . . . I'm six feet and 11 stone 7 lbs. They also falsely alleged I had made demands. I've made none, no requests, no negotiations.'

A judicial review of Ian Brady's right to die was set to be heard in Liverpool Crown Court on 28 February 2000. Under English law an adult who is competent – mentally capable – of understanding the consequences and assessing the factors involved, may refuse any treatment, including force-feeding. The House of Lords confirmed that artificial feeding is a form of medical treatment in the case of Tony Bland, a survivor of the Hillsborough stadium disaster.

In the event, Mr Justice Maurice Kay ruled that Ashworth's efforts to force-feed Ian Brady were 'reasonable'. I asked Brady how he felt about the verdict: 'I continue the death-strike despite the negative court decision re halting force-feeding.'

Brady's mother was quoted as saying that she was happy about the court's decision: 'I want him kept alive, but I was sad that he hasn't got what he wanted. It is difficult to talk him out of something once he has set his mind on it.' (I consider that this is yet another of the great under-statements of the Moors case.)

While Justice Kay was hearing Brady's application, BBC 2 television was preparing to broadcast a film in the *Modern Times* series on the Moors Murders. It was based on the contact the journalist Duncan Staff had with Myra Hindley and the 150 pages of letters she sent him. Duncan Staff wrote, 'She had received countless requests to tell her story and refused them all.' I thought this claim was a little far-fetched, since Myra had been doing little else than tell her story for years.

The fact is that Myra Hindley received visits from and corresponded with many people over the years, and eventually gave a detailed account of her version of the murders and her relationship with Ian Brady to Peter Timms and Peter Topping in 1987. The transcript of her 'confessions' was published in 1989, in Topping's book, as Duncan Staff acknowledged in the *Guardian* of 29 February 2000. Myra could not, of course, maintain the façade of total innocence with her visitors and correspondents after the Topping book was published. She did, however, enlarge upon the reasons for her involvement in the events she belatedly admitted to in her face-to-face and written contact with her friends both inside and outside the prison. Some of her reasons found their way into print. She has talked and written in detail about the way she was allegedly abused by Brady. This is a matter of public record.

Duncan Staff writes that Myra could not bring herself to talk about the murder of Lesley Ann Downey: 'I'm sorry, Duncan, I just can't deal with it.' This is a strange comment. Myra had spoken in detail about the child's death to Peter Topping years before. Ian Brady, of course, would say that there were two obvious reasons why she couldn't talk about it. Firstly, her participation in the final minutes of Lesley's life is preserved on tape. It was the one murder that she could not extract herself from. The second reason is even simpler, according to Brady: she murdered Lesley with her own hands. The truth about the Moors Murders was never going to come from the lips of Myra Hindley – not even on the BBC.

Soon after the programme was screened, the House of Lords endorsed the Home Secretary's ruling that Myra Hindley would die in prison. This meant that she had exhausted all of her possible appeal procedures in British courts. Undaunted, Myra lodged an appeal to the European Court of Human Rights. Her appeal was still awaiting a hearing when she died.

Before her appeal she had suffered a cerebral aneurysm – a swelling artery – a condition exacerbated by her forty-a-day smoking habit. She already suffered from angina, high blood pressure and the brittle bone disease osteoporosis. Before her operation for the aneurysm, Myra told her lawyers that she did not want to be kept alive artificially if she lapsed into a coma. She added that none of her organs were to be given for transplant after she died.

Myra was transferred to Highpoint, a Category C prison in Suffolk, called 'Hi-Di-Highpoint' by the cynics for its lax regime. She was given her own furnished room and was allowed to do some undemanding work. Myra cut off many of her contacts with the outside world after her aneurysm. She suffered a suspected stroke at Highpoint, and her mobility was curtailed when she broke a thigh in the prison's gym. The injury never fully healed and she walked with a stick.

The Human Rights Act came into force in the UK in October 2000. This act, and a favourable ruling in Strasbourg in another case, would pave the way for another mandatory lifer, Anthony Anderson, to challenge the Home Secretary's powers in the House of Lords in October 2002 – a month before Myra died.

*   *   *   *   *

On 30 September 2000, exactly one year after beginning his hunger strike, Brady made a new appeal to be allowed to starve himself to death. Following Brady's complaints about his treatment and the decision to force-feed him, Ashworth commissioned an independent review of their actions. Professor David Sines of South Bank University in London conducted the investigation He concluded that the hospital's decision to transfer Brady and feed him was a correct one. However, Professor Sines said that the way in which the move was organised was 'fundamentally flawed'. Senior managers failed to prepare Brady for their actions or take reasonable steps to secure his co-operation. He had never displayed any violence towards the hospital staff and might well have gone voluntarily. The report acknowledges that a psychiatrist called in by Brady's solicitors to give an independent assessment said he thought that their client was capable of making an informed and rational decision to refuse food.

Ashworth responded to one of Professor Sines' criticisms by saying that Brady had received no advance warning in order to avoid leaks to the media.

Ian Brady sent out his Christmas cards early, in October 2000. He feared that the doctors at Ashworth were about to medicate him forcibly with psychotropic drugs, 'in order to silence me and dislocate legal actions in progress.'

The well-known barrister Michael Mansfield QC was apparently preparing to defend Ian Brady's renewed attempt to obtain legal recognition for his right to starve himself to death when he was called away to defend the man charged with the murder of the television personality Jill Dando. In June 2001, Justice Jackson ruled against Ian Brady's petition. Brady commented: 'Unfortunately there is a legal requirement that before one can reach the higher, morally superior European Court of impartial judges, one must first waste time and energy on fruitless application to English courts and politically briefed judges.'

A month or so earlier, a senior official at Ashworth described Brady shuffling about the ward with a plastic tube protruding from his nose: 'I've never seen anyone more resigned to death,' the official said. 'Some of us wonder why we go to such lengths to keep him alive when he wants so badly to die.'

The population of the UK was required to complete a census form in June 2001. Ian Brady commented: 'Didn't bother to fill in the census form. An insult offering it, by bastards who know where I am and [that I] will die.'

Lord Longford died on 3 August 2001. Allegedly, he remembered Myra in death by leaving £500 to her solicitor, Andrew McCooey.

Before that, after years without contact, Ian Brady had sent Lord Longford a 90th birthday card out of the blue; characteristically marked, 'Private and Confidential'. Brady was angry when Longford couldn't resist telling the *Daily Mail* about it. Despite this, Brady told me he was sad to hear the news of Lord Longford's death. He returned to the Countess of Longford a set of oil paints that her husband had sent to him a few months before. (Brady wasn't allowed to use paint thinner in Ashworth.)

I mentioned to Brady the oft-repeated story that Lord Longford never brought the correct brand of cigarettes when he visited. Brady replied: 'He never brought any to visits in the 20 years I knew him as he was a non-smoker. It didn't bother me. He was a kind person but he had his faults like everyone else. Someone worth knowing and who contributed to the world in general. A person to be missed.'

* * * * *

In September 2000 Ian Brady had reminded me about his manuscript of *The Gates of Janus*, and wrote; 'I no longer care about the pseudonym now that I'm finished.' For a long time I hadn't given a thought to what Brady used to call the 'project'. Ian suggested I write to Adam Parfrey at Feral House, the Los Angeles publisher that had scheduled to release the book in August 2001. Feral House specialise in 'exploring sociological extremes'. Adam Parfrey replied within a matter of days to say that he had put my foreword in the book because it presented a different view from that given in Colin Wilson's introduction.

The Gates of Janus was subtitled 'Serial Killing and its Analysis' and was essentially a hunting manual for the tracking down of the serial killer by the use of psychological profiling and the study of his after-image at the scene of the murder. When Brady and I were discussing his book, he said that he could have written a sequel to it: 'I could have written a second book on how to hinder and obfuscate detection, by use of proactive methods, exploitation of initiative, etc., but no socially conscious agency would publish the subversive sort of diversion, distraction and confusion. Objectively, opposition would be academic, since publication of scientific and pursuit techniques can be read by both sides anyway.'

I responded by asking whether the cultivation of forensic mystique deters more than it instructs. Brady replied, 'Probably only the arm-chair criminals – and who isn't? In any case, it is inevitable that most scientific advances can be turned judo-wise, to advantage against the creator.'

In the first part of *The Gates of Janus* Brady expounds his own personal philosophy and describes in detail what he means by relativism. The second part illustrates his approach to profiling through a study of eleven serial killers. Brady wrote his book primarily for a US readership. The killers he discusses are American – apart from two English cases: Graham Young, the poisoner, and Peter Sutcliffe, the Yorkshire Ripper. Ian Brady had met both of them in prison, as we have seen.

On Saturday, 18 August 2001, the *Daily Mail* printed an article by Colin Wilson on *The Gates of Janus*. It went out under the title: 'WHY I HELPED THIS MOST HATED MAN'. If Colin Wilson thought up this headline himself, he shouldn't have been surprised by the reaction it would evoke from Ian Brady. Wilson writes: 'Now, out of this bizarre friendship – for that is what it has become – has come a project which looks as if it is going to create a great deal of trouble for both of us.'

Brady was incandescent with anger as he read Wilson's article, which went on to state: 'This book shows Ian Brady could become a first-rate criminal profiler. That's why I believe my original hunch that he might turn out to be a real-life Hannibal Lecter, applying his expertise and insight to understanding the criminal mind, proved sound to me.'

The Gates of Janus was published in the USA, but Ashworth Hospital succeeded in a temporary court order banning its sale in the UK. There is, of course, no UK law forbidding a prisoner from writing a book. Ashworth's case was based on the grounds that the book could breach rules about patient confidentiality. Brady himself had made it clear from the beginning that he didn't want to make a penny from the book himself. What profits there were would be given to his mother, Peggy, now old and frail and almost blind. When she died on 10 February 2003, Brady ordered all profits from the book to be divided between the People's Dispensary for Sick Animals and The Royal Society for the Protection of Birds.

Colin Wilson sent the manuscript of *The Gates of Janus*, together with his own introduction, to Ashworth, so that the hospital could judge whether its rules had been broken. Within a short time, Ashworth admitted that there was nothing in the book to justify their claim for a ban and the court order was withdrawn, allowing Brady's book to be sold in the UK.

The book's publication aroused vociferous criticism from all quarters, particularly from the tabloid press and relatives of the Moors Murderers' victims. The Home Office announced a review of the law governing the rights of criminals to write following the outcry. Adam Parfrey responded by saying the decision to publish *The Gates of Janus* was not simply a commercial one: 'What is the best way to deal with the horror of Ian Brady's crimes? By consuming tabloid exploitation? Or by examining the crimes more clinically and realistically?

'People misunderstand that publishing a book that sells a couple of thousand copies [and] seriously analysing the behaviour of criminals is not the same as promoting it. The tabloids themselves that sell hundreds of thousands of copies featuring the most negligible stories of Ian Brady are the ones cynically profiting off his crimes.'

Parfrey did admit, however, that it was the British tabloid press which had aroused his interest in Brady: 'I started wondering how this guy provoked forty years of continual, obsessive coverage that uses the kind of language reserved for enemies in holy wars.' One American reviewer wondered whether, 'Brady is toying with us from his living grave at Ashworth, trying to whet the public's appetite for his life story, to be published on his death.' Several reviewers could make little sense of Peter Sotos' 'Afterword' to the book. Neither could I. One reviewer described Sotos' contribution as 'simply appalling'.

Surely Colin Wilson was naïve if he didn't expect a sharp reaction from Ian Brady after describing him as a 'loner' three times in his introduction to the book. As I observed earlier, Brady saw nothing sinister in anyone being described as a 'loner', but after ten years' correspondence, Wilson should have learned that Brady rejected such a facile classification of himself.

Further, it seems to my analysis that Wilson likes to classify. The well-worn categories appear again and again: the outsider; the rebel; the loner; the self-esteem killer, and so on. In his introduction, Wilson uses the term 'king rat' to describe Brady. He argues that 5% of the members of any group are dominant, whether they are animals, birds fishes or humans. According to Wilson, Brady was in good company: the Napoleons, Hitlers, Beethovens and Wagners were all 'king rats'.

As soon as I read Wilson's introduction, I knew what Brady would feel about yet another of Wilson's facile ragbag of a category in which to put the world and his wife. Wilson suffers from what Wittgenstein called 'a craving for generality'. To classify Ian Brady as a 'self-esteem' killer hardly approaches the complexities of the Moors Murders.

Colin Wilson wrote another article on Ian Brady, published by the *Sunday Times* on 25 November 2001. The headline on this occasion was: 'MY FRIEND IAN BRADY HAS SOMETHING TO TELL YOU'. Ian Brady told me that he had ditched Wilson by the time this article was written: 'Wilson's introduction is what I expected, simply repetition of uninformed rubbish he wrote 20 years ago before we began corresponding – easier than writing the truth; he only wanted to make money and publicity. I stopped communicating with him last September when the spineless bastard co-operated with this criminal regime by giving them a copy of my manuscript (which he shouldn't have had) and his introduction . . . I might as well have written to him in invisible ink . . . Most of Wilson's books are repetitive slabs lifted intact from earlier ones, so I knew his introduction would be the same, ignoring 10 years of correspondence.'

Colin Wilson didn't help his own case, in the article, by stating that Pauline Reade had been strangled. As we have seen, it is a matter of public record that strangulation was not the cause of Pauline's death – her throat was cut.

Any reader of *The Gates of Janus* can see that there were obviously tensions between Colin Wilson and Ian Brady. In the book, Brady devotes a few very critical paragraphs to Wilson, commenting that Wilson is deficient in his grasp of the multi-dimensional psychic factors at work in any given individual's motivations and actions.

Colin Wilson doesn't respond to Brady's criticisms in his introduction to *The Gates of Janus*. Brady was so furious with Wilson that he asked me not to mention him by name in any of my future letters. In his auto-biography, *Dreaming to Some Purpose*, published in 2004, Colin Wilson refers to Brady's break with him and comments that he was not too concerned about the split because they had exhausted all they had to say to each other. Wilson does add, however, that *The Gates of Janus* is a unique document, despite its being obsessive, paranoid, and wrong-headed.

* * * * *

There was a renewed interest in the search for Keith Bennett's gravesite during 2001. Keith's brother, Alan Bennett, had been digging on Saddleworth at weekends for some years. Duncan Staff, a reporter for the *Guardian*, had been asked to approach Myra Hindley by Alan Bennett and Professor John Hunter, a leading forensic archaeologist and founder of the Forensic Search Advisory Group. Professor Hunter's team took over 11,000 readings on Saddleworth Moor and studied aerial photographs. The moorland peat changes constantly with banks and gullies shifting up to 60ft in the last forty years.

Duncan Staff sent Ordnance Survey maps to Myra Hindley, which were hand-delivered by an intermediary. Myra responded by sending Staff a map with arrows showing the final journey Keith made with his killers. The arrows also mark Brady and Hindley's return journey and where they buried their spade. After talking with Ian Brady for years I knew how utterly misleading and futile such maps were, coming as they did from the hand of Myra Hindley. The gullibility of journalists can be almost touching at times, as I have discovered since my involvement with the Moors case.

The map was reproduced in the press in November 2001. Geoffrey Knupfer, a detective who worked with Peter Topping on the search which failed to find Keith, commented that Myra's map was of little consequence: 'We literally went down Hoe Grain and Shiny Brook and we excavated every single gully, concentrating on those where there was some peat exposed.'

I asked Ian Brady what he thought of Myra's new map, already knowing what the reply would be: 'Same old parole ploy and distancing strategy to suggest: (A) less than full knowledge and participation; (B) helpful co-operation. Totally irrelevant exercise in misinformation and misdirection.'

David Astor died early in December 2001 and Myra Hindley lost another of her most devoted friends, just four months after Lord Longford's death. Edward Fitzgerald QC, Longford's grandson-in-law, took on the battle to win over the sceptics from the two deceased campaigners for Myra's freedom. It was a thankless, impossible task.

On 28 May 2002, the European Court of Human Rights ruled against the rights of politicians to extend the tariff of serious criminals. The court ruled that when Jack Straw had been Home Secretary he had breached the human rights of Dennis Stafford, a convicted killer, by keeping him in prison longer than the Parole Board had recommended. Myra Hindley's supporters had their hopes raised yet again. Home Secretary David Blunkett reacted immediately, however, and vowed to 'do whatever is necessary' to ensure that the likes of Hindley would die behind bars. Ironically, a month before the European Court's decision, the play, *And All the Children Cried*, opened at the West Yorkshire Playhouse in Leeds. The two-women play tells of Myra and Gail, two child-killers waiting in prison for a meeting before the parole board. Some relatives of the Moors victims attacked the showing for prolonging their suffering and grief.

Brady wrote to me early in July 2002 in order to make me heir to his property. He was anxious that his possessions, held in the main store at Ashworth, would be pilfered and sold and wanted me to collect them as soon as possible. I would receive his 'cell' property after his death. In the event, Ashworth were happy to deliver all of the store property to my home address. Five large boxes arrived at my door in late July. As I have already mentioned, the contents were Brady's furniture, books, videos, tapes, numerous small personal items and a variety of papers.

I was surprised to find a number of compact discs among the items and asked Ian Brady if he had a CD player. A true vinyl afficionado, he replied: 'No, I like to hear the scratches.'

* * * * *

Ian Brady's mother Peggy, by then 92 and virtually blind, was admitted into Manchester Royal Infirmary – close to her council home in Hathersage Road, Longsight – in September. She asked to see her son before she died. The request was put to Home Secretary David Blunkett and he sanctioned Brady's visit, under police guard, on 25 September. York House in Hathersage Road was closed to all normal visitors, while Brady sat for just over an hour at Peggy's bedside in October Ward before leaving her for the last time.

Although she was thought to be close to death at the time of Brady's visit, Peggy survived for another four months. She died on 10 February 2003. I asked Brady how he felt about her death. He replied: 'As she worked and was independent all her life, she would have found "hospital" and "care" worse than a prison. So she is now better off.'

CHAPTER TWENTY-FIVE

TO DENY OUR NOTHINGNESS

Throughout my hours of conversations with Ian Brady, and our years of correspondence, I became aware of a peculiar kind of spiritual schizophrenia in his life. I am not thinking of a clinical diagnosis of schizophrenia, the stock in trade of psychologists and psychiatrists. Brady told me that he had been classified as a schizophrenic in prison and the Liverpool secure hospital. I am not qualified to offer an opinion on Ian Brady's mental health from a purely medical point of view. Nevertheless, Brady wrote in *The Gates of Janus* that he could evaluate the integrity and calibre of a psychiatrist, 'usually within the first ten minutes of a discussion, and decide whether to persevere or dismiss him or her as mechanistic'.

I am thinking of something else entirely – a spiritual or philosophical schizophrenia. I shall attempt to describe this after a few pages of explanation.

In the opening pages of this book, I discussed briefly how Ian Brady's assumptions about the purposelessness of life were in harmony with the convictions of so many of modern-day philosophers and scientists. Brady called his view 'existential' or 'moral relativist'. Right and wrong are a matter of geography. There are no acts that are intrinsically good or evil. The locality decides the difference between the two. In *The Gates of Janus*, Brady writes: 'No act in itself has inherent qualities of good or evil that is not made so by the audience.'

The French atheist Albert Camus is remembered by many people for saying that life is absurd. One passage in Brady's copy of Camus' *The Rebel* has been heavily highlighted:

The sense of the absurd, when one first undertakes to deduce a rule of action from it, makes murder seem a matter of indifference, hence, permissible. If one believes in nothing, if nothing makes sense, if we can assert no value whatsoever, everything is permissible and nothing is important. There is no pro or con; the murderer is neither right nor wrong. One is free to stoke the crematory fires, or to give one's life to the care of lepers. Wickedness and virtue are just accident or whim.

In our conversations and his letters to me, Ian Brady invariably used images from the philosopher Friedrich Nietzsche to illustrate his own relativist standpoint, particularly from Nietzsche's classic *Thus Spake Zarathustra*. Before quoting Zarathustra, we could add that Brady has put himself in good philosophical company by marking another passage in *The Rebel*, where Camus quotes Nietzsche: 'The advantages of our times; nothing is true, everything is permitted.'

Zarathustra had spent ten years alone in the mountains before descending to the people in the valley – his 'down-going'. Brady loved to quote Nietzsche's intoxicating prose. Zarathustra embodies the 'Great Self-Contempt' – contempt for all man-made barriers. Zarathustra delivers his devastating message to the people. God is dead. The 'Ultimate man' will replace the 'ape' man has become. Zarathustra speaks:

Man is a rope, fastened between animal and Superman – a rope over an abyss.

I love those who do not know how to live except their lives be a down-going, for they are those who are going across.

I entreat you, my brothers, remain true to the earth, and do not believe those who speak to you of superterrestrial hopes! They are poisoners whether they know it or not.

Nietzsche, of course, saw himself as the prophet announcing the Death of God, a philosopher ahead of his time. He had seen the lighting: another generation would hear the thunder. Nietzsche allows Zarathustra to speak for him: 'They do not understand me: I am not the mouth for these ears.'

Nietzsche was certainly the mouth for the ears of Ian Brady. In letters to me in 1992, Brady makes it clear that he saw Nietzsche as the philosopher who spoke most radically to his own condition: 'I understood the principle instantly.' He writes: 'The Great Self-Contempt is the key to the realm of total possibility, as it leads to contempt for all manmade barriers and produces the paradox of the extraordinary becoming; of going down in order to rise above.

'The Great Self-Contempt is the wilderness to which the individual descends in order to rise above the mundane – in, if you like, a pagan sense, not that of Christ.'

Anyone who has corresponded at length with Ian Brady will be familiar with his use of the phrases 'the Great Self-Contempt' and the 'Great Down-going'. He devoted several introductory chapters of *The Gates of Janus* to describing in some detail his final reflections on his own brand of relativism, supported – he believed – by the writings of Nietzsche.

Life in itself is utterly without purpose, according to Brady; we can only give it a very transient purpose. We can be loyal to our immediate family and friends: 'We owe genuine loyalty only to our loved ones and close friends. It is to whom we give our word that matters, not the giving of it.'

Writing near to what he thought as the end of his life, Brady observed that his views had not changed on this fundamental point: 'At this moment I continue to value personal loyalty and friendship even more. The coining of golden rules is not always the prerogative of those with the gold.'

In a letter of May 1993, Brady commented: 'Trust and loyalty were a weakness, a vanity with me. I would trust certain people to prove they could trust me. But, when or if they broke the bond, I felt free to deal with them in any way I chose; no more rules, except destruction by their own methods.'

When I first heard these thoughts from Brady's lips, I reacted as anyone would, with a very obvious question. He and Myra Hindley had violated the 'microcosms' – Brady's term – of other people by murdering their loved ones. Shouldn't they seek revenge?

He responded immediately to my question and said, 'Of course!' If he had been a friend or close relative of any of the Moors victims, he would have done everything in his power to kill 'Brady and Hindley'. He believed that all the venom poured on himself and Myra Hindley was completely justified, if it came from the lips of the victims' loved ones.

Brady would add to this that even if vengeance were exacted, it would be ultimately nothing more than a passing gesture in a meaningless cosmos. Brady would say that we are all in prison. It's called the 'human condition'. André Malraux put it evocatively: 'The greatest mystery is not that we have been flung at random among the profusion of the earth and the galaxy of the stars, but that in this prison we can fashion images of ourselves sufficiently powerful to deny our nothingness.'

Ian Brady would regard his loyalty to his 'loved ones' as an image to deny his own nothingness, albeit in a very fleeting sense. His victims have a family and friends who have images of their own denial of a purposeless life and total life imprisonment for Brady and Hindley is central to their images. Given the choice, Brady would have preferred the executioner's rope.

I referred briefly in the introduction to the fact that many contemporary philosophers and scientists share Ian Brady's basic view that life is without any ultimate meaning. The pre-eminent scientist associated with the view that human beings are a product of their selfish genes is Richard Dawkins of Oxford University. I noted earlier that Dawkins regards questions about the purpose of life as 'silly'.

For Dawkins and his followers there are, in effect, the 'saved' and the 'lost' – to use the distinction drawn by old-time fundamentalist preachers. The 'lost' are those who do not accept that scientific truth is the only truth there is. The 'saved' are those who agree with Dawkins. After all these centuries, the theologians are the new 'lost'.

As Dawkins put it: 'Theologians don't do anything, don't affect anything, achieve anything, don't even mean anything.' One would have thought that a scientist, such as Dawkins, would have shown a more positive and naturalistic interest in an endangered species which is – apparently – about to become extinct, and whose demise he is actively promoting.

As a scientist, Dawkins would be aware of the life of Sir Isaac Newton, widely regarded as the greatest scientist of all time. Newton's *Principia* is also commonly regarded as the greatest scientific book ever written. Yet Newton himself apparently viewed his scientific studies only as amusing diversions. Throughout his life his main interest was in theology and related studies. His personal relationship with God was the most important thing for him. If he were alive today, however, and if some people had their way, he – like the professors of theology at Oxford – would be unemployable if he wanted a job that involved his main fascination.

In parallel, the influential American theologian, Paul Tillich, addressed what he believed to be the central question facing mankind at the end of the twentieth century. This was the threat of 'meaninglessness' in all aspects of life. Tillich grappled with this issue in many of his books, and particularly in *The Courage to Be* – being about the 'courage' to say 'yes' to life.

Both Tillich and Ian Brady described themselves as existentialists but had radically different ways of saying 'Yes' to existence. Brady's way led to murder and finally a longing for death in a universe that led only to chaos. By contrast, Paul Tillich wrote: 'Even in the despair about meaning being affirms itself through us. The act of accepting meaninglessness is itself a meaningful act. The vitality that can stand the abyss of meaninglessness is aware of a hidden meaning within the destruction of meaning.'

The closest Ian Brady came to the point Tillich is making is when he admitted that his own nihilistic view needed itself to have the illusion of meaning. In one letter to me he wrote: 'Evil, like its opposite, must be sustained by illusion, for it brings with it an understanding of the futility of life when all actions are permissible and equally meaningless. Emptied of forbidden desires, we still desire contrast, the illusion of meaning.' Paul Tillich's final book, *My Search for Absolutes*, is an intellectual biography and a distillation of his lifetime's quest for truths that transcend their cultural and local expressions.

Paul Tillich shared the conviction of the Danish philosopher Søren Kierkegaard, who wrote that we should 'relate ourselves relatively to the relative, and absolutely to the absolute'. As we have seen, many contemporary scientists believe the theologians searching for ultimate truth are on a wild goose chase and should devote themselves to something more worthwhile. They argue that we are products of our genes, selfish genes, and nothing more. All talk of purpose is fanciful.

I have included the following few paragraphs for those who have an interest in the contemporary theoretical issues that are part of the climate in which all talk of meaning, or purpose in life, are discussed. Today, the issues of reductionism and so-called postmodernism are of central concern for intellectuals in many fields. I have tried to show, in different ways, how vital the question of reductionism, in particular, is for our understanding of the worth of human life – or the lack of it – in the shadow of the motivations of Ian Brady and – to a lesser extent – Myra Hindley.

Brady thought that he and Hindley were straws in the wind that is blowing us into the Brave New World, one where there are no absolutes. For me, this prospect sounds like a diabolical nightmare.

There are several thinkers who could have been chosen as representatives of modern-day reductionism. But I shall stay with Richard Dawkins and Peter Atkins, since I have already made a few observations about them.

Thinkers, who deny that we are each directed by our genes, and that their self-perpetuation is the origin of even our altruistic acts, have challenged Dawkins and his militaristic tribe. One of them is the respected American writer James Hillman in his *The Force of Character*. Hillman refers to the selfish-gene theory and is very pertinent to the subject of my own discussion in all the chapters leading to the present one. Hillman denies that if you scratch an altruist, a hypocrite bleeds:

> That theory discounts generosity, conceiving it to be indirectly promoting the species' gene pool. It discounts our wish for the welfare of others, including the conservation of nature and the preservation of history. It makes self-sacrifice merely the selfish gene's manipulation in aid of its own survival. Psychopaths think this way too, which to my elderly mind means that the selfish gene theory, even while it promotes evolution, gives authoritative backing to the selfish individualism of psychopathy, and is, in effect, a psychopathic idea.

Felipe Fernández-Armesto, in his book, *So You Think You're Human?* argues that scientifically explicable morality is a contradiction in terms and that without a spiritual dimension our future will be 'post-human'.

Some philosophers have supported James Hillman's scientific criticisms of the evolutionary relativism and the bleak prophets of postmodernism. One of the most widely respected of these is the American philosopher, Ken Wilber. In *A Brief History of Everything*, Wilber writes:

> Everything is 'socially constructed' – this is the mantra of the extremist wing of postmodernism. They think that different cultural worldviews are entirely arbitrary, anchored in nothing but power or prejudice or some 'ism' or another.
>
> If the constructivist stance is taken too far, it defeats itself. It says, all worldviews are arbitrary, all truth is relative and merely culture-bound, there are no universal truths. But that stance itself claims to be universally true. It is claiming everybody's truth is relative except mine, because mine is absolutely and universally

true. I alone have the universal truth, and all you poor schmucks are relative and culture-bound.

This is the massive contradiction hidden in all extreme multi-cultural postmodern movements. And their absolute truth ends up being very ideological, very power-hungry, very elitist in the worst sense.

This extreme constructivism is really just a postmodern form of nihilism: there is no truth in the Kosmos, only those notions that men force on others. This nihilism looks into the face of the Kosmos and sees an unending hall of mirrors, which finally show it nothing but its own egoic nastiness reflected to infinity. And the hidden core of that nihilism is narcissism: truth is ignored and replaced with the ego of the theorist.

We can ignore the philosophical terms in these paragraphs and still see the essential point Ken Wilber is making. This passage is a very lucid criticism of the brand of relativism advocated by Ian Brady and his strange bedfellows in academic science and philosophy. It's a distillation of the kind of criticism I put to Brady over the years. The flaw in Brady's position – and those philosophers and scientists who unwittingly share it with him – is the fiction of the separate ego, 'egoic nastiness reflected to infinity', and his naïve view of religion.

It has to be said, of course, that the philosophers and scientists referred to would find Brady's actions utterly abhorrent.

With the philosopher Mary Midgley, Dawkins and Atkins are dealing with someone more of their own size. She cuts them down to a reasoned version of their actual height. In a series of books she carefully spells out how many scientists are simply blind to the huge philosophical pre-suppositions they make. The titles of her books speak for themselves: *Science as Salvation*; *Evolution as a Religion*; *Heart and Mind*; *Wisdom, Information and Wonder* and *Science and Poetry*, to mention just a few. At the time of writing, her latest book is *The Myths We Live By*, in which she discusses the ludicrous, damaging and extreme claims made by Dawkins, Atkins and their ilk concerning the omnicompetence of science, their megalomania or, as Ken Wilber would say, 'egoic nastiness reflected to infinity'. It is colonialism and imperialism all over again. But this time it is in the name of science.

With careful steps, Mary Midgley attempts to show that scientists, like everyone else, live in a wider context of myths. Wittgenstein wrote: 'We feel that even when all possible scientific questions have been answered, the problems of life remain completely untouched.' Wittgenstein, being Wittgenstein, would not have come to that view without a great deal of thought. Dawkins and Atkins write as though intellectuals of the stature of Wittgenstein had never existed.

In the months leading up to the final break with Myra Hindley, Ian Brady taunted her about her return to Catholicism, asking her in one letter how all the millions of China could be accommodated in heaven. This is a question a child might ask.

The alternative views to Brady's nihilism are many and varied. Let me briefly describe just one of these.

In the oriental philosophies and religions, the state of illusion is the 'vision of separateness', severed consciousness, the illusion of the separate ego. In the Hindu view, the Divine is playing all the parts. Each little self is the big Self wearing a mask. This stands in diametrical contrast to the many contemporary individuals who, like Ian Brady speak of the supremacy of 'relativity'.

From the viewpoint of much oriental religious philosophy, everything is fundamentally related. Relativity is the most secure thing there is. The enlightened can say to anyone, *Tat tvam asi* – That Thou Art – you are it, the Divine. The point of life is to wake up from the sleep of normal consciousness, the dull normal world as it is experienced on a wet Monday morning. This 'normalcy' is surprise-free; it's in the bag; it's the way it's going to be.

An old Hindu story makes the point. A man had been captured, tortured for years, but refused to utter a word. His captors decided to execute him. As the executioner plunged his sword into the prisoner's stomach, the victim looked into his executioner's eyes and spoke for the first time – Tat tvam asi – you are the Divine but you are lost in the vision of separateness, lost in the belief in your own separate reality.

To be truly, consciously 'related' is to be alive to the other person's misery. This 'relativism' has no place for the disconnected, willing ego. To be aware of the other person is to have a 'me too' feeling and is the genuine basis for compassion. As the great psychologist C. G. Jung observed: 'Consciousness and suffering are synonymous.'

E. M. Cioran, in *Tears and Saints*, quotes Brady's much-admired Dostoevsky: 'Suffering is the cause of consciousness'. People belong to two categories, those who have understood this, and the others.

I once raised the question of compassion with Ian Brady. He replied in July 1993: 'You make a good point (in the "all is vanity" dialectics) about compassion: the "me too" factor. But where does self-pity end or begin? In human relationships, I believe the dichotomy is more or less fifty-fifty – half compassion for the person, half compassion from self-identification. Now if you had said, compassion for animals, insects, etc., you would've hit on what I consider to be the highest sense of compassion, the most genuine despite the inescapable self-identification.'

An ancient image of this alternative to Brady's 'relativism' is that of a spider's web, heavy with morning dew. Each dewdrop reflects the whole web, and each dewdrop in the reflection is doing the same, ad infinitum. The whole of reality can be reflected in a single dewdrop. A classical Zen text is called *Moon in a Dewdrop*. The Buddha was once asked how it was possible to prevent a dewdrop from drying up. He answered, 'Cast it into the ocean.'

These observations, brief as they are, describe the radical alternative to the relativism of much scientific and philosophical writing, unwittingly attracting the likes of Ian Brady. Brady would say, of course, that his brand of 'relativism' had taken shape long before he had encountered the writings of congenial intellectuals. He was, in fact, contemptuous of such academics: 'The academic moral relativists are a bore, skirting the axiomatic and socially embarrassing in favour of pretentious nit-picking, which is what society is all about, eluding its own stink.'

Those offering alternatives to the relativists' claim, explicitly or implicitly, argue that there is something wrong with the normal, everyday consciousness, which is the sacred cow of many forms of relativism. The philosophical schizophrenia I mentioned at the beginning of this chapter relates to the fact that Ian Brady experienced what, for him, were profound challenges to the consensus of the dull normal state of consciousness. As he spoke of them, he clearly believed that his experiences were anything but Huxley's 'measly trickle', an image I referred to in the early pages of this book.

Brady's flatland version of moral relativism seems shallow and trivial in the light of the altered states he claims to have experienced first-hand. His arid, abstract pronouncements on moral relativism, to borrow an image Brady himself sometimes used, have all 'the depth of a gnat's piss'.

To take just one example, in one letter to me Ian Brady described an experience that puts a question mark against the dreary, bleak relativism he advocated in other contexts. The experience took place as he sheltered under a tree after being caught in a heavy shower while he was out riding his bicycle. The deluge stopped as suddenly as it had begun. He looked upwards and the tree he was lying under 'shimmered like a shower of diamonds': 'The freshly washed earth and air exuded purity. To anyone pantheistically attuned, as I was, it seemed to whisper benign messages in a nescient language needing no translation. The birds felt it. Awareness of shadowy presences evokes a trance-like state of a depth of the sublime unknown to the mundane consciousness we pitifully call real. It's as though we have forgetfully wandered into some normally incontiguous, eclipsed dimension of all-consuming wonder that completely erases our normal faculties. We enter the awareness unconditionally, revelling in its brightness. If we try to coerce it, make it subject to our will, it vanishes as though shielding its purity and modesty.'

Brady occasionally spoke of his experiences of *satori*. This is the Japanese word for the experience of sudden enlightenment in Zen Buddhism. I had taught courses on Oriental religious philosophy and Zen Buddhism for years and had written a book on Zen itself. I was particularly interested in what Brady had to say on the subject. He told me that these sudden changes in his consciousness were often triggered when he was in the open air early on frosty mornings. He described these as spiritual experiences. There were books on Zen in Brady's property and he had obviously pursued the subject.

It would take us too far off the track to discuss this issue in detail. Besides, most readers will find it ludicrous to mention enlightenment and Ian Brady in the same breath. It strained my credulity, but I decided to listen and try to make sense of it. I will make a few more general observations and then take three less rarefied and recurring concrete experiences in Brady's life.

I mentioned in an earlier chapter that one of the first books Ian Brady gave me was by Colin Wilson: *New Pathways in Psychology – Maslow and the Post-Freudian Revolution*. Wilson had sent the book to him as a gift. The past few decades have seen the emergence of a generation of psychologists and philosophers, such as Abraham Maslow, who have widened the scope of psychology to embrace what are sometimes called 'altered states' and modifications of consciousness which, in earlier periods, would be classified as 'mystical'. These new psychologies are often called 'transpersonal' or 'integral'.

A few sentences in Maslow's *Religions, Values, and Peak-Experiences* may be helpful for anyone unfamiliar with the subject: 'To sum up . . . the two religions of mankind tend to be the peakers and the non-peakers, that is to say, those who have private, personal, transcendent, core-religious experiences easily and often and who accept them and make use of them, and, on the other hand, those who have never had them or who repress or suppress them.'

Brady has made his own notes in the margins of Colin Wilson's book. Many would doubt the 'peak' status of one of Brady's marginal notes: 'Spiritual lightness after non-stop sex-athletics and drinking.' I asked him about this comment: 'I learned how to induce ultra-awareness and experience high-energy whatever the circumstances. Nature had put mystical awareness and the sexual in close proximity. Over a weekend I would go straight through the hours with "dissipation" – relentless alcohol, cigarettes and sex. I loved to step out into the cold air on frosty Sunday mornings and exchange the fumes of alcohol and tobacco for fresh air. Each breath was like liquid energy, reinvigorating the spirit. The heart came into the mouth of all my senses. I was spiritually and physically honed. My body was illuminated and limned by an inner psychic force. I felt spiritually higher than the passing sallow-faced churchgoers, staring down at the gray pavements as they dragged themselves to the weekly ritual. I felt no hostility towards them. I was too happy. Yet I reminded myself that I had to keep an alcoholic balance; walk a tightrope between the hunger for stimulation and overindulgence which would lead to tiredness and boredom.'

Ken Wilber has probably done more than any other contemporary philosopher to explore the states of human consciousness. His first book set out the ground for his life's work: *The Spectrum of Consciousness*. Wilber has repeated again and again, in several books which followed, that every identifiable state of consciousness – from the most primitive to the most sublime – can be experienced pathologically.

In religious literature, there are the metaphors of the 'Black Buddha' and the 'Dark Christ'. If it is light on the top, it is dark underneath. One of the central ideas of Carl Gustav Jung was that the Shadow is a reality in everyone's consciousness. Ben-Ami Scharfstein's book *Mystical Experience* has a chapter entitled 'Psychotic Mysticism'. Even serial killers are human and susceptible to 'peak' experiences, though they might respond to them in a psychotic way.

Brady commented in *The Gates of Janus*, 'Not even serial killers are entirely what you expect. Sometimes they can be the rope across the spiritual abyss, between man and his failed aspirations.' (Brady was alluding to the 'rope' metaphor in the passage from Nietzsche's *Thus Spake Zarathustra* quoted earlier.) From a certain point of view Brady

390 IAN BRADY – THE UNTOLD STORY OF THE MOORS MURDERS

could be described as a psychotic mystic. Psychotic, because no one kills another human being in a state of wonder.

I will comment on just three experiences that were seminal in Brady's life, as I have described it. They were each 'peak' experiences in their own way, however pathologically Brady may have interpreted them. They were re-experienced by Brady time after time.

The first of Brady's experiences is the least ambiguous of the three. The young Ian was on holiday with the Sloans. He climbed a hill and gazed across Loch Lomond and the wilderness beyond. Brady wrote that it was as though, 'I had suddenly been propelled through an invisible barrier and arrived in another dimension.' It was, he wrote, an 'atavistic vision'. The boy from the Gorbals had known nothing but its rat-infested streets and tenements. He was intoxicated. As an adult, Ian Brady reflected on his experience: 'Time and again, years into the future, I was to have days like these.'

Ian went on holiday with his mother, Peggy, to Tobermory and was even more deeply moved by the feral wilderness: 'This was the true reality. This was real power . . . absolutely free and unconstrained . . . derangement of versatile delight.'

Many years later, in *The Gates of Janus*, the mature Ian Brady reflected on this power:

Most people have vague intimations of this recondite power. Standing on a vacant shore, staring over oceanic plains, the soothing surge of the void fills them with renewed life. Unknown presences whisper. Arcane meanings beyond language are experienced. Silent music.

Some may interpret the metaphysical revitalisation as a religious experience. Others a pagan power source, causing them to laugh and dance with savage delight at the cosmic insignificance of humanity. The nature of unconditional freedom is instinctively seized and wielded.

There are countless reports of this kind of experience of ecstatic wonder at the natural world in mystical literature. Brady's ecstasy in the Scottish wilderness gave him a new affinity with the natural stone of the Gorbals tenements. Even in later years, when he lived in Manchester and travelled north to visit Glasgow, he would press his forehead against the stone buildings and whisper, 'I'm back'.

He once explained that Myra soon became familiar with this dimension of his life: 'When we were in the countryside, Myra watched as I placed my hand on trees and rocks to absorb energy from them. When Myra drove me to Glasgow – sometimes we would be there and back within twenty-four hours – I felt a current of energy flow through me as I stepped out of the car on to the pavement. I was galvanised too by pressing my hand against a tenement block. To others these would be lifeless surfaces but to me they were sentient and charged with life. We communicated with each other.'

For the remainder of his life, Brady could be what he called 'pantheistically attached' to his possessions, as I noted earlier. Whenever he gave me a typewriter or video recorder he would use the phrase.

The second experience was Brady's encounter with the 'green face' of Death, on Paisley Road, when he was fifteen years old. I described it fully in an earlier chapter and will just select a few sentences to bring out the significance of the experience for him.

Brady said that he entered a new dimension of heightened being. It was, he said, a profound revelation or occult visitation. It would give the reason for all else that was to follow for the rest of his life: 'So there was more to life than I imagined . . . Why had no one prepared me for this experience? . . . I felt on the brink of a revelation.'

Brady himself compared the experience with that of religious converts. Death would become his deity. The green radiance would always remind him of death. His experience of the colour green would make him feel close to death without making him fearful of it. It was a warm, pleasant feeling. Decades later, he would say to me, 'There is only one divine *deus ex machina* – God from the machine – in my universe. Everything else is heedless of our intellectual arrogance and our naïve psychological fantasies about our own importance in the scheme of things.'

The teenage Brady would not have known how his experience was redolent with religious imagery. He compared it with a religious experience, but I doubt whether even as an adult he realised just how close the comparison was.

The phenomenon of Death itself as a deity is an ancient theme in religious traditions and mythologies. Death, for example, is a deity in Mayan religion. Yama is the death deity in Hinduism. In the Buddhist *Tibetan Book of the Dead*, Death is also a deity.

The colour green is also widely associated with death in the religious memory and literary sagas. The skin of Yama in Hindu iconography is green. Everything associated with the deity of Death is green in Tibetan Buddhist art. Most obviously of all, in the Arthurian legends of the Holy Grail, the Green Knight is the grim reaper in disguise. Sir Gawain accepts the tempting challenges made by the Green Knight and agrees to meet him in the Green chapel one year later.

The temptations of the Buddha resemble those of Sir Gawain. In both cases, death incarnate functions as the master of initiation. The imagery in these stories is about the mystery of dying to the transient individuality. Death himself bestows the gift of the green girdle of death to the initiate. The fear of death had been overcome.

Ramana Maharshi (not the Maharishi of Beatles' fame) provides the classic twentieth-century instance of a youth being transformed by an overwhelming experience of death. He died in 1950. He and Ramakrishna are regarded as the two great, enlightened Hindu sages of modern times.

When I first heard Ian Brady describe his experience of greenness and death, I was taken aback by the resemblance it had to classic cases of initiation. The American psychologist Robert Johnson has written a brilliant series of books in which he interprets familiar religious stories and sagas in Jungian terms. In his book, *He – Understanding Masculine Psychology*, he explains the story of the Quest for the Holy Grail as an inner reality, an experience of the soul, a quest for a transformation of consciousness which will open the floodgates of the true reality that conventional reality allows us to experience only in a cataclysmically reduced form. Robert Johnson explains:

> The myth is telling us that a youth can blunder into the Grail castle sometimes in his midadolescence without earning it or even asking for it. Perhaps every boy in his adolescence spends at least one day in the Grail castle and experiences this perfection . . .
>
> Usually a man has repressed this, but if he will remember back, somewhere there was a moment when he stumbled into the Grail castle. This usually happens around fifteen or sixteen years of age. There is that morning or that perfect day . . . a boy wakes up with something new in him – a power, a perception, a strength, a vision. This is his Grail castle . . . he will never be the same again.
>
> The Grail experience is dangerous . . . too much of it or the experience of it at the wrong time is an invitation to a psychotic experience. The drawbridge can click shut too soon, and one is trapped and cannot get out.

Ian Brady, aged fifteen, seems to have had the kind of experience Robert Johnson describes but had become a psychotic victim – the drawbridge clicked too soon. Brady should have been freed from the fear of death, not impelled to bring death into the lives of other people without any reservation. It's significant that, as an adult, Brady used the imagery of the Grail Quest to describe his search for an opportunity to steal enough money to free him from the need to work, calling this sought-after great prize his 'Holy Grail'.

Brady may well have had a genuinely psychological encounter with the Grail within himself, his true self, but interprets it psychotically as the mundane act of stealing other people's money for his own egocentric ends. He confused 'the many splendoured thing' with a pile of stolen banknotes.

The third of Ian Brady's experiences is the *black light* referred throughout the story I have told. As Brady remarks, 'All my senses would become supranormal. It was an unspeakable flux in sensual perception.' Often in situations of danger, everything seemed to be luminous, as though outlined – to use Brady's image – with liquid electricity. As I mentioned much earlier, Brady chose *Black Light* as the title of his autobiography. His experience of *black light* made the everyday world seem mundane: 'I sank into deep depression when I returned to normal sensibilities.' *Black light* gave Brady 'a spiritual certainty beyond mundane religions.'

As with the first two of Brady's experiences, the third one of luminosity resembles many accounts recorded in religious literature. In Christianity the classic instance is of Christ on the mount of Transfiguration, where he appears to be luminous to his disciples, transfigured as Moses was said to be on Mount Sinai. In a very different religious tradition, Zen Buddhism, the awakened mind, has the 'shining trance' and sees the world as 'wondrous being'. Brady actually used the word 'transfiguration' to describe his experience of the 'black light'. In their book, *Seeing the Invisible*, Meg Maxwell and Verena Tschudin, have collected several accounts by individuals who have experienced luminosity in ways that are akin to Brady's own descriptions of the phenomenon.

To take just one of many individuals in modern times, Ken Wilber writes about his experiences of light and luminosity in his published diary, *One Taste*. Several people who have taken LSD speak in similar terms. But, some individuals have truly bad trips. Albert Hofmann, the man who first discovered LSD, described his first experience of the drug: 'I thought I had died and was in hell. My next door neighbor was transformed into a demonic figure.'

We could say that Ian Brady's experience of *black light* was something like a bad trip. Brady wasn't filled with a feeling of love and compassion, as many have been who have been in similar states of consciousness. On the contrary, the experience was triggered by the situation of threat and danger to him. It gave him the power to respond violently. Again, we have to conclude that Brady's response to this third experience was psychotic. Brady himself probably realised this when he described the experience as one of *black* light.

I have been trying here to look at the spiritual schizophrenia in Ian Brady's life. These two worlds are the threads that have run through all of the chapters in this book. If we can believe his account, he had experiences that sublimely transcended the wretched, money-grubbing world of theft and the mercilessly cruel world of child murder. In direct contrast, he also experienced the sense of life as without purpose and meaning, which he expressed through the arid, wretched language of relativism and reductionism that is ready to hand in the writings of the academics who are clearly immune to attacks of mystery and the sublime, and who will not be content until they have reduced philosophy to utter boredom.

These two worlds in Ian Brady's mind never met. They were like the friends who occupied the different compartments in his life. This is the mantra that has been humming beneath the surface of every page of this book. This is *real* schizophrenia and all of us experience it in our own way, although it is a world that is far removed from Ian Brady's. We experience the sublime in our lives, the point where *eternity* intersects *time* – the road less travelled. Yet, it seems, we often choose *time* – time after time, after time.

This is, in a profound sense, one of the deep factors that led to the ghastly nightmare of the Moors Murders. If only those two worlds had met in the consciousness of Ian Brady and he had chosen the other road.

In parts of Manchester, or some other city today, perhaps, Pauline Reade, John Kilbride, Keith Bennett, Lesley Ann Downey and Edward Evans would be looking forward to seeing their own children when they visit on Sunday.

CHAPTER TWENTY-SIX

IT'S ALL OVER NOW, BABY BLUE

On Friday, 15 November 2002, a journalist from the *Daily Mail* telephoned to tell me that news was 'coming through on the wires' that Myra Hindley was at death's door. He asked me if I could obtain a reaction from Ian Brady. Just before 5 o'clock on the same afternoon a journalist from the *Daily Mirror* also telephoned to tell me that Myra was dying. I was watching the television news when I picked up the telephone. I responded to his news with: 'She's not dying; she's just died.'

Myra had died of bronchial pneumonia at West Suffolk hospital in Bury St Edmunds. She had been admitted to the hospital under the false name of Christine Charlton after a suspected heart attack. Father Michael Teader had given her the last rites at 6 a.m. on the day she died. Her final words were cries for her mother, who was living in a Manchester nursing home. She was 82 and too frail to travel to see her daughter.

Policemen kept watch over Myra's corpse in case intruders attempted to defile it. She was guarded in death as she had been in life. The journalist Nicci Gerrard wrote in the *Observer* that it was as though her body was 'like radioactive waste with an after-life'.

Twenty funeral directors in the region were approached to carry out the necessary arrangements. All of them turned down the requests, fearing the damage to their businesses. A funeral director in the north of England eventually agreed to accept the job. The cost of the funeral was taken from Myra's savings, estimated to be £340. She had asked for Albinoni's *Adagio* to be played.

Myra wanted just twelve people to attend the cremation service at Cambridge City Crematorium. Included in the group was her former lesbian lover, Nina Wilde. The funeral took place in the evening after the crematorium's normal working day. There was a strong police presence to meet any public disturbance. In the event, very few people turned up to watch the proceedings and there were no angry protests.

Journalist Richard Ingrams wondered in his *Observer* column whether the newspapers, which had for days been milking the story to death, were disappointed that the anticipated mob outside the crematorium never materialised. The crowd of journalists waiting to record the obscene chants outnumbered the few members of the public who turned up to witness the end of a forty-year-old tabloid story. Ingrams added that this suggests it was only the press who had maintained an interest in Myra Hindley and that the public at large had ceased to be interested in her years ago.

There was just one bunch of white freesias left outside the entrance of the crematorium, along with a hand-written message on a card: 'Rest in peace, Myra.' Freesias, as we have seen, were the flowers which meant the presence of Lesley Ann for her mother Ann West.

Myra Hindley died before the House of Lords were about to give a ruling on the right of the Home Secretary to override the tariff given by trial judges in life sentence cases. The current Home Secretary, David Blunkett, was spared the controversy over Myra Hindley's possible release. The Manchester City police had been considering charging Myra with the murders of Pauline Reade and Keith Bennett.

The day after Myra's death the leading article in the *Guardian* reflected on her treatment by the judicial system: 'The Parole board . . . had the independence to ignore the label tied round her neck by the tabloids – the most evil woman in Britain. Crime has enough difficult causes already without adding the supernatural. Her overlong imprisonment demeaned our society.'

Myra's friend and former confessor, Peter Timms, commented that her treatment was 'a scar on the judicial system'. Dr Colin Morris, speaking on BBC radio sometime before Myra's death, commented:

We have much to learn about overcoming evil from Jewish survivors of the Nazi death camps. They have been relentless in the pursuit of justice for the victims of the Holocaust but they also resolved not to allow the rest of their days to be dominated by underlying hatred and bitterness, otherwise evil would have won, for such negative feelings are almost as destructive of life as the death camps themselves.

The tragedy is that for the public to remain obsessed with Myra Hindley and her crimes after thirty years is in itself a form of imprisonment.

Ian Brady commented to me once that, 'we should nurture some conscious retention of the will to understand, even when understanding is not synonymous with liking. To be hated is unfortunate, but to hate can be unbearable.'

The inquest into Myra's death took place on 23 January 2003. It was revealed that she was on a daily cocktail of drugs for a long list of ailments: osteoporosis, angina, insomnia, hypertension, raised cholesterol, depression, menopausal symptoms, headaches, back pain, asthma, bronchitis, arthritis and irritable bowels.

At the close of the hearing, Greater Suffolk coroner Peter Dean asked all those present in court to stand for a minute's silence in tribute to Myra Hindley's victims. Ironically, Myra had died on the day of Britain's Children in Need Appeal.

David Smith, now 54, was asked for his thoughts on Myra's death. Speaking in the village of Oughterard, where he ran a bed and breakfast house with his second wife, Mary, Smith said that the news of Myra's death caused him no emotion: 'She was the most evil and by far outstrips Brady. The night she was cremated, I had a feeling something good was happening. They were burning her and that meant that there isn't a place on this earth that she will exist.

'To say that I am a victim is to denigrate what happened to all the people who ended up buried on the moors. But I do feel a sense of peace now.'

The *Sun* newspaper claimed that Myra Hindley's ashes were scattered in the presence of a few of her relatives and friends in Stalybridge Country Park, Cheshire, in late February 2003. The beauty spot, known to Myra before her life with Ian Brady, is just twelve miles from Saddleworth Moor. The story was given the full tabloid treatment, including a photograph, alleged to be of the ashes on the ground in a gully above Walkerwood Reservoir. Predictably, there was also a picture of one of the Moors victims' relatives standing near the spot.

In the wake of Myra's death, Keith Bennett's mother, Mrs Winnie Johnson, pursued the possibility of the police charging Ian Brady belatedly with the murder of her son and Pauline Reade. However, the Crown

Prosecution Service announced early in March 2003 that Brady would not be charged since there was no realistic prospect of a conviction. Three months later, detectives visited Brady in Ashworth Hospital to ask him for some guidance on the location of Keith Bennett's grave. The *Sun* claimed that Brady refused to help the police.

A spokesman for Keith Bennett's family responded: 'He has always refused to help end our torment.' Ian Brady, in fact, had visited Saddleworth Moor with Inspector Peter Topping on two occasions to find Keith's grave. I asked Brady about the newspaper reports. In a letter of August 2003, he said simply; 'The Bennetts suffer from amnesia. Not that it matters now.'

Some months before writing these resigned words, Ian Brady had asked for a public hearing in front of a mental health tribunal to show that he was not insane. If he proved his case, Brady would be transferred back into the prison system and have the right to continue his hunger strike without being force-fed. He repeated to me; 'I look forward to death alone.'

Brady was granted his right to a hearing before a mental health tribunal in September 2003 and, at the time of writing, was due to have this before the end of the year. A year after Myra was freed from prison through death, Ian Brady was fighting to enter prison again.

Joan Baez's version of Bob Dylan's 'It's All Over Now, Baby Blue' always reminded Brady and Hindley of the final murder, that of Edward Evans in October 1965. Brady told me so. The record had been on sale in the shops for a month before Edward's death. I didn't ask Ian Brady for his thoughts on Myra's death. I knew what his response would be. Silence.

Millions of lovers the world over, through all time, have eventually become nothing to each other. This was so with Ian Brady and Myra Hindley. As we have seen, Brady said he loved Myra still 'for the innocent times' they had together.

As the drama of the Moors Murders moved to its final scene, Myra Hindley was longing for life to begin, while Ian Brady was restless for life to end. Myra pipped her lover at the post. It wasn't the win she was hoping for. Yet, if her Christian faith was real, it was life nevertheless.

On a bitterly cold November night of freezing rain, Myra Hindley's coffin was escorted by police through the stone entrance of Cambridge City Crematorium. She passed beneath the gateway bearing the Latin words *Mors Janua Vitae* – 'Death is the Gateway to Life' – her own Gates of Janus.

Ian Brady, alone in his cramped room, flicked across the television channels to avoid the late-night news coverage of Myra's funeral. He was absorbed in his own invading belief – life is the gateway to death. As one of Brady's favourite authors, E. M. Cioran, put it, in *The Trouble With Being Born*: 'Over the gate of our cemeteries should be written: "Nothing is Tragic. Everything is Unreal".'

CONCLUSION

WHERE HE HAS GONE, I HAVE GONE. WHAT HE HAS DONE, I HAVE DONE.

Ian Brady woke every morning hoping he would die that day: 'Death makes life worthwhile. It's balm for the hopeless. Death is the architect of all emotion,' he wrote to me on my birthday in January 1994. It was a less desperate time for him, even though he had just passed his 56th birthday, having been in captivity for almost thirty years: 'Death holds the stopwatch and we all race to experience as much as possible before our time is up. Without death, life would have no zest, no value, and offer only boredom and atrophy, and a craving for oblivion. I favour oblivion.'

Oblivion was the last thing on Myra Hindley's mind. She was hoping to be free one day. Yet she had only eight years of life left when Brady wrote this letter to me. Her first words to detectives, after Ian Brady's arrest, could be a subtitle for this book. She had gone where he had gone; she had done what he had done. The victims' relatives were completely justified in their claims that Myra Hindley was an equal participant with Brady in the Moors Murders.

The whole saga has been a nightmare for hundreds of people for forty years. This book has been based on Ian Brady's life and his version of events. As I grew to know him over the years, I could see that the question of his release was absolutely out of the question. Yet he outlived his former lover, who was five years younger and hoping for her eventual release.

As he saw his own end drawing ever closer, Brady admitted that his adult life had been the story of prolonged catastrophe. His criminal career was a complete failure by his own standards. He had fallen down on his own cherished 'no connecting thread' precaution. He had left incriminating evidence everywhere – on paper, in photographs, on tapes – quite apart from the major miscalculation of trusting David Smith to keep quiet about witnessing murder. The police's evidence against Brady and Hindley made the Moors Murders an open-and-shut case.

As we have seen, Ian Brady described his fundamental outlook on life as 'existential' – the intense immediacy and awareness of sheer existence and the unrepeatable present moment: 'seize the day'. There are, of course, different forms of existentialism. There is the atheistic French brand found in the writings of Jean-Paul Sartre, who spoke of human existence as a 'useless passion'. As Sartre's book *Nausea* implies, reality makes some existentialists sick.

Brady's own brand of existentialism is derived from Dostoevsky's characters. Their lives are often ones of pain upon pain and unrelenting inner agony. In the end, Brady didn't act on his own philosophical advice: 'A person should consciously choose whether to exist as a grey daub on a grey canvas, or as an existential riot of every colour of the spectrum.'

During my conversations with him, Brady showed little enthusiasm for my own preferred existentialist writer, the troubled Danish Christian Søren Kierkegaard, who was arguably the first existentialist in the modern sense of the term.

Kierkegaard's advice, to match that given above by Brady, is to live your life in a way which, if it were put in the form of a play on stage, would make the audience weep with ecstasy. Ian Brady's audience has screamed with anger.

Underlying all of Kierkegaard's writings is the experience of intense 'inwardness' that makes a person an 'individual'. Brady sometimes quoted Albert Camus: 'An intense feeling carries with it its own universe, magnificent or wretched as the case may be.'

In June 2001 Ian Brady recalled a conversation we had had some time before: 'As I said once, years ago, fame and infamy are delusions, and one day earth will be as barren as the moon, nothing and no one even remembered. I once sat on a mountain at 3 a.m. or so in the morning, thinking such thoughts, only the darkness and stars for company. Puts things in perspective – all is vanity, humankind being no more significant than insects in universal terms.

'If you were to sit on that mountain your whole life you'd probably be more aware of reality than those below scuttling around in a frenzy of delusion and trivia till they die and disappear without trace – even world wars less than a flea breaking wind; hydrogen bombs not even equivalent to a distant spark of static electricity.'

This was Ian Brady's 'magnificent and wretched' universe. They were different worlds for him. They were the two fundamental compartments of his life. In this book, I have tried to show that these two worlds never met. This was the true schizophrenia in his life. The sublime experiences of the Scottish wilderness and atmospheric, haunting cobbled alleyways of the Gorbals felt no echo in the screams of children on the barren wilderness of Saddleworth Moor or in the cramped, squalid matchbox rooms of number 16 Wardle Brook Avenue.

As Myra Hindley eased the car out of the horseshoe scoop to make the descent from Saddleworth Moor, having just helped Ian Brady to bury Pauline Reade, she felt that God had died. She was the first and only convert to Ian Brady's world and had ritualised her new citizenship with the murder of a sixteen-year-old girl.

Malraux wrote that, 'Death is the irrefutable proof of the absurdity of life. Nothing – no divine thought, no future recompense – can justify the end of a human existence.' The Jewish writer Elie Wiesel, a survivor of Auschwitz and a Nobel Peace Prize winner, acknowledged the truth of Malraux's words but responded with a passage from the Talmud that echoes the two universes that Ian Brady, quoting Camus, called the wretched and the magnificent: 'Whoever kills a human being, it is as though he has destroyed the world; whoever saves a man, it is as though he has saved the world.'

At the end of a documentary on Myra Hindley, broadcast in September 2003, the narrator's voice informs the viewers that many of the people involved in the Moors case are dead and concludes: 'Even after her death, monster Myra lives on. Will she ever die?'

I have the same question about Ian Brady in mind and conclude with a poem by the late Ken Smith, writer in residence to Wormwood Scrubs prison between 1985 and 1987. The poem is in Ken Smith's evocative collection, *Shed: Poems 1980–2001*. I sent a copy to Ian Brady. He wrote back: 'Thanks for the poem by Ken *Smith* (that name pursues me!). Interesting that the final line captures the truth.'

BRADY AT SADDLEWORTH MOOR

Out, this is air, abrupt and everywhere,
the light and sky all one blaze of it.
Count them eleven clear hours of wind
over the world's tops into my face –

this old bleached-out moon always adrift
through the bad dreams of the neighbourhood.
In my ten thousand days I count this day:
the moor, all its space and vastness

I hear them say I say. I find nothing
in all four corners of the wind
where stones haven't changed, tumps, gullies
one blue blur of heather and upland grass

where one grave looks much like another.
Think how many years the rain fell I felt
my heart in my chest a fist of sour dust
forming in the acids of my discontent –

but it knows one thought: nothing's forgot
though my vision's bad, my sanity debateable.
I can forget, I can remember, I can be mad,
I will never be as free again, ever.

Nor will anyone be free of me. Count on it.

In the opening pages of this book I commented that memory forgets many
things, but not what *should* have happened. It is impossible to be a
hypocrite and pretend when we dream. Dreams, like lightning and the sun,
are self-luminous. Brady sometimes remembered the days when the *black
light* gleamed, but when he woke from his fretful slumbers in Ashworth
Hospital, he accepted the guilt which his dreams remorselessly forced him
to feel on waking.

Sometimes when I phoned him, the nurse who answered told
me that he was lying on his bed, fully clothed and fast asleep.
Brady always complained that he should have been woken up if there
was a telephone call. He told me time and again that the first thought

when his eyelids flickered to face the dawn was, 'I am the Moors Murderer.'
Brady sometimes quoted E. M. Cioran's words in Tears and Saints: 'Life
is too full of death for death to add anything to it.' Nevertheless, he longed
for death and rewrote the Prayer Book in his sleep, as he revealed in one
letter to me: 'Let Death be the power and the glory for ever and ever . . .'
No more nightmares. Never again to be haunted by the terrified stare in
Pauline's eyes. Never again to hear John's cry in the mist, Keith's shout
in the wilderness, Lesley Ann's screams or Edward's dying murmur.
Oblivion.

Ian Brady clutched a meagre crumb of comfort some mornings when
waking. He thought of a line he had once read in Wormwood Scrubs: 'Life
is a dream, they tell, waking to die.'

POSTSCRIPT, MAY 2017

Before the end Ian Brady gave me his final thoughts. These reflections
consisted of two hundred handwritten pages. He asked me to delete repetitions
before sending a typed version on to his solicitor in London. The following is
a selection from this.

> Full forty years from my prison planet I have watched your changeling
> world diminish, doing as much to you as little for me. So I have returned
> for a few departing final observations and clarifications, my suspended
> animation disturbed by recent historical events on your side of the void.

The unstructured format is intentional, styled as a lengthy, almost stream-of-
consciousness personal letter.

> With Myra dead and me on the brink, always scheduled to die in
> captivity anyways, certain long withheld information can be safely
> revealed for the first time, particularly in regard to our final year of
> freedom together.

> We always avoid irresponsible or gratuitous employment of guns,
> not wishing to leave ballistic footprints. And contrary to later tabloid
> slurs, we never shot at animals for sport or target practice. When Myra
> personally wished to experience the capacity of the .38 Smith and
> Wesson snub nose, she had the opportunity to cancel a liability we had
> up in Yorkshire.

Fortunately the evening was bright and fine for a lengthy stretching of the legs over rough terrain. As we reached the chosen appointed spot Myra affected some trouble with her shoe. Halting, ostensibly to wait for her, I gave the landscape a 360-degrees with the binoculars. For the all clear I then casually distanced myself from the target by several paces while maintaining a particular song that was in the current hit parade as the trigger.

Luckily the single shot went straight through and high, obviating any need for messy ballistic retrieval. The brown peat naturally absorbed all surface traces. The usual depersonalisation and disposal procedures were completed smoothly and without incident at the pre-prepared nearby site. Frequent post-incident scans indicated a clear run, and back at the car we relaxed with a whisky, listening to the radio tuned to Radio Caroline and discussing remaining logistics to sanitise the car interior before nightfall.

Although mutually gratified by the successful conclusion of the operation and the strategic security it ensured, the mundane ease of the operation was not only curiously unsatisfying but also philosophically lacking, a sentiment encapsulated in the Peggy Lee song 'Is That All There Is?'

Another theme in the 'final observations' concerns Brady's own mental states in his captivity.

Statistically, psychotic symptoms are considered more valid grounds for transfer to a mental hospital. And the linchpin of psychosis consists of delusional, hallucinatory experience and history. In Gartree prison I therefore began to manufacture and exhibit symptoms, reinforcing them with a devised false history that, hitherto, I had supposedly managed to conceal for a fear of ridicule.

I had embarked on a subtle number of other psychotic symptoms – distraction, preoccupation, withdrawal, etc, avoiding explanation or engagement of any description. Simultaneously, whenever I had to be seen to be eating, I later regurgitated so that my weight continued to fall dramatically, and I was moved to the hospital wing of the prison. Whenever a prison warder thought I was unaware that I was being watched, I would either move my lips as though speaking to an invisible presence or answering imaginary 'voices', or sometimes actually speak the words aloud, simulating agitation and anger.

Occasionally I would focus my attention on the radio (switched off) or radiator while having these supposedly unseen conversations. At night I would pace my cell talking aloud to myself and gesticulating at an imaginary person. I had also stopped going to bed, remaining in a chair huddled over the radiator and mumbling whenever I heard prison warders stealthily approaching to observe me through the spyhole. My letters to people outside also had to show degrees of irrationality and paranoia, of course – which was the most demeaning and hardest part of all. It is one thing to perform secretly behind prison walls, but quite another to sacrifice one's expectation and self-esteem in the eyes of relatives and friends.

Fortunately, without acting out of character in the role I was playing, I could periodically return to being my normal self and obtain some relief from the constant stress of performing by having conversations with intelligent individuals.

I had to sustain enactment of all these symptoms, and more, for well over a year, maintaining the consistency of pattern and theme.

One night, after regurgitating food, I slipped on the wet floor and fractured my hand, the bones being brittle as my weight had fallen to under eight stone. But I maintained the appearance of irrationality by not reporting the broken bone, knowing that someone would eventually notice how swollen my hand had become.

When asked to explain how it happened, I returned to my psychotic role, stating I had punched the wall in rage, knowing they would attribute the rage to the delusional characters I was arguing with. This was only one example of how I had to keep innovating to sustain the image of a well-rounded psychotic in florid mode, feigning forgetfulness selectively and, paradoxically, therefore having to retain a good memory.

Because on top of all this I was having to field interviews with doctors, specialists and Home Office officials, and stay in character when talking to other prisoners, some of whom could be informers or provocateurs set to test me by the authorities.

Suffice it to say that, if ever called upon to prove the success of my marathon performance, I could now give a detailed account of very day, action and conversation I had during that period of simulated 'psychotic breakdown', even though it took place over twenty years ago.

I possess almost total recall of every significant event in my life.

Authors, journalists, academics etc I've been corresponding with for over four decades frequently express astonishment not at all my memory but also on how I've managed to stay so mentally alert and balanced during, and in spite of, forty years' horrendous captivity. But frankly I can't claim credit for it, no more than I could for continuing to breathe. It just happened so. In fact, satirically, I often muse that one would have to be mad to survive such, or even wish to.

As I strove to seize meaningful existence via psychotic burlesque, Myra's gate fever was making her public utterances increasingly innovative and damaging to me.

Ian Brady's Health Review Tribunal was held in June 2013. He had been hoping the panel would rule that he was not mentally ill so he could be transferred to a normal prison where he would have the option to starve himself to death. It was the first time Ian Brady had been seen in public for four decades. During his evidence at the tribunal he had claimed that he was simply a 'petty criminal' and said his killings had been 'recreational', merely 'existential' experiences. One journalist who attended the tribunal said that Brady's evidence was just a wall of noise, paralegal jargon he had picked up over the years. It was no surprise that the hearing ruled that Brady would not be returned to the prison system.

The Daily Mirror issued a front-page exclusive report of Brady's 'dementia' on 2 January 2014, the date of his seventy-sixth birthday. Most of the material in the article consisted of the comments of Brady's health advisor, Jackie Powell, who had visited him regularly since 1999. She said something which chimed with my own experience of meeting Ian Brady: 'No one who meets him could ever deny that he had a very sharp mind. He is highly intelligent and insisted on dealing with things on his own terms.' She commented that getting dementia was his worst nightmare. Her most recent meetings with Brady had shown that the glint had gone out of his eyes and he just seemed to be waiting to die. 'He looked gaunt and grey like a frail old man'

Near the end, he said to me that he had three regrets. The first: 'I regret having lived this long, though it hasn't been wasted, as you will discover on my departure. I always took if necessary by proxy.'

The second regret moved him most profoundly: 'I am immensely grateful and proud to have emanated from and experienced the old Gorbals before it was demolished. I only regret that I failed to fully appreciate and took for granted the vast number of good and loyal people I knew during my lifetime. But that's human nature – gloriously imperfect and randomly selective from moment to moment. The most loyal of all being Myra, who compacted to die if we were ever trapped beyond salvation of the guns. I forgave her for what years of captivity and parole extortion inevitably wrought in terms of enforced compromise and betrayal, and I trust she forgave my like retaliation.'

The third reflection is on crime: 'I caution stereotyped hacks that a life entirely devoted to criminal pursuits, to a degree more than good sense and necessity demands, will find it as tedious and soul-diminishing as prison itself. Only those with nothing to gain or lose ever totally experience freedom.'

I have my own final thoughts. One is that of Carl Jung, paradoxically admired by Ian Brady. Jung wrote that human beings cannot live a meaningless life, and that the sole purpose of existence is to kindle a light in the darkness of being.

Another is the conclusion drawn by Victor Frankl, who survived the death camps and was a victim of the Nazi ideology many have found echoes of in the Moors murders. Frankl believed that each of us have our own inner concentration camp. We are prisoners of our own thoughts. Brady and Hindley embodied this truth in a cruelly sadistic way as they gave flesh to their own private holocaust.

My abiding memory of Ian Brady is of a returning stare through a haze of cigarette smoke.

Keith Bennett's mother Winnie died of cancer early in September 2012 without knowing where her son had been buried. An untouched plot of earth next to her own grave was reserved for the remains of her son, should he ever be found on the high barrenness of Saddleworth Moor.

BIBLIOGRAPHY

Babuta, Subniv and Bragard, Jean-Claude, Evil, Weidenfeld and Nicolson, London, 1988
Birch, Helen, edited, Moving Targets, Virago, London, 1993
Brady, Ian, The Gates of Janus, Feral House, Los Angeles, 2001
Camus, Albert, The Myth of Sisyphus, Random House, New York, 1955
– The Rebel, Penguin, Harmondsworth, 1962
Cioran, E. M., Anathemas and Admirations, Quartet Books, London, 1992
– On the Heights of Despair, The University of Chicago Press, Chicago, 1992
– Tears and Saints, The University of Chicago Press, Chicago, 1995
– The Trouble With Being Born, Archade Publishing, New York, 1998
Cohen, Stanley and Taylor, Laurie, Psychological Survival, Penguin, Harmondsworth, 1972
Dostoevsky, Fyodor, Crime and Punishment, Penguin, Harmondsworth, 1951
Eunson, Eric, The Gorbals: An Illustrated History, Richard Stenlake Publishing, Catrine, 1996
Fernández-Armesto, Felipe, So You Think You're Human?, Oxford University Press, Oxford, 2004
Fido, Martin, To Kill and Kill Again, Carlton, London, 2001
Garrett, Geoffrey and Nott, Andrew, Cause of Death, Robinson, London, 2001
Gibson, A. Boyce, The Religion of Dostoevsky, SCM, London, 1973
Glasser, Ralph, Growing Up in the Gorbals, House of Stratus, Thirsk, 2001
Goodman, Jonathan, The Moors Murders: The Trial of Myra Hindley and Ian Brady, David &
    Charles, London, 1986
Harrison, Fred, Brady and Hindley – Genesis of the Moors Murders, Grafton, London, 1987
Hart, Christine, The Devil's Daughter, New Author Publications, Essex, 1993
Hick, John, Evil and the God of Love, Macmillan, London, 1966
Hillman, James, The Force of Character, Random House, New York, 1999
Huxley, Aldous, Do What You Will, Watts, London, 1936
Johnson, Pamela Hansford, On Iniquity, Macmillan, London, 1967
Johnson, Robert A., He, Harper & Row, New York, 1989
Jones, Janie, The Devil and Miss Jones, Smith Gryphon, London, 1993
Jones, Judith and Beatrix Campbell, And All the Children Cried, Oberon Books, London, 2002
Jones, Richard Glynn, Killer Couples, Berkley Books, New York, 1987
Jung, C. G., The Psychology of Nazism, Princeton University Press, Princeton, 1989
Levy, Neil, Moral Relativism: A Short Introduction, One World, Oxford, 2002
Longford, Lord, The Grain of Wheat, Collins, London, 1974
Lucas, Norman, The Child Killers, Arthur Barker, London, 1970
Marchbanks, David, The Moor Murders, Leslie Frewin, London, 1966
Maslow, Abraham H., Religions, Values, and Peak-Experiences, Penguin, New York, 1976
McArthur, A. and Kingsley Long, H., No Mean City, Corgi Books, Neville Spearman edition, 1956
Melechi, Antonio, Fugitive Minds, Heinemann, London, 2003
Midgley, Mary, Wickedness, Routledge, London, 2001
– The Myths We Live By, Routledge, London, 2003
Nietzsche, Friedrich, Thus Spoke Zarathustra, Penguin, Harmondsworth, 1961
Potter, John Deane, The Monsters of the Moors, Elek, London, 1966
Prince, Michael, Murderous Places, Blandford, London, 1989
Quiller-Couch, Arthur (ed.), The Oxford Book of English Verse: 1250–1918, Clarendon Press,
    Oxford, 1957
Ritchie, Jean, Myra Hindley – Inside the Mind of a Murderess, Grafton, London, 1991
Russell, Bertrand, Mysticism and Logic and Other Essays, Edward Arnold, 1918
Sanford, John A., Evil – The Shadow Side of Reality, Crossroad, New York, 1988
Scharfstein, Ben-Ami, Mystical Experience, Penguin, Baltimore, 1974
Sparrow, Gerald, Satan's Children, Oldhams, London, 1966
Staff, Duncan, The Lost Boy, Bantam, London, 2007
Stanford, Peter, The Outcasts' Outcast, Sutton, Stroud, 2003
Stein, Murray, edited, Jung On Evil, Princeton University Press, Princeton, 1995
Steiner, George, In Bluebeard's Castle, Faber & Faber, London, 1971
– Nostalgia for the Absolute, House of Anansi Press, Toronto, 2004

Syme, Anthony, Murder on the Moors, Horwitz Publications, Sydney, 1966
Tillich, Paul, The Courage To Be, Fontana, London, 1962
– My Search for Absolutes, Simon & Schuster, New York, 1967
Topping, Peter, Topping – The Autobiography of the Police Chief in the Moors Murder Case, Angus
    & Robertson, London, 1989
West, Ann, For The Love of Lesley, Allen, London, 1989
Wiesel, Elie, Evil and Exile, University of Notre Dame, Indiana, 1990
Wilber, Ken, A Brief History of Everything, Gill & Macmillan, Dublin, 1996
Williams, Emlyn, Beyond Belief, Pan, 1978
Wilson, Colin, The Outsider, Victor Gollancz, London, 1956
Wilson, Robert, Devil's Disciples, Express Newspapers, London, 1986
– Return to Hell, Javelin Books, London, 1988

ACKNOWLEDGEMENTS

The author and publisher are grateful for permission to quote from the following:
The Force of Character by James Hillman, Random House Inc., 2001.
A Brief History of Everything by Ken Wilber. Copyright 1996, 2000 by Ken Wilber. Reprinted by
    arrangement with Shambhala Publications, Inc., Boston, www.shambhala.com.
Avowed Intent by Lord Longford, Little, Brown – Time Warner Books UK, 1994.
Shed: Poems 1980–2001 by Ken Smith, Bloodaxe Books, 2002.
The Gates of Janus by Ian Brady, Feral House, 2001.
God in the Shower: Thoughts from Thought for the Day by Colin Morris, Macmillan, 2002.
Religions, Values, and Peak Experiences by Abraham Maslow, 1976, the Estate of A. H. Maslow.
Do What You Will by Aldous Huxley, 1936, the Aldous Huxley Literary Estate.
Mysticism and Logic and Other Essays by Bertrand Russell, Edward Arnold 1918. The Bertrand
    Russell Peace Foundation.
The Second Coming by W. B. Yeats, A. P. Watt Ltd on behalf of Michael B. Yeats.
The Rebel by Albert Camus, Penguin Books. Translated by Anthony Bower (Hamish Hamilton 1953,
    Peregrines 1962). Translation copyright 1953 by Anthony Bower.
Crime and Punishment by Fyodor Dostoevsky, reproduced by permission of Penguin Books Ltd.
    Translated with an introduction by David Magarshack (Penguin Classics 1951, reprinted 1966).
    Copyright David Magarshack.
Crime and Punishment by Fyodor Dostoevsky, reproduced by permission of Penguin Books
    Ltd. Translated with an introduction by David McDuff (Penguin Classic 1991). Translation,
    introduction and notes copyright David McDuff, 1991.
On Murder by Brian Masters, Hodder and Stoughton, 1994, reproduced by permission of Brian
    Masters.
'Way of the world' by Auberon Waugh, the Daily Telegraph, October 1994, reproduced by
    permission of the Estate of Auberon Waugh.
'My father met Ian Brady' by Angela Neustatter, the Guardian, March 2000, reproduced by
    permission of Angela Neustatter.
'That girl shouldn't have been out at that time of night' by Yvonne Roberts, the Observer, November
    2002, reproduced by permission of Yvonne Roberts.
'Ian Brady in hot water', the Daily Telegraph, 1970, copyright Telegraph Group Limited 1970.
'Journey into darkness', the Guardian, 2000 and 'Looking for Keith', the Guardian, 2001, by Duncan
    Staff, reproduced by permission of Duncan Staff.
'My Story: The "normal, happy girl" who Became the "Icon of Evil" ' by Myra Hindley, the
    Guardian, 1995, copyright the Guardian.
'How I ended Moors Murderers' reign of evil', Manchester Evening News, November 2002.
'The Moors Murders', Chameleon TV 1999.
The Psychology of Nazism by C. G. Jung, Routledge, 1988.

INDEX